Lecture Notes in Artificial Intelli

Edited by J. G. Carbonell and J. Siekmann

Subseries of Lecture Notes in Computer Science

Rogier M. van Eijk   Marc-Philippe Huget
Frank Dignum (Eds.)

Agent
Communication

International Workshop on Agent Communication, AC 2004
New York, NY, USA, July 19, 2004
Revised Selected and Invited Papers

 Springer

Series Editors

Jaime G. Carbonell, Carnegie Mellon University, Pittsburgh, PA, USA
Jörg Siekmann, University of Saarland, Saarbrücken, Germany

Volume Editors

Rogier M. van Eijk
Frank Dignum
Utrecht University
Institute of Information and Computing Sciences
3508 TB Utrecht, The Netherlands
E-mail: {rogier, dignum}@cs.uu.nl

Marc-Philippe Huget
ESIA-LISTIC
B.P. 806, 74016 Annecy, France
E-mail: Marc-Philippe.Huget@univ-savoie.fr

Library of Congress Control Number: 2005920596

CR Subject Classification (1998): I.2.11, I.2, C.2.4, C.2, D.2, F.3

ISSN 0302-9743
ISBN 3-540-25015-8 Springer Berlin Heidelberg New York

Springer is a part of Springer Science+Business Media

springeronline.com

© Springer-Verlag Berlin Heidelberg 2005
Printed in Germany

Typesetting: Camera-ready by author, data conversion by Scientific Publishing Services, Chennai, India
Printed on acid-free paper   SPIN: 11394303   06/3142   5 4 3 2 1 0

Preface

In this book, we present a collection of papers around the topic of agent communication. The communication between agents has been one of the major topics of research in multiagent systems. The current work can therefore build on a number of previous Workshops of which the proceedings have been published in earlier volumes in this series. The basis of this collection is formed by the accepted submissions of the Workshop on Agent Communication held in conjunction with the AAMAS Conference in July 2004 in New York. The workshop received 26 submissions of which 14 were selected for publication in this volume. Besides the high-quality workshop papers we noticed that many papers on agent communication found their way to the main conference. We decided therefore to invite a number of authors to revise and extend their papers from this conference and to combine them with the workshop papers. We believe that the current collection comprises a very good and quite complete overview of the state of the art in this area of research and gives a good indication of the topics that are of major interest at the moment.

The papers can roughly be divided over the following five themes:

- social commitments
- multiparty communication
- content languages
- dialogues and conversations
- speech acts

Although these themes are of course not mutually exclusive they indicate some main directions of research. We therefore have arranged the papers in the book according to the topics indicated above.

The first three papers focus on the role of social commitments in agent communication. In the first paper, Nicoletta Fornara, Fransesco Viganò and Marco Colombetti explore the role of social commitments in defining the semantics of agent communication in the context of artificial institutions. *Roberto Flores, Philippe Pasquier and Brahim Chaib-draa* formalize the dynamics of social commitments, where they stress the role of commitment messages as coordination devices to advance the state of joint activities. In the subsequent contribution, *Ashok Mallya and Munindar Singh* use social commitments as a semantic underpinning of a formal framework to reason about the composition of interaction protocols.

The next two contributions involve communication between more than two agents. *Gery Gutnik and Gal Kaminka* address the representation of interaction protocols by means of Petri nets. In particular, the authors focus on protocols for overhearing in which more than two agents are involved. The theme of multiparty communication is further elaborated in the contribution of *Marc-Philippe Huget and Yves Demazeau*, where a communication server for multiparty dialogue is described.

The following two contributions focus on the role of vocabularies, ontologies and content languages in agent communication. *Jurriaan van Diggelen, Robbert-Jan Beun, Frank Dignum, Rogier van Eijk and John-Jules Meyer* study the characteristics and properties of communication vocabularies in multiagent systems with heterogeneous ontologies. *Mario Verdicchio and Marco Colombetti* deal with another aspect of content languages: the formal expression of temporal conditions.

The first paper of the section on dialogues and conversations is by *Jarred McGinnis and David Robertson* who define a general language for the expression of dynamic and flexible dialogue protocols. The flexibility of protocols is further elaborated in the contribution of *Lalana Kagal and Tim Finin* where conversation specifications and conversation policies are defined in terms of permissions and obligations. The authors introduce techniques to resolve conflicts within the specifications and policies and provide an engine that allows agents to reason about their conversations. In the next paper, *Joris Hulstijn, Mehdi Dastani and Frank Dignum* study the coherence of agent conversations. In particular, they show how constraints on the context of messages can be used to establish coherent dialogues. The importance of the context is also stressed in the contribution of *Matthias Nickles, Michael Rovatsos and Gerhard Weiss* who study the effects of social interaction structures on the semantics of messages. *Mirko Viroli and Alessandro Ricci* look at communication from the perspective of coordination. In their approach, agents coordinate their activities via artifacts that specify the successive actions of the interaction protocol.

The last four contributions of the volume are centered around the semantics of speech acts. *Karim Bouzouba, Jamal Bentahar and Bernard Moulin* develop a computation model to study the semantics of speech acts in dialogues between agents and humans. In the subsequent contribution, *Peter McBurney and Simon Parsons* propose a set of speech acts together with an interaction protocol for argumenation for which they provide an operational semantics. In the contribution of *Marcus Huber, Sanjeev Kumar and David McGee*, a repertory of speech acts is provided, where the semantics of the acts is defined in terms of joint intentions. Finally, *Shakil Khan and Yves Lesperance* study the semantics of speech acts in terms of the agents' knowledge, intentions and commitments and show how this can be integrated into a planning framework.

To close, we would like to take this opportunity to thank the members of the Program Committee, the external reviewers and the authors of submitted papers for enabling us to edit this exciting volume on the *Developments in Agent Communication*.

Utrecht, November 2004   Rogier van Eijk
                                                        Marc-Philippe Huget
                                                        Frank Dignum

Workshop Organization

Organizing Committee

Rogier van Eijk	Utrecht University, Utrecht, The Netherlands
Marc-Philippe Huget	Laboratoire LEIBNIZ, Institut IMAG, France
Frank Dignum	Utrecht University, Utrecht, The Netherlands

Program Committee

Leila Amgoud	IRIT (France)
Brahim Chaib-draa	Laval University (Canada)
Phil Cohen	Oregon Health and Science University (USA)
Marco Colombetti	Politecnico di Milano (Italy)
Mehdi Dastani	Utrecht University (The Netherlands)
Amal El Fallah-Seghrouchni	University of Paris 6 (France)
Frank Guerin	University of Aberdeen (UK)
Mark d'Inverno	Westminster University (UK)
Andrew Jones	King's College, London (UK)
Yannis Labrou	Fujitsu Laboratories (USA)
Nicolas Maudet	University of Paris 9 (France)
Peter McBurney	University of Liverpool (UK)
Simon Parsons	Brooklyn College, City University of NY (USA)
Shamima Paurobally	University of Southampton (UK)
Nico Roos	Maastricht University (The Netherlands)
Munindar Singh	North Carolina State University (USA)
Gerhard Weiss	Technical University Munich (Germany)
Michael Wooldridge	University of Liverpool (UK)

External Reviewers

Sanjeev Kumar
Jan Broersen
Roberto Flores
Jamal Bentahar
Philippe Pasquier
Michael Rovatsos
Matthias Nickles

Table of Contents

Section V: Speech Acts

Agent Communication and Institutional Reality*

Nicoletta Fornara[1], Francesco Viganò[1], and Macro Colombetti[1,2]

[1] Università della Svizzera italiana, via G. Buffi 13, 6900 Lugano, Switzerland
{nicoletta.fornara, francesco.vigano, marco.colombetti}@lu.unisi.ch
[2] Politecnico di Milano, piazza Leonardo Da Vinci 32, Milano, Italy
marco.colombetti@polimi.it

Abstract. In this paper we propose to regard an Agent Communication Language (ACL) as a set of conventions to act on a fragment of institutional reality, defined in the context of an artificial institution. Within such an approach, we first reformulate a previously proposed commitment-based semantics for ACLs. In particular we show that all commonly used types of communicative acts can be defined in terms of a single basic type, namely *declarations*, within an artificial institution that we call Basic Institution. We then go on defining special institutions, that augment the Basic Institution by adding ontological and normative elements. Finally, as an example of a special institution we give a partial definition of the institution of English Auctions.

1   Introduction

In the last few years the concept of *social commitment* has been largely used by a growing number of researchers to define the semantics of Agent Communication Languages (ACLs). After the first studies carried out by Singh and by Colombetti [28, 5], further investigations have been carried out from an operational point of view [12, 19], following a logical approach [30], and in the field of argumentation studies [1, 3]. The main advantages of this approach are that commitments are objective and independent of an agent's internal structure, and that it is possible to verify whether an agent is behaving according to the given semantics.

Social commitments are used to represent the evolution of social relationships among agents during interactions. Communicative acts are then viewed as actions carried out to modify such relationships by creating, updating or cancelling commitments according to a predefined set of shared rules [30, 13]. More precisely, communicative acts are regarded as a sort of *institutional actions*, that is, as actions performed within an *institution* to modify a fragment of social reality [25]. Defining the semantics of an ACL has therefore two sides: one side is the definition of the institutional effects brought about by the performance of communicative acts; the other side is the definition of the social context in which

---

* Supported by Swiss National Science Foundation project 200021-100260, "An Open Interaction Framework for Communicative Agents".

agents can carry out institutional actions, and that we call an *(artificial) institution*. Indeed, our main tenet is that without the definition of an appropriate institution it is impossible to specify the semantics of an ACL.

This paper is structured as follows. In Section 2 we introduce the fundamental concepts on which we base our treatment of agent communication, namely the concepts of an *institutional action*, of a *convention*, and of a "counts as" relationship between an *instrumental action* and the corresponding communicative act. In Section 3 we define the institutional actions that can be performed on commitments. In Section 4 we describe the Basic Institution (i.e., the institution that regulates the management of commitments) and introduce the concept of a special institution. In Section 5 we give a partial description of a specific case of a special institution, that is, the institution of English Auctions. In Section 6 we briefly remark on related work present in this volume. Finally in Section 7 we draw some conclusions and delineate some directions for future work.

2   Fundamental Concepts

We view a multiagent system (MAS) as a technological extension of human society, by which individual persons and human organizations can delegate the execution of institutional actions to the artificial system. Examples of such actions are establishing appointments, signing contracts, and carrying out commercial transactions. For this reason there are strong connections between some aspects of a MAS and some aspects of human society, and therefore the concepts used to model a MAS interaction framework have to reflect some crucial characteristics of their human counterpart.

The context within which artificial agents operate can be modelled as consisting of a set of *entities* that can have *natural* or *institutional* attributes, that is, attributes that exist only thanks to the common agreement of the interacting agents (or more precisely of their users). For example, the color of a book is a natural attribute, while the book's price and its owner are institutional attributes. Natural attributes are assumed to reflect the physical properties of the corresponding entities of the real world, and typically cannot be changed by artificial agents (unless the agent controls a physical robot). On the contrary, institutional attributes can be affected by *institutional actions* performed by purely software agents.

2.1   Institutional Actions

Institutional actions are particular types of actions [7] that are crucial for the formalization of communicative interactions taking place in open interaction frameworks. The effect of institutional actions is to change institutional attributes, that exist only thanks to common agreement. Therefore, agents cannot perform such actions by exploiting causal links occurring in the natural world, as it would be done to open a door or to remove a physical object. Rather, as we shall see, institutional actions are performed on the basis of a shared set of conventions.

Because of their intrinsic social nature, a crucial condition for the actual performance of institutional actions is that they must be *public*, that is, made known to the relevant agents by means of some action that can be directly executed by an artificial agent. It is therefore natural to assume that all institutional actions are performed by sending suitable messages to the relevant agents. An example of institutional action, that will be discussed in Section 5, is the act of opening an auction; as we shall see, an agent (the auctioneer) can perform such an action by sending a suitable message to the relevant group of agents (the participants). However, the act of sending the message is merely instrumental, and should not be confused with the institutional action of opening the auction.

We define institutional actions by specifying their *preconditions* and *postconditions*, therefore abstracting from the way in which such actions are concretely carried out. More precisely, an institutional action is characterized by:

- an *action name* followed by a possibly empty list of *parameters*;
- a possibly empty set of *(ontological) preconditions*, that specify the values that certain institutional attributes must have for the action to be meaningful (for example, opening an auction is meaningful only if the auction is not already open);
- a nonempty set of *postconditions*, that specify the values of certain institutional attributes after a successful performance of the action.

2.2   Instrumental Actions

As we have already remarked, an institutional action is performed by executing an instrumental action, conventionally associated to the institutional action. In the human world such instrumental actions vary from certain bodily movements (raising one's arm to vote), to the use of specific physical tools (waving a white flag to surrender), to the use of language (saying "the auction is open" to open an auction). In a system of artificial agents, it is natural to assume that all institutional actions are performed by means of a single type of instrumental actions, namely exchanging a message.

For the purposes of the current treatment, a message consists of: a *message type*, a *sender*, one or more *receivers*, and a *content*. The action of exchanging a message will be represented with the following notation:

exchMsg($message\_type, sender, receiver(s), content$)

Note that here *sender* and *receiver* are just fields of a message. That such fields correctly represent the agent that actually sends the message and the agents to which the message is delivered has to be guaranteed by the underlying message transport system.

2.3   The "Counts as" Relation

Following Searle [25], the construction of social reality in the human world is possible thanks to *constitutive rules* of the form X *counts as* Y *in* C; in the particular case where X and Y are actions, the performance of an action of type X in context C can count as performing an action of type Y. Similarly, in an artificial system, thanks to shared *conventions*, the action of exchanging a particular message can "count as" the execution of some institutional action, if certain *contextual conditions* are satisfied.

According to Searle's Speech Act Theory [24], *declarations* are the particular category of communicative acts whose point is to bring about a change in the institutional reality in virtue of their successful performance. By definition the content of a declaration describes precisely the institutional changes that it brings about. Therefore, we take messages of type *declare* as the fundamental means to perform institutional actions. The convention that binds the exchange of a *declare* message to the performance of the institutional action (*iaction*), described in its content, can be described as follows:

$$\mathsf{exchMsg}(\mathsf{declare}, sender, receiver, iaction(parameters)) =_{conv}$$
$$iaction(parameters)$$

By itself, however, a convention is not sufficient to guarantee the successful performance of an institutional action by the exchange of a *declare* message: indeed, some additional conditions about the agent that sends the message and about the state of system must be satisfied. In general, an agent must be *authorized* to perform an institutional action; for example, only the auctioneer can open an auction by sending a suitable message to the participants. Further *contextual conditions* about the state of the system, expressed by suitable Boolean expressions, may be required; for example, it may be established that an auction is validly opened only if there are at least two participants.

Assuming that every agent in the interaction system has an identifier (*agent_id*), authorizations will be represented with the following notation:

$$\mathsf{Auth}(agent\_id, iaction(parameters), contextual\_conditions)$$

Our notion of authorization should not be confused with the notion of *permission*. The distinction we make between these two concepts is similar to the one between institutionalized power and permission proposed by Jones and Sergot in [16]. While authorizations are necessary conditions for the performance of institutional actions, permissions (like obligations) are brought about by *norms* (see Section 4.2), that is, by rules that affect the normative positions of the agents in the system. The crucial difference between authorizations and permissions is highlighted in the cases when they are not granted. If an agent is not authorized to perform an institutional action, a performance of the corresponding instrumental action does not count as a performance of the institutional action (the institutional action is thus not executed). On the contrary, if an authorized agent performs an institutional action without permission, the institutional action is successfully performed, but the agent violates a norm and it may be sanctioned for its behavior.

In the specification of an interaction system it is useful to express authorizations in term of the *roles* filled by agents, in order to abstract from the concrete agents that will be actually involved in an interaction. For example, the authorization to open and close an auction is granted to the agent that fills the role of the auctioneer, independently of its individual identity.

The concept of a role is very broad: for example, it is possible to regard social commitments as institutional entities that define two roles: the *debtor* of the commitment and its *creditor*. This fact appears to be general; that is, roles are defined relative to an institutional entity. We can then abstractly define the authorization to perform a specific institutional action (with given parameters) associating it to a role defined in the context of a specific institutional entity (*ientity*):

Auth(*ientity.role, iaction(parameters), contextual_conditions*)

In a concrete interaction, the authorizations associated to roles need to be transformed into authorizations of an actual agent in the system. Such transformation can be obtained searching among all the institutional entities present in the system the ones that match the description given through the parameters of the institutional action, and then creating a concrete authorization for each agent having the role indicated in the abstract authorization.

3   A Commitment-Based Agent Communication Language

The semantics of ACLs that we have proposed in [12, 13] is based on the assumption that the performance of a communicative act in a multiagent system has the effect of changing the social relationship between the sender and the receiver, and that this change can be represented by means of an institutional entity, that is, *social commitment*. To specify the meaning of various types of communicative acts in terms of effects on commitments, it is necessary to define an ontology of commitment and the institutional actions necessary to operate on commitments.

3.1   The Ontology of Commitment

We regard a commitment as an entity with the following attributes: a *debtor*; a *creditor*; a *content*; a *state*, used to keep track of the temporal evolution of the commitment. Commitments will be represented with the following notation:

Comm(*state, debtor, creditor, content*)

The content of a commitment can be represented by means of a *temporal proposition* (for a detailed treatment of temporal propositions see [13, 6]), that is, a proposition about a state of affairs or about the performance of an action, referred to a specific interval of time. At every time instant, a temporal proposition has a truth value, that can be *undefined, true, or false.*

The state of a commitment undergoes a life cycle, described by the state diagram of Figure 1, and can change as an effect of the execution of institutional actions (solid lines) or of environmental events (dotted lines). Relevant events are due to the change of the truth-value of the commitment's content.

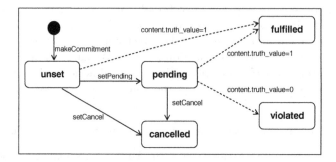

Fig. 1. The life-cycle of commitments

The creditor of a commitment can be a single agent or a group of agents. It is important to remark that a commitment taken with a group of agents need not be equivalent to a conjunction of commitments taken with every member of the group. This point has been thoroughly analyzed in the literature [4, 8] but is behind the scope of this paper.

Institutional Actions on Commitment. The institutional actions that operate on commitments are defined below; preconditions and effects are described using Object Constraint Language (OCL) [23].

- $name$: makeCommitment($debtor, creditor, content$)
  pre : not Comm.$allInstances \rightarrow exists(c|c.$debtor $= debtor$
          $and\ c.$creditor $= creditor\ and\ c.$content $= content$)
  $post$: Comm.$allInstances \rightarrow exists(c|c.$state $=$ unset and
          $c.$debtor $= debtor\ and\ c.$creditor $= creditor\ and\ c.$content $= content$)
- $name$: setCancel($debtor, creditor, content$)
  pre :   Comm.$allInstances \rightarrow exists(c|(c.$state $=$ unset $or\ c.$state $=$ pending)
          $and\ c.$debtor $= debtor\ and\ c.$creditor $= creditor\ and\ c.$content $= content$)
  $post$: Comm.$allInstances \rightarrow exists(c|c.$state $=$ cancel and
          $c.$debtor $= debtor\ and\ c.$creditor $= creditor\ and\ c.$content $= content$)
- $name$: setPending($debtor, creditor, content$)
  pre :   Comm.$allInstances \rightarrow exists(c|c.$state $=$ unset and
          $c.$debtor $= debtor\ and\ c.$creditor $= creditor\ and\ c.$content $= content$)
  $post$: Comm.$allInstances \rightarrow exists(c|c.$state $=$ pending and
          $c.$debtor $= debtor\ and\ c.$creditor $= creditor\ and\ c.$content $= content$)

It is often useful to define *institutional macro-actions*, that is, actions whose execution coincides with the sequential execution of a list of existing institutional actions, conceived of as a single transaction. For example:

$name$: makePendingComm($debtor, creditor, content$) $=_{def}$
makeCommitment($debtor, creditor, content$), setPending($debtor, creditor, content$)

3.2   Communicative Acts Libraries

As we already discussed in Section 2, the exchange of a message of type declare can be considered as the universal act for the performance of institutional actions; in particular, every type of communicative act can be performed by means of a declaration. This means that, at least in principle, an ACL can be defined on the basis of a single type of messages[1].

To make a more natural set of communicative acts available to human developers, we now define a library of messages that gets closer to FIPA ACL [15]. The content of all messages defined below is a temporal proposition, that is, a description of a state of affairs or the description of a physical action referred to a certain interval of time. The symbol $=_{def}$ means that performing the action on the left-hand side is the same as performing the action on the right-hand side.

- exchMsg($inform, sender, receiver, content$) $=_{def}$ exchMsg(declare, $sender,$ $receiver$, makePendingComm($sender, receiver, content$))
- exchMsg($request, sender, receiver, content$) $=_{def}$ exchMsg(declare, $sender,$ $receiver$, makeCommitment($sender, receiver, content$))
- exchMsg($accept, sender, receiver, content$) $=_{def}$ exchMsg(declare, $sender, receiver$, setPending($sender, receiver, content$))
- exchMsg($reject, sender, receiver, content$) $=_{def}$ exchMsg(declare, $sender, receiver$, setCancel($sender, receiver, content$))

4   Artificial Institutions

The word *institution* is used in the literature with different meanings. An institution can be seen as an established organization (especially of a public character) with a code of law, like for example a hospital or a university. With a different meaning, the word is used to refer to a set of concepts that exist only thanks to the common agreement of a community of agents, like for example in the case of money, ownership, or marriage.

In multiagent systems research the term *artificial institution* is commonly used to refer to a specific organization or to an abstract pattern that regulates the interaction among agents [9] [29]. On the contrary, we use the term "artificial institution" to refer to the abstract description of shared concepts and rules that regulate a fragment of social reality. In this perspective a concrete organization is a reification of one or more artificial institutions. In our view, the specification of an institution consists of the following components:

- the *core ontology*, that is, the definitions of the institutional concepts introduced by the institution and of the institutional actions that operates on them;

---

[1] Carrying out a communicative act by declaration corresponds to a *performative execution* of the communicative act [26]. In human languages, however, only the communicative acts that are completely overt may have a performative execution; certain communicative acts, like for example the act of insinuating, cannot be performed by declaration, because they intrinsically contain a concealed component.

- a set of *authorizations* specifying which agents are empowered to perform the institutional actions;
- a set of *norms* that impose *obligations* and *permissions* on the agents that interact within the institution.

Of course, in order that the proposed model can actually be used in real applications it is necessary that the fundamental concepts, used to define the structure of institutions, are collectively accepted by the designers and users of open interaction frameworks.

4.1   The Basic Institution

The Basic Institution is the institution that defines and regulates the management of commitments, which we regard as the fundamental concept of every interaction. In the previous section commitment has been introduced as an institutional entity, together with a set of institutional actions to operate on it. We showed that commitments can be used to define basic types of communicative acts that can be performed by exchanging *declare* messages.

As discussed in Section 2, the "count as" relation between the action of exchanging a message and the associated institutional action takes place if some conditions are satisfied; more precisely, the sender of the message must be authorized to perform the institutional action and some contextual conditions must hold. We have also shown how authorizations can be associated to roles.

We now define a set of authorizations concerning the creation and the manipulation of commitments. Such authorizations will be associated to the two roles introduced by commitments themselves: the role of *debtor* and the role of *creditor*. Moreover, we assume a universal role, *RegAgt*, that every registered agent plays throughout its lifetime.

- Any registered agent can create an *unset* commitment with any other registered agent as debtor or creditor:

  Auth(RegAgt, makeCommitment(*debtor, creditor, content*));

- the debtor of an *unset* commitment can set it to *pending*:

  Auth(Comm(*debtor, creditor, content*).debtor, setPending(*debtor, creditor, content*));

- the debtor of an *unset* commitment can set it to *cancelled*:

  Auth(Comm(unset, *debtor, creditor, content*).debtor, setCancel(*debtor, creditor, content*));

- the creditor of a commitment can set it to *cancelled*:

  Auth(Comm(*debtor, creditor, content*).creditor, setCancel(*debtor, creditor, content*)).

Note that these authorizations allow an agent to perform all communicative acts defined in Section 3.2. These basic authorizations may be modified or new ones may be introduced within special institutions (see Section 5).

In general, institutions also define sets of norms to regulate the behavior of agents. In our current view, the Basic Institution specifies no norms. However, norms are introduced by most special institutions, and in particular by the special institution of English Auctions described in Section 5. Therefore, in the next subsection we give a detailed description of our concept of norm.

4.2   Norms

In a special institution, the execution of an action by an authorized agent often needs to be regulated by another fundamental component of artificial institutions, that is, a system of *norms*. For example, the auctioneer of an English Auction not only is authorized to declare who is the winner, but he is also obliged to do so in certain circumstances. Furthermore, there are conditions under which it is forbidden to the auctioneer to declare an agent as the winner (for instance during a period of time reserved for offers).

Norms prescribe which institutional actions should or should not be executed among those that are authorized. In doing so, norms play an important function, in that they make an agent's behavior at least partially predictable and allow agents to coordinate and plan their actions according to the expected behavior of the others, as studied in [21, 2]. In particular, we think that norms can be used to specify protocols, because they can dictate that in certain circumstances an agent ought to send a given type of message, or react to a message in a specific way, to comply with the regulations of a specific institution. How this can be done will be shown in Section 5.

We regard norms as event-driven rules that fire under appropriate conditions and, by doing so, create, update or cancel commitments affecting a predefined set of agents. At an abstract level, a norm is part of the definition of an artificial institution; its instances then regulate and are bounded to the organization that reifies the institution. Agents are liable to all the norms associated to the roles they play in an institution.

A norm is defined within an institution, observes an entity of an institution, is activated by an event concerning such an entity, and then fires if certain contextual conditions are met. Typically, interesting event types are the filling of a role by an agent, a value change of an institutional attribute, the reaching of certain instant of time, and so on.

When a norm fires, it is applied to a collection of *liable agents*, that are described by a suitable selection expression; in general, the collection of liable agents corresponds to the set of agents that play a given role in the institution. For every liable agent, the norm creates, updates or cancels a set of commitments.

The general structure of a norm can be described as follows:

within *context_name*: *ientity*
on *e*: *event_type*
if *contextual conditions* **then**

foreach *agent* **in** *selection expression*
do {*commitmentActionDescription*}$^+$

Many studies have been devoted to the analysis of the relationship holding between norms and commitments, which is often perceived as a fundamental aspect of institutions [9] and organizations [4]. For example in [10] commitments are viewed as a specialization of norms, while in [4] and [27] norms are a special kind of commitments, called *metacommitments*.

From our point of view, norms are not themselves commitments, but rules that manipulate commitments of the agents engaged in an interaction. In fact, norms are associated to roles rather than to individual agents; they do not have a debtor or a creditor, and strictly speaking they cannot be fulfilled or violated. Indeed, what can be fulfilled or violated is not a norm, but a commitment created by the application of a norm.

There are, in conclusion, two types of commitments: the ones created by individual agents through the execution of communicative acts, and the ones created by norms and acquired by an agent in virtue of its role in an institution.

5   English Auction

In this section we will briefly describe an example[2] of a *special institution*, concerning the specification of a widely studied interaction framework: the English Auction. The formalization proposed exploits the conventional nature of this type of interaction, making explicit the social concepts and rules that constitute and regulate the interaction.

In the literature there are other attempts to specify the English Auction, like for instance the one proposed by FIPA [14] and the one presented in a previous work of ours [13]. But we think that the definition of the English Auction as a special institution overcomes some drawbacks of those formalizations. In particular in the approach presented in [14] the commitments between the winner and the auctioneer are created only when the auction is closed. On the contrary in the current formalization and in [13] commitments are undertaken by the agents during the auction.

Another important advantage of this approach with respect to [13] is that the explicit formalization of the context of the interaction simplifies the content of the exchanged messages. For instance if the context is not made explicit, the auctioneer of an English Auction has to accept a bid of a participant, committing the auction house to give the product to that participant, on condition that no higher bids will be submitted. Otherwise the context can be made explicit for example by introducing the role *current_winner* and a norm that creates a commitment for the *current_winner* to pay the *ask_price* to the auction house, and a commitment for the auction house to give the *product* to the *current_winner* of

---

[2] A complete example appears in the forthcoming Technical Report USI-Com-ITC-01, May 2004.

the last round. Using this formalization, the content of the exchanged messages for bidding and for declaring the winner are simple institutional actions, as will be shown in the next section.

5.1   The English Auction Ontology (EAOntology)

Entities. The ontology of the English Auction consists of some institutional entities and is described by the class diagram reported in Figure 2. The fundamental entity called *EnglishAuction* is identified by its *id* and can assume three different states: *unset*, during the registration phase, *open* and *closed*. An *EnglishAuction* has a *product* that will be sold at the *ask_price*, which starts from the *reservation_price* and increases until there are no more bids or the maximum number of rounds (*max_round*) is reached.

An agent that takes part in an English Auction can fill the role of *participant* or of *auctioneer*. In each *Round*, participants can only raise their *Bids* and the highest bidder is declared the *current_winner*. During one auction we assume that an agent cannot be both a participant and an auctioneer, while it must be a participant in order to be allowed to become a *current_winner*. Furthermore, all the agents that are related to the auction are gathered in the *EAGroup*.

Other concepts that are fundamental for every MAS, like *Agent* and *IndividualAgent*, are assumed to be defined in external ontologies.

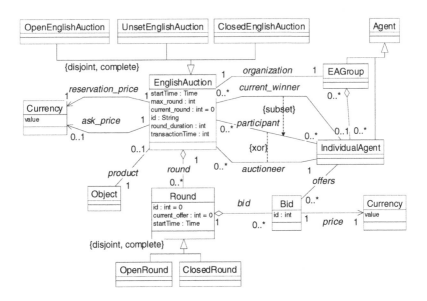

Fig. 2. Class diagram representing the English Auction ontology

Institutional Actions. The institutional actions that operate on *EnglishAuction* entities allow agents to open and close the auction, to set the *current_winner* or a new *ask_price*, to open and close a round and to make a bid.

To describe an institutional action a slight extension of OCL is needed. In fact, using the terminology introduced in [7], object oriented specifications usually treat actions as events, because they only model state changes in the world. Instead, an action is an event brought about by an agent, and may have different effects depending on which authorized agent has performed it. For example, the act of bidding creates a new offer for the bidder and not for other agents. Therefore, we introduce a new reserved word, *actor*, that is used to refer to the agent that is performing the action. Below we formally define some of the institutional actions made available by the EAOntology. The action for opening an auction is:

$name$: openAuction($auct\_id$)
pre :   UnsetEnglishAuction.$allInstances \rightarrow exists$(id = $auct\_id$)
$post$:   OpenEnglishAuction.$allInstances \rightarrow exists$(id = $auct\_id$)

The action for setting the *ask_price*, that can only rise, is:

$name$: setAskPrice($auct\_id, price$)
pre :   OpenEnglishAuction.$allInstances \rightarrow exists$(id = $auct\_id$
            and ask_price.value $< price$)
$post$:   OpenEnglishAuction.$allInstances \rightarrow exists$(id = $auct\_id$
            and ask_price.value $= price$)

The action for making a bid:

$name$: makeBid($auct\_id, price$)
pre : $let\ a$: OpenEnglishAuction = OpenEnglishAuction.$allInstances \rightarrow$
            $select$(id = $auct\_id$)
            a.round $\rightarrow select$($r \mid r.oclIsTypeOf$(OpenRound)).bid $\rightarrow$
            $select$($actor$ = offers) $\rightarrow isEmpty$() $and\ a$.ask_price.value $< price$)
$post$: $let\ round$: Round = EnglishAuction.$allInstances \rightarrow$
            $select$(id = $auct\_id$).round $\rightarrow select$(a.current_round)
            $round$.current_offer = $round$.current_offer@pre + 1 $and\ round$.bid $\rightarrow$
            $select$($b \mid not\ round$.bid@$pre \rightarrow including$($b$) $and\ b$.offers = $actor$
            $and\ b$.price.value = $price\ and\ b$.id = $round$.currentOffer) $\rightarrow sizeOf$() = 1

This action is successful only if the offered price is higher than the *ask_price* and if the bidder has not yet offered in the current round. Its effect is to increment the number of offers and to create a new *Bid*.

5.2   Authorizations

Participant are authorized only to make bids:

Auth(EnglishAuction$_{id}$.participant, makeBid($id, price$))

Auctioneers are authorized to perform all other actions defined by the EAOntology. For example:

Auth(EnglishAuction$_{id}$.auctioneer, openAuction(id))
Auth(EnglishAuction$_{id}$.auctioneer, setAskPrice($id, price$))

5.3   Norms

Due to space limitations we will describe the main phases that characterize an auction, reporting only an example of the required norms.

During the registration phase, when an agent fills a role, a suitable norm forbids it to execute any action on *EnglishAuction* entities. This to prevent agents from executing ontologically impossible institutional actions, thus causing system overload due to the exchange of useless messages.

In every phase of the interaction, the auctioneer is obliged to do a specific action among those it is authorized to perform, and it is forbidden from doing any of the others. Therefore, the norms concerning the auctioneer have a recurrent pattern.

When the auction is declared open, the auctioneer should set the reservation price and open a new round, during which the participants can bid. Unlike the auctioneer, a participant has the *permission* to make a bid but it is not obliged. Therefore, when a round is opened, its commitment not to bid has to be cancelled, but no obligation to do so is created.

After the *round_duration* has elapsed, participants are prohibited from making more bids, while the auctioneer is committed to close the round, and, if there is a valid offer, to proclaim the *current_winner* and the new *ask_price*, otherwise it must close the auction. For example the following norm defines the obligation of the auctioneer relative to the operation of setting the ask price when a round is closed.

within r: Round
on e: $changeState(r)$
if $r.oclIsTypeOf$(CloseRound) *and* r.bid $\rightarrow notEmpty()$ **then**
  foreach $agent$ **in** r.englishAuction.auctioneer
  do
   foreach $comm$ **in** Comm.$AllInstances \rightarrow select$(debtor $= agent$ *and*
    creditor $= r$.englishAuction.organization *and*
    content.$match$(not setAskPrice(r.englishAuction.id, $-$)))
   do
   setCancel($comm$.debtor, $comm$.creditor, $comm$.content)
   makePendingComm($agent$, r.englishAuction.organization,
    (setAskPrice(r.englishAuction.id, r.bid $\rightarrow select(b1, b2 \mid b1 <> b2$ *implies*
    $b1$.price.value $\geq b2$.price.value).price.value $\rightarrow asSet()$), [now, now $+ \delta$], $\exists$))
   makePendingComm($agent$, r.englishAuction.organization,
    (not closeRound (r.englishAuction.id),
    [now, $time\_of$(closeAuction(r.englishAuction))], $\forall$))

Where δ is the time allowed to the agent to fulfill its obligation. When an agent fills the role of *current_winner*, a norm obliges it to buy the *product* on sale at the price of its last bid and forces the auctioneer to sell it. Finally, if *max_round* is not reached the auctioneer has to open a new round, otherwise it should close the auction.

6   Discussion

In this section we compare our approach with other proposals presented in this volume.

In [11] Flores et al. propose an ACL semantics based on four levels: compositional, conversational, commitment state, and joint activity. The first level, used to express the meaning of messages in term of commitments, characterized by a life cycle based on states and transitions, is very close to our proposal. However, Flores et al. do not face the problem of describing the content of messages and commitments. A further difference of their approach is that in order for a commitment to become active either the debtor or the creditor have to accept it; this is an interesting change in the life cycle of commitment that we intend to investigate in our future works. The introduction of the other levels for specifying the semantics of messages is very interesting, even if we think that these levels do not change the semantics of messages but introduce new conditions for the correctness of messages; such conditions look like to soundness conditions of interaction protocols treated in [13].

A semantics based on objective and external concepts is also given in [22], where the meaning of communicative acts is described in terms of the expected future actions of the interacting agents. We think that such an approach could be applied to collaborative systems, where the assumptions about communication regularities and the existence of recurrent pattern are usually verified. Instead, we think that such empirical semantics is difficult to apply to open and competitive systems. In fact, in such systems communication regularities are not guaranteed, because the set of the interacting agents can change, and very few assumptions can be made about how agents behave.

In [31] Viroli and Ricci propose a model of agent communication that does not rely on the exchange of ACL messages, but it is based on coordination artifacts. In their view, coordination artifacts mediate agent communication by offering to agents a set of operating instructions for sending and receiving information. One of the most remarkable differences between communication performed through artifacts and messages is that agent communication is not synchronized and, in general, agents do not know who their addresses are. We agree with Viroli and Ricci that their approach is not a competitor of ACLs, because they involve different scenarios.

In [18] Mallya and Singh propose an algebra for combining protocols to obtain more flexible conversations. In their approach, commitments are viewed as means for engineering protocols. As we showed in Section 4.2, norms can describe protocols; thus it would be interesting to study in depth how different institutions can be combined, how a designer can guarantee normative coherence, or how a conversation can reach the same communicative state by following alternative paths.

In [20] McBurney and Parson claim that the communicative act library of FIPA-ACL lacks in the coverage of agent argumentation. For this reason, they introduce a set of performatives that can be integrated in FIPA-ACL and define both a declarative and operational semantics for each act. Although we agree with McBurney and Parson that agents often have to deal with uncertainty, this does not mean that the most general semantics of assertions is to commit an agent to provide evidence when challenged. In fact, following Searle's Speech Act Theory, we think that the semantics of assertive acts is to commit the speaker to the truth of the propositional content. The semantics defined in [20] is a particular case, relevant when agents are involved in an argumentation process, because their behaviour is regulated by a specific set of norms that are characteristic of argumentation. For example, a norm can state that when an agent makes an assertion, if it is challenged it should either provide reasons to justify its point of view, or retract the assertion. Thus, we perceive the performatives described in [20] as a set of illocutionary acts that can be performed within a special institution devoted to argumentation.

In [17] Kagal and Finin present a preliminary model of conversation specification and policies using permissions and obligations. The approach to model and constrain agent interactions using normative concepts is similar to the one presented in this paper, where we describe the English Auction Protocol by means of norms that restrict the set of communicative actions available for an agent at each step of the interaction. We did not distinguish between conversation specification and policies, because our norms are suitable to express both cases. Our approach is more detailed in modelling institutional reality, which is regulated by a set of norms; we also propose to distinguish between authorization (or power) and permission. Kagal and Finin's declarative approach to the formalization of norms is fit for developing a reasoning engine for artificial agents, our operational approach is particularly suitable to check if an agent is behaving in accordance with the system of norms. Finally, a very interesting topic of research faced by Kagal and Finin, that we intend to investigate in future works, is the problem of resolving conflicts between norms using for example meta-policies.

7   Conclusions

In this paper we have defined an ACL as a set of conventions to act on a fragment of institutional reality, defined in the context of an artificial institution, called the Basic Institution. Within such an approach, we proposed a commitment-based semantics for an ACL, and showed that all commonly used types of communicative acts can be defined in terms of a single basic type, namely declarations. Then we have defined special institutions, that augment the Basic Institution by adding ontological and normative elements, and showed how a well known interaction framework, the English Auction, can be regarded as a special institution, its interaction protocol being defined as a set of norms.

We believe that our approach helps clarifying the strict relationships holding between language, institutional reality, and interaction rules in a MAS. Moreover, we believe that the adoption of an operational modelling style makes our proposal reasonably easy to implement. In fact, we plan to implement our framework as an extension of JADE in the near future.

References

1. L. Amgoud, N. Maudet, and S. Parsons. An argumentation-based semantics for agent communication languages. In F. V. Harmelen, editor, *Proceedings of the European Conference on Artificial Intelligence (ECAI-2002)*, pages 38–42, Lyon, France, 2002. IOS Press.
2. M. Barbuceanu, T. Gray, and S. Mankovski. Coordinating with obligations. In K. P. Sycara and M. Wooldridge, editors, *Proceedings of the 2nd International Conference on Autonomous Agents (Agents'98)*, pages 62–69, New York, 1998. ACM Press.
3. J. Bentahar, B. Moulin, and B. Chaib-draa. Commitment and argument network: A new formalism for agent communication. In F. Dignum, editor, *Advances in Agent Communication, International Workshop on Agent Communication Languages, ACL 2003, Melbourne, 2003*, volume 2922 of *LNCS*, pages 146–165. Springer, 2004.
4. C. Castelfranchi. Commitments: From individual intentions to groups and organizations. In V. Lesser, editor, *Proc. First International Conference on Multi-Agent Systems*, pages 528–535, San Francisco, USA, 1995. AAAI-Press and MIT Press.
5. M. Colombetti. A commitment–based approach to agent speech acts and conversations. In *Proc. Workshop on Agent Languages and Communication Policies, 4th International Conference on Autonomous Agents (Agents 2000)*, pages 21–29, Barcelona, Spain, 2000.
6. M. Colombetti, N. Fornara, and M. Verdicchio. A social approach to communication in multiagent systems. In J. A. Leite, A. Omicini, L. Sterling, and P. Torroni, editors, *Declarative Agent Languages and Technologies*, volume 2990 of *LNAI*, pages 191–220. Springer, 2004.
7. M. Colombetti and M. Verdicchio. An analysis of agent speech acts as institutional actions. In C. Castelfranchi and W. L. Johnson, editors, *Proc. AAMAS 2002*, pages 1157–1166, Bologna, Italy, 2002.
8. F. Dignum and L. Royakkers. Collective obligation and commitment. In *In Proc. of 5th Int. conference on Law in the Information Society*, Florence, Italy, 1998.
9. M. Esteva, J. A. Rodríguez-Aguilar, C. Sierra, P. Garcia, and J. L. Arcos. On the formal specification of electronic institutions. In F. Dignum and C. Sierra, editors, *Agent Mediated Electronic Commerce, The European AgentLink Perspective (LNAI 1991)*, pages 126–147. Springer, 2001.
10. F. Lopez y Lopez and M. Luck. Modelling Norms for Autonomous Agents. In E. Chavez, J. Favela, M. Mejia, and A. Oliart, editors, *Proceedings of Fourth Mexican International Conference on Computer Science*, pages 238–245, 2003.
11. R. Flores, P. Pasquier, and B. Chaib-draa. Conversational Semantics with Social Commitments. In F. Dignum, R. van Eijk, and M. Huget, editors, *Developments in Agent Communication*, LNAI, page in this volume. Springer Verlag, 2004.

12. N. Fornara and M. Colombetti. Operational specification of a commitment-based agent communication language. In C. Castelfranchi and W. L. Johnson, editors, *Proc. AAMAS 2002*, pages 535–542, Bologna, Italy, 2002.
13. N. Fornara and M. Colombetti. Defining interaction protocols using a commitment-based agent communication language. In J. S. Rosenschein, T. Sandholm, M. Wooldridge, and M. Yokoo, editors, *Proc. AAMAS 2003*, pages 520–527, Melbourne, Australia, 2003.
14. Foundation for Intelligent Physical Agents. FIPA English Auction Interaction Protocol Specification. http://www.fipa.org, 2001.
15. Foundation for Intelligent Physical Agents. FIPA Communicative Act Library Specification. http://www.fipa.org, 2002.
16. A. Jones and M. J. Sergot. A formal characterisation of institutionalised power. *Journal of the IGPL*, 4(3):429–445, 1996.
17. L. Kagal and T. Finin. Modeling Conversation Policies using Permissions and Obligations. In F. Dignum, R. van Eijk, and M. Huget, editors, *Developments in Agent Communication*, LNAI, page in this volume. Springer Verlag, 2004.
18. A. U. Mallya and M. P. Singh. A Semantic Approach for Designing Commitment Protocols. In F. Dignum, R. van Eijk, and M. Huget, editors, *Developments in Agent Communication*, LNAI, page in this volume. Springer Verlag, 2004.
19. P. McBurney and S. Parsons. Posit spaces: a performative model of e-commerce. In J. S. Rosenschein, T. Sandholm, M. Wooldridge, and M. Yokoo, editors, *Proc. AAMAS 2003*, pages 624–631, 2003.
20. P. McBurney and S. Parsons. Locutions for argumentation in agent interaction protocols. In F. Dignum, R. van Eijk, and M. Huget, editors, *Developments in Agent Communication*, LNAI, page in this volume. Springer Verlag, 2004.
21. Y. Moses and M. Tennenholtz. Artificial social systems. *Computers and AI*, 14(6):533–562, 1995.
22. M. Nickles, M. Rovatos, and G. Weiss. Empirical-Rational Semantics of Agent Communication. In F. Dignum, R. van Eijk, and M. Huget, editors, *Developments in Agent Communication*, LNAI, page in this volume. Springer Verlag, 2004.
23. Object Management Group, OMG . Object Constraint Language Specification 1.4. http://www.omg.org/, 2003.
24. J. R. Searle. *Speech Acts: An Essay in the Philosophy of Language*. Cambridge University Press, Cambridge, United Kingdom, 1969.
25. J. R. Searle. *The construction of social reality*. Free Press, New York, 1995.
26. J. R. Searle and D. Vanderveken. *Foundations of Illocutionary Logic*. Cambridge University Press, Cambridge, UK, 1984.
27. M. P. Singh. An ontology for commitments in multiagent systems: Toward a unification of normative concepts. *Artificial Intelligence and Law*, 7:97–113, 1999.
28. M. P. Singh. A social semantics for agent communication languages. In *Proceedings of IJCAI-99 Workshop on Agent Communication Languages*, pages 75–88, 1999.
29. J. Vazquez and F. Dignum. Modelling electronic organizations. In V. Marik, J. Muller, and M. Pechoucek, editors, *Multi-Agent Systems and Applications III*, volume 2691 of *LNAI*, pages 584–593. Springer, 2003.
30. M. Verdicchio and M. Colombetti. A logical model of social commitment for agent communication. In J. S. Rosenschein, T. Sandholm, M. Wooldridge, and M. Yokoo, editors, *Proc. AAMAS 2003*, pages 528–535, Melbourne, Australia, 2003.
31. M. Viroli and A. Ricci. Instruction-Based Semantics of Agent Mediated Interaction. In F. Dignum, R. van Eijk, and M. Huget, editors, *Developments in Agent Communication*, LNAI, page in this volume. Springer Verlag, 2004.

Conversational Semantics with Social Commitments

Roberto A. Flores, Philippe Pasquier, and Brahim Chaib-draa

Université Laval, Département d'Informatique et de Génie Logiciel,
Sainte-Foy, Québec, Canada G1K 7P4
{flores, pasquier, chaib}@damas.ift.ulaval.ca

Abstract. Message semantics are traditionally defined in terms of mental states, which is a trend that is criticized for assuming the sincerity and cooperativeness of agents. To circumvent these limitations, several proposals have been put forth to define the semantics of messages using social commitments. We follow this trend and present a conversational model where the meaning of messages is based on their use as coordinating devices advancing conversations that advance the state of social commitments and the state of the activities in which agents participate.

1 Introduction

Agent communication languages (ACLs) mandate the common elements upon which *coherent conversations* (4) can take place. The most influential ACLs in the agent community are KQML (5) and its *de facto* successor FIPA-ACL (8), which define the semantics of messages using mental states, and the sequencing of messages through conversation protocols. The main reasons to challenge the viability of these approaches in open environments lie on the practical impossibility of agents to verify that uttered messages comply with their semantic definitions without assuming the goodwill of interlocutors to abide by them (*sincerity condition*) (20), and the disassociation between message definitions and their use in conversations (17). As an alternative to circumvent these limitations, a second trend has emerged that makes use of the notion of social commitments to define coherent conversations. Notably within this trend is the work advanced in (7; 9; 11; 24), which support various aspects of conversational coherence.

We borrow from these experiences and propose an approach to define the conversational semantics of messages, i.e., the meaning that messages could have according to their use in conversations. To this end, we drew inspiration from the study of language use (3), which highlights two complementary types of meaning: *speaker's meaning*, which is based on the use of messages for the communication of intent, and *signal meaning*, which is based on the use of messages as coordinating devices advancing the state of joint activities.

We advocate this latter type of meaning and conceptualize messages as coordinating devices that advance conversations that advance the state of social commitments that advance joint activities, where the states of conversations, commitments and activities are part of the common ground of interacting agents.

R.M. van Eijk et al. (Eds.): AC 2004, LNAI 3396, pp. 18–32, 2005.

Following this view, we propose a model where the meaning of messages is incrementally defined based on the following levels: a *compositional level*, where the meaning of messages is given by the relationship of instances in a message (e.g., agents and the roles they play in a commitment); a *conversational level*, where the meaning of messages is given based on their occurrence as part of a conversation in which agents concur to advance the state of commitments; a *commitment state level*, where the meaning of messages is given according to the state of the commitments these messages manipulate; and a *joint activity level*, where the meaning of messages is given according to their use in joint activities.

In Section 2, we describe social commitments and their life cycle, i.e., the states in which a commitment could be, as well as the transitions between these states. In particular, we focus on transitions that are accomplished through the exchange of messages. This is followed (in Section 3) by our view of agents as image holders, where an image is an agent representation that stores both the messages that the agent represented has exchanged with the agent holding the image, and the commitments these agents have established through these communications. It is in this context that we derive our definitions of shared utterance and shared commitment. Based on these notions, we present (in Section 4) our four-level model upon which messages could be incrementally defined, and illustrate its application by defining a *call for proposals* message in a Contract Net Protocol (22) activity. We then conclude with brief remarks on related work.

Throughout this paper, we use the Object-Z specification language (21) to formalize definitions. We chose this language mainly due to the straightforwardness it affords to translate definitions into object-oriented implementations.

2   Social Commitments

The notion of *social commitments* (2; 19; 23) has been advanced as a way to raise expectations about other agents' performances. Specifically, a social commitment can be defined as an engagement in which an agent (the debtor) is responsible relative to another agent (the creditor) for the performance of an action.[1].

We share with others (e.g., (1; 12; 10)) the view that social commitments have a life cycle made of states and transitions between states. As shown in Figure 1, a commitment could be either *accepted* or *rejected* according to whether or not agents are engaged in it. If accepted, a commitment is either *active, violated* or *fulfilled*; if rejected, it is either *inactive* or *cancelled*. Commitments can move between states through four transition types: *adoption*, where an inactive commitment becomes accepted; *violation* and *fulfilment*, where an active commitment becomes violated or fulfilled, respectively; and, *discharge*, where an accepted commitment becomes cancelled. Initially, all commitments are inactive, but can become accepted upon adoption. Adopted commitments are classified as either active, violated or fulfilled based on the state of achievement of their conditions of satisfaction (i.e., whether these conditions could be met, cannot be

---

[1] We do not explicitly consider propositional content in this paper.

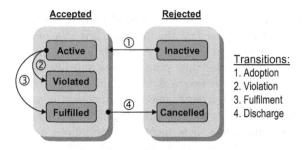

Fig. 1. Social Commitment states

met, or have been met, respectively), and can become cancelled upon discharge. It is worth noticing that violation and fulfillment depend on the conditions of satisfaction and that adoption and discharge are accomplished through (conversational) agreement. We model only conversational transitions and assume that transitions based on the conditions of satisfaction are carried out automatically.

2.1   Social Commitment Messages

We see messages as communicative actions where a speaker sends to an addressee a (non-empty) set of conversational tokens. We identify four tokens for the negotiation of commitments: *propose*, which indicates a social commitment operation (either to adopt or to discharge a commitment), and a time interval by which a reply to this proposal is expected; *accept* and *reject*, which are replies indicating either an acceptance or rejection to modify a social commitment state; and *counter*, which simultaneously rejects a modification and proposes a different one to be considered instead. We further specify utterances as events marking the occurrence of communicative actions at a certain moment in time.

2.2   Achieving Conversational Transitions

It is one thing to define communicative acts and quite another to describe how they are used and what they can accomplish in conversations. To that end, we use an interaction protocol called *protocol for proposals* (*pfp*) (6) as the fundamental vehicle to adopt and discharge commitments. As shown in Figure 2, the protocol starts with a proposal (i.e., a communicative act containing a *propose* token) from agent a to agent b. This message can be followed (before the expiration of a reply deadline) by the interaction patterns α or β. Interaction pattern α indicates that either agent b sends an accepting message to agent a, or that the interaction continues with pattern β (but with agents a and b's participatory roles inverted, that is, the role of the agent that in pattern α was agent a will be agent b in pattern β, and likewise for agent b). Interaction pattern β indicates that agent a sends a rejection or counterproposal message to agent b, in which case the interaction follows (before the expiration of a reply deadline) by either pattern α or pattern β. All replies except a counterproposal terminate

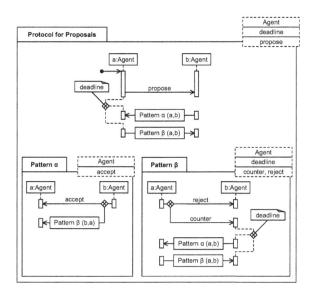

Fig. 2. The *protocol for proposals*

the protocol; and when an acceptance is issued, both *a* and *b* simultaneously apply the proposed and accepted social commitment operation to their record of social commitments.

3   Images and Agents

We conceptualize agents as image holders, and images as agent representations listing utterances and commitments. To restrict complex constructs (e.g., agents holding images that hold images, *ad infinitum*, of other agents), we limit these definitions through the following two properties: first, agents only capture utterances in which they are involved as either the speaker or the addressee (thus circumventing intricate ascriptions, such as agents being thought to have witnessed other agents' communications); and, second, communications are reliable (i.e., issuing an utterance implies that the speaker and the addressee are aware that it occurred). These properties help us capture the shared state of witnessed utterances, in the same spirit as that of shared-basis common ground (3).

Images are specified as repositories of utterances and social commitments, where each social commitment is associated with a unique state. As such, we define (as shown below) a mapping between a social commitment and a state.

$$SocialCommitmentState == \downarrow SocialCommitment \times \downarrow State$$

This definition does not preclude (as a function would do) that agents establish duplicated commitments, i.e., commitments that have the same debtor, creditor and action but different states. This feature requires common constructs and policies to unambiguously manipulate commitments and keep their shared state consistent as they undergo transitions. Rather than providing a unique identifier field as part of the structure of commitments, we kept the minimal debtor-creditor-action structure and specified that all identical commitments could only undergo conversational transitions through independent utterances, which guarantees that each duplicated commitment maps to a unique state.

As shown below, an image is specified as an *UtteranceHolder* and a *Social-CommitmentHolder*, where the former holds a set of utterances occurring at different times. On the other hand, a *SocialCommitmentHolder* (not shown) holds a set of social commitment states in which identical adopted (or discharged) commitments were proposed and accepted using different utterances.

$$
\begin{array}{|l}
\hline \textit{Image} \underline{\hspace{8cm}} \\
\textit{UtteranceHolder} \\
\textit{SocialCommitmentHolder} \\
\hline
\end{array}
$$

$$
\begin{array}{|l}
\hline \textit{UtteranceHolder} \underline{\hspace{6cm}} \\
\hline
\textit{witnessed} : \mathbb{P}\ \textit{Utterance} \\
\hline
\forall\ u_1, u_2 : \textit{witnessed}\ \big|\ u_1 \neq u_2 \bullet u_1.\textit{time} \neq u_2.\textit{time} \\
\hline
\end{array}
$$

As shown below, we define agents as entities that hold images. To this end, we first define the class *ImageHolder*, which specifies a function mapping agents and images, and where 1) an image only holds utterances whose speaker or addressee is the agent this image represents, 2) an image only holds commitments where its agent is the creditor or debtor, and 3) an image has records of all the utterances that have changed the state of all the adopted and discharged commitments it holds. Lastly, we specify agents as image holders, where each held image records utterances in which the agent is either the speaker or addressee, and commitments where the agent is either the creditor or debtor.

$$
\begin{array}{|l}
\hline \textit{Agent} \underline{\hspace{7cm}} \\
\textit{ImageHolder} \\
\hline
\forall\ \textit{agent} : \downarrow \textit{Agent};\ \textit{image} : \textit{Image}\ \big| \\
\quad \textit{image} = \textit{awareof}(\textit{agent}) \\
\bullet\ (\forall\ \textit{utterance} : \textit{image.witnessed} \\
\quad \bullet\ \textit{self} \in \textit{utterance.speechact.performers})\ \land \\
\quad (\forall\ \textit{time} : \textit{Time} \\
\quad \bullet\ \forall\ \textit{sc} : \text{dom}(\textit{image.commitments}(\textit{time})) \\
\quad\quad \bullet\ \textit{self} \in \{\textit{sc.creditor}, \textit{sc.debtor}\}) \\
\hline
\end{array}
$$

┌─ *ImageHolder* ───

  awareof : ↓*Agent* → *Image*
  ─────────────────────────────
  ∀ *agent* : ↓*Agent*; *image* : *Image* |
    image = *awareof*(*agent*)
  • (∀ *utterance* : *image.witnessed*
    • *agent* ∈ *utterance.speechact.performers*) ∧
    (∀ *time* : *Time*
    • (∀ *sc* : dom(*image.commitments*(*time*))
      • *agent* ∈ {*sc.debtor*, *sc.creditor*}) ∧
      (∀ *add* : ↓*Adopted* |
        add ∈ ran(*image.commitments*(*time*))
      • *add.adopt.proposal* ∈ *image.witnessed* ∧
        add.adopt.acceptance ∈ *image.witnessed*) ∧
      (∀ *del* : ↓*Discharged* |
        del ∈ ran(*image.commitments*(*time*))
      • *del.discharge.proposal* ∈ *image.witnessed* ∧
        del.discharge.acceptance ∈ *image.witnessed*))

└───

3.1   Sharing Utterances and Commitments

An utterance is shared between its speaker and addressee if they are aware that the utterance has been witnessed by both of them—which holds true given our assumption of reliable communications. Thus, an utterance is shared if its speaker and addressee hold images in which they have witnessed its occurrence.

┌───

  SharedUtterance : *Utterance* → 𝔹
  ─────────────────────────────
  ∀ *u* : *Utterance*
  • *SharedUtterance*(*u*) ⇔
    (∀ *agent* : *u.speechact.performers*
    • ∃ *speaker*, *addressee* : *Image* |
      speaker = *agent.awareof*(*u.speechact.speaker*) ∧
      addressee = *agent.awareof*(*u.speechact.addressee*)
    • *u* ∈ *speaker.witnessed* ∧
      u ∈ *addressee.witnessed*)

└───

Likewise, a social commitment is shared between two agents if these agents are the creditor and debtor of the commitment and if they have images in which this commitment has the same state. Accordingly, that a shared commitment is in an adopted or discharged state implies that agents also share the proposing and accepting utterances that brought the commitment to its current state.

$SharedSocialCommitments : Time \times \downarrow Agent \times \downarrow Agent \rightarrow \mathbb{P}\, SocialCommitmentState$

$\forall\, t : Time;\; a_1, a_2 : \downarrow Agent$

- $SharedSocialCommitments(t, a_1, a_2) =$
  $\{sc : SocialCommitmentState \,|$
  $\quad \forall\, agent : \{a_1, a_2\}$
  - $\exists\, i_1, i_2 : Image \,|$
    $\quad i_1 = agent.awareof(a_1)\; \wedge$
    $\quad i_2 = agent.awareof(a_2)$
    - $sc \in i_1.commitments(t)\; \wedge$
      $sc \in i_2.commitments(t)\}$

4   Message Definitions

Based on the above specifications, we incrementally built our message definitions through four levels: at the *compositional level*, where messages can be classified according to type and identity of their constituents; at the *conversational level*, where the significance of messages is given based on their occurrence as part of conversations seeking agreement to advance the state of commitments; at the *commitment state level*, where meaning is given according to the state of manipulated commitments; and at the *joint activity level*, where meaning is given according to the use of messages as part of joint activities.

4.1   Compositional Level

This level sets the foundations to build our message classification. Definitions at this level identify messages based on the type and identity of their components. These definitions are independent of the occurrence of messages as utterances, and allow their analysis outside the scope of conversations.

In the context of the *pfp*, agents agree on the conversational transition of social commitment states. In this view, a message is a well formed proposal (defined through the *ToPropose* function below) if it contains a *propose* conversational token whose speaker and addressee are the creditor and debtor of the proposed commitment. Similarly, a message is a well formed reply (as defined in *ToReply*) if there is a *reply* token (either an *accept*, *reject* or *counter*) whose speaker and addressee are the creditor and debtor of the commitment, and if there is no other reply token referring to this commitment (thus avoiding ambiguity on the termination of a *pfp* instance within a single message).

$ToPropose : ToSpeak \rightarrow \mathbb{P} \downarrow Propose$

$\forall\, s : ToSpeak$

- $ToPropose(s) =$
  $\{p : \downarrow Propose \,|$
  $\quad (p \in s.tokens)\; \wedge$
  $\quad (s.performers = \{p.proposing.commitment.creditor,$
  $\qquad\qquad\qquad\qquad\quad p.proposing.commitment.debtor\})\}$

$ToReply : ToSpeak \rightarrow \mathbb{P} \downarrow Reply$

$\forall s : ToSpeak$
- $ToReply(s) =$
  $\{r : \downarrow Reply \mid$
  $(r \in s.tokens) \wedge$
  $(s.performers = \{r.replying.commitment.creditor,$
  $\qquad\qquad\qquad r.replying.commitment.debtor\}) \wedge$
  $(\nexists r_1 : \downarrow Reply \mid$
  $\quad r_1 \in s.tokens \wedge$
  $\quad r_1 \neq r$
  - $r_1.replying.commitment = r.replying.commitment)\}$

These definitions can be used to specify other messages with more refined meanings. For example, acceptances and rejections could be defined as messages containing an accept and reject token (respectively) that are well formed replies; and counterproposals could be defined as messages containing a counter token that is a well formed proposal and rejection. Other feasible definitions are an offer, which could be a proposal where the speaker is the debtor of the commitment, and a request, where the hearer is the debtor of the commitment.

4.2   Conversational Level

This level builds upon the compositional level, and indicates the significance of messages once they are uttered. Definitions take into account the time when an utterance was issued, the previous utterances that are shared between its speaker and addressee, and its occurrence as part of a *pfp* instance.

To support definitions at this level, we specify *SharedProposals* (below) to refer to all proposals shared by two agents, within a certain time interval, that contain a propose token matching a given commitment operation. Likewise, *Shared-Replies* (not shown) refers to all shared replies that occurred in a time interval.

$SharedProposals : Interval \times \downarrow Agent \times \downarrow Agent \times \downarrow Operation \rightarrow \mathbb{P}\ Utterance$

$\forall i : Interval;\ a_1, a_2 : \downarrow Agent;\ op : \downarrow Operation$
- $SharedProposals(i, a_1, a_2, op) =$
  $\{u : SharedUtterances(a_1, a_2) \mid$
  $\quad i.from \leq u.time \leq i.until \wedge$
  $\quad (\exists p : ToPropose(u.speechact)$
  - $p.proposing = op)\}$

Based on these definitions, we specify that a proposal between two agents at a given time is a sound attempt to reach agreement (as shown in *SoundProposal* below) if 1) there exists (at the given time) a shared utterance between these agents that proposes the given commitment operation, and 2) this proposal can be replied, which we specify simply as having the reply time in the proposal start after the utterance of the proposal.

$SoundProposal : Time \times \downarrow Agent \times \downarrow Agent \times \downarrow Propose \rightarrow \mathbb{B}$

$\forall\, time : Time;\ agent_1, agent_2 : \downarrow Agent;\ propose : \downarrow Propose$
- $SoundProposal(time, agent_1, agent_2, propose) \Leftrightarrow$
  $(SharedProposals(at(time), agent_1, agent_2, propose.proposing) \neq \varnothing) \wedge$
  $(time < propose.reply.from)$

Likewise, the function *SoundReply* (below) specifies that a reply is sound if, at the time it occurs, there is a proposal that could be answered and has not been answered yet. This outcome is achieved by the partial functions *proposed*, which maps each shared proposal that could be replied at the given time to a set of replies that could answer it; and *replied*, which maps a subset of the proposals in *proposed* with one of its corresponding replies, where each reply replies to only one proposal. Thus, a reply would be sound if there are unanswered proposals, i.e., if the proposals in *replied* is a proper subset of proposals in *proposed*.

$SoundReply : Time \times \downarrow Agent \times \downarrow Agent \times \downarrow Reply \rightarrow \mathbb{B}$

$\forall\, t : Time;\ s, a : \downarrow Agent;\ r : \downarrow Reply$
- $SoundReply(t, s, a, r) \Leftrightarrow$
  $(\forall\, proposed : Utterance \nrightarrow \mathbb{P}\, Utterance\,\big|$
     $\mathrm{dom}\, proposed =$
         $\{u : SharedProposals(before(t), s, a, r.replying)\,\big|$
           $\exists\, p : ToPropose(u.speechact)\,\big|$
             $p.reply.from \leq t \leq p.reply.until \wedge$
             $p.proposing = r.replying$
             - $proposed(u) = SharedReplies(within(p.reply.from, t), s, a, r.replying)\}$
  - $\forall\, replied : Utterance \nrightarrow Utterance\,\big|$
     $\forall\, u : \mathrm{dom}\, replied$
     - $replied(u) \in proposed(u) \wedge$
       $(\nexists u_1 : \mathrm{dom}\, replied\,\big|$
         $u_1 \neq u$
         - $replied(u) = replied(u_1))$
  - $\mathrm{dom}\, replied \subset \mathrm{dom}\, proposed)$

Based on the above, we define that an utterance would be a proposal if it is a well formed, sound proposal (as shown in *Proposing* below).

$Proposing : Utterance \rightarrow \mathbb{P}\downarrow Propose$

$\forall\, u : Utterance$
- $Proposing(u) =$
  $\{p : ToPropose(u.speechact)\,\big|$
    $SoundProposal(u.time, u.speechact.speaker, u.speechact.addressee, p)\}$

Likewise, an utterance would be a reply (as defined in *Replying* below) if it is a well formed, sound reply.

$Replying : Utterance \rightarrow \mathbb{P} \downarrow Reply$

$\forall\, u : Utterance$
- $Replying(u) =$
  $\{r : ToReply(u.speechact) \,|$
  $SoundReply(u.time, u.speechact.speaker, u.speechact.addressee, r)\}$

In the same manner as it was explained in the compositional level, definitions at this level could also be specialized to create other more refined definitions, such as accepting, rejecting, offering and requesting, among others.

4.3   Commitment State Level

This level builds upon the conversational level, and refines the definitions of messages according to the shared state of the commitment being manipulated. As such, an utterance proposing the discharge of a social commitment (as indicated in *ProposingStateDischarge* below) would be one that contains a propose token attempting to delete an accepted social commitment.

$ProposingStateDischarge : Utterance \rightarrow \mathbb{P}\, SocialCommitmentState$

$\forall\, u : Utterance$
- $ProposingStateDischarge(u) =$
  $\{sc : SocialCommitmentState \,|$
  $\exists\, p : Proposing(u);\ a : Accepted \,|$
  $p.proposing \in Delete$
  - $sc = (p.proposing.commitment \mapsto a)\ \wedge$
    $sc \in SharedSocialCommitments(u.time, u.speechact.speaker,$
    $u.speechact.addressee)\}$

This definition could then be refined as a withdrawal (as indicated in *Withdrawal*, shown below) if the involved commitment is in an active state, and if its discharge is being proposed by the same agent that proposed its adoption. Likewise, this definition could be refined as a *Release* (not shown) if the proposing and proposed agents are the creditor and debtor of the withdrawn commitment.

$Withdrawal : Utterance \rightarrow \mathbb{P}\, SocialCommitmentState$

$\forall\, u : Utterance$
- $Withdrawal(u) =$
  $\{sc : ProposingStateDischarge(u) \,|$
  $\forall\, a : Active \,|$
  $a = state(sc)$
  - $a.adopt.proposal.speechact.speaker = u.speechact.speaker\}$

4.4   Joint Activity Level

The joint activity level builds upon the commitment state level, and refers to the meaning given to messages when they are used as part of joint activities. In retrospect, the meaning of messages is not only given by their constituents, their use as devices advancing the state of commitments, and the shared state of the commitments they refer to, but also by the type of actions these commitments bring about, and by the roles that interacting agents play in these actions.

To exemplify this point, we refer to a contract net joint activity defined in (7), which specifies a manager and a bidder roles that interact to bring about three interdependent actions: one in which the bidder produces a bid, a second one in which the manager evaluates the bid, and a third one in which (if offered by the manager) the bidder performs the then-bid now-contract. These actions were defined in independent activities with independent roles, and then merged into the contract net activity, where dependencies between roles and actions were defined, e.g., the bid resulting from the bidding action is the bid evaluated in the evaluating action, the bidder is the producer of a bid and the executor of the contract. In this view, a *call for proposals* message (below) would be one in which a manager requests to a bidder the adoption of a commitment where the bidder produces a bid (which indicates the requirements she could fulfill).

Message definitions at this level could be used by designers to specify the roles that agents could be programmed to play in activities, or by deliberative agents to dynamically direct their conversations based on the messages issued and the commitments they entail (which is an approach explored in (15)).

$CallforProposals : Utterance \rightarrow \mathbb{P}\, SocialCommitmentState$

$\forall\, u : Utterance\,|$
  $u.speechact.speaker \in Manager \wedge$
  $u.speechact.addressee \in Bidder$
- $CallforProposals(u) =$
  $\{sc : RequestingAdoption(u)\,|$
    $\forall\, act : ToOfferPerformance\,|$
      $act = (commitment(sc)).action$
      - $act.producer = u.speechact.addressee \wedge$
      $act.receiver = u.speechact.speaker\}$

4.5   Resolving Ambiguities in Transitions When Duplicated Commitments Exist

A few issues must be resolved to keep the consistency of shared commitments during transitions when duplicated commitments exist, and when commitments can only be identified through a creditor, debtor and action descriptors. In this section we explore these issues during conversational and satisfaction transitions.

On the one hand, conversational transitions must unambiguously identify the commitment that is being referred to in utterances. Ambiguity could arise if 1) a reply occurs at a time when more than one proposal with identical commitments could be answered, since this may result in agents selecting different proposals as the one being replied to; and 2) a subsequent reply occurs that is regarded by one of the agents as answering the remaining proposal while the other agent does not (e.g., if the reply time of the message that the latter agent retained as unanswered has expired), and this reply is an acceptance changing the state of a social commitment, since it will result in one of these agents changing the state of the referred commitment while the other agent does not. These cases result (or may result, in the case of the former) in discrepancies on the shared state of commitments: in the first case, agents hold commitments with different replied proposals; in the second case, an agent holds an accepted commitment while the other does not, which may eventually lead to a clash of their expectations of each other within the joint activity in which they participate.

These problems can be prevented either by expanding the structure of communicated commitments with a disambiguating feature (e.g., the time when the proposal being answered was issued, a unique commitment identifier), by engaging on a subsequent dialog requesting the explicit identification of the proposal being replied (e.g., asking for the time when the proposal occurred), or by mandating that agents use the same criteria to select the proposal being replied (e.g., a reply answers the proposal whose reply time expires first). Although we do not model these strategies, we intuitively favor that agents engage in dialogues, rather than augmenting the structure of communicated commitments with proprietary information, or attempting to standardize the functionality of agents, which would be impossible to enforce in open environments.

On the other hand, satisfaction transitions deal with the issue of identifying the performances that satisfy accepted commitments. That an agent holds identical active commitments only means that it has recorded those commitments given independent conversational transitions, not necessarily that these commitments will be satisfied as many times as recorded. Since the possibility of optimizing performances (i.e., whether one performance satisfies all identical commitments or if independent performances are required) may be bound by the expectations of involved agents, they are not modelled in our analysis. Rather, we assume that transitions based on conditions of satisfaction are automatically traversed according to the state of these conditions.

5   Related Work

Conversations and social commitments have been the subject of previous studies. Some efforts have aimed at the study of social commitments in argumentation (23), in which the evolution of conversations is motivated by the commitments that are implied (and not necessarily made explicit) in communications. Of particular interest are the proposals furthered in (14; 18). Other efforts have focused on the mechanics of conversations based on the operations advancing the state of social commitments, which is a view independent of the intentional motives behind their advancement. We share this view, and aim at the identification of public elements binding the evolution of conversations. In addition to our proposal, there are other approaches pursuing this goal, such as those advanced by Fornara and Colombetti (9) (who specify messages categorized as speech acts whose meaning is given by operations to manipulate the state of commitments), and Yolum and Singh (24) (who specify that messages have meaning according to operations and reasoning rules applied to commitments). We share with these approaches the view that part of the meaning of messages is based on the (shared) state of commitments, and with the practical aspects of *pre-commitments* (indicating a sequencing of messages establishing commitments) and *conditional commitments* (indicating a sequencing of commitments), which we model through the *pfp*, and the constraints in agent roles and joint activities, respectively.

Sensible differences between our approaches include the pragmatics of commitment state transitions, which in the above approaches tend to be restrictive. For example, that a commitment can be created only by its debtor (24, p. 530) (whereas a creditor should be able to create a commitment in the context of an offer)[2], and that a commitment can be cancelled only by its creditor (9, p. 536) (whereas a debtor could cancel a commitment if sanctions were applied) are too stringent for practical purposes. Differently, the incremental nature of our model distinguishes these aspects, and allows others to be considered. As an example, we have been exploring the role of sanctions to complement our model (16).

Lastly, an additional concern noted in (13) regarding (24), is the view that commitment operations should not be unilaterally applied but rather must be jointly approved by interacting agents (unless mandated by the context or by meta-commitments). Although we endorse this view, our current analysis is restricted to explicit manipulations approved by consensus, as afforded by the *pfp*, for any conversational transition adopting or discharging social commitments.

6 Conclusions

As noted in (3), utterances are signals with two complementary types of meaning: *speaker's meaning*, which is defined in terms of their use for the communication of intent, and *signal meaning*, which is defined in terms of their use as coordinating devices to advance joint activities. The subtle but important difference between these types of meaning resides on what is understood by the issuing of a signal: whereas speaker's meaning appeals to the reasons for advancing a joint activity, signal meaning puts forth a token that is meant to advance the joint activity.

Within the multiagents community, message semantics has traditionally emphasized speaker's meaning, as reflected by FIPA-ACL and KQML's use of speech acts and mental states for their message definitions. This approach is superb to communicate intent, since agents can readily know the intended meaning of a message by just observing its definition rather than by inferring its meaning from the context of interaction. However, these definitions are given independently of any joint activity, and their application to open environments is maimed by the assumption that agents are always sincere and cooperative.

Signal meaning, on the other hand, has been kept as a low profile component of meaning and is not addressed by these standardizing efforts. We contend that this type of meaning must be taken into account as part of message definitions.

---

[2] See (13, p. 369) for a discussion on this issue.

We explored this possibility in the context of messages aiming at the negotiated manipulation of social commitment states. We chose this type of messages due to the fitness of social commitments to coordinate the expectations of agents and provide a point of reference to advance the state of their interactions.

Following this perspective, we proposed a four-level incremental model that focuses on the characteristics of messages (*compositional level*) that agents use in conversations (*conversational level*) to advance the state of social commitments (*commitment state level*) that advance their joint activities (*joint activity level*). Lastly, we explored the feasibility of *pfp* messages to describe signal meaning given their support for building flexible and modular conversation protocols (7).

Acknowledgements

We are grateful for the support received from the National Science and Engineering Research Council (NSERC) of Canada.

References

[1] J. Bentahar, B. Moulin, and B. Chaib-draa. Commitment and argument network: A new formalism for agent communication. In F. Dignum, editor, *Advances in Agent Communication*, volume 2922 of *Lecture Notes in Artificial Intelligence*, pages 146–165. Springer Verlag, 2004.

[2] C. Castelfranchi. Commitments: From individual intentions to groups and organizations. In *Proceedings of the 1st International Conference on Multi-Agent Systems*, pages 41–48, San Francisco, CA, June 1995.

[3] H.H. Clark. *Using language.* Cambridge University Press, 1996.

[4] R.T. Craig and K. Tracy. *Conversational Coherence: Form, Structure, and Strategy.* Sage Publications, 1983.

[5] T. Finin, Y. Labrou, and J. Mayfield. KQML as an agent communication language. In J.M. Bradshaw, editor, *Software Agents*, pages 291–316. MIT Press, 1997.

[6] R.A. Flores and R.C. Kremer. To commit or not to commit: Modelling agent conversations for action. *Computational Intelligence*, 18(2):120–173, 2003.

[7] R.A. Flores and R.C. Kremer. A principled modular approach to construct flexible conversation protocols. In A.Y. Tawfik and S.D. Goodwin, editors, *Advances in AI: Canadian AI 2004*, volume 3060 of *Lecture Notes in Computer Science*, pages 1–15, London, Canada, May 2004. Springer Verlag.

[8] Foundation for Intelligent Physical Agents (FIPA). http://www.fipa.org.

[9] N. Fornara and M. Colombetti. Operational specification of a commitment-based agent communication language. In C. Castelfranchi and W.L. Johnson, editors, *Proceedings of the 1st International Joint Conference on Autonomous Agents and Multiagent Systems*, pages 535–542, Bologna, Italy, July 2002.

[10] N. Fornara, F. Vigano, and M. Colombetti. Agent communication and institutional reality. In R. van Eijk, M-P. Huget, and F. Dignum, editors, *this volume*, Lecture Notes in Computer Science. Springer Verlag, 2004.

[11] M.A. Labrie, B. Chaib-draa, and N. Maudet. Diagal: A tool for analyzing and modelling commitment-based dialogues between agents. In Y. Xiang and B. Chaib-draa, editors, *Advances in Artificial Intelligence*, volume 2671 of *Lecture Notes in Artificial Intelligence*, pages 353–369. Springer Verlag, 2003.

[12] A.U. Mallya and M.P. Singh. A semantic approach for designing commitment protocols. In R. van Eijk, M-P. Huget, and F. Dignum, editors, *this volume*, Lecture Notes in Computer Science. Springer Verlag, 2004.

[13] P. McBurney and S. Parsons. The posit spaces protocol for multi-agent negotiation. In F. Dignum, editor, *Advances in Agent Communication*, volume 2922 of *Lecture Notes in Artificial Intelligence*, pages 364–382. Springer Verlag, 2004.

[14] S. Parsons, P. McBurney, and M.J. Wooldridge. The mechanics of some formal inter-agent dialogues. In F. Dignum, editor, *Advances in Agent Communication*, volume 2922 of *Lecture Notes in Artificial Intelligence*, pages 329–348. Springer Verlag, 2004.

[15] P. Pasquier and B. Chaib-draa. The cognitive coherence approach for agent communication pragmatics. In J.S. Rosenschein, T. Sandholm, M.J. Wooldridge, and M. Yokoo, editors, *Proceedings of the 2nd International Joint Conference on Autonomous Agents and Multiagent Systems*, pages 544–552, Melbourne, Australia, July 2003. ACM Press.

[16] P. Pasquier, R.A. Flores, and B. Chaib-draa. The enforcement of flexible social commitments. In 5th *International Workshop on Engineering Societies in the Agents World*, Lecture Notes in Artificial Intelligence. Springer Verlag, 2004.

[17] J. Pitt and A. Mamdani. Some remarks on the semantics of FIPAs agent communication language. *Autonomous Agents and Multi-Agent Systems*, 2(4):333–356, 1999.

[18] C.A. Reed. Dialogue frames in agent communication. In *Proceedings of the 3rd International Conference on Multiagent Systems (ICMAS 98)*, pages 246–253, Paris, France, 1998. IEEE Press.

[19] M.P. Singh. Social and psychological commitments in multiagent systems. In *AAAI Fall Symposium on Knowledge and Action at Social and Organizational Levels*, Monterey, California, November 1991.

[20] M.P. Singh. Agent communicational languages: Rethinking the principles. *IEEE Computer*, 31(12):40–47, December 1998.

[21] G. Smith. *The Object-Z Specification Language*. Kluwer Publishers, 2000.

[22] R.G. Smith. The contract net protocol: High-level communication and control in a distributed problem solver. *IEEE Transactions on Computers*, 29(12):1104–1113, 1980.

[23] D.N. Walton and E.C.W. Krabbe. *Commitment in Dialogue: Basic Concepts of Interpersonal Reasoning*. State University of New York Press, 1995.

[24] P. Yolum and M.P. Singh. Flexible protocol specification and execution: Applying event calculus planning using commitments. In C. Castelfranchi and W.L. Johnson, editors, *Proceedings of the 1st International Joint Conference on Autonomous Agents and Multiagent Systems*, pages 527–534, Bologna, Italy, July 2002.

A Semantic Approach for Designing Commitment Protocols*

Ashok U. Mallya and Munindar P. Singh

Department of Computer Science,
North Carolina State University,
Raleigh, NC 27695-7535, USA
{aumallya, singh}@ncsu.edu

Abstract. Protocols enable unambiguous and smooth interactions among agents, and commitments among agents are a powerful means of developing protocols. Commitments allow flexible execution of protocols and help agents reason about protocols and plan their actions accordingly, while at the same time providing a basis for compliance checking. Multiagent systems that employ commitment-based interaction can conveniently and effectively model business interactions because the autonomy and heterogeneity of agents mirrors real-world businesses. Such modeling, however, requires multiagent systems to host a rich variety of interaction protocols that can capture the needs of different applications. We show how a commitment-based semantics for protocols provides a basis for refining and aggregating protocols. We propose an approach for designing commitment protocols wherein traditional software engineering notions such as refinement and aggregation are extended to apply to protocols. We present an algebra of protocols that can be used to compose protocols by refining and merging existing ones, and does this at a level of abstraction high enough to be useful for real-world applications.

1   Introduction

Multiagent systems where the agents are autonomous and heterogeneous are a convenient and accurate model for describing and enacting many real life processes and interactions. While autonomy and heterogeneity are what make the multiagent paradigm attractive, heterogeneity gives rise to incompatibility and autonomy to unpredictability. Agents need to understand each other and behave in predictable ways for their interactions to be fruitful. To achieve consensus and smooth interaction between agents, standards are required, as in most distributed systems. Web Services are an example of how standards allow heterogeneous systems to interact with each other. Recent efforts for Web Service *choreography*—which deals with the way services interact—and *orchestration*—which deals with the way services are composed using other services—address service inter-actions [12] similar in spirit to agent interaction protocols. Agent interaction, however,

---

* We thank Amit Chopra and Nirmit Desai for valuable comments. This research was supported by the NSF under grant DST-0139037.

R.M. van Eijk et al. (Eds.): AC 2004, LNAI 3396, pp. 33–49, 2005.

requires higher-level abstractions to deal with the rich variety of interactions found in multiagent systems.

Interaction Protocols. A protocol is a description of the steps involved in an interaction. Protocols make interactions coherent and easy to implement. The use of protocols has successfully solved the problem of standardization in areas such as computer networks. Likewise, the heterogenous and distributed structure of multiagent systems necessitates clear protocols to govern any interaction. Network protocols explain the steps to be taken in great detail, sometimes even enumerating all possible events that can occur. For example, the Session Initiation Protocol (SIP), which is used to set up phone calls over the Internet, describes every message that has to be sent for setting up and tearing down calls and also every possible resultant reply for the message [14]. By contrast, multiagent systems require protocols to be specified at a high level of abstraction, to accommodate the complexity of agent systems, and to not overwhelm protocol designers with unnecessary details.

While protocols are needed to force an agent to behave in a predictable manner, they should also allow flexibility of execution. A protocol that allows only one sequence of steps does not let its participants leverage their autonomy. A restrictive protocol, however, is not always bad. If a protocol allows only a single computation, checking whether the participants are compliant with the protocol is trivial. Any step that does not agree with the protocol signals a violation. As protocols become more flexible, however, compliance verification becomes harder, since many choices are offered to the participants at any step of the protocol. Consequently, protocol design is an exercise in finding the right balance between flexibility of execution and ease of compliance checking.

Motivation. The tradeoffs between execution and verification to be borne in mind while designing a protocol make protocol design a nontrivial undertaking. It requires human expertise and knowledge of the application domain. To reduce unnecessary effort and to prevent reinventing the wheel, designers should be able to create new protocols by refining or combining existing protocols whose properties are well understood. In such a situation, a sound theory of composition of protocols and a classification of protocols in a hierarchy backed by formal semantics would aid protocol designers and take from them some of the burden of ascertaining the properties of the protocols being designed. An algebra of protocols is needed as the basis for protocol composition. Such an algebra should support operators that allow merging of protocols into a refined protocol which preserves certain properties of the merged protocols.

Our central claim is that protocols have properties as a whole, rather than being just a sequence of steps. We develop a protocol algebra which is at once a high-level abstraction of protocols and a useful tool for composing protocols and reasoning about them, as we demonstrate with an example.

Contribution. Our main contribution is in developing an algebra for composing protocols. Just as conceptual modeling in general involves abstractions such as refinement and aggregation, so must conceptual modeling of protocols. This algebra we develop provides the underpinnings of such abstractions for protocols. The algebra is a high-level abstraction that relates to real-world interaction protocols, and hence is easy for protocol designers to understand. We also demonstrate how the use of commitments allows reasoning about protocols that leads to richer interaction patterns from existing ones. Further, we outline how a hierarchy of protocols can be generated based on commitments. This hierarchy aids reasoning about which protocol is the most general for a given process.

Organization. The rest of this paper is organized as follows. Section 2 introduces the technical background, and some illustrative examples that are used throughout the paper. Section 3 develops our theory of semantics of protocol subsumptions, introduces the protocol algebra and demonstrates its utility in composing protocols. Section 4 summarizes the paper, identifies related work in the field, and charts out future directions.

2   Technical Framework

We represent protocols as transition systems similar in spirit to finite state machines. These protocols generate computations or *runs*, which are sequences of states that a valid protocol execution can go through. We devise a hierarchical classification based on the runs generated by protocols. Runs are composed of *states* that the protocol computation (execution) goes through based on the *actions* that the participants in the given protocol perform. This classification forms the basis of our work. Next, we introduce commitments, discuss some scenarios from our running example, and then define the basic technical concepts needed for our semantics.

2.1   Commitments in Protocols

Commitments among agents are an abstraction of contracts that exist in the real world [3, 15]. Commitments lend coherence to interactions because they help agents plan based on the actions of others, and they are, in principle, enforceable. Commitment-based protocols are more flexible than traditional formalisms like Finite State Machines and Petri nets [20, 22]. By specifying the states that need to be reached in terms of commitments, they can allow multiple paths to achieve a state, and consequently create a flexible protocol specification.

A commitment $C(x, y, p)$ denotes that the agent x is responsible to the agent y for bringing about the condition p. Here x is the *debtor*, y the *creditor*, and p the *condition* of the commitment, expressed in a suitable formal language. Commitments can also be *conditional*, denoted by $CC(x, y, p, q)$, meaning that x is committed to y to bring about p if q holds.

Commitment Operations. Commitments are created, satisfied, and transformed in certain ways. Conventionally, six operations are defined on commitments. These are the CREATE(x, C), the CANCEL(x, C), the RELEASE(y, C), the ASSIGN(y, z, C), the DELEGATE(x, z, C), and the DISCHARGE(x, C). The ASSIGN(y, z, C) operation replaces y with z as C's creditor and the DELEGATE(x, z, C) operation makes z the new debtor of the commitment C. A detailed exposition of all these operations is given in [15] and is omitted here, for brevity.

The DISCHARGE$(\cdot, \cdot, \cdot)$ operation satisfies a commitment. A commitment is said to be *active* if it has been created, but not yet discharged.

2.2 Running Example

As a real world example, we consider a variant of the NetBill protocol [17] used by a customer's agent to purchase a book from an online bookstore's agent. We identify four distinct, but related, scenarios that can arise during this purchase interaction. Each of these scenarios requires a different amount of effort from the participants in terms of protocol execution, planning, and coordination. Both agents would benefit from being able to compare scenarios to choose the one that best serves their interests.

1. The customer asks the bookstore for a price quote on a book, and upon receiving a quote from the bookstore, accepts the bookstore's offer. The bookstore sends the book, and the customer pays. Figure 1(a) shows this interaction. This interaction sequence belongs to the *purchase* protocol.
2. The bookstore is willing to refund the price of returned books. This scenario is similar to the previous scenario till the book is delivered to the customer, but is longer, since the customer then returns the book for a refund. Figure 1(b) shows this interaction.
3. The customer delegates the payment to a third party, e.g., a bank. Such a situation is not very different from using a credit card to pay for goods, and is shown in Figure 1(c).
4. The customer wants insured shipping, and the bookstore's existing shipper does not insure goods. The bookstore negotiates with and contracts out the actual shipping to a shipper. Here, the shipper delivers the books to the customer, after which the shipper is paid by the bookstore. To complicate matters, the customer pays the bookstore via its bank like in the previous scenario. This scenario is shown in Figure 2.

In Figures 1(a), 1(b), 1(c), 2, 4(a), and 4(b), ellipses represent states, named s_i. Solid arrows are labeled by the messages that are passed between the participating agents. These messages correspond to actions that the agents take. Note that each of these figures represent a possible scenario, i.e., a *run* of the protocol. Also, states of the runs are drawn in different columns (also called swimlanes in UML parlance) to show the interacting agents clearly even though states are maintained by all interacting agents.

Table 1 explains the meanings of the states that the first scenario runs through. Table 3 shows the meanings of the messages passed, where, c represents the customer, b, the bookstore, g, the book that the customer is interested in buying, and k, the customer's bank. The *delegate* message relates to corresponding commitment operation.

2.3 Propositions

Propositions capture facts about what conditions hold, what commitments have been made, and whether these commitments have been fulfilled. The propositions used in a protocol are assumed to be understood by agents involved in the protocol. In the *purchase* example, we use the propositions given in Table 2. In addition to these, active commitments are also represented as propositions, as we shall explain when discussing states.

Table 1. Meaning of states in the purchase protocol

State	Meaning
s_1	Customer has asked the bookstore the price of the goods. No commitments made.
s_2	Bookstore has quoted a price for the said goods. The bookstore is now willing to send the goods if the customer promises to pay for them
s_3	Customer has agreed to the bookstores price. The customer is willing to pay the price if the books are delivered.
s_4	Bookstore has delivered the book.
s_5	Customer has paid for the book.

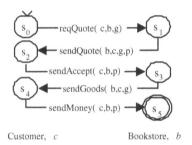

Customer, c Bookstore, b

(a) Purchase protocol scenario 1

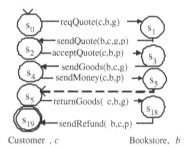

Customer , c Bookstore, b

(b) Purchase protocol scenario 2– goods are returned for a refund

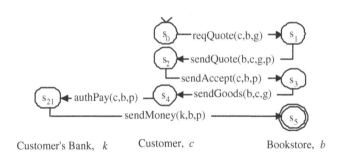

Customer's Bank, k Customer, c Bookstore, b

(c) Purchase protocol scenario 3– customer pays via bank

Fig. 1. Three scenarios of the purchase example

2.4   Actions

Agents perform actions to bring about changes in the world. In our framework, actions are modeled as messages sent by an agent to other agents. Just like an action, a message sent by an agent can affect the state of a protocol in which the agent partic-

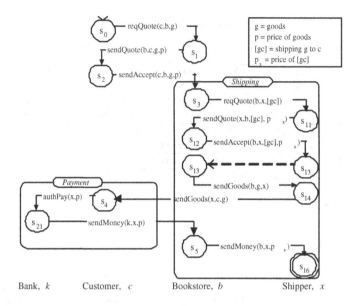

Fig. 2. Purchase protocol scenario 4– shipping via a separate shipper and payment via bank

ipates. Messages may be implemented in different ways. For example, filling a form with credit card information and submitting it over the web is a message that represents a transfer of funds. The set of actions is denoted by $\mathbb{A}$. The meanings of actions used in our *purchase* example are given in Table 3. In addition to the actions shown, $\mathbb{A}$ also contains actions corresponding to commitment operations. For example, $\mathbb{A}$ contains an action *delegate*(c, k, C) corresponding to the operation *delegate*(c, k, C), where C is a commitment made by c.

2.5   States

A protocol has many *states* that it goes through, during the course of its execution. A state is a snapshot of the world and is labeled by the set of propositions that are true in it. That is, a state is an assignment of truth values to propositions. For example, state s_1 of the *purchase* example is labeled by the set $\{reqQuote(c, b, g)\}$ and state s_0 by $\{\mathsf{true}\}$. We denote the label of a state s by $[s]$. Table 4 shows the labels that are assigned to states in the *purchase* protocol. The set of states is denoted by $\mathbb{S}$. We include in this set a unique start state s_ϕ, which is labeled by the set $\{\mathsf{true}\}$. In the *purchase* example, $s_0 = s_\phi$.

2.6   Runs

A run is one possible execution sequence of a protocol. A protocol can allow many computations, or *runs*. A run is a sequence of states $\langle s_0 \ldots s_i \ldots \rangle$. In this paper, we consider only non-empty runs except in a special protocol described in Section 3.3.

The operator $\prec_\tau$ orders states temporally with respect to a run τ, so that $s_i \prec_\tau s_j$ implies that s_i occurs before s_j in the run τ.

Table 2. Meanings of propositions used in the purchase protocol

Proposition	Meaning
$reqQuote(c, b, g)$	c has requested a quote for g from b.
$quote(b, c, g, p)$	b quotes to c price p for g, i.e., b will deliver if c commits to pay upon delivery. This is represented by $CC(b, c, goods(b, c, g), acceptQuote(c, b, g, p))$.
$acceptQuote(c, b, g, p)$	c has accepted the price p that b quoted for g, i.e, c commits to pay if the goods are delivered. This is represented by $CC(c, b, pay(c, b, p), goods(b, c, g))$
$goods(b, c, g)$	g has been delivered to c by b.
$pay(c, b, p)$	The amount p has been paid to b by c.
$return(c, b, g)$	g has been returned to b by c.
$refund(b, c, p)$	The amount p has been refunded to c by b.

Table 3. Meanings of actions (modeled as messages) in the purchase protocol

Message	Meaning
$reqQuote(c, b, g)$	c asks b what the price of g is.
$sendQuote(b, c, g, p)$	b quotes price p to the c, for g.
$sendAccept(c, b, g, p)$	c accepts the price p quoted by b for g. c is now committed to pay if the book is sent to it.
$sendGoods(b, c, g)$	b sends g to c.
$sendMoney(c, b, p)$	c sends the money p to b.
$delegate(c, k, C)$	c delegates the commitment C to k.
$returnGoods(c, b, g)$	c returns g to b.
$sendRefund(b, c, p)$	b refunds the money p to c.
$authPay(c, b, p)$	c authorizes its bank to pay the amount p to b. Essentially c delegates $C(c, b, p)$ to k.

2.7 Protocols

Computationally, a protocol corresponds to a set of computations that it allows. These can be captured as a set of runs where any of the runs that *subsume* the given runs may be realized. That is, each run in a protocol defines a sequence of steps that must be performed in the same order relative to each other. The concept of subsumption of runs is introduced shortly. A protocol is represented as a transition system as defined by a tuple $\langle \mathbb{A}, \mathbb{S}, s_0, \Delta, \mathbb{F}, \mathbb{R} \rangle$ where

- $\mathbb{A}$ is a set of actions,
- $\mathbb{S}$ is a set of states,
- s_0 is the initial state, $s_0 \in \mathbb{S}$,
- Δ is a set of transitions, $\Delta \subseteq \mathbb{S} \times \mathbb{A} \times \mathbb{S}$,
- $\mathbb{F}$ is a set of final states, $\mathbb{F} \subseteq \mathbb{S}$, and
- $\mathbb{R}$ is a set of roles (or participants).

Table 4. State labels in the purchase protocol

State	Associated Label
s_0	$\{\text{true}\}$
s_1	$\{reqQuote(c,b,g)\}$
s_2	$\{quote(b,c,g,p)\}$
s_3	$\{\mathsf{C}(b,c,goods(b,c,g)),\mathsf{CC}(c,b,pay(c,b,p),goods(b,c,g))\}$
s_4	$\{goods(b,c,g),\mathsf{C}(c,b,pay(c,b,p))\}$
s_5	$\{goods(b,c,g),pay(c,b,p)\}$
s_{21}	$\{goods(b,c,g),\mathsf{C}(k,b,pay(k,b,p))\}$
s_{17}	$\{goods(b,c,g),pay(c,b,p)\}$
s_{18}	$\{goods(b,c,g),return(c,b,g),\mathsf{C}(b,c,refund(b,c,p))\}$
s_{19}	$\{goods(b,c,g),return(c,b,g),refund(b,c,p)\}$

Δ contains transitions of the form $\langle s_i, a, s_j \rangle$, where $s_i, s_j \in \mathbb{S}$ and $a \in \mathbb{A}$. Here s_i is the source of the transition and s_j its destination. Such a transition advances a computation that is in state s_i to state s_j when an action a is performed, i.e., when the message corresponding to a is sent and received. In other words, a run can be generated from a protocol by the successive concatenation of transitions beginning from the initial state of the machine. The concatenation of a transition to a run appends the destination of transition to the run if the source of the transition matches the last state of the run. Consequently, a run $\langle s_0 s_1 s_2 \dots s_n \rangle$ can be generated by a machine whose initial state is s_0, and whose transition set contains the elements $\langle s_0, \_, s_1 \rangle$, $\langle s_1, \_, s_2 \rangle$ and so on till $\langle s_{n-1}, \_, s_n \rangle$, where $s_n \in \mathbb{F}$. The set of all such runs is denoted by $[\![P]\!]$.

Protocols are specified by propositions and actions that cause states to change. The semantics of actions are given in terms of commitments such as those shown in Table 3. Given the actions and their semantics, the formalization of a protocol is straightforward. The transition function of a protocol can be specified explicitly as state-action-state triples or as a set of rules that are complied into such triples for runtime efficiency. Two example transition mechanisms for commitment-based protocols are [22] and [4]. For example, Tables 2, 3, and 4, along with a set of rules for determining the new state given the old state and the action taken would define the purchase protocol.

3   Reasoning About Protocols

This section describes our theory of comparison of protocols and protocol refinements. Section 3.1 defines how states are deemed similar to one another, Section 3.2 defines subsumptions of runs, and Section 3.3 uses comparisons of commitment-operation based propositions to relate different protocols.

3.1   Similarity of States

States form the fundamental components of runs, and are labeled by sets of propositions. Any comparison of states, therefore, must be based on comparing propositions.

In this section, we introduce three state-similarity functions ι, σ, and $\alpha_{A,P}$, all based on commitment propositions, and show how these help relate different runs.

A *state-similarity function* f is a mapping from a state to a set of states, i.e., $f : \mathbb{S} \mapsto 2^{\mathbb{S}}$.

Definition 1. *A state s_i is similar to a state s_j under the state-similarity function f if and only if $s_j \in f(s_i)$.*

State-similarity under the function f is denoted by $[f\rangle$. That is, $s_i[f\rangle s_j \iff s_j \in f(s_i)$.

Identity State-Similarity. ι is the identity state-similarity function. That is, $s_i[\iota\rangle s_j$ if and only if s_i and s_j are labeled by same set of propositions. $\iota(s_i) = \{s_j | [s_i] = [s_j]\}$.

$[\iota\rangle$ is reflexive, symmetric, and transitive.

Creditor State-Similarity. As another state-similarity function, consider σ. Under σ, a state s_i is similar to a state s_j if in the two states all the participants of the protocol have the same commitments being made towards them, regardless of which agent makes it. Since the creditor of a commitment is immaterial under σ and a *delegate*$(\cdot, \cdot, \cdot)$ action changes the creditor of a commitment, σ can be defined as $\sigma(s_i) = \{s_j | s_j$ can be reached by a finite number of *delegate*$(\cdot, \cdot, \cdot)$ actions from $s_i\}$

As an example, consider states s_4 and s_{21} from the of the example scenarios. These states are similar under σ because, as described in Table 4, these states have propositions representing commitments that differ only in their creditors.

$[\sigma\rangle$ is reflexive, symmetric, and transitive.

Role-and-Commitment State-Similarity. A state s_i is similar to a state s_j under $\alpha_{A,P}$, where A is a set of roles and P is a set of propositions, if the commitments made by any role in A to any other role in A, and the propositions in P that hold at s_i, also hold at s_j.

3.2 Subsumption of Runs

Our theory of comparing protocols is based on a notion of *subsumption* of the runs specified by a protocol. $[\![f\rangle$ denotes subsumption operator over runs. The operator $[\![f\rangle$ is an order-preserving mapping from one run to another, and depends on the function f.

Definition 2. *A run τ_j subsumes a run τ_i under function f if and only if, for every state s_i that occurs in τ_i, there occurs a state s_j in τ_j that is similar under f, and s_j has the same temporal order relative to other states in τ_j as s_i does with states in τ_i.*

$\tau_j[\![f\rangle \tau_i \iff \forall s_i \in \tau_i, \exists s_j \in \tau_j : s_j \in f(s_i)$ and $\forall s_i' \in \tau_i, \exists s_j' \in \tau_j : s_j' \in f(s_i') \Rightarrow (s_i \preceq_{\tau_i} s_i' \Rightarrow s_j \preceq_{\tau_j} s_j')$ That is, longer runs subsume shorter ones, provided they have similar states occurring in the same order. Consider the identity state-similarity function ι. Under ι, a run τ_j subsumes all its subruns. $[\![\iota\rangle$ is reflexive and transitive.

- **Reflexivity.** Every run subsumes itself under ι.
- **Transitivity.** If $\tau_j[\![\iota\rangle \tau_i$, and $\tau_k[\![\iota\rangle \tau_j$, then $\tau_k[\![\iota\rangle \tau_i$, since τ_k has all states of τ_j in proper temporal order, and τ_j in turn has all states of τ_i in proper temporal order.

Let τ_1, τ_2, and τ_3 be the runs shown in Figures 1(a), 1(b), and 1(c) respectively. We then have $\tau_2[\![\iota]\!\rangle\tau_1$. Also, $\tau_3[\![\iota]\!\rangle\tau_1$. However, τ_1 subsumes neither τ_2 nor τ_3, because τ_3 has a state s_{21}, whose label does not match any state label in τ_1, and τ_2 has states s_{18} and s_{19}, whose labels do not match any state label in τ_1. Run τ_3 does not subsume τ_2 because of s_{21}, and τ_2 does not subsume τ_3 because of s_{18} and s_{19}.

Next, we consider run subsumption under the creditor state-similarity function σ. Here, $\tau_2[\![\sigma]\!\rangle\tau_1$. Also, since $s_{21} \in \sigma(s_4)$, $\tau_1[\![\sigma]\!\rangle\tau_2$. Run τ_3 subsumes both τ_1 and τ_2 for the same reason, but neither τ_1 nor τ_2 subsumes τ_3, since neither of them have states that are σ-similar to s_{18} and s_{19}.

$[\![\sigma]\!\rangle$ is reflexive and transitive.

- **Reflexivity.** Every run subsumes itself under σ, since $[\![\sigma]\!\rangle$ is reflexive over states.
- **Transitivity.** If $\tau_j[\![\sigma]\!\rangle\tau_i$, and $\tau_k[\![\sigma]\!\rangle\tau_j$, then $\tau_k[\![\sigma]\!\rangle\tau_i$, since τ_k has all states of τ_j in the same temporal order, τ_j has all states of τ_i in the same temporal order, and σ is transitive over states.

Figure 3(a) shows the subsumption relation between the runs τ_1, τ_2, and τ_3 under the identity function ι and Figure 3(b), under σ.

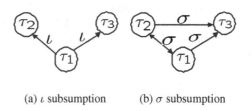

(a) ι subsumption   (b) σ subsumption

Fig. 3. Subsumption of purchase protocol runs under ι and σ

3.3   The Protocol Algebra

Operationally, the runs allowed by a protocol completely characterize that protocol. A protocol that allows many runs is better than one that allows a few runs, since the many-run protocol affords more choice and flexibility in protocol execution to the participants. Short runs are better because they require fewer messages. The definition of the subsumption of protocols reflects these intuitions.

Every protocol P is considered to belong to a *frame* with enough propositions in it to label all states that can occur in $[\![P]\!]$. A frame serves as a common ontology for the propositions used by a protocol. Frames provide an upper bound on the universe of discourse of a protocol.

Definition 3. *A protocol P_j subsumes a protocol P_i under the function f if and only if, every run in $[\![P_i]\!]$ subsumes, under f, a run in $[\![P_j]\!]$.*

$$P_j[\![f]\!\rangle P_i \iff \forall \tau_i \in [\![P_i]\!] \, \exists \tau_j \in [\![P_j]\!] : \tau_i[\![f]\!\rangle\tau_j \tag{1}$$

If P_j is a protocol that has short runs and P_i is a protocol that has long runs only, then P_j subsumes P_i as long as each of P_i's runs subsumes at least one of P_j's runs. Since long runs subsume shorter ones, protocols with long runs are subsumed by protocols with short runs. The protocol-subsumption relation $[\![\iota]\!\rangle$ is reflexive and transitive because of the reflexivity and transitivity of run subsumption under ι.

We now introduce our protocol algebra as consisting of two operators (*merge* and *choice*), their identity elements ($\mathbb{1}$ and $\mathbb{O}$, respectively), and an ordering relationship (subsumption, as defined above). *Merge* and *choice* are closed under frames meaning that their result always belongs to the union of the frames of their argument protocols.

Merge. The merge operator, denoted by $\otimes_f$, splices two protocols under a state-similarity function f so that refined protocols can be created from existing ones. A merge of two protocols is a meshing of the runs of the protocols. Formally, $P \otimes_f Q = R$ such that $[\![R]\!] = \{r \mid \exists r_p \in [\![P]\!], \exists r_q \in [\![Q]\!], r[\![f]\!\rangle r_p \text{ and } r[\![f]\!\rangle r_q\}$.

Protocol concatenation is a special case of the merge operator. The concatenation of two protocols is equivalent to performing one protocol followed by the other.

Choice. The result of a choice $\oplus$ of two protocols P and Q is a protocol R, whose set of runs $[\![R]\!]$ contains exactly those runs that exist in the sets $[\![P]\!]$ and $[\![Q]\!]$, so that choosing a run from $[\![R]\!]$ is equivalent to choosing a run from either $[\![P]\!]$ or a run from $[\![Q]\!]$. Formally, $P \oplus Q = R$ such that $[\![R]\!] = [\![P]\!] \cup [\![Q]\!]$.

Constants. The properties of the merge operator lead us to define two protocols, $\mathbb{O}$ and $\mathbb{1}$. The $\mathbb{O}$ protocol is an "impossible" protocol, which does not have any runs. $\mathbb{O} = \{\}$. The $\mathbb{1}$ protocol is a "trivial" protocol which allows the zero-length run. $\mathbb{1} = \{\tau_\phi\}$. The $\mathbb{O}$ and the $\mathbb{1}$ protocols form the bottom and the top element, respectively, of a protocol hierarchy based on the merge function. All protocols are subsumed by the $\mathbb{1}$ protocol and all protocols subsume the $\mathbb{O}$ protocol.

Formal Results. We briefly present some formal results, which simplify reasoning about protocols using our algebra. Since each run in $[\![P \otimes_f Q]\!]$ subsumes a run each from $[\![P]\!]$ and from $[\![Q]\!]$, the following properties apply to the merge operator

1. The merge operator refines the protocols being merged.
   $P[\![f]\!\rangle(P \otimes_f Q)$
   $Q[\![f]\!\rangle(P \otimes_f Q)$
2. Since $P \otimes_f Q$ belongs to a frame that is the union of the frames of P and Q, the merge of a protocol with itself yields the same protocol (idempotence).
   $P[\![f]\!\rangle(P \otimes_f P)$
   $(P \otimes_f P)[\![f]\!\rangle P$
   $(P \otimes_f P) = P$
3. The merge operator is commutative and associative.
   $P \otimes_f Q = Q \otimes_f P$
   $P \otimes_f (Q \otimes_f R) = (P \otimes_f Q) \otimes_f R$
4. Merge distributes over choice.
   $P \otimes_f (Q \oplus M) = (P \otimes_f Q) \oplus (P \otimes_f M)$

5. The merge of any protocol with $\mathbb{1}$ gives that protocol and the merge of any protocol with $\mathbb{O}$ gives $\mathbb{O}$. In this way, the $\mathbb{1}$ protocol is the identity element and the $\mathbb{O}$ is the nil element for merge.
$$P \otimes_f \mathbb{1} = P$$
$$P \otimes_f \mathbb{O} = \mathbb{O}$$

Choice also supports idempotence, commutativity, and associativity. The choice of a protocol with $\mathbb{1}$ yields $\mathbb{1}$ and the choice of a protocol with $\mathbb{O}$ yields that protocol itself.

1. Idempotence.
   $$(P \oplus P) = P$$

2. Commutativity.
   $$(P \oplus Q) = (Q \oplus P)$$

3. Associativity.
   $$P \oplus (Q \oplus R) = (P \oplus Q) \oplus R$$

4. Choice with $\mathbb{1}$ and $\mathbb{O}$
   $$P \oplus \mathbb{1} = \mathbb{1}$$
   $$P \oplus \mathbb{O} = P$$

Applying the Algebra. Now we discuss how the algebra can be applied to create new protocols. The choice operator $\oplus$ allows us to choose between runs belonging to different protocols. This operator can be used, for example, when multiple ways of payment exist, such as payment by credit card, or payment by personal check. The result of the choice operator is a protocol whose set of runs is larger and thus offers more choices than the individual protocols to which the choice was applied.

The merge operator is more interesting. As an example of its application, consider the run shown in Figure 1(c). This run belongs to the merge of the simple purchase shown in Figure 1(a) and payment, shown in Figure 4(a). The merge is performed under the creditor state-similarity function σ.

As a more complicated, consider a run of the refined purchase example as shown in Figure 2. This run belongs to the refined purchase protocol, which is the result of a merge of the simple purchase, the shipping, and the payment protocols. The state-similarity function used here is $\alpha_{A,P}$. Under $\alpha_{A,P}$, A is a set of agents, p, a set of propositions, and two states are similar if all commitments between agents agents in A and all propositions in P that exist in one state also exist in the other. Under $\alpha_{A,P}$, where A denotes the set containing the participants of *Shipping*, i.e., $\{b, x, c\}$, and P denotes the set of all propositions that are used in *Shipping*, we see that the *Shipping* run shown in Figure 4(b) is subsumed by the refined *Purchase* run shown in Figure 2. Specifically, the states $s_3, s_{11}, s_{12}, s_{13}, s_{14}, s_5$, and s_{16} of refined *Purchase* are $\alpha_{A,P}$-similar to the states $s_{10}, s_{11}, s_{12}, s_{13}, s_{14}, s_{15}$, and s_{16} of *Shipping* respectively. Similarly, the states s_4 and s_{21} of the refined *Purchase* are similar to states s_{20} and s_{21} of *Payment* under $\alpha_{A,P}$, where A denotes $\{c, k\}$ and P denotes the set of all propositions used in *Payment*. Consequently, the refined *Purchase* run subsumes *Payment*. Note that Figure 2 shows

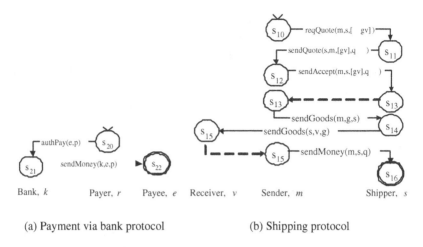

(a) Payment via bank protocol   (b) Shipping protocol

Fig. 4. A payment and a shipping protocol

only one run of the refined purchase protocol. Given the semantics of the merge operator, the refined purchase protocol allows more runs, since all valid interleavings of runs of the merged protocols are allowed. One such run could be where the shipping protocol is started before the first step of the purchase protocol. In practice, data dependencies and temporal state ordering are specified to filter the set of runs generated by interleaving.

4   Discussion

We wish to develop rich abstractions methodologies that will ease the development of large-scale open systems. This paper is part of our ongoing research in that direction.

The framework presented in this paper is intended to serve as the foundation for developing design-time tools, not for automated, runtime composition. Complete automation of protocol composition would require a complete specification of the behavior of a protocol. We believe that this is rarely the case when dealing with complex agent interaction protocols that can find applications in business processes modeling or Web Service composition. Most realistic settings require considerable context sensitive information, which may be encoded as policies local to the agent. Such contexts may be based on social motivations such as trust, economics, and profit, which can change unpredictably. The autonomy of agents in a multi-agent system allows agents to behave differently under different contexts. It is this dynamic behavior that makes the agent paradigm attractive for application to open systems, and cannot be statically specified for all but the simplest of agents. Our framework helps develop tools that aid protocol designers in tailoring an existing protocol to meet their requirements by automatically verifying properties of the designed protocol. An overview of the motivations for this work and of the applications we envision for it is provided in [16].

Our understanding of protocols as specifications of the minimum states that a computation should contain is analogous to the minimal process execution semantics as defined in the MIT Process Handbook [11]. There is an underlying assumption that concise specifications are better than elaborate ones, since flexibility of a protocol is desirable in business applications where opportunities can be profitably exploited. In some cases, however, a maximal execution semantics might be applicable, e.g., in a protocol for which compliance checking is costly or difficult or where unexpected actions are undesirable.

4.1   Literature

Our work relates to and draws both from well established and emerging fields. Business processes have received much attention lately because of the economic benefits of cross-enterprise business. Coordination and interaction protocols have been studied by the agent research community so that agent conversations and interaction can be computationally realized. We list here selected literature from both areas.

Workflows and Processes. Business processes have been traditionally automated as workflows. Recently, the web service model has been applied to process automation.

Workflows have been studied extensively as Petri-net based models of business processes [18, 19]. The Workflow Management Coalition (WfMC) is a standards body that has created a reference model for workflows [5]. This model has two basic parts, a modeling and an enactment part. The model prescribes a workflow engine as the system that executes the workflow. These models specify a rigid sequence of steps. Workflows require human intervention to handle most exceptions. Because of their inflexibility, workflows have had only limited success.

The MIT Process Handbook [11] is a project that aims to create a hierarchy of commonly used business processes. Based on this hierarchy, Grosof and Poon [8] develop a system to represent and execute business rules.

Of late, web services have been touted as the solution to the business interoperability problem. The need for process composition and interoperability has led to the development of standards for orchestration and choreography of web services [12]. Orchestration refers to intra-service planning and choreography to an overall view of inter-service coordination. Here, we shall mention only two important standards, WSCI and BPEL4WS. The Web Services Choreography Interface (WSCI) is an XML-based language that describes a service interface by the flow of messages sent and received by the service. The standard, however, looks at protocols one level lower than our view, since each WSCI specification corresponds to a role in our scheme. The Business Process Execution Language for Web Services (BPEL4WS) is currently the most widely used web services standard for describing business processes [1]. However, BPEL4WS is no more than a procedural script encoded in XML.

Fu and colleagues [7] develop methods to verify if a given web service will adhere to a given conversation protocol. Their work develops formal results about verification of protocol compliance for protocols based on finite state machines. Hamadi and Benatallah [9] develop a protocol algebra for petri nets and show its applicability to workflows and web services. However, this approach suffers from the same pitfalls as workflows modeled using Petri nets.

Interaction Protocols. Yolum and Singh [22] give one of the first accounts of the use of commitments in modeling agent interaction protocols and the flexibility that it affords the participating agents. Fornara and Colombetti [6] describe how commitments relate to FIPA-ACL messages and demonstrate with an example. Both approaches highlight the benefits of a commitment-based approach to interaction protocol design.

Johnson *et al.* [10] develop a scheme for identifying when two commitment-based protocols are equivalent. Their scheme, however, is simplistic, classifying protocols based solely on their syntactic structure. Our work provides stronger results about the relationships between protocols from an application point of view and relates better to the Web Services approach.

Bussmann *et al.* [2] present a design methodology to aid in the selection of a protocol from a library of existing protocols to apply to agent-based control applications. They identify criteria like the number of agents, the number of roles, and the number and kind of commitments and use these to select a protocol from an existing pool of interaction protocols. This approach is quantitative, and lacks a formal semantics to base the methodology on.

Pitt and Mamdani [13] describe a semantics for agent interaction protocols using the Belief-Desire-Intention (BDI) theory. Using this semantics, they outline the design of a system of agent plans that are instantiated by agents to carry on conversations with other BDI agents. In our work, an agents beliefs, desires, and intentions are private to that agent. We work with social commitments which are observable by all agents and whose breach is easier to verify.

In more recent work, Vitteau and Huget [21] describe an approach for designing agent interaction protocols using modular *micro-protocols*. This scheme is similar to our protocol design proposal in spirit. However, Vitteau and Huget do not provide a formal basis for putting protocols together.

4.2 Conclusions and Directions

The above is a semantic approach to commitment protocols that yields a simple algebra for protocols. This algebra provides a basis for conceptual reasoning about protocols in terms of refinement and aggregation, which is essential if we are to engineer protocols that way other software systems are engineered. To our knowledge, this work is unique in formulating the problem of problem design at a conceptual level. Partly, it derives it uniqueness from a careful consideration of the commitments that underlie protocols in multiagent settings.

This work opens up some interesting challenges. One, it would help consider how the algebra will work with more subtle kinds of state similarity functions. Two, the abstractions supported by our algebra must be woven into a methodology for designing protocols. Three, such methodologies should be supported by tools that give appropriate reasoning assistance to designers.

References

1. BPEL. Business process execution language for web services, version 1.1, May 2003. www-106.ibm.com/developerworks/webservices/library/ws-bpel.

2. Stefan Bussmann, Nicholas R. Jennings, and Michael Wooldridge. Re-use of interaction protocols for agent-based applications. In *Proceedings of the 3rd International Workshop on Agent-Oriented Software Engineering*, 2002.

3. Cristiano Castelfranchi. Commitments: From individual intentions to groups and organizations. In *Proceedings of the AAAI-93 Workshop on AI and Theories of Groups and Organizations: Conceptual and Empirical Research*, 1993.

4. Amit Chopra and Munindar P. Singh. Nonmonotonic commitment machines. In Marc-Philippe Huget and Frank Dignum, editors, *Proceedings of the AAMAS-03 Workshop on Agent Communication Languages and Conversation Policies*, 2003.

5. Layna Fischer, editor. *The Workflow Handbook 2004*. Future Strategies Inc., Lighthouse Point, FL, 2004. Compendium of standards and articles by the Workflow Management Coalition (WfMC).

6. Nicoletta Fornara and Marco Colombetti. Defining interaction protocols using a commitment-based agent communication language. In *Proceedings of the 2nd International Joint Conference on Autonomous Agents and Multiagent Systems (AAMAS)*, pages 520–527. ACM Press, July 2003.

7. Xiang Fu, Tevfik Bultan, and Jianwen Su. Realizability of conversation protocols with message contents. In *Proceedings of the 2004 International Conference on Web Services*, pages 96–105. IEEE Computer Press, 2004.

8. Benjamin N. Grosof and Terrence C. Poon. SweetDeal: Representing agent contracts with exceptions using XML rules, ontologies, and process descriptions. In *Proceedings 12th International Conference on the World Wide Web*, pages 340–349, 2003.

9. Rachid Hamadi and Boualem Benatallah. Proceedings of the 14th Australasian Database Conference. In Xiaofang Zhou and Klaus-Dieter Schewe, editors, *ADC*, volume 17 of *Conferences in Research and Practice in Information Technology*, pages 191–200. Australian Computer Society, February 2003.

10. Mark W. Johnson, Peter McBurney, and Simon Parsons. When are two protocols the same? In Marc-Philippe Huget, editor, *Communication in Multiagent Systems: Agent Communication Languages and Conversation Policies*, volume 2650 of *LNAI*, pages 253–268. Springer-Verlag, Berlin, 2003.

11. Thomas W. Malone, Kevin Crowston, and George A. Herman, editors. *Organizing Business Knowledge: The MIT Process Handbook*. MIT Press, Cambridge, MA, 2003.

12. Chris Peltz. Web service orchestration and choreography. *IEEE Computer*, 36(10):46–52, October 2003.

13. Jeremy Pitt and Abe Mamdani. Communication protocols in multi-agent systems. In Frank Dignum and Mark Greaves, editors, *Issues in Agent Communication*, volume 1916 of *Lecture Notes in Artificial Intelligence*, pages 160–177. Springer, 2000.

14. J. Rosenberg, H. Schulzrinne, G. Camarillo, A. Johnston, J. Peterson, R. Sparks, M. Handley, and E. Schooler. SIP: Session initiation protocol. IETF Proposed Standard. Available as an RFC at http://www.ietf.org/rfc/rfc3261.txt.

15. Munindar P. Singh. An ontology for commitments in multiagent systems: Toward a unification of normative concepts. *Artificial Intelligence and Law*, 7:97–113, 1999.

16. Munindar P. Singh, Amit K. Chopra, Nirmit V. Desai, and Ashok U. Mallya. Protocols for processes: Programming in the large for open systems. In *Onward! at the 19th ACM Conference on Object Oriented Programming, Systems, Languages, and Applications*, 2004.

17. Marvin A. Sirbu. Credits and debits on the Internet. *IEEE Spectrum*, 34(2):23–29, February 1997.

18. Wil van der Aalst, Jörg Desel, and Andreas Oberwis, editors. *Business Process Management: Models, Techniques, and Empirical Studies*, volume 1806 of *Lecture Notes in Computer Science*. Springer-Verlag, Berlin, 2000.

19. Wil van der Aalst and Kees van Hee, editors. *Workflow Management Models, Methods, and Systems*. MIT Press, Cambridge, MA, 2002.
20. Mario Verdicchio and Marco Colombetti. Commitments for agent-based supply chain management. *ACM SIGecom Exchanges*, 3(1):13–23, 2002.
21. Benjamin Vitteau and Marc-Philippe Huget. Modularity in interaction protocols. In Frank Dignum, editor, *Advances in Agent Communication*, volume 2922 of *Leture Notes in Artificial Intelligence*, pages 291–309. Springer, 2004.
22. Pınar Yolum and Munindar P. Singh. Flexible protocol specification and execution: Applying event calculus planning using commitments. In *Proceedings of the 1st International Joint Conference on Autonomous Agents and MultiAgent Systems (AAMAS)*, pages 527–534. ACM Press, July 2002.

A Scalable Petri Net Representation of Interaction Protocols for Overhearing[*]

Gery Gutnik and Gal Kaminka

The MAVERICK Group, Computer Science Department, Bar-Ilan University
52900 Ramat Gan, Israel
{gutnikg ,galk}@cs.biu.ac.il

Abstract. In open distributed multi-agent systems, agents often coordinate using standardized agent communications. Thus, representing agent conversations is an important aspect of multi-agent applications. Lately, Petri nets have been found to provide certain advantages comparing to other representation approaches. Radically different approaches using Petri nets to represent multi-agent interactions have been proposed, and yet relative strengths and weaknesses of these approaches have not been examined. Moreover, no approach was shown to provide a comprehensive coverage of advanced standardized communication aspects such as those found in FIPA interaction protocols. This paper presents (i) an analysis of existing Petri net representation approaches in terms of their scalability and appropriateness for different tasks; (ii) a novel scalable representation approach, particularly suited for monitoring open systems; and (iii) a skeletal procedure for semi-automatically converting FIPA interaction protocols to their Petri net representations. We argue that the representation we propose is comprehensive, in the sense that it can represent all FIPA interaction protocol features.

1 Introduction

Open distributed multi-agent systems often involve multiple, independently-built agents performing mutually dependent tasks. To allow different agents designs to be developed independently, without having to consider the internal design of other agents, the coordination of the activities is often accomplished using standardized inter-agent interactions, typically by communications. Indeed, the multi-agent community has been investing a significant effort in developing standard communication languages to facilitate sophisticated multi-agent systems (e.g., FIPA communication standards [4]). These languages define agent interaction protocols that rely on pre-defined communicative acts for a variety of system tasks, ranging from simple queries, to complex negotiations by auctions and bidding. For instance, FIPA Contract Net Protocol [4] defines possible sequences of concrete messages that allow the interacting agents to negotiate.

Ideally, interaction protocols should be represented in a way that allows performance analysis, validation and verification, automated monitoring, debugging, etc. Various formalisms have been proposed for such purposes. However, Petri nets

---

[*] This research was supported in part by BSF grant #2002401.

R.M. van Eijk et al. (Eds.): AC 2004, LNAI 3396, pp. 50–64, 2005.
© Springer-Verlag Berlin Heidelberg 2005

have been shown to offer significant advantages in representing multi-agent interactions, compared to other approaches [2,8,9,10]. Specifically, Petri nets are useful in validation and testing, automated debugging and monitoring [13] and dynamic interpretation of interaction protocols [3].

Unfortunately, existing literature on using Petri nets to represent multi-agent interactions leaves open several questions. First, different approaches to represent multi-agent interactions have been introduced, and yet their relative strengths and weakness have not been investigated. Second, most previous investigations have not provided a systematic comprehensive coverage of all issues that arise in representing complex protocols such as the standardized FIPA interaction protocols.

This paper addresses these open challenges. We analyze and compare existing approaches to representing interactions using Petri nets (Section 3). This comparison is done based on the type of Petri net chosen, its choice of representing individual or joint states, and explicit representation of messages. We then present a novel scalable representation that uses Colored Petri nets in which places explicitly denote joint conversation states and messages (Sections 4). This representation can be used to cover essentially all features used in FIPA conversation standards, including interaction building blocks, communicative act attributes (such as message guards and cardinalities), protocol nesting and temporal aspects (e.g., deadlines and duration). Finally, we provide a skeletal algorithm for converting FIPA conversation protocols in AUML, i.e. *Agent UML*, (the chosen FIPA representation standard [4,11]) to Petri nets (Section 5). Section 6 concludes.

2 Background

We begin first with a brief overview of Petri nets, and then survey existing approaches that use Petri nets in representing multi-agent interactions.

Petri nets are a graphical representation for describing systems in which multiple concurrent states may exist. An early elaboration of Petri nets is called Place/Transition nets (*PT-nets*), while another high-level extension is called Colored Petri nets (*CP-nets*) [6].

A PT-net is a bipartite directed graph where each vertex is either a place (typically denoted by circles) or a transition (rectangles). Arcs are directed edges connecting places to transitions and vice versa. A place can contain tokens (small black dots). An assignment of tokens to places is called *a marking*. Arcs may have associated integer *expressions*, which determine the number of tokens associated with the corresponding arc. A transition is *enabled* if and only if the marking of its input places satisfies the appropriate arc expressions. It then *fires*, carrying tokens from its input places, per the output arc expressions, to its output places.

In CP-nets, tokens carry information, called *color* [6]. Token color may be simple or complex, e.g. a tuple. Each place contains only tokens of a specified color. CP-net arc expressions are also extended, to allow complex expressions over colored token variables associated with the corresponding arcs. CP-nets also use *transition guards,* boolean expressions over token color attributes, which determine transition firing. CP-nets contain additional extensions, which can be useful in representing complex AUML features. Further detail can be found in [5].

We now turn to using Petri nets to explicitly represent multi-agent conversations. All Petri net representation approaches of this type use places to represent interaction states, and Petri net transitions to represent transitions between interaction states. Net marking represents the current state of interaction. However, previous investigations take different design choices within this general approach.

Individual Roles and CP-Nets. Most investigations choose to separately represent individual roles within the interaction, rather than represent joint interaction states. In this approach, separate places are used for separate roles in the interaction, and thus different markings distinguish a conversation state where one agent has sent a message, from a state where the other agent received it. Typically, the net for each individual role is built separately, and then these nets are either merged into a single net [2,8,9], or simply connected together using Petri net fusion places, or other means [3,14]. All these investigations use CP-nets to represent multi-agent interactions. As shown later in the paper, the use of token color allows compact representation of multiple conversations using the same net.

Joint-State Representations Using PT-Nets. In contrast, a limited number of investigations model conversations using PT-nets with joint conversation states [10,13].[1] In joint state representations, each net place is at once a representative of the conversation state of all agents. Typically, markings represent only valid conversation states (thus the nets ignore transmission delay, etc.), and synchronization protocols are implicitly assumed to underlie the conversation, to make sure that the agents are synchronized [12].

3   Analysis of Key Representations

The survey of related work presented above indicates that previous investigations have introduced rather different approaches to the modeling of multi-agent interactions using Petri nets. This section offers a comparative analysis of these approaches on the basis of several criteria: scalability (Section 3.1), and suitability for monitoring tasks (Section 3.2).

3.1 Scalability

We have classified previous approaches based on (i) their representation of individual conversation states vs. joint states, and on (ii) their utilization of token color. We now show how these two independent features affect the scalability of the chosen representation in terms of the number of conversations.

In principle, for a conversation that has R roles, with M messages, a representation which explicitly differentiates the conversation state of each role would have $O(MR)$ places: For every message there would be two individual places for the sender (before sending, and after sending), and similarly two more for each receiver (before

---

[1] Though authors claim otherwise, they in fact ignore color, using CP-nets as if they were PT-nets. For instance, Nowostawski et al. [10] duplicate portions of Petri net to represent multiple conversations, rather than using color tokens within a single net.

receiving and after receiving). All possible joint states (i.e. message sent and received, sent and not received, not sent but incorrectly believed to have been received, not sent and not received) can be represented. In cases where all joint states must be represented (including all erroneous states), this representation is preferable to an explicit joint-state representation which would require $O(M^R)$ places.

However, many applications only require representation of valid conversation states (message not sent and not received, or sent and received). For instance, the specification of the FIPA interaction protocols [4] implicitly assumes the use of underlying synchronization protocols to guarantee delivery of messages [12]. Under such assumption, for every message, there are only two joint states regardless of the number of roles: before the message is sent, and after the message is sent and received. The number of places representing joint conversation states grows (linearly) in this case only with the number of messages – $O(M)$.

We now turn to examining the use of color tokens. In principle, CP-nets and PT-nets are equivalent from a computational perspective [6], in much the same way the high level programming languages are no more powerful in principle than assembly. However, when representing conversations, a significant difference between PT-nets and CP-nets is their scalability. A PT-token corresponds to a single bit. The information it conveys is a function of the place it is marking. As a result, it is impossible to represent several concurrent conversations in the same PT-net, since the tokens representing the different states of the conversations may overwrite each other, or cause the net to fire erroneously. Therefore, representing C concurrent conversations–all of the same interaction protocol–would require $O(C)$ PT-nets.

In contrast, however, colored tokens can be differentiated, even when multiple tokens mark the same net. For instance, in the representation we present in Section 4, token colors carry information about the sender and receivers of messages, about the time in which the message was sent, etc. This information allows us to represent multiple concurrent conversations–of the same protocol–on a single CP-net structure. Note that we save only on the number of nets explicitly represented–the number of tokens for representing C conversations is $O(C)$ in either a PT-net or CP-net approach.

There are some additional differences between CP-nets and PT-nets, in terms of features that support representation of FIPA interaction protocols, such as guards, sequence expressions, cardinalities and timing [4]. Representation of FIPA attributes is straightforward using the additional information carried by token color (a more detailed discussion can be found in [5]).

Table 1. Scalability Comparison

	PT-nets	CP-nets
Individual States	**Space: O(MRC)**	**Space: O(MR)** [2],[3],[8],[9],[14]
Joint States	**Space: O(MC)** [10],[13]	**Space: O(M)**

Based on the above, it is possible to make concrete predictions as to the scalability of different approaches with respect to the number of agents. Table 1 above shows the space complexity of different approaches, given that we model C conversations, each with a maximum of R roles, and M messages. The table also cites relevant investigations.

3.2 Monitoring Conversations

There are many different uses for a representation of an interaction: To monitor its progress, to detect faults [13], to verify or analyze its features, etc. We focus here on monitoring, and distinguish two settings, depending on the information available to the monitor.

In the first type of setting, the monitor, representing the conversation, has access to the state of the conversation in one or more of the participants, but not to the messages being exchanged. This would be the case, for instance, if a participant in a conversation is monitoring its own progress. In this case, the participant has access to its own conversation state, but likely, does not have direct knowledge on whether messages were sent or received by others. Therefore, messages are not explicitly represented, except as transitions that take the conversation from one place to another (regardless of whether these places are represented individually or jointly). By placing tokens in the appropriate conversation places, an agents' state can be inferred. Then, letting the corresponding transition fire implies the message being sent and received. Previous works that have taken this approach include [2,8,9].[2]

In the second type of settings, the monitor has knowledge of the messages being sent and received, but does not necessarily know the internal conversation state. It monitors conversations by tracking the messages (e.g., through overhearing [7]). This could be done either from an individual perspective, or in settings of a global monitor that does not have direct knowledge of the conversation state of each agent. However, this requires the use of separate message places. In this type of representation, a state place and a message place are connected via a transition to a new state. A monitoring agent in this case places a token in the appropriate message place whenever it intercepts a message. Together with conversation state places, these tokens allow the conversation to transition from one conversation state to a new conversation state only based on explicit knowledge of the message being sent or received. In principle, given the current state, the new conversation state can be inferred from "observing" a message. Previous work that has used explicit message places include [2,3,10,13,14].

4 Scalable Representation for Overhearing

In this section, we focus on developing a scalable representation for overhearing. The design choices are dictated by the insights gained in the previous section. Thus, the clear choice in terms of scalability is the approach combining CP-nets with places representing joint interaction states. In addition, since in overhearing we only expect to have knowledge of messages being exchanged, we use explicit message places. Unfortunately, previous investigations did not explore this design, though the work in [13] explores similar ideas using PT-nets.

---

[2] In the same publication, Cost et al. [2] also use the other approach.

We now show how various simple and complex AUML interaction features, used in FIPA conversation standards [4], can be implemented using the proposed CP-net representation.

We begin by examining a simple agent conversation building block, corresponding to a FIPA asynchronous message, which we first show in AUML (Figure 1-a) and then using our CP-net representation (Figure 1-b). Here, $agent_1$ sends an asynchronous message msg to $agent_2$. In Figure 1-a, the msg communicative act is shown by the arrow connecting the lifelines of the corresponding agents. The stick arrowhead denotes that msg is passed asynchronously (see [1,4,11] for AUML details).

To represent the same conversation using a CP net, we first identify net places and transitions. The representation we develop uses two types of places, corresponding to messages and joint conversation states (as previously described). Figure 1-b shows the asynchronous message implementation using our CP-net model. This CP-net shows three places and one transition connecting them. The A_1B_1 and the A_2B_2 places are agent places, while the msg place is a message place. The A and B capital letters are used to denote the $agent_1$ and the $agent_2$ individual interaction states respectively. We have indicated the individual and the joint interaction states over the AUML diagram in Figure 1-a, however these details are omitted later on in the paper. The A_1B_1 place indicates a joint interaction state where $agent_1$ is ready to send the msg message to $agent_2$ (A_1) and $agent_2$ is waiting to receive the corresponding message (B_1). The msg message place corresponds to the msg sent and received. The interception of the msg (and placing a corresponding token) causes the agents to transition to the A_2B_2 place. This place corresponds to the joint interaction state in which $agent_1$ has already sent the msg communicative act to $agent_2$ (A_2) who has received it (B_2).

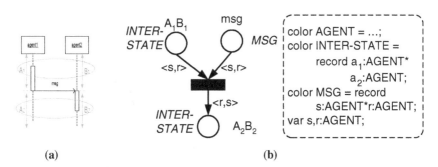

(a)   (b)

Fig. 1. Asynchronous message interaction (a) AUML (b) CP-net representations

The CP-net implementation in Figure 1-b introduces the use of token colors to represent additional information about agent interaction states and communicative acts of the corresponding interaction. The token color sets are defined in the net declaration (dashed box in Figure 1-b). The syntax follows standard CP-notation [6]. The *AGENT* color is used to identify agents participating in the corresponding interaction. This color is further used to construct the two net compound color sets.

The first color set is *INTER-STATE*. This color set is related to the net agent places and it is applied to represent agents corresponding to the appropriate joint interaction states. The *INTER-STATE* color token is a tuple (record) $<a_1,a_2>$, where a_1 and a_2 are *AGENT* color elements of the interacting agents. We apply the *INTER-STATE* color set to model concurrent conversations using the same CP-net. The second color set is *MSG*. The *MSG* color set describes interaction communicative acts and it is associated with the net message places. The *MSG* color token is a record $<s,r>$, where the s and r elements determine the sender and the receiver agents of the corresponding message.

Therefore, in Figure 1-b, the A_1B_1 and the A_2B_2 places are associated with the *INTER-STATE* color set, while the *msg* place is associated with the *MSG* color set. The place color set is written in italic capital letters next to the corresponding place. Furthermore, we use the s and r *AGENT* color type variables to denote the net arc expressions. Thus, given that the output arc expression of both the A_1B_1 and the *msg* places is $<s,r>$, the a_1 and a_2 elements of the agent place token must correspond to the s and r elements of the message place token. Consequently, the net transition occurs if and only if the addressed agents of the message correspond to the interacting agents.

Figures 2 through 4 show similar mappings between AUML representation of FIPA building blocks, and their CP-net equivalents. Figure 2 shows synchronous message passing, denoted through the filled solid arrowhead, meaning, that an acknowledgement of *msg* communicative act must always be received by *agent₁* before the interaction protocol may proceed. Figure 3 shows a more complex interaction, called XOR-decision. In this interaction, the sender can send only one of the two possible messages to the designated recipients. The figure shows the use of a joint state for the three agents (the $A_1B_1C_1$ place). Figure 4 shows another complex interaction, the OR-parallel interaction, in which the sender can send one or two communicative acts (inclusively) to the designated recipients simulating an inclusive-or. As shown, *agent₁* can send message *msg₁* to *agent₂* or message *msg₂* to *agent₃* or both.

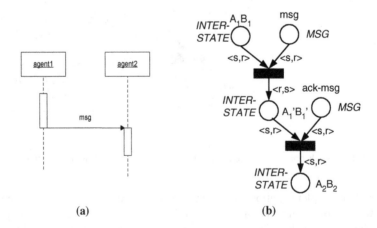

Fig. 2. Synchronous message interaction (a) AUML (b) CP-net representations

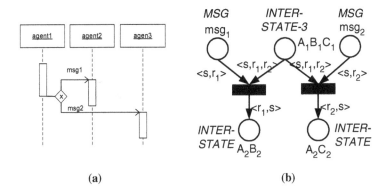

Fig. 3. XOR-decision messages interaction (a) AUML (b) CP-net representations

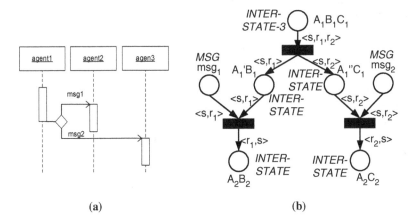

Fig. 4. OR-parallel messages interaction (a) AUML (b) CP-net representations

We now extend our technique to facilitate the implementation of additional interaction aspects useful in describing multi-agent conversation protocols. First, we use CP-nets to represent interaction message attributes used by FIPA conversation standards such as guards, sequence expressions, cardinalities, etc [4]. Second, we demonstrate representation of multiple agent concurrent conversations using the same CP-net.

Figure 5-a demonstrates a conditional agent interaction using AUML. This interaction is similar to Figure 1-a above, except for the use of the message guard-condition *[condition]*. Its semantics are that *msg* is sent if and only if the *condition* is true. Fortunately, message guard-conditions can be mapped directly to a CP-net transition guard (indicated next to the corresponding transition using square brackets in Figure 5-b). The transition guard guarantees that the transition is enabled if and only if the transition guard is true.

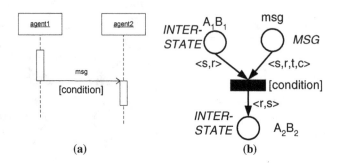

Fig. 5. Message guard-condition (a) AUML (b) CP-net representations

In Figure 5-b, we also demonstrate the CP-net implementation to message type and content attributes. For that purpose, we define two additional colors. The first, *TYPE* color, determine a message type, while the second, *CONTENT* color, represents message content. Furthermore, we extend the *MSG* color set, previously defined, to allow information passing between agents. Thus, the *MSG* color token is a record $<s,r,t,c>$, where the s and r elements has previous interpretation and the t and c elements define the message type and content.

Additional communicative act attributes include message sequence-expression and cardinality. In FIPA [4], sequence-expressions denote a constraint on the message sent from an agent: m denotes that the message is sent exactly m times; $n..m$ denotes that the message is sent n up to m times; *{*}* denotes that the message is sent an arbitrary number of times.

In this paper, we focus on a non-FIPA extension commonly used–the broadcast sequence expression, which denotes the broadcast sending of a message to all recipients on a list. In Figure 6 we show its representation using CP-nets. For this purpose, we define an *INTER-STATE-CARD* color set. This color set is a tuple $(<a_1,a_2>, i)$ consisting of two elements. The first tuple element is an *INTER-STATE* color element, which denotes the interacting agents as before. The second tuple element is an integer i that counts the number of messages already sent by an agent–message cardinality. This element is initially assigned to 0. The S_1R_1 place is of color *INTER-STATE-CARD*. Two additional colors are *BROADCAST-LIST* (defining the sender's list of receivers) and *TARGET* (index into this list).

The key novelty in Figure 6 is the use of the condition on the first transition, coupled with the arc looping back to S_1R_1. The initial marking of S_1R_1 is a single token $(<s,TARGET(0)>,0)$, pointing at the first receiver on the broadcast list as the target, with message cardinality counter initiated to 0. On the other hand, the msg_1 message place initially contains multiple tokens. Each of these tokens represents the msg_1 message addressed to a designated receiver on the broadcast list. The S_1R_1 place token and the appropriate msg_1 place token together enable the corresponding transition. It fires, thus representing the sending of msg_1 to the first receiver on the broadcast list.

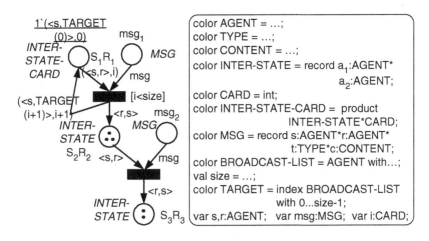

Fig. 6. Broadcast in CP-net representation

The arc looping back to S_1R_1 has an arc expression which increments the index i. Thus after the initial firing, a new token is placed in S_1R_1, pointing at the next recipient on the broadcast list. This recipient is matched with the appropriate token in the msg_1 place, and again the transition would fire, indicating transmission and receipt of msg_1 by the second receiver. The process continues while the condition on the transition holds, i.e., while the index i is smaller the size of the broadcast list.

The use of token color allows multiple conversations to be concurrently tracked using the same CP-net. For instance, in Figure 6, let the sender agent be called $agent_1$ and its broadcast list contain agents $agent_2,...,$ $agent_6$. Suppose $agent_1$ has already sent msg_1 to all agents on the broadcast list, but has only received the msg_2 reply from $agent_3$, $agent_4$ and $agent_6$. The CP-net marking for this state would be: (i) The S_2R_2 place marked $\{<agent_2, agent_1>, <agent_5, agent_1>\}$; and (ii) the S_3R_3 place marked $\{<agent_1, agent_3>, <agent_1, agent_4>, <agent_1, agent_6>\}$. The different tokens, that are distinguishable because of the token color, differentiate concurrent conversations involving $agent_1$, using the same CP-net. This is a significant improvement over PT-net representations.

Due to space constraints, we cannot show how the proposed CP-net representation is amenable to represent *all* FIPA AUML building blocks (and additional features, such as deadlines and nested protocols). The reader is referred to [5] for such details.

5   Algorithm and Concluding Example

Previous investigations have explored various machine-readable Petri net representations. However, interaction protocols are typically specified in human-readable form (e.g., in AUML [1,11]). The question of how to systematically translate an interaction protocol specification into a machine-readable form has been previously ignored. We present a semi-automated procedure for transforming an AUML protocol diagram of two interacting agents to its CP-net representation. While not fully automated, we believe that it represents a significant step towards fully automatic translation. We apply this algorithm on a complex multi-agent conversation protocol that involves many of the interaction aspects already discussed.

The procedure is presented in Figure 7. Its input is an AUML diagram, and its output is a corresponding CP-net representation using joint states and explicit message places. The CP-net is constructed in iterations: The algorithm essentially creates the conversation net by exploring the interaction protocol breadth-first, while avoiding cycles. Lines 1-2 create and initiate a queue and the output CP-net respectively. The queue, denoted by S, holds the initiating agent places for the current iteration. These places correspond to interaction states that initiate further conversation between the interacting agents. In lines 4-5, an initial agent place, A_1B_1, is created and inserted into the queue.

We enter the main loop in line 8 and set *curr* to the first initiating agent place in S. Lines 10-13 create the CP-net components of the current iteration. First, in line 10, message places, associated with *curr* agent place, are created using *CreateMessagePlaces*. These places correspond to communicative acts, which take agents from the joint interaction state *curr* to its successor(s). Then, in line 11, we create agent places that correspond to interaction state changes as a result of these

---

Algorithm $CreateConversationNet$ (**input** : $AUML$, **output** : CPN)

1: S $\leftarrow$ **new** *queue*
2: CPN $\leftarrow$ **new** CP - net
3:
4: A_1B_1 $\leftarrow$ **new** *agent place with color information*
5: S.*enqueue* (A_1B_1)
6:
7: **while** S **not** *empty* **do**
8: *curr* $\leftarrow$ S.*dequeue* ()
9:
10: MP $\leftarrow$ $CreateMessagePlaces$ $(AUML, curr)$
11: RP $\leftarrow$ $CreateResultingAgent$ $Places$ $(AUML, curr, MP)$
12: (TR, AR) $\leftarrow$ $CreateTransitionsAndArcs$ $(AUML, curr, MP, RP)$
13: $FixColor$ $(AUML, CPN, MP, RP, TR, AR)$
14:
15: **foreach** *place p* **in** RP
16:    **if** *p was not created in current iteration*
17:       **continue**
18:    **if** *p* **is not** *terminating place*
19:       S.*enqueue*(p)
20: **end foreach**
21:
22: CPN.*places*   = CPN.*places* $\bigcup MP \bigcup RP$
23: CPN.*transitions* = CPN.*transitions* $\bigcup TR$
24: CPN.*arcs*   = CPN.*arcs* $\bigcup AR$
25: **end while**
26:
27: **return** CPN

Fig. 7. AUML to CPN Conversion Procedure

messages associated with *curr* agent place. Then, in *CreateTransitionsAndArcs* (line 12), these places are connected through transitions and arcs, using the CP-net building blocks described previously, and in [5]. Finally, we add token color elements to the CP-net structure, implementing attributes using *FixColor* (line 13).

Lines 15-20 determine agent places that are inserted into *S* for further iteration. Only non-terminating agent places, corresponding to non-terminal interaction states, are inserted into *S* (lines 18-19), with the exception of places that have already been handled (lines 16-17). Completing the iteration, the output CP-net, denoted by *CPN*, is updated according to the current iteration CP-net components in lines 22-24. The loop iterates as long as *S* contains places that have not been handled. Finally, the resulting CP-net is returned (line 27).

To demonstrate this algorithm, we now use it to construct a CP-net of the FIPA Contract Net Interaction Protocol [4] (shown in AUML in Figure 8). In this protocol, the *Initiator* agent issues *m* calls for proposals using a *cfp* message. By a given deadline, each of the *Participants* may send either a *refuse* message (terminating the interaction), or a *propose* message containing a counter-proposal. Once the deadline expires, the *Initiator* evaluates received proposals and selects agents to perform the requested task. Selected participants are sent an *accept-proposal* message, while others are sent a *reject-proposal*. Selected participants carry out their task, and upon completion, send either an *inform-done*, an *inform-result*, or a *failure* message.

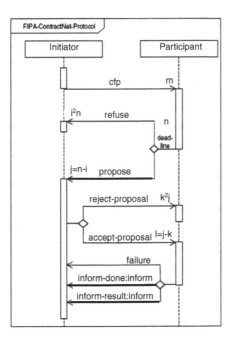

Fig. 8. FIPA Contract Net using AUML

We now use the algorithm introduced above to create a CP-net for this protocol, in four iterations of the main loop. The algorithm begins with the creation (and insertion into S) of the I_1P_1 place, of *INTER-STATE* color. Thus, in the first iteration, the *curr* variable is set to I_1P_1. The algorithm creates net places, which are associated with the I_1P_1 place, i.e. a *cfp* message place and an I_2P_2 resulting agent place. Then, the three places are connected using the asynchronous message building block shown in Figure 1-b. Next, the color sets of the corresponding places are determined, and the algorithm also handles the broadcast sequence-expression attribute of the *cfp* message, as shown in Figure 6. Accordingly, the color set associated with I_1P_1 place, is changed to the *INTER-STATE-CARD* color set. The I_2P_2 is not a terminating place (*Initiator* is waiting for a response from *Participants*) and is thus inserted into the S queue.

In the second iteration, *curr* is set to the I_2P_2 place. A *Participant* can send either a *refuse* or a *propose* messages, and thus appropriate message places are created. Then, the I_3P_3 and I_4P_4 agent places, corresponding to the results of the messages, are created. The I_2P_2, *Refuse*, I_3P_3, *Propose* and I_4P_4 places are connected using the XOR-decision described in Figure 3-b. Then, the deadline sequence expression of both the *refuse* and the *propose* messages is implemented as shown in [5]. The I_3P_3 place (resulting from *refuse*) is a terminal interaction state, while the I_4P_4 place represents a non-terminal state. Thus, only I_4P_4 is inserted into S.

For lack of space, we now skip over the final two iterations of the main loop, to the resulting CP net (Figure 9). The only items of interest in these skipped iterations involve the creation of the guard conditions on the transitions (see Figure 5-b), and the abstraction of the two inform messages (*inform-done*, *inform-result*) into a single message place marked *inform*. A detailed discussion of their creation is provided in [5].

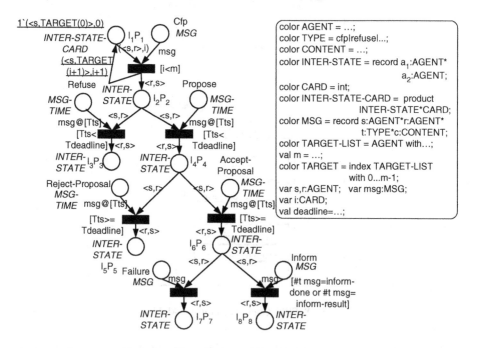

Fig. 9. FIPA Contract Net using CP-net

Although this procedure can convert many 2-agent protocols in AUML to their CP-net equivalents, it does not address the general n-agent case. We leave this development to future work.

6 Summary and Conclusions

Over recent years, increasing attention has been directed at representations of agent conversations. In particular, there is an increasing interest in using Petri nets to model multi-agent interactions [2,9,10,14]. Unfortunately, features of competing approaches with respect to scalability and suitability for different tasks have not been analyzed. Furthermore, no procedures were provided that guide the conversion of an interaction protocol given in AUML (the FIPA standard human-readable representation [4,11]) to any of the Petri net representations.

This paper sought to address these open questions. First, we analyzed key features in existing representation approaches. We have shown that (i) when representing valid conversations, a CP-net, where places denote joint conversation states, scales better than other approaches; (ii) message places are necessary for tracking conversations by overhearing. Unfortunately, previous work did not examine this combination of CP-nets with joint states and message places.

We therefore developed this representation to target scalable overhearing and monitoring tasks. We provided building blocks allowing this representation to model complex multi-agent conversations as defined by FIPA [4]. Finally, we have presented a skeleton semi-automated procedure for converting an AUML protocol diagrams to an equivalent CP-net, and demonstrated its use on a challenging FIPA conversation protocol.

We believe that the proposed technique can assist and motivate continuing research on representing conversations for tasks other than overhearing, e.g., debugging [13], automated monitoring [7], etc.

References

1. AUML site (2004). Agent UML, at www.auml.org.
2. Cost, R. S., Chen, Y., Finin, T., Labrou, Y. & Peng, Y. (2000). Using Coloured Petri Nets for a Conversation Modeling. In Dignum, F. & Greaves, M. (Eds.), Issues in Agent Communications, pp. 178-192. Springer-Verlag.
3. Cranefield S., Purvis M., Nowostawski M. & Hwang P. (2002). Ontologies for interaction protocols. In Proceedings of AAMAS-02.
4. FIPA Specifications (2004). FIPA Specifications, at www.fipa.org/specifications/index.html.
5. Gutnik, G. & Kaminka, G.A. (2004). A comprehensive Petri net representation for multi-agent conversations. MAVERICK Technical Report 2004/1, Bar-Ilan University, at www.cs.biu.ac.il/~maverick/tech-reports/.
6. Jensen, K. (1997). Coloured Petri Nets. Basic Concepts, Analysis Methods and Practical Use. Springer-Verlag.
7. Kaminka, G.A., Pynadath, D.V. & Tambe, M. (2002). Monitoring Teams by Overhearing: A Multi-Agent Plan-Recognition Approach. JAIR, 17, 83-135.

8. Lin, F., Norrie, D. H., Shen, W. & Kremer, R. (2000). A schema-based approach to specifying conversation policies. In Dignum, F. & Greaves, M. (Eds.), Issues in Agent Communications, pp. 193-204. Springer-Verlag.

9. Mazouzi, H., Fallah-Seghrouchni, A. E. & Haddad, S. (2002). Open protocol design for complex interactions in multi-agent systems. In Proceedings of AAMAS-02.

10. Nowostawski, M., Purvis, M. & Cranefield, S. (2001). A layered approach for modeling agent conversations. In Proceedings of Workshop on Infrastructure for Agents, MAS and Scalable MAS, pp. 163-170. Montreal, Canada.

11. Odell, J., Parunak, H. V. D. & Bauer, B. (2001). Agent UML: A formalism for specifying multi-agent interactions. In Ciancarini, P. & Wooldridge, M. (Eds.), Agent-Oriented Software Engineering, pp. 91-103. Springer-Verlag, Berlin.

12. Paurobally S., Cunningham J. & Jennings N. R. (2003). Ensuring consistency in the joint beliefs of interacting agents. In Proceedings of AAMAS-03.

13. Poutakidis, D., Padgham, L. & Winikoff, M. (2002). Debugging multi-agent systems using design artifacts. In Proceedings of AAMAS-02.

14. Purvis, M. K., Hwang, P., Cranefield, S. J. & Schievink, M. (2002). Interaction Protocols for a Network of Environmental Problem Solvers. In Proceedings of iEMSs-02.

First Steps Towards Multi-party Communication

Marc-Philippe Huget and Yves Demazeau

Leibniz-MAGMA,
46, Avenue Felix Viallet,
38031 GRENOBLE, France
{Marc-Philippe.Huget, Yves Demazeau}@imag.fr

Abstract. Agent communication is currently a one-to-one communication, that is, a communication *la Shannon* from a sender to a receiver via a communication channel. Such approach is restrictive in the context of multiple agents interacting each other. In this paper, we propose to extend agent communication to multi-party communication, that is, communication with several agents. Each agent is able to react to the message even if it is not the addressee. We describe in this paper the communication server for multi-party communication.

1 Introduction

Early work in agent communication take roots in distributed system communication and as a consequence, favor one-to-one communication: a speaker communicates with an addressee [7]. Even if this approach could be quite efficient in some specific cases where it is unnecessary to have auditors and overhearers, such approach is rather restrictive and does not offer good support for argumentation and multiagent communication. Agents are not able to hear the dialogue moves from other agents and cannot react in a specific way. For instance, in argumentation, it is interesting for agents to hear moves from other agents in case they disagree with the argument or to defend an argument if they agree and the speaker has no more argument to give. Argumentation is not the unique domain of interest for multi-party communication as suggested in [8] where it is used in training. Few work exist on multi-party communication, we can only quote [8], [2] and [6]. The first one focuses on multi-modal multi-party dialogues where verbal and non-verbal behaviors are used for dialogues, focus of attention and initiative. The second one concentrates on a system for multi-party dialogues based on a blackboard. Finally, in the third one, Ricordel *et al.* describe multi-dialogism based on the Ethernet protocol, that is, agents are on a ring and receive messages serially.

The work presented here proposes a communication server for multi-party communication. This work is related to the one described in [2]. The communication server depicts three different modes of communication: (1) public where speaker, addressees, auditors and overhearers can hear the message (see [2] for a

R.M. van Eijk et al. (Eds.): AC 2004, LNAI 3396, pp. 65–75, 2005.
© Springer-Verlag Berlin Heidelberg 2005

detailed description of these roles), (2) mute where only speaker and addresses hear the message. However, other agents are aware of this conversation, and finally (3) private where the conversation is not disclosed outside the speaker and addresses. Other agents are unaware of this conversation. There are two structures for communication: (1) a forum and (2) within the environment. The first option is used when messages have to be stored and retrieved by agents joining during the communication. The forum is similar to those used in chats on the Internet. Forums are preferable for argumentation systems. The second option is used when agents share a common "physical" environment and in specific applications where it is more efficient and simpler to use the environment as communication medium. An outstanding example is the use of MASSIVE in the Lord of the Rings movie to realize the battle of Helm's deep. Each fighter indicate his attack to his opponent. The opponent adequately answers to this attack. Coordination and cooperation are two other examples of multi-party communication that can be efficiently performed via the environment.

A comparison between our approach and the one in [2] is given in Section 8.

The remaining of this paper is structured as follows. Section 2 describes the differences between agent communication and multiagent communication. Section 3 presents the three different modes of communication in our approach: public, mute and private communications. The next three sections depicts these modes of communication. Section 7 presents applications of the public mode of communication. Finally, Section 8 compares our approach and the one in [2]. Section 9 concludes the paper and gives future directions of work.

2   Agent Communication Versus Multiagent Communication

Agent communication (opposed to multiagent communication) is a one-to-one communication, that is a speaker utters speech acts to a single addressee. One-to-many agent communication, such as the one we can found in the Contract Net protocol [1] is artificial since it corresponds to many one-to-one communication. Bidders cannot hear offers from other agents to make proposals. Actually, there are several features that characterize one-to-one communication:

- Communications are between two agents: a speaker and an addressee,
- Communications are privileged to two agents. That is, it is not possible for other agents to hear these communications,
- Entering and leaving communications are subject to agreement from other agents, particularly in dialogue games where there are dedicated speech acts for this purpose [5] and
- Termination of communications is necessarily known before beginning the communication.

Some features seem to be in opposition with the idea of multiagent systems. The remaining of this section reviews these features in the basis of a multiagent communication. This will give us the structure for multiagent communication and the features that should have the communication server.

1. Except private conversations that should not be disclosed, communications should not be restricted to a communication between two agents. It is frequently the case in human conversations that humans intervene in conversations where they are not either the speaker or the addressee. This is due to the fact that humans hear the content of the conversation (or bribes of it) and consider of importance to give their opinion. Multiagent communication should depict this feature of a communication where, potentially, all agents can hear the conversations, except if the conversation is considered as private. Actually, one needs three different kinds of communication: communications with potentially many hearers, private communications but agents are able to *see* that agents are whispering and finally, private communications where agents outside of the communication are unaware of this communication,

2. Multiagent communication should be like *reactive communication* based on pheromones, that is, it is only possible for agents to hear communications close to them and not communications that are too far. It is then important to add the notion of earshot, earshot can be from whispering (private communications) to harangue where even further agents can hear,

3. Multiagent systems are open systems, as a consequence, agents can enter and leave at any moment during the conversation. It should be the same in multiagent communication. One issue arises from this openness: addressees can disappear before the message arrives to them. Multiagent communication needs, more than before, to be asynchronous in the sense agents in a protocol should have an exit if the participant to the protocol is no longer present,

4. Termination of communications is not necessarily decided before beginning the communication. Termination can happen if no more communication is needed—there is no more argument against a proposal—, or if a certain event appears such as weariness in a long-lasting negotiation or an external event modifies the subject of the communication—the subject of dispute is no longer present,

5. Finally, a main difference lays in the turn taking of multiagent communication. In a one-to-one communication, especially for protocols, agents know when they have to speak but this is not necessarily the case in multiagent communication: some agents can interrupt other agents or they can monopolize the conversation. It is then required to augment the framework to consider these features and above all, the ability to avoid an agent to speak if it speaks too frequently or if it monopolize the conversation.

3   Three Modes of Communication

Agent communication is based on Shannon's ideas [7], that is, a message is sent from a sender to a receiver via a medium also called a communication channel. As a consequence, communication between agents is private to these agents. It is then not possible to send the same message to all the agents and to see the answers without using a multicast or a broadcast mechanism. Moreover, *hearing* the message assumes that the agent is recognized as member of this communication. An agent cannot overhear the communication and intervene if needed. In our proposal, this mode of communication is called the *private* mode since this thread of communication is only visible to which belonging to it. We consider as well two other modes of communication: the *public* mode and the *mute* mode. Actually, the public mode comes from the Internet multi-party communication where chats and forums are accessible to everybody and even if a message is addressed to a specific addressee, everybody can read the message, and they can answer to the message. We really are in a many-to-many communication. Finally, the mute mode corresponds to private conversations in theater. Other agents can see that these agents discuss together but they cannot hear what it is said.

The two main modes are the public and the private modes. The mute mode is frequent on chats and forums when two persons want to exchange messages without disclosing them to other persons. We add this mode to be consistent with this approach but this mode is of limited use for the moment in agent communication. It may have an application in human-lifelike applications and games. The interest in comparison with the private mode is other agents are aware of this communication and can infer some beliefs such as these agents are acquainted, they share a secret or they are friends, which are impossible in private mode.

These three different modes of communication are described on a technical point of view in following sections. They are all supported by a communication server.

4   Public Communication

As stated above, the public communication is based on the Internet multi-party communication where potentially, all agents are able to "hear" the message. The agent communication not only contains the sender and the addressees but auditors and overhearers as well. If we want to allow auditors to hear this message, it is necessary either to "open" this channel to everybody or to send the message to all the agents. The latter approach is too resource-consumptive to be used, above all if the number of agents is quite high. Chats and forums on the Internet are using a dedicated "area" where everybody can read the different messages as they arrive to the chat server. We follow two different approaches for our public mode: (1) a forum communication and (2) an environment-based communication. The difference between the two approaches remain in the way to handle communication. For instance, it is possible to consider gathering one or two hundred people in the same piece to discuss, it is more difficult for hundreds or thousands people, without speaking about location management and how to transmit speech, etc. These problems are solved on the Internet where it is possible to gather thousands of people without any further effort. We follow the same idea in agent communication where public communication via the environment is reserved for small multi-party communication whereas the forum is used for more important multi-party communication.

4.1   Forum Communication

Forum communication is used when communication is purely verbal and does not require to be immersed within an environment. Argumentation and auctions are examples of communication that can be addressed by a forum. Forums are equivalent to the ones found on the Internet, that is, a shared zone where one or several threads of conversation run concurrently. For sake of simplicity, we restrict to one thread and several subsequent threads derived from the main thread. Subsequent threads are used to clarify some points in the current conversation. Clarifying a message content is an example of subsequent thread since it deserves the main thread. Forums are created on request of agents for a particular need. For instance, the agent wants to open an auction to sell an item.

When an agent begins a new dialogue in forum mode, the communication server creates a forum with one participant and posts the message. Then, the communication server advertises this forum to other agents. The way of advertising can be done along different modes:

1. The sender identifies an agent role to which the advertisement should be sent,
2. The sender gives an advertisement to be sent to all the agents,
3. The sender gives no advertisement, the message is sent to all the agents.

The communication server updates as well the list of ongoing forums. It creates a slot that contains the list of participants and the advertisement if it exists. This list is used by agents to access it if they do not have received the advertisement—in the context of open systems or when they were not addressed by the advertisement. This list only contains the public and the mute communications. All the messages post on the forum are stored. One of the interest to store the message is for agents that join during the conversation. It is then possible for them to find what the current state of the conversation is. They just have to execute the protocol on the different messages posted. Turn taking is not restricted and agents can speak freely when they need to. Termination in multi-party communication is ensured either by the communication server and by the agents. The communication server checks that some agents are not present in the communication only to slow it down. If it is the case, it removes them from the communication. Removing agents is performed on request of agents that found some agents are opposed to terminate the communication in short time. Such decision is difficult to define since it is required to consider what slowing down the communication means. For instance, in a one-to-one negotiation, it corresponds that agents do not change their proposal and iterate on it infinitely. Removal decision is *ad hoc* to the domain of communication.

The main difference with Internet forums is the use of protocols and the restriction to only one thread of conversation. An example of public communication via forums is given in Section 7.

4.2   Environment-Based Communication

The first mode of communication in public communication is the forum mainly used for verbal conversations where the immersion of agents within environment is not important. The mode of communication, we present here, makes the assumption that agents communicate via the environment. Thus, sending a message does not correspond to send it to a dedicated communication channel but propagating in the environment. A similar approach already exists in MANTA [3] where this time, the message is a pheromone. One reason for agents to choose this mode of communication is the need to coordinate or to cooperate with other agents. This mode of communication is driven as well by some specific applications such as human-lifelike applications or games. For instance, a wargame can use this approach to coordinate platoons or to help soldiers in danger. An outstanding example of communication via the environment is the use of MASSIVE for the battle of Helm's deep in the Lord of the Rings movie. Attacks are passed via the environment to allow opponents to react to this attack. They then reduce the complexity of agents by leveraging down their perception requirements: there is no vision process to recognize an opponent and his attack.

Messages are released in the environment with a specific force and a decrement of 1. It means that the force of the message is total at the source location but decreases by 1 for each cell far from the source. The further the message is from its source, the weaker it is. An example of message release is given on Figure 1. Agent *agent*1 sends a message *inform* with a force of 4 and a decrement of 1. Agent *agent*2 hear the message since it is within earshot but not Agent *agent*3 since it is out of earshot.

Contrarily to communication via forums, messages are not stored for newcoming agents. Moreover, messages are substituted by new ones if earshot of a new message is on some cells of a previous message. We use as well the direction of the agent, that is, a message is more easily heard if the speaker watches the

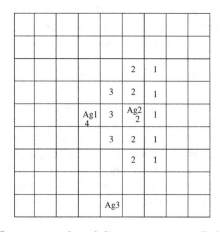

Fig. 1. Environment-based Communication in Public Mode

recipient than the speaker has its back to the recipient. The message is written in the environment along an arc of a circle. The structure of the environment modifies as well the possibility to hear the message. For this particular communication server, we consider that messages can go through walls by a decrement of 3.

When an agent begins a new dialogue in environment-based mode, the communication server retrieves the force of the message and updates the environment with this message. That is, it propagates the message within the environment and decrements the force of the message based on the distance between the current location and the source as shown on Figure 1. Reading messages for addressees is performed by perceiving the environment and retrieving the message. This is only possible if the agent is within the earshot. A timestamp is associated to messages. When the timestamp is passed, the message is removed from the environment. The same approach is used for pheromones in MANTA to avoid considering outdated information [3].

5   Mute Communication

Mute communications are certainly the less frequent mode of communication in multiagent systems. The aim of this mode of communication is to offer some privacy to agents during the conversation. It means that other agents outside the communication are aware of this communication but cannot hear the content. This mode of communication is frequent in theater when several characters move away and discuss—usually for a plot. Mute communication receives less attention for the moment in multiagent communication. Actually, it is similar to private communication except that other agents are aware of this communication. However, we do a slight modification in comparison with theater private conversations since it is not possible to spy on the communication and to disclose the content. The interest in this mode of communication is to reveal to other agents that some agents are acquainted. Agents can infer beliefs about this private conversation. For instance, in games, it can imply that some relationships exist between characters and it can affect the way to play.

Two elements have to be taken into account when communicating in mute mode. Privacy of the communication has to be ensured and agents outside the communication have to be aware of this communication. The support for mute communication is a forum only accessible for the participants. It means that the communication server controls the access to the forum and only agents granted by the participants can access it. New participants are chosen either by the leader of the communication—if it exists—or on a vote of all the participants. If most of the participants agree, new participants can enter the discussion. The communication server saves a list of all the forums that currently run. It is straightforward for agents to retrieve the list and know agents involved in forums.

6   Private Communication

Our mode of private communications is similar to current one-to-one communication. It means it is not possible for agents outside the participants of the communication to be aware of this communication. We adopt the same approach than for mute communications, that is, the communication server uses a forum to store the message exchanged during this communication but this time, this forum does not appear in the list of ongoing forums. The use of this forum is the one described in Section 4.1.

7   Multi-party Communication Application

Previous sections depict three different modes of communication, respectively public communication, mute communication and private communication. In this section, we describe two examples of public communication.

Public mode in multi-party communication can be used for auctions for instance. The current protocol for auctions such as English auction or Dutch auction waits for a deadline to select the winner. Agents know whether they win or lose the turn but they do not know which agent wins the turn. As a consequence, they cannot infer some beliefs about the interest of other agents in the auction. Moreover, they do not know which agents are attending this auction. Using public communication via a forum can simplify the protocol and let the auction closer to human auctions. A modified version of the English auction protocol is shown on Figure 2. The main differences are in the treatment of proposals and winner notification. In the usual English auction protocol, each participant can accept the bid via an *inform* message [4]. After deadline, the auctioneer informs bidders whether it accepts the bid or not. In terms of messages, if n participants are willing to bid, there are $2n$ messages used whereas in human auctions, there are only two messages: one from the first bidder and one from the auctioneer. Thanks to the forum communication, it is possible to reduce the number of messages to two messages and to increase the quantity of information, participants can use to infer strategies on other participant. Since the bid is posted on the forum, other participants are aware of this proposal and know they no longer propose. A message from the auctioneer is required to inform which agent wins the turn in case several agents bid at the same moment. Mute mode or private mode can be used for the final phase of auctions, that is, paying for the item won.

An illustrative example where public communication via the environment can be used is the battle of Helm's deep in the Lord of the Rings-The Two Towers where orcs and humans are agents and they fight together. Opponents do not perceive what other agents do but perceive a message sent in the environment by their direct opponent and react as they want. In this approach, the communication is restricted to informing opponents of what is the attack, but it is possible to think about using this communication to coordinate fighters and help fighters in danger. Another classical example in multiagent systems is the

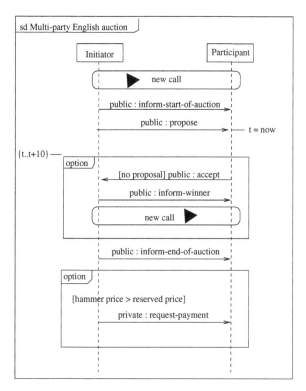

Fig. 2. English Auction Protocol in the Context of Multi-Party Communication

MANTA project where communication between ants and cocoons is performed via environment propagation.

8   Comparison with Dignum and Vreeswijk's Approach

The proposal made in [2] is the closest to ours. In this one, a blackboard system is used for multi-party dialogues. On the reading of this paper, we can infer several differences between the two approaches:

1. An unique blackboard system is proposed whereas we consider several forums, one per conversation. It means that either the system in [2] is more complex since it is required to extract between several threads of conversation or agents are restricted to only one conversation at a time,
2. The system is closed in [2]. It is then not possible to add new agents during the conversation. As a consequence, no policy has to be defined to restrict the access to a forum. In our approach, the system is open and agents can enter and leave when they desire to. Moreover, entering a communication is accepted after the agreement of the participants.

3. Dignum and Vreeswijk use computational dialectic to direct agent communication. Moreover, communication is unaddressed. In our approach, messages are addressed to addressees even if all agents potentially can read them. We still use protocols to direct communications.

4. Without any reasons—except maybe the termination issue—, agents speak alternatively and on a fixed number of rounds in [2]. It is a restrictive approach. There is no fixed number of rounds in our approach since termination is decided both by the communication server and agents.

5. There is no private communications in [2]. As a consequence, it is not possible for agents to discuss without noticing other agents.

These two approaches are not contradictory but complementary. It could be interesting to consider mixing our communication server with the computational dialectic defended by Dignum and Vreeswijk since our communication server is not dedicated to a specific way to address the communication.

9   Conclusion

Agent communication is still a one-to-one communication, that is, the communication is between a speaker and an addressee and auditors and overhearers are not considered. This has some impact on communication and for instance in argumentation where it is not easily possible for agents to defend or attack arguments of other agents if they are unable to hear them, they can only defend their own arguments. The idea defended in this paper is to offer one-to-many and many-to-many communication to agents. As a consequence, messages are addressed to all the agents that can hear them. We propose three modes of communication: public communication similar to forums on the Internet, mute communication similar to private conversations but other agents are aware of these conversations and finally, private communication similar to current one-to-one communication. Other agents are unaware of these communications. Public communications are supported by either a forum or by the environment. The forum allows agents to communicate via a many-to-many communication. Each agent which is participant in this forum can hear the message and answer if it wants even if it is not the addressee of the message. The second support—the environment—is particularly suited for coordination and cooperation. Agents only communicate with agents close to them and as a consequence, maybe those that are the most able to help them. An outstanding example is battles in games where communication via the environment can coordinate platoons.

Multi-party communication generates new issues that have to be solved for efficient communications. That is, turn-taking, termination and entering communications have now to be considered from a theoretical point of view, for instance considering how multiple parties affect dialogue games or argumentation systems. The example of English auction in Section 7 presents a reduction in the number of messages when using multi-party communication in comparison with one-to-one communication. It could be interesting to define what are the advantages in terms of number of messages when passing from one-to-one communication to multi-party communication and how protocols are modified to answer to multi-party communication. These two topics are in our agenda.

References

1. R. Davis and R. G. Smith. Negotiation as a metaphor for distributed problem-solving. *Artificial Intelligence*, 20:63–109, 1983.
2. F. Dignum and G. Vreeswijk. Towards a testbed for multi-party dialogues. In M.-P. Huget and F. Dignum, editors, *AAMAS 2003 Workshop on Agent Communication Language and Conversation Policies (ACL 2003)*, Melbourne, 2003, July 2003.
3. A. Drogoul. *De la simulation multi-agents à la résolution collective de problème. Une étude de l'émergence de structures d'organisation dans les systèmes multi-agents.* PhD thesis, Universit Paris 6, 1993.
4. FIPA. Fipa interaction protocol library specification. Technical Report XC00025, FIPA, 2000.
5. P. McBurney. *Rational Interaction*. PhD thesis, Department of Computer Science, University of Liverpool, 2002.
6. P.-M. Ricordel, S. Pesty, and Y. Demazeau. About conversations between multiple agents. In *First International Conference of Central Eastern Europe on Multi-Agent Systems (CEEMAS)*, St Petersbourg, June 1999.
7. C. E. Shannon. A mathematical theory of communication. *The Bell System Technical Journal*, 27, 1948.
8. D. Traum and J. Rickel. Embodied agents for multi-party dialogue in immersive virtual worls. In *Proceedings of the First International Conference on Autonomous Agents and Multi-Agent Systems (AAMAS 2002)*, Bologna, Italy, July 2002.

Optimal Communication Vocabularies and Heterogeneous Ontologies

Jurriaan van Diggelen, Robbert Jan Beun, Frank Dignum, Rogier M. van Eijk, and John-Jules Meyer

Institute of Information and Computing Sciences,
Utrecht University, The Netherlands
{jurriaan, rj, dignum, rogier, jj}@cs.uu.nl

Abstract. In this paper, we will consider the alignment of heterogeneous ontologies in multi agent systems. We will start from the idea that each individual agent is specialized in solving a particular task and therefore requires its own specialized ontology that is, in principle, not understandable for other agents. This heterogeneity of ontologies, of course, poses problems for the communication between agents. In our framework, we assume that the agents share some minimal common ground which can be used to learn new concepts. We will discuss which concepts of the different ontologies the agents should learn from each other in order to establish a communication vocabulary that enables optimal communication.

1 Introduction

The World-Wide Web has enabled people to access a vast amount of information from distributed sources all over the world. Due to its rapidly increasing size, and the scattered nature of the information resources available, it is becoming more and more difficult for humans to find the information they are interested in. This problem has given rise to research on the enhancement of the current infrastructure with machine processable semantics. In the future, this would enable computer agents to use and understand information on the web, and so assist humans in performing tasks on the internet.

In [10], for example, a future scenario is described in which a travel-agent assists a customer in planning a holiday trip to the United States. The agent not only finds a cheap flight, but also investigates the prices for camper rental, suggests other transport possibilities, and finds out which licenses are required for campsites on the way. Basically, it does everything that your travel agency does for you these days. Before this scenario can be made reality, some important barriers have to be overcome. One of them is that agents must be able to communicate with each other. A fundamental problem in communication is caused by the heterogeneity of the underlying knowledge sources, or more specifically, of the underlying ontologies ([18]). For instance, a travel-agent may encounter another agent that offers a "mobile home". The travel-agent should be able to recognize

R.M. van Eijk et al. (Eds.): AC 2004, LNAI 3396, pp. 76–90, 2005.

that this offer concerns a concept that he himself would refer to as a "camper". However, when the travel-agent encounters an agent offering a "mobile phone", it should recognize that this offer will not fulfil its desire to rent a camper.

Over the last decade, some important progress has been made towards the standardization of agent communication languages (ACL's), e.g. KQML ([7]), FIPA ACL ([1]). However, these standards mainly focus on the syntax of messages and the semantics of performatives. The semantics of the *content* of a message is not specified by the ACL standard, but by the ontology which is used. The content of a message will only be correctly conveyed if the receiving agent knows the ontology of the sending agent. In an open multi agent system (MAS), both the situation that all agents share one and the same ontology, and the situation that every agent knows each other's ontology are not desirable. Because every agent is specialized in solving its own particular task, every agent requires its own specialized ontology. Also, the situation of making every agent acquainted with every other agent's ontology will be untenable in an open MAS.

In this paper, we will address the problem of establishing a suitable communication vocabulary in a formal and abstract way. We will specify a framework which contains those elements that are relevant for the problem, and those elements that are necessary in order to make the problem solvable. Every agent has its own specialized ontology that is, in principle, not understandable for other agents. To provide a starting point for the agents to understand each other's ontologies, we assume that there is a common ground in which each private ontology of an agent is rooted. This common ground enables them to uncover the relations of foreign concepts with their private concepts. In this paper, we will construe this common ground as a *ground ontology*. This implies that all the terms used in a private ontology can be expressed as a complex of basic terms defined in this ground ontology. We will also introduce the notion of a *communication vocabulary*. Although agents are unable to communicate their private concepts directly, they can use this communication vocabulary to express private concepts in an efficient manner without using the complex and, for communication purposes, inefficient definitions of the ground ontology.

We will focus on the desirable properties of the communication vocabulary and specify which concepts are most suited to become part of this vocabulary. On the one hand, the vocabulary should contain enough concepts to enable the agents to express all things with sufficient accuracy. On the other hand, it should contain as few concepts as necessary in order not to burden the agents with superfluous concepts.

In the next section we will discuss the backgrounds of the problem and review related work. In section 3 we will give the formal definitions of the framework, and discuss the place of the ground ontology and the communication vocabularies in the system. In section 4 we will discuss the various possibilities for the communication vocabulary. Section 5 presents our conclusions and indicates steps for further research.

2   Background and Related Work

Within an agent's knowledge representation, a distinction can be drawn between the description of intensional knowledge, concerning general knowledge about a problem domain, and the description of extensional knowledge, concerning a particular problem [4]. The former will be referred to as the agent's ontology, and the latter as the agent's assertional knowledge base. An agent's ontology is usually thought to be changeless, whereas an agent's assertional knowledge base is subject to change, as it represents the current state of the world. The ontology describes the agent's commitment on how to view the world. The assertional knowledge base is described in terms of the concepts defined in the ontology. As a consequence, the things that can be expressed well about the current state of the world are heavily dependent on the concepts defined in the ontology.

One of the strong points of a MAS is that it enables one to partition the problem space of a complex system into smaller problems which can be solved by individual agents ([13]). This means that each agent requires its own specialized ontology which is tailored to its own specific task. Therefore, the problem of integrating heterogeneous ontologies is not just a matter of reaching agreement among system developers to use one common standard. In fact, the presence of heterogeneous ontologies is inherent to the task division in multi agent systems.

However, disparities in the agents' conceptualizations pose problems for the communication between agents. One of the characteristics commonly ascribed to agents is that of exhibiting *social* behavior. In the context of the distinction between ontological and assertional knowledge, the social nature of agents will be apparent in the communication of *assertional* knowledge. As has been argued above, an agent's ontology represents its changeless knowledge about a problem domain. Therefore, it is useless for one agent to communicate its ontological knowledge to another agent, as the other agent will not be willing to change this type of knowledge anyway. However, it does make sense for agents to communicate assertional knowledge, as this characterizes itself by being subject to change, representing the current state of the world.

Because assertional knowledge is defined in terms of the concepts introduced in the ontology, communicating assertions becomes problematic when heterogeneous ontologies are involved. There is no guarantee that, when one agent sends an assertion in terms of its private ontology to another agent, the meaning of this assertion is also conveyed to the other agent. The receiving agent may be unfamiliar with the terms used in the assertion, or, even worse, may assign different meanings to these terms.

In the knowledge representation community, the problem of integrating heterogeneous ontologies has been given a lot of attention lately. Several tools have been developed in order to merge and align ontologies (e.g. Chimaera [11], Prompt [12]). However, these tools require human intervention to ensure correct mappings. In open multi agent systems, inter-ontology mappings have to be established on such a large scale that this prerequisite is unacceptable.

The foundation for intelligent physical agents (FIPA) has recognized the problems for agent communication caused by heterogeneous ontologies. In [2] this problem is given attention by specifying the communicative interface to a service that assists agents in aligning their ontologies. However, the internal implementation of a service that performs this task (a task which they characterized as *very difficult, and not always possible to realize*) is left to system developers. We agree with the observation that ontology alignment is very difficult, yet indispensable for MAS's. Therefore, we believe that a formal and theoretical underpinning is essential at this point in order to identify the relevant components and investigate their nature.

Only recently, a few approaches have been proposed which address the problem of aligning heterogeneous ontologies in MAS's. In [19], an approach is described in which the agents use machine learning techniques to learn the meaning of each others concepts. The initial clues on the meaning of foreign concepts are provided by the instances of those concepts. This resembles the approach taken in [17], where overlaps in instance data are the main driving force behind the characterization of foreign concepts in terms of upper- and lower bounds of private concepts. In [5], the authors describe how agents can autonomously derive transformation functions (i.e. *glue code*) to translate between heterogeneous ontologies. In this approach, it is assumed that a common underlying theory exists to which the private ontologies of the agents are linked.

All these approaches have in common that they aim at providing the agents with a set of shared concepts in which they can express their private knowledge (or similarly, with some shared understanding of each others concepts). In our framework, this set of shared concepts is present in the communication vocabulary. However, whereas the approaches described above focus on how the agents are to derive the communication vocabulary, in this paper we focus on its structure and desirable properties.

Every approach that deals with fully automatic alignment of ontologies presupposes some form of common ground to find inter-ontology mappings. In some cases this common ground is provided by shared instances (as in [19], [17]), in other cases there exist some shared ground terms (as in [5], [6]), and in yet other cases there are pointable objects which are observable by both agents (as in [15]). In this paper we have chosen for a ground ontology as common ground which provides a set of shared ground terms that the agents use to define their private concepts. Since the main focus of this paper is on the communication vocabulary and not on the ground ontology, our results are still relevant when the agents have a different kind of common ground at their disposal.

3   General Framework

3.1   Representation of Ontologies

Ontologies may take a variety of forms which differ in representation format and expressivity ([8]) (e.g. Ontolingua ([9]), OWL ([3]). We will abstract away from representational differences by adopting one syntax which is used by all agents. Furthermore, because the inheritance relation almost without exception lies at the core of an ontology, we will restrict ourselves to taxonomic structures with disjointness relations.

Ontologies will be formalized using a language $\mathcal{L}$, which is equal to the description logic language $\mathcal{ALC}$ without roles. The semantics of $\mathcal{L}$ is based on interpretations of the form $\mathcal{I} = (\Delta^{\mathcal{I}}, \cdot^{\mathcal{I}})$, where $\Delta^{\mathcal{I}}$ is the domain and $\cdot^{\mathcal{I}}$ is the interpretation function that maps every concept to a subset of $\Delta^{\mathcal{I}}$ and every individual to an element of $\Delta^{\mathcal{I}}$. Given a set of *atomic concepts A*, *complex concepts* can be formed using concept constructors. The following constructs are available:

- A, where $A^{\mathcal{I}} \subseteq \Delta^{\mathcal{I}}$
- $\top$, where $\top^{\mathcal{I}} = \Delta^{\mathcal{I}}$
- $\bot$, where $\bot^{\mathcal{I}} = \emptyset$
- $\neg C$, where $(\neg C)^{\mathcal{I}} = \Delta^{\mathcal{I}} - C^{\mathcal{I}}$
- $C \sqcap D$, where $(C \sqcap D)^{\mathcal{I}} = C^{\mathcal{I}} \cap D^{\mathcal{I}}$
- $C \sqcup D$, where $(C \sqcup D)^{\mathcal{I}} = C^{\mathcal{I}} \cup D^{\mathcal{I}}$

The notation $\mathcal{L}(\mathcal{C})$ is used to denote the set of complex concepts in $\mathcal{L}$ over the set of atomic concepts $\mathcal{C}$. Statements can be used to define one of the following:

- **subsumption:** $C \sqsubseteq D \Leftrightarrow C^{\mathcal{I}} \subseteq D^{\mathcal{I}}$
- **equality:** $C \doteq D \Leftrightarrow C^{\mathcal{I}} = D^{\mathcal{I}}$
- **membership:** $C(a) \Leftrightarrow a^{\mathcal{I}} \in C^{\mathcal{I}}$

We say that $\mathcal{I}$ is a model of a set of statements Γ, if $\mathcal{I}$ satisfies every statement in Γ. We say that Γ entails a statement γ, i.e. $\Gamma \models \gamma$, if and only if every model of Γ also satisfies γ.

An *ontology O* is defined as a tuple $\langle T, \mathcal{C} \rangle$. $\mathcal{C}$ is the set of atomic concepts and T is a TBox consisting of a set of statements of the form: $A \doteq C$ or $A \sqsubseteq C$, where $A \in \mathcal{C}$, and $C \in \mathcal{L}(\mathcal{C})$. It is assumed that the definitions in T are *unique* (i.e. no concept occurs more than once at the right hand side of some axiom), and *acyclic* ([4],p.52).

Among atomic concepts, a distinction can be drawn between *primitive concepts* and *defined concepts*. Primitive concepts are those that only occur at the right hand sides of the TBox statements, whereas defined concepts occur somewhere on the left hand side of a TBox statement. Since we assume that the TBox definitions are unique and acyclic, the TBox is *unfoldable* ([4],p.310). This means that every defined concept can eventually be written in terms of primitive concepts. The unfolding of concept C with respect to TBox T is written as $[C]_T$ and can be obtained by recursively substituting the defined concepts in the formula by their definitions in T.

3.2   Ontologies in Multi Agent Systems

A multi agents system is defined as: $\mathcal{A} = \{x_1..x_n\}$. An agent x_i is defined as a tuple with one component containing the knowledge base $KB_i = \langle O_i, A_i \rangle$, where $O_i = \langle T_i, \mathcal{C}_i \rangle$ is the ontology, and A_i is the set of membership statements, constituting an ABox. A membership statement takes the form $C(a)$, where $C \in \mathcal{C}$, $a \in \Delta$. $C(a)$ holds iff $a^{\mathcal{I}} \in C^{\mathcal{I}}$.

In our framework, the communication vocabulary is also formalized as an ontology. For the agents to adapt to a communication vocabulary, they must be able to uncover the relations of the concepts in the communication vocabulary with the concepts in their private ontologies. For that reason we have introduced the ground ontology which is shared by the entire MAS and in which every private concept of each individual agent can eventually be defined. Formally, this implies that every primitive concept in each agent's ontology is present in this ground ontology. Even with a small set of ground concepts (i.e. concepts in the ground ontology), an enormous quantity of complex concepts can be formed. This enables every agent to adopt its own specialized world view, while keeping the possibilities for interoperability open. The following definition formalizes the notion of grounding an ontology.

Definition 1. *Grounding Ontologies*
An ontology $O_i = \langle T_i, C_i \rangle$ is grounded in the ground ontology $O_g = \langle T_g, C_g \rangle$ if for all $C \in C_i$ holds that $[C]_{T_i} \in \mathcal{L}(C_g)$

We assume that for all agents x_i it holds that their private ontology O_i is grounded in O_g. This assumption to facilitate the integration of heterogeneous knowledge sources, is similar to that proposed by the SENSUS methodology ([16]). The main characteristic of this methodology is that one large ontology (with more than 50,000 concepts) is used as a skeletal foundation for the domain specific ontologies. As all ontologies built using this methodology share a common underlying structure, merging and aligning them will become much easier.

Example 1. Consider the ontology of agent x_1 (the Camper rental Agent), $O_1 = \langle T_1, C_1 \rangle$, which is grounded in the ground ontology presented in figure 1.

$T_1 = \{$ *OneBedCamper $\doteq$ Vehicle $\sqcap$ Shelter $\sqcap$ WeightsMoreThan1Ton $\sqcap$ $\neg$WeightsMoreThan2Ton $\sqcap$ $\neg$ ElectronicEquipment $\sqcap$ YellowThing , ForestCamper $\doteq$ Vehicle $\sqcap$ Shelter $\sqcap$ WeightsMoreThan2Ton $\sqcap$ $\neg$ ElectronicEquipment $\sqcap$ GreenThing , HappyHolidayCamper $\doteq$ Vehicle $\sqcap$ Shelter $\sqcap$ WeightsMoreThan2Ton $\sqcap$ $\neg$ ElectronicEquipment $\sqcap$ YellowThing* $\}$
$C_1 = \{$ *OneBedCamper, ForestCamper, HappyHolidayCamper* $\}$

The ontology of the camper rental agent characterizes its personal view on the world, which consists of campers. This ontology enables agent x_1 to store camper related knowledge efficiently. However, it leaves limited possibility to store other kinds of knowledge, as it has been tailored to the camper domain. The shared ground assumption becomes apparent in the definitions of its private concepts of C_1. The concepts used in these definitions all belong to the concepts of the ground ontology, namely C_g.

3.3   Communication Vocabularies

The concept names used in an agent's private ontology are not understandable to other agents. However, their definitions in terms of ground concepts *are*. An obvious solution to the communication problem would be to use the definition of a private concept in communication, instead of the private concept itself. However, this is not the preferred approach, as concept definitions are generally

$T_g = \{$ *TangibleThing* $\sqsubseteq \neg$ *IntangibleThing* ,
YellowThing $\sqsubseteq$ *TangibleThing* ,
GreenThing $\sqsubseteq$ *TangibleThing* $\sqcap \neg$ *YellowThing,*
WeightsMoreThan1Kg $\sqsubseteq$ *TangibleThing,*
WeightsMoreThan1Ton $\sqsubseteq$ *WeightsMoreThan1Kg* ,
WeightsMoreThan2Ton $\sqsubseteq$ *WeightsMoreThan1Ton* ,
Artifact $\sqsubseteq$ *TangibleThing* $\sqcap$ *ManMade* ,
Shelter $\sqsubseteq$ *TangibleThing,*
ElectronicEquipment $\sqsubseteq$ *Artifact* $\sqcap \neg$ *Shelter,*
CommunicationDevice $\sqsubseteq$ *Artifact,*
Vehicle $\sqsubseteq$ *Artifact* $\sqcap \neg$ *CommunicationDevice,*
Building $\sqsubseteq$ *Artifact* $\sqcap \neg$ *ElectronicEquipment* $\sqcap \neg$ *CommunicationDevice* $\}$
$\mathcal{C}_g$ = $\{$ *TangibleThing,*   *IntangibleThing,*   *YellowThing,*   *GreenThing,*
WeightsMoreThan1Kg,   *WeightsMoreThan1Ton,*   *WeightsMoreThan2Ton,*   *Artifact,*
ManMade, Shelter, ElectronicEquipment, CommunicationDevice, Vehicle, Building$\}$

Fig. 1. Example Ground Ontology

very large. Communicating directly in terms of ground concepts would lead
to long messages, resulting in a high bandwidth load, and large amounts of
data to be processed. The rationale behind introducing a defined concept in
an ontology, is to enable the agent to store information using only one atomic
concept instead of storing it using a complex structure of primitive concepts.
Likewise, the rationale behind adopting a communication vocabulary, is to enable
the agent to communicate a complex concept using only one defined concept,
instead of communicating it using a complex structure of primitive concepts.

From this perspective, the intuition behind the communication vocabulary
links up with a common technique from information theory, where frequently
used symbols are encoded in a smaller number of bits than the rarely used
symbols, e.g. as in Morse codes, or Huffman codes. These codes enable one to
reduce the average size of messages sent over some communication channel.

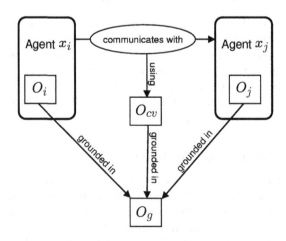

Fig. 2. General framework

To enable agents to uncover the relations with their private ontologies, the communication vocabulary is grounded in the ground ontology. The situation is illustrated in figure 2. Note that the set of concepts of agent x_i (i.e. C_i) denotes the set of concepts in which its assertional knowledge is expressed. There may be (ground) concept names that occur in T_i that are not member of C_i. The set of concepts in the ground ontology (i.e. C_g) is used to refer to all concepts that occur in T_g.

4   Properties of Communication Vocabularies

An optimal communication vocabulary is defined as the smallest set of concepts to be used in communication, while remaining sufficiently accurate. In this section we will formalize this notion.

4.1   Concept Equivalence Relative to an Ontology

When an agent is committed to a certain ontology, it has decided to view the world only in terms of those concepts defined in its ontology. The agent can store only those things that are expressible using the concepts in its ontology and the concept constructors in the language $\mathcal{L}$. Foreign concepts can therefore be characterized solely in terms of their relations with the concepts in the agent's ontology. Suppose the following membership statement is sent: $C(a)$, where C is a concept in the ground ontology. The only thing that matters to the receiving agent is what implications this statement carries concerning membership of the concepts in its private ontology. Such an implication w.r.t. a concept D in its private ontology, can be one of the following:

1. It can be derived that a is also member D, i.e. $D(a)$
2. It can be derived that a is not member of D, i.e. $\neg D(a)$
3. Neither 1, nor 2 holds, i.e. $D(a)$ cannot be proven, and $\neg D(a)$ cannot be proven.

A derivation of type 1 can be made if and only if $C \sqsubseteq D$ holds (specific-to-general reasoning). A derivation of type 2 can be made if and only if $C \sqsubseteq \neg D$ (reasoning with disjointness). The agent remains ignorant about $D(a)$ and $\neg D(a)$ if neither $C \sqsubseteq D$, nor $C \sqsubseteq \neg D$ can be proven.

Elaborating on these ideas, two foreign concepts can be regarded equivalent w.r.t. an ontology if they stand in the same relation to the concepts in the ontology. This can be formalized as follows:

Definition 2. *Concept Equivalence Relative to an Ontology*
Given a ground ontology $O_g = \langle T_g, C_g \rangle$, and an ontology $O = \langle T, C \rangle$ which is grounded in O_g. The concepts $C, D \in \mathcal{L}(C_g)$ are equivalent relative to the ontology O, written as $C \equiv_O D$ iff

- *For all $E \in \mathcal{L}(C) : (T_g \models C \sqsubseteq [E]_T) \Leftrightarrow (T_g \models D \sqsubseteq [E]_T)$*
- *For all $E \in \mathcal{L}(C) : (T_g \models C \sqsubseteq \neg[E]_T) \Leftrightarrow (T_g \models D \sqsubseteq \neg[E]_T)$*

Example 2. Consider the ontology of agent x_2: the PhonedealerAgent, $O_2 = \langle T_2, C_2 \rangle$, where:

$T_2 = \{$ *KermitPhone* $\doteq$ *ElectronicEquipment* $\sqcap$ *CommunicationDevice* $\sqcap$ $\neg$ *WeightsMoreThan1Kg* $\sqcap$ *GreenThing* , *TweetyPhone* $\doteq$ *ElectronicEquipment* $\sqcap$ *CommunicationDevice* $\sqcap$ $\neg$ *WeightsMoreThan1Kg* $\sqcap$ *YellowThing* $\}$
$C_2 = \{$ *KermitPhone*, *TweetyPhone* $\}$

Relative to the ontology of agent x_1, the following concept equations, and non-equations, hold:

1. $[KermitPhone]_{T_2} \equiv_{O_1}$ *CommunicationDevice* $\sqcap \neg$ *WeightsMoreThan1Kg*
2. $[KermitPhone]_{T_2} \equiv_{O_1}$ *CommunicationDevice*
3. $[KermitPhone]_{T_2} \equiv_{O_1}$ $\neg$ *Vehicle*
4. $[KermitPhone]_{T_2} \not\equiv_{O_1}$ *Artifact*

A graphical representation of these four equations is shown in the four squares of figure 3. These figures can be interpreted as Venn diagrams, where the ovals represent concepts. The three black ovals at the left represent the three concepts in the ontology of agent x_1. The striped ovals represent concepts that belong to the ground ontology. The little vertically striped oval at the right represents the concept $[KermitPhone]_{T_2}$. The horizontally striped area that varies from figure to figure, represents: (*CommunicationDevice* $\sqcap \neg$ *WeightsMoreThan1Kg*), *CommunicationDevice*, $\neg$ *Vehicle* and *Artifact* respectively.

The first square in Figure 3 shows that the concept *KermitPhone* is equivalent to the concept *CommunicationDevice* $\sqcap \neg$ *WeightsMoreThan1Kg* relative to the ontology of x_1. That is because they are both disjoint with all concepts in the ontology of x_1. The same holds for equations 2 and 3. Equation 4 however, is different. The vertically striped oval is disjoint with all black ovals, whereas the horizontally striped oval overlaps them. It *does* make a difference to agent x_1 whether an individual belongs to the concept *KermitPhone* or to the concept *Artifact*. From membership of *KermitPhone*, the camper rental agent can derive that this individual is not a member of any of its private concepts. From membership of *Artifact*, the agent remains ignorant about membership of its private concepts.

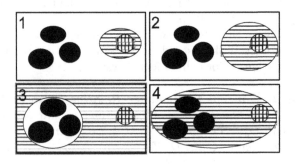

Fig. 3. Relative concept equations

4.2   Common Communication Vocabularies

Communication vocabularies (cv's) are specified for a communication pair of the form $cp = \langle x_i, x_j \rangle \in \mathcal{A} \times \mathcal{A}$, where x_i is the sending agent and x_j is the receiving agent. The cv is specified as an ontology O_{cv} which is shared by both agents. The sending agent uses the cv by making sound translations of messages stated in private concepts ($\in \mathcal{L}(\mathcal{C}_i)$) to messages stated in shared concepts ($\in \mathcal{L}(\mathcal{C}_{cv})$). To preserve soundness, an agent translates a private concept to a shared concept which is equivalent to or more general than the original concept. In the extreme case, an agent translates a private concept C to the shared concept $\top$. Although such a translation will definitely be sound, an assertion of the form $\top(a)$ does not contain any information about the individual a for the receiving agent. The price of translating knowledge in more general terms is information loss ([14]). Since an optimal communication vocabulary should contain concepts which the agents can use to be *sufficiently accurate*, the shared concepts should not be too general. The intuition behind the following definition is that the sending agent should be allowed to translate its private assertion into a more general concept in the communication vocabulary, as long as the translated concept remains equivalent with the original concept relative to the receiving agent's ontology.

Definition 3. *Lossless Communication Vocabulary*
Given a ground ontology O_g, the communication vocabulary O_{cv} is lossless for the communication pair $\langle x_i, x_j \rangle$ iff for all $C \in \mathcal{L}(\mathcal{C}_i)$, there exists $D \in \mathcal{L}(\mathcal{C}_{cv})$, s.t.

- $T_g \models [C]_{T_i} \sqsubseteq [D]_{T_{cv}}$
- $[C]_{T_i} \equiv_{O_j} [D]_{T_{cv}}$ *holds, given O_g*

Example 3. The following are examples of lossless cv's for the phone dealer agent to the camper rental agent, i.e. the communication pair $\langle x_2, x_1 \rangle$:

1. $\mathcal{C}_{cv} = \{KermitPhone,\ TweetyPhone\}$
   $T_{cv} = T_2$
2. $\mathcal{C}_{cv} = \{LightCommDevice\}$
   $T_{cv} = \{LightCommDevice \doteq CommunicationDevice \sqcap$
   $\neg\ WeightsMoreThan1Kg\}$
3. $\mathcal{C}_{cv} = \{Conveyance\}$
   $T_{cv} = \{Conveyance \doteq Vehicle\}$

The first cv is lossless because agent x_2 does not have to translate its private knowledge in the shared vocabulary. Using the second cv, x_2 can translate all its private concepts (*KermitPhone* and *TweetyPhone*) to *LightCommDevice*, which is subjectively equivalent with the original concepts w.r.t. the ontology of agent x_1. The third cv enables x_2 to translate its private concepts into $\neg\ Conveyance$, providing for a lossless cv. The following is *not* a lossless cv:

$\mathcal{C}_{cv} = \{ManMadeObject\}$
$T_{cv} = \{ManMadeObject \doteq Artifact\}$

This is because *ManMadeObject* is *not* subjectively equivalent with *Kermit-Phone*, w.r.t. agent x_1.

When a communication vocabulary is used by more communication pairs, we speak of a common communication vocabulary. It is lossless if it is a lossless communication vocabulary for each communication pair.

Definition 4. *Lossless Common Communication Vocabulary*
A common communication vocabulary O_{cv} is lossless for the set of communication pairs $CP \subseteq (\mathcal{A} \times \mathcal{A})$ iff O_{cv} is a lossless communication vocabulary for all elements of CP.

Example 4. The first three cv's from example 3 are lossless common communication vocabularies for $\{\langle x_2, x_1 \rangle, \langle x_1, x_2 \rangle\}$.

As has been argued before, the number of non-private concepts an agent must learn for communication purposes should be kept as small as possible. Therefore, besides being lossless, an *optimal* common communication vocabulary is minimal in size.

Definition 5. *Optimal Common Communication Vocabulary*
A common communication vocabulary $O_{cv} = \langle T, C \rangle$ is optimal for the set of communication pairs $CP \subseteq (\mathcal{A} \times \mathcal{A})$ iff

- *O_{cv} is a lossless common communication vocabulary for CP*
- *There is no lossless common communication vocabulary for CP: $O'_{cv} = \langle T', C' \rangle$, such that $\#C' < \#C$*

The notation $\#C$ is used to denote the number of elements in set C.

Example 5. The second and the third cv from example 3 are optimal common communication vocabularies for $\{\langle x_2, x_1 \rangle, \langle x_1, x_2 \rangle\}$. The first cv is not, because it contains superfluously many concepts. Consider another example: the ontology of the travel-agent, i.e. agent x_3 is described as:

$T_3 = \{ SoloCamper \doteq Vehicle \sqcap Shelter \sqcap WeightsMoreThan1Ton$
$\sqcap \neg WeightsMoreThan2Ton \sqcap \neg ElectronicEquipment, FamilyCamper \doteq Vehicle$
$\sqcap Shelter \sqcap WeightsMoreThan2Ton \sqcap \neg ElectronicEquipment, Hotel \doteq Building$
$\sqcap \neg Vehicle \sqcap Shelter \sqcap WeightsMoreThan2Ton$
$C_3 = \{ SoloCamper, FamilyCamper, Hotel \}$

The following is an optimal common communication vocabulary for the communication pairs $\{\langle x_i, x_j \rangle | i, j \in \{1..3\} \wedge i \neq j\}$:

$C_{cv} = \{ LightCommDevice, SoloCamper, FamilyCamper \}$
$T_{cv} = \{ LightCommDevice \doteq CommunicationDevice \sqcap \neg WeightsMoreThan1Kg,$
$SoloCamper \doteq Vehicle \sqcap Shelter \sqcap WeightsMoreThan1Ton$
$\sqcap \neg WeightsMoreThan2Ton \sqcap \neg ElectronicEquipment, FamilyCamper \doteq Vehicle$
$\sqcap Shelter \sqcap WeightsMoreThan2Ton \sqcap \neg ElectronicEquipment \}$

The concept *LightCommDevice* is required for the communication between the Phone dealer agent with the other two agents. The distinction between telephones with different colors is not present in the cv, as it is irrelevant to the two other agents. Likewise, the camper rental agent (x_1) has specified its campers at a finer granularity than the travel-agent (x_3). The communication vocabulary only provides for concepts in which distinctions are made that are relevant to both x_1 and x_3.

4.3   Distributed Communication Vocabulary

As opposed to a common communication vocabulary, when distributed cv's are used, different cv's may be assigned to different communication pairs. As will become apparent, distributed cv's may lead to a smaller amount of shared concepts that the individual agents will have to adopt. Cv's are distributed using a distribution function, defined as follows:

Definition 6. *Communication Vocabulary Distribution Function*
A communication vocabulary distribution function $\mathcal{O}_{cv}$ for the set of communication pairs $CP \subseteq (\mathcal{A} \times \mathcal{A})$ is defined as a function that assigns a communication vocabulary to every element $cp \in CP$.

The lossless property can be formulated for cv distribution functions as follows:

Definition 7. *Lossless cv Distribution Function*
The cv distribution function $\mathcal{O}_{cv}$ is lossless for the set of communication pairs CP iff for all $cp \in CP$: $\mathcal{O}_{cv}(cp)$ is a lossless communication vocabulary for cp.

An agent x_i must know all communication vocabularies which are assigned to the communication couples of the form $\langle x_i, x_j \rangle$ or $\langle x_j, x_i \rangle$ (where x_j is an arbitrary agent $\in \mathcal{A}$). Therefore it is useful to define the operator $\upharpoonright$ which collects all communication pairs in which agent x_i is involved.

Definition 8. *Projection*
Let $CP \subseteq (\mathcal{A} \times \mathcal{A})$ be a set of communication pairs, then the projection of CP to the agent x_i is defined by $CP \upharpoonright x_i = \{cp | cp \in CP \wedge \exists x_j \in \mathcal{A}(cp = \langle x_i, x_j \rangle \vee cp = \langle x_j, x_i \rangle)\}$

The costs for an agent to adopt a cv distribution function is defined as the total number of concepts from the cv's it has to know to adopt it.

Definition 9. *Costs*
Given a cv distribution function $\mathcal{O}_{cv}$ for CP.
$costs_{x_i}(\mathcal{O}_{cv}) = \#(\bigcup_{cp \in (CP \upharpoonright x_i)} \mathcal{O}_{cv}(cp))$

The optimal cv distribution function is both lossless and minimizes the total costs that is involved to adopt it.

Definition 10. *Optimal cv Distribution Function*
The cv distribution function $\mathcal{O}_{cv}$ is optimal for the set of communication pairs CP iff

- *$\mathcal{O}_{cv}$ is a lossless cv distribution function.*
- *There is no lossless cv distribution function $\mathcal{O}'_{cv}$ such that:*
  $\sum_{x_i \in \mathcal{A}} costs_{x_i}(\mathcal{O}'_{cv}) < \sum_{x_i \in \mathcal{A}} costs_{x_i}(\mathcal{O}_{cv})$

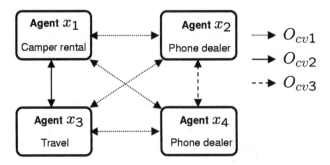

Fig. 4. cv distribution function of example 6

Note that the optimal common cv from definition 5 can be seen as a special case of an optimal cv distribution function, namely one that maps every communication pair to the same communication vocabulary. Therefore, the total costs for the agents to adopt an optimal cv distribution function will never be larger than the costs to adopt an optimal common cv. However, in many cases the total costs to adopt a cv distribution function will be smaller, as will become apparent in the following example.

Example 6. Suppose another phone dealer agent (x_4) joins the community. The ontology of x_4 is:

$T_4 = \{$ *GreenPhone* $\doteq$ *ElectronicEquipment* $\sqcap$ *CommunicationDevice* $\sqcap \neg$ *WeightsMoreThan1Kg* $\sqcap$ *GreenThing* , *YellowPhone* $\doteq$ *ElectronicEquipment* $\sqcap$ *CommunicationDevice* $\sqcap \neg$ *WeightsMoreThan1Kg* $\sqcap$ *YellowThing* $\}$
$C_4 = \{$ *GreenPhone, YellowPhone* $\}$

Now, consider the following optimal cv distribution function for $\{\langle x_i, x_j\rangle | i, j \in \{1..4\} \wedge i \neq j\}$. The distribution of the cv's over the communication pairs is illustrated by figure 4. The content of the cv's is as follows:

$C_{cv1} = \{Phone\}$
$T_{cv1} = \{$ *Phone* $\doteq$ *CommunicationDevice* $\sqcap \neg$ *WeightsMoreThan1Kg* $\}$
$C_{cv2} = \{FamilyCamper, OnePersonCamper\}$
$T_{cv2} = \{$ *FamilyCamper* $\doteq$ *Vehicle* $\sqcap$ *Shelter* $\sqcap$ *WeightsMoreThan2Ton* $\sqcap \neg$ *ElectronicEquipment, OnePersonCamper* $\doteq$ *Vehicle* $\sqcap$ *Shelter* $\sqcap$ *WeightsMoreThan1Ton* $\sqcap \neg$ *WeightsMoreThan2Ton* $\sqcap \neg$ *ElectronicEquipment*$\}$
$C_{cv3} = \{GreenPhone, YellowPhone\}$
$T_{cv3} = \{$ *GreenPhone* $\doteq$ *ElectronicEquipment* $\sqcap$ *CommunicationDevice* $\sqcap \neg$ *WeightsMoreThan1Kg* $\sqcap$ *GreenThing* , *YellowPhone* $\doteq$ *ElectronicEquipment* $\sqcap$ *CommunicationDevice* $\sqcap \neg$ *WeightsMoreThan1Kg* $\sqcap$ *YellowThing* $\}$

This cv distribution function requires agents x_1 to x_4 to learn the following concepts:

1: $\{Phone, FamilyCamper, OnePersonCamper\}$
2: $\{Phone, GreenPhone, YellowPhone\}$

3: *{Phone, FamilyCamper, OnePersonCamper}*
4: *{Phone, GreenPhone, YellowPhone}*

Note that an optimal *common* cv would consist of *{FamilyCamper, OnePerson-Camper, GreenPhone, YellowPhone}*. A common cv would require all agents to adopt four concepts, whereas the use of distributed cv's requires them to adopt only three concepts. This benefit occurs when several groups of agents with different focus areas are present within the MAS. In MAS's consisting of many heterogeneous agents, this benefit may be considerably large. Another advantage of a distributed cv is that it allows local adjustments of the cv when new agents join the MAS, whereas common cv's always require every agent in the MAS to adjust its cv.

5   Conclusion and Future Work

In this paper we have shown how to investigate and characterize communication vocabularies in a heterogeneous multi agent system from an objective stance. To ensure that the cv enables the agents to communicate with sufficient accuracy, the ontologies of both the sending and receiving agent are relevant. This idea is manifest in the notion of a lossless cv. To minimize the number of concepts in the cv, all communication pairs have to be taken into account. This idea is manifest in the notion of an optimal communication vocabulary. Furthermore, we have presented the notion of a distributed communication vocabulary and discussed its benefits over a common cv.

This analysis can be regarded as a starting point to investigate how agents can autonomously establish appropriate communication vocabularies. In this paper we have discussed what we think should qualify as *appropriate*. We intend to continue this line of work by developing dialogue strategies which the agents can employ to establish an optimal common cv, or an optimal cv distribution function. By specifying which concepts are important to be shared within the MAS, agents can decide which concepts they should adopt in their communication vocabularies. Because the criteria are dependent on the ontologies of both agents, they need to be engaged in a *dialogue*.

Furthermore, we intend consider some extensions of our framework, for example, by enriching the ontology language with more description logic constructs.

References

1. FIPA ACL Message Structure Specification. http://www.fipa.org/specs/fipa00061/.
2. FIPA Ontology Service Specification. http://www.fipa.org/specs/fipa00086/.
3. OWL Web Ontology Language Reference. http://www.w3.org/TR/owl-ref/.
4. F. Baader, D.L. McGuinnes, and P.F. Patel-Schneider. *The description logic handbook: Theory, implementation and applications.* Cambridge University Press, 2003.
5. M. Burnstein, D. McDermott, D.R. Smith, and S.J. Westfold. Derivation of glue code for agent interoperation. *Autonomous Agents and Multi-Agent Systems*, 6(3):265–286, 2003.

6. P. Doherty, W. Lukaszewicz, and A. Szalas. On mutual understanding among communicating agents. *Proceedings of the Workshop on Formal Approaches to Multi-Agent Systems (FAMA'03)*, pages 83–97, 2003.

7. T. Finin, R. Fritzson, D. McKay, and R. McEntire. KQML as an Agent Communication Language. In N. Adam, B. Bhargava, and Y. Yesha, editors, *Proceedings of the 3rd International Conference on Information and Knowledge Management (CIKM'94)*, pages 456–463, Gaithersburg, MD, USA, 1994. ACM Press.

8. R. Jasper and M. Uschold. A framework for understanding and classifying ontology applications. *Proceedings of the IJCAI99 Workshop on Ontologies and Problem-Solving Methods(KRR5)*, 1999.

9. Stanford University Knowledge Systems Laboratory. Ontolingua. http://www.ksl.stanford.edu/software/ontolingua/.

10. M. Luck, P. McBurney, and C. Preist. Agent technology: Enabling next generation computing. *Agent link community*, 2003.

11. D. L. McGuinness, R. Fikes, J. Rice, and S. Wilder. The chimaera ontology environment. *Proceedings of the The Seventeenth National Conference on Artificial Intelligence (AAAI 2000)*.

12. Natalya Fridman Noy and Mark A. Musen. Prompt: Algorithm and tool for automated ontology merging and alignment. *In Proceedings of the National Conference on Artificial Intelligence (AAAI)*, 2000.

13. N.R. Jennings. On agent-based software engineering. *Artificial Intelligence*, 2000.

14. M. Obitko and V. Marik. Mapping between ontologies in agent communication. In *Proceedings of the CEEMAS 2003, Prague, Czech Republic*, Lecture Notes on Artificial Intelligence 2691, pages 191–203. Springer-Verlag, 2003.

15. Luc Steels. The origins of ontologies and communication conventions in multi-agent systems. *Autonomous Agents and Multi-Agent Systems*, 1(2):169–194, 1998.

16. B. Swartout, R. Patil, K. Knight, and T. Russ. Toward distributed use of large-scale ontologies. *Proceedings of the Tenth Knowledge Acquisition for Knowledge-based Systems Workshop*, 1996.

17. Y. Tzitzikas and C. Meghini. Ostensive automatic schema mapping for taxonomy-based peer-to-peer systems. In *Proceedings of the 7th International Workshop on Cooperative Information Agents*, Helsinki, Finland, 2003.

18. M. Uschold. Where is the semantics in the semantic web? *Workshop on Ontologies in Agent Systems (OAS) at the 5th Int. Conference on Autonomous Agents*, 2001.

19. A.B. Williams. Learning to share meaning in a multi-agent system. *Autonomous Agents and Multi-Agent Systems*, 8(2):165–193, 2004.

Dealing with Time in Content Language Expressions

Mario Verdicchio[1] and Marco Colombetti[1,2]

[1] Politecnico di Milano, Piazza Leonardo da Vinci 32 20133 Milano, Italy
{Mario.Verdicchio, Marco.Colombetti}@PoliMi.It
[2] University of Lugano, Via Giuseppe Buffi 13 6904 Lugano, Switzerland
Marco.Colombetti@Lu.UniSi.CH

Abstract. The ability to express temporal conditions, like for example deadlines, is extremely important in agent applications. Nevertheless, communication standards like FIPA ACL do not outline a uniform way to specify such conditions in Content Language expressions. In this paper we extend a CTL*-like temporal language with two very expressive interval operators, and integrate it with a FIPA-compatible representation of dates. We then show, by a number of selected examples, that the resulting language allows agents to express a rich assortment of temporal constraints in a very natural way.

1 Introduction

The ability to express temporal conditions, like for example deadlines, is extremely important in agent applications. Nevertheless, communication standards like FIPA ACL do not outline a uniform way to specify such conditions in Content Language expressions. In fact, the only relevant reference to time in FIPA's recommendations is given as part of FIPA SL Content Language Specification [5], which imports the ISO standard for absolute and relative dates. However, nothing is said on how dates can be combined into complex temporal constraints for SL expressions.

A language for the specification of temporal conditions should be both *general* and *natural*. By "general" we mean that all usual kinds of temporal constraints should be expressible, for example:

- absolute and relative deadlines: "the payment is due before the end of May 2004", "the payment is due within 30 days from the time of delivery;"
- absolute and relative intervals: "the auction will be open from May 1, 2004 to May 6, 2004;" "the auction will be open for 24 hours;" "tomorrow the auction will be opened;"
- periodical multi-intervals: "the auction will be open every day from 8:00 to 18:00."

Besides being general, a temporal language should allow one to express temporal conditions in a way that is natural for humans to write and to understand. Some

R.M. van Eijk et al. (Eds.): AC 2004, LNAI 3396, pp. 91–105, 2005.
© Springer-Verlag Berlin Heidelberg 2005

of these problems have already been tackled in the literature (see for example [2, 11]). However, in our opinion not all issues of interest for agent communication languages have been dealt with in details. Some extensively studied temporal languages, like CTL* [4], are very general, but they are not at all natural. In particular, such languages do not have primitive operators to specify time intervals, which appear to be a very natural means to express temporal constraints. Moreover, a temporal language should include a human-like dating system, following the Gregorian calendar and allowing for both absolute and relative dates (for a through analysis of the Gregorian calendar see [12]).

In this paper we propose a temporal language that appears to meet the previous requirements. To reach our goal we extend a CTL*-like temporal language with two very expressive interval operators, and integrates it with a FIPA-compatible representation of dates. We then show, by a number of selected examples, that the resulting language allows agents to express a rich assortment of temporal conditions in a natural way.

The paper is structured as follows. In Section 2 we specify our version of a CTL*-like temporal language. In Section 3 we define two interval operators, that allows one to use arbitrary logical expressions to define the boundaries of intervals. In Section 4 we introduce Gregorian dates and discuss a number of possible dating systems. In Section 5 we show how dates can be used in the context of interval operators and give a number of significant examples. Finally, in Section 6 we give our concluding remarks.

2   The Basic Temporal Language

This section provides new definitions which extend the temporal logic that we have begun to illustrate in [19], called $CTL^{\pm}$.

Our starting point is $CTL^{\pm}$, a temporal language close to CTL*, which is a powerful logic of branching time used to analyze and prove properties of computational systems. CTL* includes only future-directed temporal operators, and it has been proved in [7] and [9] that adding past-tense operators does not increase the logic's expressiveness. However, as stated in [10] and [14], and proved in [16], some properties of computational systems can be expressed in a far more succinct way if their logical model includes also operators that deal with the past. Thus, we extend CTL* with past-directed operators. In the literature, CTL* with past tense operators is sometimes referred to as PCTL* [15], but as the 'P' in the name of temporal logics often stands for 'propositional' [3], we prefer to call our language $CTL^{\pm}$, relying on the idea that the '+' symbol represents the future and the '−' symbol represents the past. In $CTL^{\pm}$, time is assumed to be discrete, with no start or end point, and branching only in the future. In the literature we can find temporal logic proposals that involve branching also in the past [17, 8], but we prefer to rely on the idea of "historical necessity" [18], according to which agents have no possibility of changing the past, so that they are enabled to reason about alternatives or indeterminacy only with respect to the future.

The formal language of CTL$^\pm$ is the smallest set **L** such that:

A $\subseteq$ **L**, where **A** is a suitable set of atomic formulae;
$\neg$**L** $\subseteq$ **L**, (**L** $\wedge$ **L**) $\subseteq$ **L**;
Next**L** $\subseteq$ **L**, Prec**L** $\subseteq$ **L**, (**L** Until$^\circ$ **L**) $\subseteq$ **L**, (**L** Since$^\circ$ **L**) $\subseteq$ **L**;
Cert**L** $\subseteq$ **L**.

The symbols $\neg$ and $\wedge$ come from classical propositional logic, and the intuitive meaning of the temporal operators is as follows: Next means at the next instant (in the future); Prec means at the previous instant (in the past); Until$^\circ$ means until (in the future); Since$^\circ$ means since (in the past). Cert is a *path quantifier*, which means "certainly", that is, "on every path".

Let us quickly define the formal semantics of CTL$^\pm$. Let S be a set of *states*. A CTL$^\pm$ *frame* F on S is an infinite tree-like structure on S, in which every state has exactly one *predecessor* and at least one *successor*, so that there is at most one walk between any pair of states. When state s is the predecessor of state s' we write sRs'.

A *path* in frame F is an infinite sequence $p = \langle p_0,...,p_n,...\rangle$ of states, such that for every state p_n in the sequence, state p_{n+1} is one of its successors in the frame. p_0 is called the *starting point* of path p. The subsequence of p starting from state p_n is itself a path, and it is denoted by p^n. The set of all paths that have state s as starting point are denoted by $Paths(s)$.

A CTL$^\pm$ *model* is a pair $M = \langle F,v\rangle$, where F is a CTL$^\pm$ frame and v is an evaluation function that assigns to every atomic formula in **A** a truth value for every state in S.

We now have all the necessary elements to define the truth conditions for a formula of CTL$^\pm$ in model M on path p:

$M,p \models \phi$, where ϕ is an atomic formula, iff $v(\phi, p_0) = 1$;
$M,p \models \neg\phi$ iff not $M,p \models \phi$;
$M,p \models (\phi \wedge \psi)$ iff $M,p \models \phi$ and $M,p \models \psi$;
$M,p \models$ Next ϕ iff $M,p^1 \models \phi$;
$M,p \models$ Prec ϕ iff for some path q, $q^1 = p$ and $M,q \models \phi$;
$M,p \models (\phi$ Until$^\circ$ $\psi)$ iff for some n, $M,p^n \models \psi$ and for all m such that
                          $0 \leq m < n$, $M,p^m \models \phi$;
$M,p \models (\phi$ Since$^\circ$ $\psi)$ iff for some path q and for some n,
                          $q^n = p$ and $M,q \models \psi$ and for all m such that
                          $0 \leq m < n$, $M,q^m \models \phi$;
$M,p \models$ Cert ϕ iff for all $q \in Paths(p_0)$, $M,q \models \phi$.

We have illustrated the truth conditions for propositional logic, but if we need to deal with first order logic, the introduction of the usual definitions for variable quantification is straightforward. Please note that the names of the temporal operators have been changed with respect to [19] in order to increase the readability of formulae.

Taking the temporal operators Next, Prec, Until$^\circ$, and Since$^\circ$ as primitives, we introduce the following operators:

SomFut	sometimes in the future	SomFut ϕ $=_{def}$ $true$ Until° ϕ;
SomPast	sometimes in the past	SomPast ϕ $=_{def}$ $true$ Since° ϕ;
AlwFut	always in the future	AlwFut ϕ $=_{def}$ $\neg$ SomFut $\neg\phi$;
AlwPast	always in the past	AlwPast ϕ $=_{def}$ $\neg$ SomPast $\neg\phi$.

Moreover, we can define a "weak until" and a "weak since" temporal operator, as follows:

ϕ WeakUntil° ψ $=_{def}$ AlwFut ϕ $\vee$ ϕ Until° ψ,
ϕ WeakSince° ψ $=_{def}$ AlwPast ϕ $\vee$ ϕ Since° ψ.

In the literature, there is usually a distinction between *state formulae* and *path formulae* in CTL*. A state formula is such that to establish its truth value we need to take into account only the state in which such formula is evaluated, while the truth conditions of a path formula require that we specify a path upon which the truth value of that formula is checked. For instance, an atomic formula ϕ is a state formula, because we just need to check the value of the evaluation function in the relevant state. Instead, SomFut ϕ, which intuitively means "sometime in the future ϕ will be the case", is a path formula, as we need to specify the path upon which its truth value is evaluated, that is, the possible future course of events that the modelled system may go through. Such distinction obviously has repercussions on the definition of the semantics of CTL*, in which the $\models$ symbol is inductively defined in different ways for state and path formulae, respectively [3]. As our semantics of CTL$^\pm$ kicks off from a definition that takes into account both a path and a state, which is the path's starting point, we do not need to draw any distinction, and the truth conditions of all formulae can rely on a single definition of $\models$.

It should also be noted that, as we are aiming at modelling the content language of an ACL, even if the logical framework relies on a tree-like structure with branches in the future, the agents that use such a language need not take branching into account. To understand this point, consider an agent making a statement concerning the future, like for example "the payment will be completed within tomorrow." What the agent actually means by such a statement is not that the relevant event will take place within tomorrow *on every possible path*, but that it will take place within tomorrow on the only path that will actually be realized, that is, on the *actual* path. The feature highlighted by this example is completely general: when agents refer to the future, they refer to the future states of the actual path, and not on the future states of every possible path. As a consequence, the temporal language adequate to represent the contents of agent messages is the linear sublanguage of CTL$^\pm$, that we shall call LTL$^\pm$ (with an obvious reference to LTL, the linear sublanguage of CTL*). The syntax and semantics of LTL$^\pm$ are very easy to define: it is sufficient to drop from both the grammar and the truth conditions of CTL$^\pm$ all clauses involving the Cert operator.

We now introduce some derived operators, which will be useful to deal with time intervals. The Until° operator is defined so that when the formula ϕ Until° ψ holds at the starting point of a path p in a model M, ϕ is the case until eventually ψ is true, and at the state at which ψ holds, the truth value of ϕ does not matter. We define a slightly different version of such operator, in which ϕ is required to be true also at the state at which ψ holds, as follows:

$$\phi \; \mathsf{Until} \; \psi \; =_{def} \; \phi \wedge ((\mathsf{Next} \; \phi) \; \mathsf{Until}^\circ \; \psi).$$

The relevant weakened version is defined as follows:

$$\phi \; \mathsf{WeakUntil} \; \psi \; =_{def} \; \mathsf{AlwFut} \; \phi \vee (\phi \; \mathsf{Until} \; \psi).$$

Let us define the AsSoonAs operator as follows. Formula ϕ AsSoonAs ψ holds when at the first state at which ψ is true, also ϕ is the case. In other words, ϕ is true as soon as ψ is (possibly) true. More formally, we have that

$$\phi \; \mathsf{AsSoonAs} \; \psi \; =_{def} \; (\psi \rightarrow \phi) \; \mathsf{WeakUntil} \; \psi.$$

We have introduced the $\rightarrow$ symbol of implication with the usual semantics.

3   Interval Operators

Several papers in the literature have stressed the importance of intervals within the context of temporal logics. In some cases, intervals are even considered as fundamental elements in the construction of a theory of action and time [1]. We adopt an instant-based approach, but nonetheless we see intervals as a simple yet effective way to increase our language's expressiveness. Intervals have already been exploited to deal with deadlines or performance of actions that span a certain amount of time [6, 11]. We follow the guidelines traced by these works, but go further, in that we formally describe the arithmetics to deal with dates. Moreover, our definitions are flexible enough to allow for any well formed formula of language $\mathsf{LTL}^{\pm}$ within an interval operator, not only dates.

We intend to exploit a pair of interval-based operators, corresponding to the ideas of universal and existential quantification over the instants in an interval, respectively. Intuitively, $[\phi, \psi]\chi$ is a formula that holds if as soon as ϕ is the case, from that moment on until ψ possibly holds, χ is true. In other words, the next occurrence of ϕ and the subsequent occurrence of ψ set the endpoints of an interval, at all instants of which χ must hold. Similarly, formula $\langle \phi, \psi \rangle \chi$ is the case when in the interval starting from the next occurrence of ϕ and ending at the next state at which ψ is the case, there exists an instant at which χ is true. Here follow the formal definitions:

$$[\phi, \psi]\chi \; =_{def} \; (\chi \; \mathsf{WeakUntil} \; \psi) \; \mathsf{AsSoonAs} \; \phi;$$
$$\langle \phi, \psi \rangle \chi \; =_{def} \; (\neg(\neg\chi \; \mathsf{WeakUntil} \; \psi)) \; \mathsf{AsSoonAs} \; \phi.$$

The notation we use to represent these interval operators should not induce one to think that they are dual with respect to each other. In fact,

$$[\phi, \psi]\chi \; \leftrightarrow \; \neg\langle \phi, \psi \rangle \neg\chi$$

is not a valid formula. Here we provide a sketch of the proof. We show that in a model in which ϕ is never the case $[\phi, \psi]\chi$ is valid (1), while $\neg\langle \phi, \psi \rangle \neg\chi$ is not (2). According to the definition of the $[\;]$ operator, $[\phi, \psi]\chi$ is true if and only if

$(\chi$ WeakUntil $\psi)$ AsSoonAs ϕ

is the case, which, by the AsSoonAs operator's definition, is equivalent to

$(\phi \rightarrow (\chi$ WeakUntil $\psi))$ WeakUntil ϕ.

In a model in which at every state ϕ is false, this last formula is valid, as the outer WeakUntil's left hand side is a conditional whose antecedent is always false. Statement 1 has thus been proved. From the definitions of the $\langle\,\rangle$ and the AsSoonAs operators, we know that $\langle\phi, \psi\rangle\neg\chi$ is equivalent to

$(\phi \rightarrow \neg(\chi$ WeakUntil $\psi))$ WeakUntil ϕ.

Again, in the model we are considering, this formula is valid, as ϕ is false at every state, which means that its negation cannot be valid, thus proving Statement 2.

We are interested in discovering what the real dual operators of [ ] and $\langle\,\rangle$ look like, and in checking whether they may lead to some significant action expression, but such tasks are beyond the scope of this work.

According to the relevant definitions, any formula of language LTL$^{\pm}$ can work as an endpoint of the interval an operator is referring to. For instance, the formula

$[Arrival(Mario), Departure(Mario)]Lodge(Mario, Algonquin)$

means that at all instants between Mario's next arrival and his successive departure, he will be lodging at the Algonquin Hotel. In this example, two formulae referring to an event are the limits of the interval, so that a statement is made about a condition that holds between two specific events. The next section provides the definition of a special type of formulae corresponding to the dates of the Gregorian calendar that can be used in the interval operators, in order to create formulae dealing with conditions holding between specific instants of time.

4   Dates

We want to define a special type of formulae of language LTL$^{\pm}$ that can work as statements about the date (and time) associated to the states of the frame of our branching model. Our approach is as follows: we define a set $\mathcal{D}$ which is comprised of terms that correspond to a specific date, and then a function $date$, mapping every state s in $\mathcal{S}$ onto a term δ in $\mathcal{D}$, which thus can be considered as the date of that state. If we have that $date(s_1) = \delta_1$, and if state s_1 is the starting point of path p $(s_1 = p_0)$, then

$M, p \models Now(\delta_1)$

is the case. The Now predicate holds for a term δ_1 at a certain state s_1 if and only if s_1's date is δ_1.

Let us provide the formal definition of the dates set $\mathcal{D}$:

$\mathcal{D} = \{yYmMdDhHnNsSiI :$ Conditions Y, M, D, H, N, S, and I hold $\}$.

A date term is comprised of seven numeric values, each followed by a letter, which we call *date component*, indicating the meaning of such value within the context of the date itself: Y stands for 'year', M for 'month', D for 'day', H for hour, N for 'minute', S for 'second', and I for 'millisecond'. As an example, the following date term δ_k,

$$\delta_k = 1975Y12M23D11H35N49S787I,$$

corresponds to 11:35:49:787 AM on December 23rd 1975.

According to this definition, milliseconds are the shortest amount of time that can taken into account in our dating system. This is just a working hypothesis, and can be easily changed so that smaller time quanta, like microseconds, can be considered.

The conditions that must be followed in order to have a valid date term are the following:

(Y) $y \in \mathbf{Z}_0$, that is, the year number must be an integer value, not including zero; in our conventions, positive integers correspond to A.D. years, negative integers to B.C. years;

(M) $1 \le m \le 12$, the month number's boundaries are obvious;

(H) $0 \le h \le 23$;

(N) $0 \le n \le 59$;

(S) $0 \le s \le 59$;

(I) $0 \le i \le 999$, and so are the limiting values of hours, minutes, seconds, and milliseconds.

Illustrating Condition D, which deals with days, is a little more complicated, as the range of the day number d depends both on the month (January, February, and April have all different lengths, for instance), and on the year (Februaries are one day longer during a leap year). We then have to define a subset of $\mathbf{Z}_0$, which we call LY (Leap Years), comprised of all the integer values that correspond to a leap year, as follows:

$$LY = \{y \in \mathbf{Z}_0 : (y \bmod 4 = 0 \wedge y \bmod 100 \neq 0) \vee y \bmod 400 = 0\}.$$

Condition D is the case if and only if all the following four sub-conditions hold:

(D1) if $m \in \{1; 3; 5; 7; 8; 10; 12\}$ then $1 \le d \le 31$;

(D2) if $m \in \{4; 6; 9; 11\}$ then $1 \le d \le 30$;

(D3) if $m = 2$ and $y \in LY$ then $1 \le d \le 29$;

(D4) if $m = 2$ and $y \notin LY$ then $1 \le d \le 28$.

Function *date* provides a correspondence between states in $\mathcal{S}$ and date terms in $\mathcal{D}$. We will illustrate how different hypotheses about such function lead to building dating systems in our branching model with specific characteristics.

Let us first introduce a total order relation $<$ in $\mathcal{D}$. If $\delta_1, \delta_2 \in \mathcal{D}$, we will write $\delta_1 \le \delta_2$ to mean that the two dates are the same or $\delta_1 < \delta_2$.

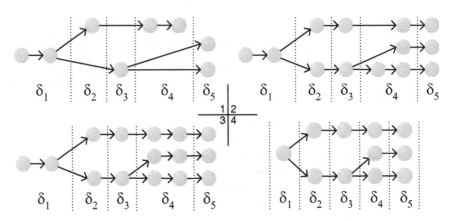

Fig. 1. Different dating systems according to different axioms

4.1   Dating Systems

The simplest assumption that we can make to introduce a meaningful dating system in frame F is that dates go by following the same direction as the states in the frame, as follows:

(A) $\forall s, s' \in \mathcal{S} \;\; sRs' \rightarrow date(s) \leq date(s')$.

Sector 1 of Figure 1 illustrates a part of a dating system that results from such a *date* function: either two consecutive states s and s' are in the same "date zone", that is, share the same date, or the latter's date is greater than the former's.

Axiom A is weak enough to allow for "empty dates" on some paths. In our terminology, a date δ is said to be empty on a path p if p's starting point has a smaller date than δ, and no state belonging to the path has δ as its date. For instance, δ_3 is empty on a path depicted in sector 1 of Figure 1, while δ_4 is empty on another path.

If we want to avoid empty dates, we have to make a stricter assumption, as in the following axiom:

(B) $\forall s, s' \in \mathcal{S} \;\; sRs' \rightarrow date(s) = date(s') \vee date(s') = flw(date(s))$,

where, given a date δ, function flw is supposed to return the following date, as in the example below

$$flw(1999Y12M31D23H59N59S999I) = 2000Y1M1D0H0N0S0I.$$

With such an assumption, the dating system would look like the example in sector 2 of Figure 1.

Providing a definition of the flw function is not trivial, as we have to take all the rules that regulate the Gregorian calendar into account. We will rely on another function $(+)$ which allows us to add a date and an amount of time. Then we will define the flw function as adding one millisecond (our smallest time quantum) to a date: $flw(\delta) = \delta + 1I$. Section 4.3 deals with time amounts and provides a formal definition of the '+' function.

Further restrictions can be imposed on function *date*. In secotr 2 of Figure 1 we can see that on different paths the sets of states that have δ_4 as their date have different cardinalities. We may want to avoid such condition by imposing that every date in $\mathcal{D}$ corresponds to a set of states that has the same cardinality on every path in the frame whose starting point comes before that date. We need to specify this last condition to exclude those paths that start after the date we are considering, and thus are not significant. Let us define the relation that holds between a state s and a path p the state belongs to $s \in p$ iff $\exists k : p_k = s$. We use the symbol $\cap(p,\delta)$ to refer to the set of states belonging to path p whose date is δ: $\cap(p,\delta) = \{s \in p : date(s) = \delta\}$. Now we can formalize the considerations above in the form of the following axiom:

(C) $\forall \delta \in \mathcal{D} \ \exists k : \forall p \ (date(p_0) < \delta \rightarrow |\cap(p,\delta)| = k)$.

A model in which both Axioms B and C hold is depicted in sector 3 of Figure 1.

Finally, we can impose the condition that the flow of successive states and the flow of consecutive dates coincide, that is, if state s' is a successor of state s, then $date(s')$ immediately follows $date(s)$. This is formalized in Axiom D, and a relevant model is shown in sector 4 of Figure 1:

(D) $\forall s, s' \in \mathcal{S} \ sRs' \rightarrow date(s') = flw(date(s))$.

In general, no dating system can be considered better than the others. In our opinion, the properties that characterize the multiagent system that has to be modelled following our approach should suggest the best choice.

4.2   Partial Dates

To increase the language's expressiveness, we extend date set $\mathcal{D}$ by introducing what we call *partial dates*, that is, dates that are comprised of only some of the components of a date. $2004Y$, $5M1D$, and $30N$ are examples of partial dates. To provide the relevant formal definition, let DC be the set of the date components we have already dealt with, and introduce a total order relation $\prec$ on such set, as follows:

$DC = \{Y; M; D; H; N; S; I\}, \ Y \prec M \prec D \prec H \prec N \prec S \prec I.$

Moreover, for every component K in DC, we write $K(\delta)$ to refer to the value of that component in date δ. The set $\tilde{\mathcal{D}}$ ($\tilde{\mathcal{D}} \supseteq \mathcal{D}$) of partial dates can then be defined as follows:

$$\tilde{\mathcal{D}} = \{k_1 K_1 ... k_j K_j : 1 \le j \le 7,$$
$$\exists \delta \in \mathcal{D} : 1 \le l \le j \ \rightarrow \ K_l(\delta) = k_l,$$
$$1 \le p < q \le j \ \rightarrow \ K_p \prec K_q\}.$$

Given a partial date $\tilde{\delta}$, we say that it is subsumed by a date δ when all the date values in $\tilde{\delta}$ are the same as the relevant values in δ, and we write $\tilde{\delta} \sqsubseteq \delta$. For instance, we have that $2000Y7M \sqsubseteq 2000Y7M30D15H30N24S741I$. Of course, given a partial date, there is more than one complete date that subsumes it, and every complete date subsumes itself. Again, we rely on the *Now* predicate to state that a partial date holds at a certain state. We extend the truth conditions for the dates in $\mathcal{D}$ as follows:

$$\forall \tilde{\delta} \in \tilde{\mathcal{D}} \ M, p \models Now(\tilde{\delta}) \ \text{ iff } \ \exists \delta \in \mathcal{D} : \tilde{\delta} \sqsubseteq \delta \text{ and } M, p \models Now(\delta).$$

We can also provide the general truth conditions for dates, whether complete or partial, as follows:

$$\forall \delta \in \tilde{\mathcal{D}} \ M, p \models Now(\delta) \ \text{ iff } \ p_0 = s, \ date(s) = \delta', \ \delta \sqsubseteq \delta'.$$

4.3   Time Amounts

So far, we have considered only absolute dates, but if we want to deal with relative deadlines or intervals, we have to introduce what we call *time amounts*. $\mathcal{A}$ is the set of time amounts, as follows:

$$\mathcal{A} = \{yYmMdDhHnNsSiI : y, m, d, h, n, s, i \in \mathbf{N}\}.$$

Time amounts are comprised of the same components as dates, but without any restriction upon their values. For the sake of simplicity, we omit the components whose value is zero, so that when we have a time amount like the following,

$40D12H0N0S0I,$

we write $40D12H$. Even if their appearance is the same, partial dates and time amounts cannot be confused, as they are used in different contexts. Partial dates can work as limits within interval operators, while time amounts are added to complete dates to obtain other complete dates. Here follows the definition of the '+' function, which adds a time amount to a date:

$+ : \mathcal{D} \times \mathcal{A} \to \mathcal{D}$
$\delta \in \mathcal{D}, \ \ \delta = yYmMdDhHnNsSiI$
$\alpha \in \mathcal{A}, \ \ \alpha = y_\alpha Ym_\alpha Md_\alpha Dh_\alpha Hn_\alpha Ns_\alpha Si_\alpha I$
$\delta' \in \mathcal{D}, \ \ \delta' = y'Ym'Md'Dh'Hn'Ns'Si'I$
$\delta + \alpha = \delta' \text{ iff}$
$\quad i' = (i + i_\alpha) \bmod 1000, \ c_S = (i + i_\alpha) \text{ div } 1000$
$\quad s' = (s + s_\alpha + c_S) \bmod 60, \ c_N = (s + s_\alpha + c_S) \text{ div } 60$
$\quad n' = (n + n_\alpha + c_N) \bmod 60, \ c_H = (n + n_\alpha + c_N) \text{ div } 60$
$\quad h' = (h + h_\alpha + c_H) \bmod 24, \ c_D = (h + h_\alpha + c_H) \text{ div } 24$
$\quad (y', m', d') = inc^{Y^{y_\alpha}}(inc^{M^{m_\alpha}}(inc^{D^{d_\alpha + c_D}}(y, m, d))).$

Let us have a closer look at the items above. All the components from milliseconds (I) to hours (H) are dealt with in the same way. We illustrate the case of milliseconds. We add the values from the complete date δ and the time amount

α (obviously, the '+' symbol is overloaded in this context), and we calculate the integer quotient (div) and remainder (mod) with respect to the number of units of the relevant component which the next larger component is comprised of (there are 1000 milliseconds in a second, 60 seconds in a minute, and so on). The reminder $((i + i_\alpha)$ mod $1000)$ represents the number of milliseconds in the resulting date (i'), while the quotient $((i + i_\alpha)$ div $1000)$ is a carry to the next component (c_S). We go on like this up to the hour component, after which we have to change approach. We cannot rely on modular arithmetics anymore, as the number of days varies in accordance with months; the month number is periodic, but starting with 1 instead of 0, which makes the modular arithmetics trickier; years are just represented by a nonzero integer. Thus, we define functions inc^D, inc^M, and inc^Y, which calculate the new year, month, and day of a date when it is increased by one day, one month, and one year, respectively. The definitions of these functions, which are omitted due to lack of space, take into account all the issues related to the facts that months differ in the number of days, that there are leap years, and that there exists no year 0 in our conventions.

When adding time amount α to date δ, we apply the inc^D function $d_\alpha + c_D$ times, where d_α is the day component of the time amount, and c_D is the day carry that we get from the hour component H. We then add m_α months with the inc^M function, and finally apply the inc^Y function y_α times to obtain the final result δ'. Following an analogous approach, we can define a function '$-$' which subtracts a time amount from a complete date.

Let us introduce a non-rigid constant $cd()$ (current date), i.e. a functional symbol of arity zero, whose interpretation in a model M on path p is the date at p_0. This constant enables us to create some significant examples, dealing with deadlines or relative dates in the form of $LTL^\pm$ formulae.

5   Dates in Interval Operators

Formulae that are built with the *Now* predicate and date terms in $\tilde{\mathcal{D}}$ can be used in the interval operators. For example, formula

$$\langle Now(2005Y1M1D0H0N0S0I), Now(2005Y12M31D23H59N59S999I)\rangle rain$$

means that during year 2005, it rains at least once.

The use of partial dates raises an issue dealing with the end point of the interval. According to our definitions,

$$[Now(2001Y3M), Now(2004Y2M)] PhDStudent(Mario)$$

means that $PhDStudent(Mario)$ is the case from the first instant at which it is March 2001 to the first instant at which it is February 2004. We may want to include the whole duration of the latter partial date. The following operator captures this feature:

$$[\phi, \psi]^\bullet \chi =_{def} [\phi, \psi \wedge \mathsf{Next}\neg\psi]\chi.$$

Thus,

$$[Now(2001Y3M), Now(2004Y2M)]^\bullet PhDStudent(Mario)$$

means that Mario was a PhD candidate until the end of February 2004. Analogously, we have

$$\langle\phi,\psi\rangle^\bullet\chi =_{def} \langle\phi,\psi\wedge \mathsf{Next}\neg\psi\rangle\chi.$$

The following abbreviation can be very useful when we want to refer to the whole duration of a condition (possibly a date):

$$[\phi]\psi =_{def} [\phi,\phi]^\bullet\psi,$$
$$\langle\phi\rangle\psi =_{def} \langle\phi,\phi\rangle^\bullet\psi.$$

For the sake of simplicity in our notation, from now on we will omit the *Now* predicate, relying on the following definitions:

$$\forall\delta\in\tilde{D} \quad [\delta,\phi]\psi =_{def} [Now(\delta),\phi]\psi, \quad [\phi,\delta]\psi =_{def} [\phi,Now(\delta)]\psi,$$
$$\langle\delta,\phi\rangle\psi =_{def} \langle Now(\delta),\phi\rangle\psi, \quad \langle\phi,\delta\rangle\psi =_{def} \langle\phi,Now(\delta)\rangle\psi,$$
$$[\delta,\phi]^\bullet\psi =_{def} [Now(\delta),\phi]^\bullet\psi, \quad [\phi,\delta]^\bullet\psi =_{def} [\phi,Now(\delta)]^\bullet\psi,$$
$$\langle\delta,\phi\rangle^\bullet\psi =_{def} \langle Now(\delta),\phi\rangle^\bullet\psi, \quad \langle\phi,\delta\rangle^\bullet\psi =_{def} \langle\phi,Now(\delta)\rangle^\bullet\psi,$$
$$[\delta]\phi =_{def} [Now(\delta)]\phi, \quad \langle\delta\rangle\phi =_{def} \langle Now(\delta)\rangle\phi.$$

We can exploit these new definitions to write in a much simpler way the formulae above, as follows:

$$\langle 2005Y\rangle rain,$$
$$[2001Y3M, 2004Y2M]^\bullet PhDStudent(Mario).$$

The endpoints of the interval must be in the future of the *time of speech* [13] because the interval operators are defined in terms of future-directed operators like AsSoonAs and WeakUntil. As we are going to see in the next example, this means that expressing past facts requires a little more attention. Let us suppose that Nick lived in Sydney from January 2000 to December 2003 (not included). The relevant formula would then be

$$[2000Y01M, 2003Y12M]Live(Nick, Sydney).$$

The problem with this formula is evident: if such formula is stated in 2004, as there will not be any next instant at which $2003Y12M$ is the case, it will be trivially true (see the definition of AsSoonAs in Section 2), in the same way as

$$[2000Y01M, 2003Y12M]Live(Nick, Mars).$$

To dodge this problem, when dealing with past dates or with an absolute reference in time, and not a relative one to the next instant at which some condition holds, we embed the interval operators in another temporal operator, as follows:

$$\mathsf{Alw}\ \phi \quad =_{def} \mathsf{AlwFut}\ \phi \wedge \mathsf{AlwPast}\ \phi,$$
$$[[\phi,\psi]]\chi =_{def} \mathsf{Alw}[\phi,\psi]\chi.$$

Thus, stated in 2004, the formula

$$[[2000Y01M, 2003Y12M]]Live(Nick,Sydney)$$

is true, while the following formula is not:

$$[[2000Y01M, 2003Y12M]]Live(Nick,Mars).$$

We can make the same considerations and introduce analogous definitions for the other interval operators:

$$\langle\langle\phi, \psi\rangle\rangle\chi =_{def} \mathsf{Alw}\langle\phi, \psi\rangle\chi,$$
$$[[\phi, \psi]]^\bullet\chi =_{def} \mathsf{Alw}[\phi, \psi]^\bullet\chi,$$
$$\langle\langle\phi, \psi\rangle\rangle^\bullet\chi =_{def} \mathsf{Alw}\langle\phi, \psi\rangle^\bullet\chi.$$

Finally, we deal with such important temporal qualifiers as 'today', 'next year', and so on. We introduce a family of *component selection* functions $|_{K_1...K_j}$ $(1 \le j \le 7, 1 \le p < q \le j \to K_p \prec K_q)$, which enable us to obtain from a complete date a partial date comprised only of the selected components $K_1...K_j$ (of course, if $\delta' = \delta|_{K_1...K_j}$ then $\delta' \sqsubseteq \delta$). These functions can be exploited to deal with the above mentioned expressions, as follows:

$$cd()|_{YMD} = \text{today},$$
$$(cd() + 1D)|_{YMD} = \text{tomorrow},$$
$$(cd() + 1M)|_{YM} = \text{next month},$$
$$(cd() - 1Y)|_{Y} = \text{last year}.$$

Here are some examples that illustrate how we can use the operators defined so far to express the temporal constraints in Section 1 in the form of LTL$^\pm$ formulae.

"The payment is due before the end of May 2004:"
$\langle cd(), 2004Y5M\rangle^\bullet Done(payment);$

"the payment is due within 30 days from the time of delivery:"
$\langle Done(delivery), cd() + 30D\rangle Done(payment);$

"the auction will be open from May 1, 2004 to May 6, 2004:"
$[2004Y5M1D, 2004Y5M6D]^\bullet Open(auction);$

"the auction will be open for 24 hours:"
$[Done(openAuction), cd() + 24H] Open(auction);$

"tomorrow the auction will be opened:"
$\langle(cd() + 1D)|_{YMD}\rangle Done(openAuction);$

"the auction will be open every day from 8:00 to 18:00:"
$[8H, 18H] Open(auction).$

6   Conclusions

This paper aimed at tackling the task of expressing temporal constraints in a content language of a generic agent communication framework. We went on developing what we had already sketched in our previous works, the CTL$^{\pm}$ branching temporal logic, and focused on its linear sublanguage LTL$^{\pm}$. We defined a dating system with an algebra to add and subtract time amounts, and analyzed the different possible ways to relate it to the frame of our logical model. We defined several interval-based operators that are flexible enough to allow for a rich repertoire of temporal constraints, referring both to general states of affairs and to dates.

Our interval operators are defined in terms of simpler CTL* operators, so their introduction does not have any significant impact on the proof theory of CTL*. Nevertheless, the analysis of derived inference rules that take into account these new operators is an interesting research path to explore. On the contrary, dealing with dates from this perspective is more complicated, in that their algebra would have to be fully axiomatized to be taken into account by an automatic reasoner.

We believe that our proposal is powerful and natural enough to serve as a basis for a standard treatment of temporal conditions in a content language for agent communication. As we have already suggested, this is a necessary step towards the definition of an ACL capable of being used in real applications.

References

1. J. F. Allen. Towards a general theory of action and time. *Artificial Intelligence*, 23:123–154, 1984.
2. F. Dignum and R. Kuiper. Obligations and dense time for specifying deadlines. In *Proceedings of the 31st Annual Hawaii International Conference on System Sciences*, volume 5, pages 186–195. IEEE Computer Society, 1998.
3. E. A. Emerson. Temporal and modal logic. In J. van Leeuwen, editor, *Handbook of Theoretical Computer Science*, volume B, chapter 16, pages 995–1072. MIT Press, Cambridge, MA, 1990.
4. E. A. Emerson and J. Y. Halpern. 'Sometimes' and 'not never' revisited. *Journal of the ACM*, 33(1):151–178, January 1986.
5. FIPA. FIPA SL Content Language Specification. Specification, Foundation for Intelligent Physical Agents, http://www.fipa.org/specs/fipa00008/, 2002.
6. N. Fornara and M. Colombetti. Operational specification of a commitment-based agent communication language. In C. Castelfranchi and W. Lewis Johnson, editors, *Proceedings of the 1st International Joint Conference on Autonomous Agents and Multiagent Systems (AAMAS 02)*, pages 535–542. ACM Press, 2002.
7. T. Hafer and W. Thomas. Computational Tree Logic CTL* and path quantifiers in the monadic theory of the binary tree. In T. Ottman, editor, *Proceedings of the 14th International Colloquium on Automata, Languages and Programming (ICALP)*, volume 267 of *Lecture Notes in Computer Science*, pages 269–279. Springer-Verlag, Heidelberg, Germany, 1987.

8. Y. Kesten and A. Pnueli. Once and for all. In *Proceedings of the 10ᵗʰ Annual IEEE Symposium on Logic in Computer Science*, pages 25–35, San Diego, California, 1995. IEEE Computer Society Press.

9. F. Laroussinie and P. Schnoebelen. A hierarchy of temporal logics with past. *Theoretical Computer Science*, 148(2):303–324, 1995.

10. O. Lichtenstein, A. Pnueli, and L. Zuck. The glory of the past. In R. Parikh, editor, *Logics of Programs*, volume 193 of *Lecture Notes in Computer Science*, pages 196–218. Springer-Verlag, Berlin, Germany, 1985.

11. A. U. Mallya, P. Yolum, and M. P. Singh. Resolving commitments among autonomous agents. In F. Dignum, editor, *Advances in Agent Communication, Proceedings of the Interbational Workshop on Agent Communication Languages (ACL 2003)*, volume 2922 of *Lecture Notes in Artificial Intelligence*, pages 166–182. Springer-Verlag, Berlin, Germany, 2004.

12. H. J. Ohlbach and D. Gabbay. Calendar logic. *Journal of Applied Non-classical Logics*, 8(4):291–324, 1998.

13. H. Reichenbach. *Elements of Symbolic Logic*. MacMillan, New York, NY, 1947.

14. M. Reynolds. More past glories. In *Proceedings of the 15ᵗʰ Annual IEEE Symposium on Logic in Computer Science (LICS'00)*, pages 229–240. IEEE Comp. Soc. Press, 2000.

15. M. Reynolds. An axiomatization of PCTL*. Draft, Murdoch University, Perth, Australia, January 2002.

16. P. Schnoebelen. The complexity of temporal logic model checking. In *Proceedings of the 4ᵗʰ International Workshop on Advances in Modal Logic (AiML'02)*. World Scientific Publishers, 2003. To appear.

17. C. Stirling. Modal and temporal logics. In S. Abramsky, D. Gabbay, and T. Maibaum, editors, *Handbook of Philosophical Logic, Volume 2*, pages 477–563. Oxford University Press, Oxford, England, 1992.

18. R. Thomason. Combinations of tense and modality. In D. Gabbay and F. Guenthner, editors, *Handbook of Philosophical Logic, Vol II: Extensions of Classical Logic*, pages 135–165. Reidel, Dordrecht, The Netherlands, 1984.

19. M. Verdicchio and M. Colombetti. A logical model of social commitment for agent communication. In J. S. Rosenschein, T. Sandholm, M. J. Wooldridge, and M. Yokoo, editors, *Proceedings of the 2ⁿᵈ International Joint Conference on Autonomous Agents and Multiagent Systems (AAMAS 03)*, pages 528–535. ACM Press, 2003.

Realizing Agent Dialogues with Distributed Protocols

Jarred McGinnis and David Robertson

Centre for Intelligent Systems and their Applications,
University of Edinburgh,
Appleton Tower, Room 4.15,
Edinburgh EH8 9LE
j.p.mcginnis@sms.ed.ac.uk

Abstract. This paper describes a protocol language which can provide agents with a flexible mechanism for coherent dialogues. The protocol language does not rely on centralised control or bias toward a particular model of agent communication. Agents can adapt the protocol and distribute it to dialogical partners during interactions.

1 Introduction

As the programming paradigm of agency evolves, more robust, diverse, and complex agents are developed. The growing heterogeneity of agent societies will increase even further as the research and development of deliberative and communicative models produce new and interesting approaches. The need for an equally adaptive means of communication between this heterogeneous multitude also grows.

Electronic Institutions [2] and other state-based approaches are not feasible for use in open multi-agent systems with dynamic or large conversation spaces. The term conversation space is used to express every possible sequence and combination of messages that can be passed between two or more agents participating in a given agent system. Protocols provide a useful framework for agent conversations and the concern that they sacrifice agent autonomy is exaggerated. In social interactions, humans and agents must willingly sacrifice autonomy to gain utility. If I want my train tickets or cup of coffee, I must follow the implicit protocol and join the queue. It is the same for software agents. If the agent must gain a resource only available by participating in an English auction, it behooves the agent to adopt the protocol necessary for participation in the auction. Whether this is done by an explicitly defined protocol or the agent learning the protocol implicitly makes no difference to the agent's behavior within the system.

Electronic Institutions take a societal approach to agent communication. Control is top-down. Administrative agents perch above the system and keep an eye on the agents as they interact inside the system. These Administrative agents regulate participating agent's dialogical activities by forcing them to adhere to

R.M. van Eijk et al. (Eds.): AC 2004, LNAI 3396, pp. 106–119, 2005.
© Springer-Verlag Berlin Heidelberg 2005

the formal definition of the Electronic Institution. The institution is defined by a set of roles for agents, a shared dialogical framework, the division of the Institution into a number of scenes and a performative structure which dictates, via a set of normative rules, the relationships between the scenes. This provides highly reliable but very constrained multi-agent systems. Electronic Institutions is only one approach to modeling interaction protocols. There are various others [6, 5, 9]

Agent-centric approaches build systems bottom-up. These approaches attempt to pack individual agents with a model of communication which can react to a multi-agent system. Dialogical actions are not prescribed to the agent beforehand. Instead, using their model of communication agents attempt to figure out the next action to take. There are many different approaches to achieve this such as cognitive dissonance theory [13]. The concept of social commitment or obligation has been employed in [4, 20] One of the more interesting approaches is dialogue games. The papers of [14, 1, 7] all use dialogue theory and games to create flexible agent dialogues. The example given in section 4 demonstrates the use of dialogue games with the protocol language.

The protocol language described in this paper seeks a balanced approach. It utilises the useful aspects of Electronic Institutions without relying on administrative agents or statically defined protocol specifications. Agents communicate not only individual messages but the protocol and dialogue state as well. The use of protocols provides structure and reliability to agent dialogues. Yet, by describing protocols as a process rather than a fixed state-based model, the conversation space can be defined as the agent interaction progresses rather than being statically defined during the engineering process. Distributing the protocol along with the message also allows agents to communicate the social conventions of the dialogue as well as coordinate it.

Section 2 describes the protocol language and a framework for implementation. Section 3 describes how agents can adapt their protocols to create dynamic and flexible dialogues. Section 4 provides an example to illustrate the main points of the protocol language and its ability to be adapted during execution. Section 5 concludes the paper with the hazards and successes of this approach.

2   The Protocol Language

The development of the protocol language is a reaction to Electronic Institutions [17]. Although the EI framework provides structure and stability to an agent system, it comes at a cost. Integral to EI is the notion of the administrative agents. Their task is to enforce the conventions of the Institution and shepherd the participating agents. Messages sent by agents are sent through the EI. This synchronises the conversation between the conversing agents, and keeps the administrative agent informed of the state of the interaction

An unreliable keystone makes the whole of the arch defective, just as the system is now dependent on the reliability and robustness of its administrative agent. Also, this centralisation of control runs counter to the agent paradigm of distributed processing. Within the scenes of Electronic Institutions, interaction

$M \in \langle m,\mathcal{P} \rangle$ *(message)* $m \in$ a communicative act

$\mathcal{P} \in \langle S,A^{\{n\}},K \rangle$ *(Protocol)* $A \in \theta :: op.$ *(Agent Clause)*

$\theta \in \mathbf{agent}(r,id)$ $\psi \in$ a predicate

$op \in$ null $\mid \theta \mid (op)$*(Precedence)* $\mid M \Rightarrow \theta$ *(Send)* $\mid M \Leftarrow \theta$ *(Receive)*

$\quad \mid op1$ **then** $op2$ *(Sequence)* $\mid op1$ **or** $op2$ *(Choice)*

$\quad \mid op1$ **par** $op2$ *(Parallelism)* $\mid \psi \leftarrow M \Leftarrow \theta$ *(Consequence)*

$\quad \mid M \Rightarrow \theta \leftarrow \psi$ *(Prerequisite)*

Fig. 1. The abstract syntax of the protocol

protocols are defined to guarantee that agents utter the proper illocutions and utter them at the appropriate time. This is defined formally by the specifications of the EI and left to the designers of individual agents to implement. It assumes that the agent's interaction protocol covers the entire conversation space before the conversation occurs. If the interaction needs of the institution change, this would require redefinition of the Institution and re-synthesis of the individual agents. Agents are also expected to know the global state of the system and their exact position within it. In EIs this is handled by an administrative agent whose job it is to synchronise the multitude of agents involved.

The protocol language addresses some of these shortcomings of EIs but retains the benefits of implementing the EI framework. Its goal is to lessen the reliance on centralised agents for synchronisation of individual participants in the system, provide a means for dissemination of the interaction protocol and to separate the interaction protocol from the agent's rationalisations to allow the dynamic construction of protocols during the interaction. By defining interaction protocols during run-time, agents are able to interact in systems where it is impossible or impractical to define the protocol beforehand. For example, negotiation dialogues where the domain of negotiation is not fixed or unknown. Another example would be diagnosis dialogues where the course of the dialogue is determined by the information sent and not a fixed sequence of messages. The protocol language defined in Figure 1 is similar to the protocol language described in [19] for which the formal semantics have been defined. The rewrite rules in figure 2 are defined in terms of these semantics.

Figure 1 defines the syntax of the protocol language. An agent clause is composed of an agent definition and an operation. The agent definition individuates the agents participating in the conversation (id), and the role the agent is playing (r). Operations can be classified in three ways: actions, control flow, and conditionals. Actions are the sending or receiving of messages, a no op, or the adoption of a role. Control Flow operations temporally order the individual actions. Actions can be put in sequence (one action must occur before the other), in parallel (both action must occur before any further action), or given a choice point (one and only one action should occur before any further action). Conditionals are the preconditions and postconditions for operations. The message passed between two agents using the protocol consists of two parts. The first is the actual illocution (m) the agent is wishing to express. The second is the full protocol $(\mathcal{P})$ itself. This is the protocol for all agents and roles involved in the conversation. This will be necessary for the dissemination of the protocol as new agents enter the system. Other aspects of the protocol are the inclusion of constraints on the dialogue and the use of roles. An agent's activities within a multi-agent system are not determined solely by the agent, rather it is the relationship to other agents and the system itself that helps determine what message an agent will send. These can be codified as roles. This helps govern the activity of groups of agents rather than each agent individually. Constraints are marked by a '←'. These are requirements or consequences for an agent on the occurrence of messages or the adoption of roles. The constraints provide the agent with a shared semantics for the dialogue. These constraints communicate meaning and implication of the action to the agent's communicating partner. For example, an agent receiving a protocol with the constraint to believe a proposition s upon being informed of s can infer that the agent sending the protocol has a particular semantic interpretation of the act of informing other agents of propositions (i.e. The receiving agent is expected to believe s when informed of s). The '⇐' and '⇒' mark messages being sent and received. On the left-hand side of the double arrow is the message and on the right-hand side is the other agent involved in the interaction.

An agent must be able to understand the protocol, the dialogue state, and its role within the protocol. Agents need to be able to identify the agent clause which pertains to its function within the protocol and establish what actions it must take to continue the dialogue or what roles to adopt.

2.1   Implementing the Protocol Framework

A message is defined as the tuple, $\langle m,\mathcal{P} \rangle$. Where m is the message an agent is currently communicating, and $\mathcal{P}$ is the protocol written using the language described in figure 1. The protocol, in turn, is a triple, $\langle S, A^{\{n\}}, K \rangle$. S is the dialogue state. This is a record of the path of the dialogue through the conversation space and the current state of the dialogue for the agents. The second part is a set of agent clauses, $A^{\{n\}}$, necessary for the dialogue. The protocol also includes a set of axioms, K, consisting of common knowledge to be publicly known between the participants. The sending of the protocol with the messages allows agents to represent the various aspects of Electronic Institutions described [2,3]. In addition, agents themselves communicate the conventions of the dialogue. This is accomplished by the participating agents satisfying two simple engineering requirements. Agents are required to share a dialogical framework. The same is required of Electronic Institutions, and is an unavoidable necessity in any meaningful agent communication. This includes the requirements on the individual messages are expressed in a ontology understood by the agents. The issue of ontology mapping is still open, and its discussion extends beyond the scope of this paper. The second requirement obligates the agent to provide a means to interpret the received message and its protocol. The agent must be able to unpack a received protocol, find the appropriate actions it may take, and update the dialogue state to reflect any actions it chooses to perform.

$$A :: B \xrightarrow{M_i, M_o, \mathcal{P}, O} A :: E$$
$$\qquad if \quad B \xrightarrow{M_i, M_o, \mathcal{P}, O} E$$
$$A_1 \ or \ A_2 \xrightarrow{M_i, M_o, \mathcal{P}, O} E$$
$$\qquad if \quad \neg closed(A_2) \wedge A_1 \xrightarrow{M_i, M_o, \mathcal{P}, O} E$$
$$A_1 \ or \ A_2 \xrightarrow{M_i, M_o, \mathcal{P}, O} E$$
$$\qquad if \quad \neg closed(A_1) \wedge A_2 \xrightarrow{M_i, M_o, \mathcal{P}, O} E$$
$$A_1 \ then \ A_2 \xrightarrow{M_i, M_o, \mathcal{P}, O} E \ then \ A_2$$
$$\qquad if \quad A_1 \xrightarrow{M_i, M_o, \mathcal{P}, O} E$$
$$A_1 \ then \ A_2 \xrightarrow{M_i, M_o, \mathcal{P}, O} A_1 \ then \ E$$
$$\qquad if \quad closed(A_1) \wedge A_2 \xrightarrow{M_i, M_o, \mathcal{P}, O} E$$
$$A_1 \ par \ A_2 \xrightarrow{M_i, M_o, \mathcal{P}, O_1 \cup O_2} E_1 \ par \ E_2$$
$$\qquad if \quad A_1 \xrightarrow{M_i, M_n, \mathcal{P}, O_1} E_1 \wedge A_2 \xrightarrow{M_n, M_o, \mathcal{P}, O_2} E_2$$
$$C \leftarrow M \Leftarrow A \xrightarrow{M_i, M_i - \{M \Leftarrow A\}, \mathcal{P}, \emptyset} c(M \Leftarrow A)$$
$$\qquad if \quad (M \Leftarrow A) \in M_i \wedge satisfy(C)$$
$$M \Rightarrow A \leftarrow C \xrightarrow{M_i, M_o, \mathcal{P}, \{M \Rightarrow A\}} c(M \Rightarrow A)$$
$$\qquad if \quad satisfied(C)$$
$$null \leftarrow C \xrightarrow{M_i, M_o, \mathcal{P}, \emptyset} c(null)$$
$$\qquad if \quad satisfied(C)$$
$$agent(r, id) \leftarrow C \xrightarrow{M_i, M_o, \mathcal{P}, \emptyset} a(R, I) :: B$$
$$\qquad if \quad clause(\mathcal{P}, a(R, I) :: B) \wedge satisfied(C)$$

A protocol term is decided to be closed, meaning that it has been covered by the preceding interaction, as follows:

$$closed(c(X))$$
$$closed(A \ or \ B) \leftarrow closed(A) \vee closed(B)$$
$$closed(A \ then \ B) \leftarrow closed(A) \wedge closed(B)$$
$$closed(A \ par \ B) \leftarrow closed(A) \wedge closed(B)$$
$$closed(X :: D) \leftarrow closed(D)$$

$satisfied(C)$ is true if C can be solved from the agent's current state of knowledge.
$satisfy(C)$ is true if the agent's state of knowledge can be made such that C is satisfied.
$clause(\mathcal{P}, X)$ is true if clause X appears in the dialogue framework of protocol $\mathcal{P}$, as defined in Figure 1.

Fig. 2. Rules for expanding an agent clause

Figure 2 describes rules for expanding the received protocols. Details can be found in [15]. A similar language for web services is described in [16]. An agent receives a message of the form specified in figure 1. The message is added to the set of messages, M_i, currently being considered by the agent. The agent takes the clause, C_i, from the set of agent clauses received as part of $\mathcal{P}$. This clause provides the agent with its role in the dialogue. The agent then expands C_i by the application of the rules in figure 2. The expansion is done with respect to the different operators encountered in the protocol and the response to M_i. The

$$\langle C_i \xrightarrow{M_i,M_{i+1},\mathcal{P},O_i} C_{i+1},\ldots,C_{n-1} \xrightarrow{M_{n-1},M_n,\mathcal{P},O_n} C_n\rangle$$

Fig. 3. Sequence of rewrites

result is a new dialogue state, C_n; a set of output messages, O_n and a subset of M_i, which is the remaining messages to be considered,M_n. The result is arrived at by applying the rewrite rules. The sequence would be similar to figure 3. C_n is then sent as part of $\mathcal{P}$ which will accompany the sending of each message in O_n.

2.2   Features of the Protocol

Several features of the protocol language are useful for agents capable of learning and adapting to the multi-agent system in which they participate. Sending the dialogue state during the interaction provides agents with several advantages. It is no longer necessary for an administrative agent to shepherd the interaction. The sending of the protocol with the message uses the 'hot potato' approach to communication. The interaction is coordinated by which agent currently 'holds' the protocol. The reception of a message would cue an agent to action. The sending of the protocol provides a means for disseminating the social conventions for the dialogue. The most common approach is to use specifications to be interpreted by individual engineers. The protocol directly communicates the social conventions and expectations an agent has for the dialogue. Agents with the ability to learn could use the received protocol to plan ahead or modify its own social conventions to be able to communicate with other agents. The protocol language is strictly concerned with the interaction level of communication. The semantics of the language does not depend on any assumptions about the agent's internal deliberative model. All requirements for the interaction are publicly specified with the protocol. Agents with different models of deliberation are able to communicate [11].

3   Means of Adaptation

Protocols are traditionally seen as a rigid ordering of messages and processing to enable a reliable means of communication. Agent-centric approaches have tended to avoid their use, lest agents be reduced to nothing more than remote function calls for the multi-agent system. The control over agent interactions within an electronic institutions is indeed intrusive. The administrative agents of electronic institutions have complete control. The sequence of messages are dictated but also the roles an agent may adopt and the actions an agent must take within and outside of the context of the dialogue.

The protocol language of this paper does not follow this tradition. It is designed to bridge the gap separating the two approaches to agent interaction. The language is capable of representing the scenes and performative structure of electronic institutions, but it is not limited to electronic institution's inflexible model of agent interaction. The protocol language and the process of sending the protocol during execution provides agents with a means of adaptation.

In the electronic institution model, the protocol does not exist within the participating agents. It is retained by the institution itself, and designers must engineer agents that will strictly conform to the protocol which will be dictated by the administrative agents. Our approach delivers the protocol to the participating agents. Individual agents are given providence over the protocol they receive. This returns the power of the interaction to the participating agents. For example, the protocol received is not required to be the protocol that is returned.

The protocol, as described so far, already allows for a spectrum of adaptability. At one extreme, the protocol can be fully constrained. Protocols at this end of the spectrum would be close to the traditional protocols and electronic institutions. By rigidly defining each step of the protocol, agents could be confined to little more than remote processing. This sacrifice allows the construction of reliable and verifiable agent systems. At the other extreme, the protocols would be nothing more than the ordering of messages or even just the statement of legal messages(without any ordering) to be sent and received. Protocols designed this way would be more akin to the way agent-centric designers envisage agent communication. Agents using these protocols would be required to reason about the interaction to determine the next appropriate step in the dialogue. Though the protocol language is expressive enough for both extremes of the spectrum, the bulk of interactions are going to be somewhere in the middle. A certain amount of the dialogue will need to be constrained to ensure a useful dialogue can occur. This allows agents to express dynamic and interesting dialogues.

The protocol language is flexible enough to be adapted during run-time. Yet, protocols modified indiscriminately would return us to the problem facing the agent-centric approach. We would have a model for flexible communication, but no structure or conventions to ensure a meaningful dialogue can take place. It is necessary to constrain any adaptation in a meaningful way. By the examination of patterns and standards of an agent-centric approach, protocols can be construct to have points of flexibility. Portions in the dialogue can be adapted without losing the benefits of a protocol-based approach. The example below employs the rules for playing a dialogue game, the protocol language, and an amendment to the rewrite rules to allow a more dynamically constructed protocol.

4   Example

Figure 4 shows the agent clauses needed to play an Information-seeking dialogue game similar to the one defined in [12]. The dialogue game rules are simplified to clarify its implementation within the protocol. There are countless variations on the rules for any one type of dialogue game. This illustrates a continuing problem with agent-centric communication design. It is not a trivial requirement to ensure agents within a system are employing the same communicative model. This is the same with dialogue games. Subtle differences could break the dialogue. By the use of the protocol, agent can communicate their 'house' rules for the game. The rules for this particular game are as follows:

1. The game begins with one agent sending the message *question(p)* to another agent.
2. Upon receiving a *question(p)* message, an agent should evaluate *p* and if it is found to be true, the agent should reply with *assert(p)* else send an *assert(null)* which is a failure message.
3. Upon receiving an *assert(p)*, an agent should evaluate the assertion, then the agent can send an *accept(p)* or *challenge(p)* depending on whether the agent's acceptance attitude will allow.
4. Upon receiving a *challenge(p)*, an agent should send an *assert(S)*. *S* is a set of propositions in support of *p*.
5. For each proposition in *S*, repeat steps 3 and 4.
6. The game is over when all propositions have been accepted or no further support for a proposition can be offered.

Rule one is satisfied by an agent taking up the role of the 'seeker'. This provides the agent with the legal moves necessary to play that side of the information-seeking dialogue game. The other agent will receive the *question(p)* message along with the protocol of figure 4. The agent identifies the clause which it should use. In this example, the clause playing the 'provider' role. It is necessary to use constraints to fully satisfy the second rule. Part of the rule states an agent sending an *assert(p)* depends on its knowledge base and its assertion attitude, otherwise an *assert(null)* is sent. The constraint *verify(p)* is assumed to be satisfiable by the agent. The agent is free to satisfy the constraint how it prefers. This could range from a simple function call to a complex belief logic with identity evaluation. The protocol only states what conditions must be satisfied, not how. The recursive steps are handled by the roles of *eval* (evaluate) and *def* (defend) which are similarly constrained. Finally, the termination rule for the game is written as the last line in the 'evaluate' role. No more messages are sent when the remainder of the set of propositions is empty.

Similar protocols can be written to express the other atomic dialogue types. Real world dialogues rarely consist of a single dialogue game type. [8] formally describe several combinations of dialogue types. *Iteration* is the initiation of a dialogue game immediately following the finishing of another dialogue game of the same type. *Sequencing* is the similar to iteration except that the following dialogue game can be of any type. In *Parallelisation* of dialogue games, agents make moves in more than one dialogue game concurrently. *Embedding* of dialogue games occurs when during play of one dialogue game another game is initiated and played to its conclusion before the agents continue playing the first. The example involves two agents; a doctor and a patient. The patient is trying to find out whether the proposition 'patient is ill' is true (i.e. looking for a diagnosis). This is the perfect scenario to play an information-seeking dialogue game and to use the dialogue game protocol. Figure 5 and 6 shows the dialogue state as it is rewritten during the course of the dialogue.

$$agent(infoseek(P, B), A) ::$$
$$agent(provider(P, A), B) \; or$$
$$agent(seeker(P, B), A).$$

$$agent(seeker(P, B), A) ::$$
$$question(P) \; \Rightarrow \; agent(provider(P, A), B) \; then$$
$$assert(P) \; \Leftarrow \; agent(provider(P, A), B) \; then$$
$$agent(eval(P, B), A) \; or$$
$$assert(null) \; \Leftarrow \; agent(provider(P, A), B).$$

$$agent(provider(P, A), B) ::$$
$$question(P) \; \Leftarrow \; agent(seeker(P, B), A) \; then$$
$$(assert(P) \; \Rightarrow \; agent(seeker(P, B), A) \leftarrow \; verify(P) \; then$$
$$agent(def(P, A), B)) \; or$$
$$assert(null) \; \Rightarrow \; agent(seeker(P, B), A).$$

$$agent(eval([P|R], B), A) ::$$
$$accept(P) \; \Rightarrow \; agent(def([P|R], A), B) \leftarrow \; accept(P) \; or$$
$$\begin{pmatrix} challenge(P) \Rightarrow agent(def([P|R], A), B) \; then \\ assert(\mathcal{S}) \; \Leftarrow \; agent(def([P|R], A), B) \; then \\ agent(eval(\mathcal{S}, B)A) \end{pmatrix}$$
$$then$$
$$\begin{pmatrix} null \leftarrow R = [] \; or \\ agent(eval(R, B), A) \end{pmatrix}.$$

$$agent(def([P|R], A), B) ::$$
$$accept(P) \; \Leftarrow \; agent(eval([P|R], B), A) \; or$$
$$\begin{pmatrix} challenge(P) \; \Leftarrow \; agent(eval([P|R], B), A) \; then \\ assert(\mathcal{S}) \; \Rightarrow \; agent(eval([P|R], B), A) \\ \leftarrow \; justify(P, \mathcal{S}) \end{pmatrix}$$

Fig. 4. The agent clauses for the information-seeking protocol

The patient begins the dialogue by taking the initial agent clause of *infoseek* which stands for information-seeking. This step is labeled *1*. The agent applies the rewrite rules to expand the seeker role and sends the *question* to the doctor agent, step *2*. The doctor receives the message and the protocol. The applies the rewrite rules and finds the only instantiation that is possible is the unfolding of the provider role. It applies the rewrite rules and comes to the *verify* constraint which it is unable to satisfy. It cannot determine the truth value of the proposition and is unwilling to defend the proposition. It takes the other half of the *or* operator and sends the *assert(null)*. Let us assume the doctor agent is a bit more clever. It cannot currently assert that the patient is ill. It has a knowledge-base and an inference engine that allows it to figure whether the proposition is true or not, and it needs some more information from the patient. The particular kind of information would depend on each patient consultation. If this diagnosis scenario was part of an electronic institution, the institution would have to

$$agent(infoseek(\text{``patient is ill''}, doctor), patient) ::$$
$$agent(seeker(\text{``patient is ill''}, doctor), patient) \tag{1}$$

$$agent(infoseek(\text{``patient is ill''}, doctor), patient) ::$$
$$question(\text{``patient is ill''}) \Rightarrow agent(provider(\text{``patient is ill''}, patient), doctor) \tag{2}$$

$$agent(infoseek(\text{``patient is ill''}, doctor), patient) ::$$
$$question(\text{``patient is ill''}) \Rightarrow agent(provider(\text{``patient is ill''}, patient), doctor) \ then$$
$$assert(null) \Leftarrow agent(provider(\text{``patient is ill''}, patient), doctor).$$
$$\tag{3}$$

Fig. 5. The progression of the dialogue state for the patient

$$agent(infoseek(\text{``patient is ill''}, patient), doctor) ::$$
$$agent(provider(\text{``patient is ill''}, patient), doctor) \tag{1}$$

$$agent(infoseek(\text{``patient is ill''}, patient), doctor) ::$$
$$question(\text{``patient is ill''}) \Leftarrow agent(seeker(\text{``patient is ill''}, doctor), patient) \ then$$
$$assert(null) \Rightarrow agent(seeker(\text{``patient is ill''}, doctor), patient).$$
$$\tag{2}$$

Fig. 6. The progression of the dialogue state for the doctor

represent in a state diagram every possible permutation of a diagnosis scenario. This is not practical, if not impossible.

Instead, the doctor agent can use the patterns of dialogue games to structure the interaction but allow adaptations to handle any run-time dialogical needs that may arise. In the example, the doctor agent needs to ask about a different proposition before it can answer the patient's original query. This is achieved by an additional rewrite rule shown in figure 7.

This allows the agent to graft the infoseek agent clause between any term in the protocol. These rewrites can be expanded further to represent other dialogue combinations as well as domain specific rewrite rules. Figure 8 shows the sequence of dialogue states for the doctor agent capable of embedding information-seeking games. The expansions and dialogue begin the same, but rather than

$$A \xrightarrow{M_i, M_o, \mathcal{P}, \mathcal{O}} A \ then \ B$$
$$if \quad clause(P, B) \wedge isa(B, dialogue - type)$$

$$isa(infoseek, dialogue - type).$$

Fig. 7. Additional rewrite rule

$agent(infoseek(\text{``patient is ill''}, patient), doctor) ::$
$question(\text{``patient is ill''}) \Leftarrow agent(seeker(\text{``patient is ill''}, doctor), patient)$ *then*
$agent(infoseek(\text{``patient has a fever''}, patient), doctor).$

(2)

$agent(infoseek(\text{``patient is ill''}, patient), doctor) ::$
$question(\text{``patient is ill''}) \Leftarrow agent(seeker(\text{``patient is ill''}, doctor), patient)$ *then*
question(``patient has a fever'')
$\Rightarrow$ **agent(provider(``patient has a fever'', doctor), patient)**

(3)

. . .

$agent(infoseek(\text{``patient is ill''}, patient), doctor) ::$
$question(\text{``patient is ill''}) \Leftarrow agent(seeker(\text{``patient is ill''}, doctor), patient)$ *then*
question(``patient has a fever'') $\Rightarrow$
   agent(provider(``patient has a fever'', doctor), patient) *then*
assert(``patient has a fever'') $\Leftarrow$
   agent(provider(``patient has a fever'', doctor), patient) *then*
$assert(\text{``patient is ill''}) \Rightarrow agent(seeker(\text{``patient is ill''}, doctor), patient).$

Fig. 8. The progression of the dialogue state for the doctor with embedding

just sending the *assert(null)*. The agent inserts the agent definition *agent (infoseek ("patient has a fever"),patient),doctor)*. The next instance of a information-seeking dialogue is begun. The moves of the embedded dialogue game are in bold text. In this instance the patient plays the provider role and the doctor plays the seeker. The game is finished by the patient asserting "patient has a fever". The doctor, now knowing this proposition to be true, has enough knowledge to assert the original proposition posed by the patient's first question. The first information-seeking game also concludes successfully by the doctor making the diagnosis and asserting the proposition "patient is ill" is true.

5   Conclusions

The protocol language described in the paper is expressive enough to represent the most popular approaches to the agent communication. It is able to capture the various aspects of Electronic Institutions such as the scenes, performative structure, and normative rules. This enables agents to have structured and meaningful dialogues without relying on centralised control of the conversation. The language is also capable of facilitating agent-centric approaches to agent communication. Agents pass the protocol to their dialogical partners to communicate the social conventions for the interaction. Agents can adapt the received protocols to explore dynamic conversation spaces. The protocol language in this paper is not seen as a replacement for either model of agent communication.

Instead, it synthesizes the two approaches to gain the advantages of both. Protocols are used to coordinate and guide the agent's dialogue, but agents are able to adapt the protocol by using an agent-centric model for communication. The use of this communicative model constrains transformation to the agent clauses in meaningful ways. The run-time delivery provides the mechanism for communicating the protocol as well as any adaptations that are made. We are developing FIPA compliant agents which uses the ACL library and the protocol language. It is hoped that the verifiability and semantic problems associated with FIPA's ACL can be mitigated by the use of the protocol language to communicate the performative's semantics during their use.

This approach does raise new issues which have not been addressed in this paper. One issue concerns restricting changes to the protocols. There are certainly dialogues where certain agents will be restricted from modifying the protocols or dialogue which require portions of the protocol to remain unchanged. There is also the issue of malicious agents. An agent could attempt to modify the dialogue state or the protocol in some dubious manner. The public expression of the protocol would certainly impede the naughty agent from gaining much from this activity, but the issue still needs to be addressed more fully. There is also some concerns with the amount of data being transmitted and the possibility of situations which do not require transmission of the dialogue state or the agent clauses. For example, agents who routinely communicate together or are known to maintain the dialogue state themselves. This remains for future work along with development of a vocabulary of generic transformations which can be proved *a priori* or verified to retain semantic and syntactical continuity of the protocols.

The protocol language has already been shown to be useful for a number of agent purposes. A scheduling program has been developed using the protocol written in Prolog and using LINDA. A Java-based agent framework also exists which uses an XML representation of the protocols. Separating the protocol from the deliberative and communicative models of agency makes definition and verification simpler tasks. Tools have already been developed which use model-checking for automatic verification [18]. The protocol language has been used to implement the generic dialogue framework of [8] and the negotiation game described in [10].

Acknowledgments

The authors of this paper would like to thank the anonymous reviewer of this paper whose extremely useful and thorough comments were greatly appreciated.

References

1. Mehdi Dastani. Negotiation protocols and dialogue games. In Jörg P. Müller, Elisabeth Andre, Sandip Sen, and Claude Frasson, editors, *Proceedings of the Fifth International Conference on Autonomous Agents*, pages 180–181, Montreal, Canada, 2001. ACM Press.

2. Marc Estava, Juan A. Rodriguez, Carles Sierra, Pere Garcia, and Josep L. Arcos. On the formal specifications of electronic institutions. *LNAI*, pages 126–147, 2001.

3. Marc Esteva, Juan A. Rodrguez-Aguilar, Josep Ll. Arcos, Carles Sierra, and Pere Garcia. Institutionalising open multi-agent systems. In *proceedings of the Fourth International Conference on MultiAgent Systems (ICMAS'2000)*, pages 381–83, Boston, 2000. ICMAS.

4. Robert A. Flores and R.C. Kremer. To commit or not to commit: Modelling agent conversations for action. *Computational Intelligence*, 18(2):120–173, May 2002.

5. Roberto A. Flores and Niek Wijngaards. Primitive interaction protocols for agents in a dynamic environment. In *Proceedings of the 12th Workshop on Knowledge Acquisition, Modeling and Management (KAW '99)*, pages 3-2-1:3-2-20, October 1999.

6. Foundation for Intelligent Physical Agents. Fipa interaction protocol library specification, 2000.

7. Nicolas Maudet and Fabrice Evrard. A generic framework for dialogue game implementation, 1998.

8. Peter McBurney and Simon Parsons. Games that agents play: A formal framework for dialogues between autonomous agents. *Journal of Logic, Language and Information*, 11(3):315–334, 2002.

9. Peter McBurney and Simon Parsons. A denotational semantics for deliberation dialogues. *Proceedings of the Third International Joint Conference on Autonomous Agents and Multiagent Systems - Volume 1 (AAMAS'04)*, 2004.

10. Peter McBurney, Rogier van Eijk, Simon Parsons, and Leila Amgoud. A dialogue-game protocol for agent purchase negotiations. *Journal of Autonomous Agents and Multi-Agent Systems. (In press).*, 2002.

11. Jarred McGinnis, David Robertson, and Chris Walton. Using distributed protocols as an implementation of dialogue games. Presented EUMAS 2003, December 2003.

12. Simon Parsons, Peter McBurney, and Michael Wooldridge. The mechanics of some formal inter-agent dialogues. In *Workshop on Agent Communication Languages*, pages 329–348, 2003.

13. Philippe Pasquier, Nicolas Andrillon, and Brahim Chaib-draa. An exploration in using the cognitive coherence theory to automate agents's communicational behavior. In *Agent Communication Language and Dialogue workshop*, Melbourne, Australia, 2003. AAMAS'03.

14. Chris Reed. Dialogue frames in agent communication. In Y. Demazeau, editor, *Proceedings of the Third International Conference on Multi-Agent Systems(ICMAS-98)*, pages 246–253. IEEE Press, 1998.

15. David Robertson. A lightweight coordination calculus for agent social norms. In *Declarative Agent Languages and Technologies*, New York, USA, 2004. a full day workshop occuring as part of AAMAS'04.

16. David Robertson. A lightweight method for coordination of agent oriented web services. In *Proceedings of AAAI Spring Symposium on Semantic Web Services*, California, USA, 2004.

17. Chris Walton and Dave Robertson. Flexible multi-agent protocols. Technical Report EDI-INF-RR-0164, University of Edinburgh, 2002.

18. Chris D. Walton. Model Checking Multi-Agent Web Services. In *Proceedings of the 2004 AAAI Spring Symposium on Semantic Web Services (To Appear)*, Stanford, California, March 2004.

19. Chris D. Walton. Multi-Agent Dialogue Protocols. In *Proceedings of the Eighth International Symposium on Artificial Intelligence and Mathematics*, Fort Lauderdale, Florida, January 2004.
20. Pinar Yolum and Munindar P. Singh. Flexible protocol specification and execution: Applying event calculus planning using commitments. In *Proceedings of the 1st International Joint Conference on Autonomous Agents and MultiAgent Systems (AAMAS)*, July 2002.

Modeling Communicative Behavior Using Permissions and Obligations

Lalana Kagal and Tim Finin

University of Maryland Baltimore County,
1000 Hilltop Circle,
Baltimore, MD 21250, USA
{lkagal1, finin}@cs.umbc.edu

Abstract. In order to provide flexible control over agent communication, we propose an integrated approach that involves using positive and negative permissions and obligations to describe both conversation specifications and policies. Conversation specifications are described in terms of the speech acts that an agent can/cannot/must/must not perform based on the sequence of messages received and sent. On the other hand, conversation policies restrict how the specifications are used and are defined over the attributes of the sender, receiver, message content, and context in general. Other policies like management, social, privacy etc. are defined at a higher level of abstraction and restrict the general behavior of agents. Whenever they deal with communication, the higher level policies are translated into conversation policies using the syntax and semantics of the specific communication language being used. Agents use a policy engine for reasoning over conversation specifications and applicable policies in order to decide what communicative act to perform next. Our work is different from existing research in communication policies because it is not tightly coupled to any domain information such as mental states of agents or specific communicative acts. The main contributions of this work include (i) an extensible framework that can support varied domain knowledge and different agent communication languages, and (ii) the declarative representation of conversation specifications and policies in terms of permitted and obligated speech acts.

1 Introduction

Multi-agent systems assume that agents interact and collaborate to satisfy their goals. Agent communication plays a very important part in these systems. A *conversation* can be defined as a sequence of communicative acts exchanged between interacting agents towards satisfying a particular goal [1, 2, 3]. In order for a conversation to be meaningful, it should follow some structured specifications. However, these conversation specifications or interaction protocols solely define the order in which communicative acts can be performed and do not take into consideration the content of the message, the attributes of the sender or the recipient or any other context. Similar to Phillips [3], we propose that along with

R.M. van Eijk et al. (Eds.): AC 2004, LNAI 3396, pp. 120–133, 2005.
© Springer-Verlag Berlin Heidelberg 2005

conversation specifications, agents should use policies that define constraints over different aspects of the conversation in order to provide more flexible control over agent communication. This also allows the communication modules of agents to be less dependent on the communication protocols permitting the modification of conversation specifications and policies without requiring the modules to be changed.

We believe that similar mechanisms should be used to reason over and integrate specifications and policies allowing agents to understand and apply both uniformly. As positive and negative authorization and obligation policies can be used to model different kinds of behavior [4], by representing conversation specifications and policies, they can also be used to represent ideal communicative behavior.

We differentiate between conversation specifications that define the order of communicative/speech acts and policies that affect how conversation specifications are used and how conversations are carried out. *Conversation specifications*, or interaction protocols as they are known within FIPA [5], define the order in which communicative acts can occur within a conversation. For example, on receiving a REQUEST communicative act, an agent can reply with REFUSE or AGREE [5]. On the other hand, we define *conversation policies* as restrictions on communication based on the content of the communicative act, the attributes of the sender and recipient including their beliefs, desires and intentions and other context like the current team they belong to, the time of day, and their location. For example, a conversation policy would *oblige* an agent to provide an evasive answer to a QUERY about a political issue in an office setting but *permit* it to provide a more truthful answer in a social setting. We also consider other policies like privacy, work, and social that may establish additional restrictions and limitations on the communicative capabilities of the agent. Consider an agent that has a privacy policy prohibiting it from disclosing the SSN of the user. Though the conversation specification provides the set of communicative acts the agent can use to reply to a QUERY, its privacy policy prohibits it from responding to any query involving the SSN of the user. Conversation specifications define all possibilities that can be used in a certain sequence of speech acts, whereas conversation policies and other higher policies narrow what is allowed by and broaden what is required by specifications. As there is a possibility of conflict between specifications and policies, we assume that conversation policies are always of higher priority than the specifications.

As an example, we describe the recent issue with the Medicare prescription drug bill in the United States [6] in terms of agent communication. According to the CNN article, Rick Foster, chief actuary for the Centers for Medicare and Medicaid Services, stated that he was asked not to answer questions from congressional Democrats regarding the cost of the bill before a series of key votes last summer. We describe how this would have worked within a multi-agent system driven by our conversation specifications and policies. Agents, including Foster, would have a conversation specification that states that in response to a QUERY, the agent is *permitted* to use either AGREE followed by an INFORM/FAILURE or REFUSE or ignore the message. The work policy would state that all government employees are *obliged* to answer queries from the congressional Democrats. However, agency chief Thomas Scully, enforces a temporary policy of the highest priority on Foster stating that Foster is *obliged* to REFUSE all queries from congressional Democrats regarding the estimated cost of the Medicare prescription drug bill until the end of summer. There also exists a sanction associated with the failure to fulfill this obligation which states that Foster could lose his job.

Whenever Foster receives a message, he reasons over his conversation specifications and policies to figure out how he should respond. When he receives a QUERY from a congressional Democrat asking about the estimated cost of the bill he knows from the conversation specifications that the correct response is AGREE or REFUSE. As his work policy *obliges* him to answer all queries from congressional Democrats, under normal circumstances Foster would agree. However, as Scully's temporary policy overrides the work policy and because of the associated sanction, Foster follows Scully's policy and REFUSEs the query. Scully's policy could also include rules *obliging* Foster to send an evasive reply to the congressional Democrats instead of refusing to answer.

2   Framework

Our framework mainly involves using permissions and obligations to control the communicative behavior of agents. It includes techniques for (i) describing conversation specifications using a specific agent communication language, (ii) defining conversation policies, (iii) resolving conflicts within specifications and policies using meta-policies, and (iv) using a policy engine to reason over the domain knowledge, specifications, policies, and meta-policies to enable an agent to decide what speech act it can/must use next.

2.1   Overview

A communicative or speech act is defined in terms of the set of actions that are implied when an agent makes an utterance. Generally, there are three actions that can be identified; (i) locution, which is the action of uttering the speech act, (ii) illocution, which deals with the conveying of the intentions of the sender, and (iii) perlocution, which are actions that occur due to the illocution.

Though our work has been done in OWL [7], a web ontology language used to describe metadata about entities, for conciseness and ease of explanation, we use expressions in predicate logic to describe speech acts, positive and negative deontic objects, and policies.

– A *communicative or speech act* is performed by an agent to achieve a certain intention. A speech act is usually assumed to have two main components; the performative and the proposition.
  We describe a communicative act as a tuple

```
performative(Sender, Receiver, Proposition)
```

For example, a QUERY-REF speech act of FIPA sent from agentX to agentY asking agentY what he believes the values of the included proposition to be

```
query-ref(agentX, agentY, estimatedCostOfBill(Cost))
```

- Domain actions are actions that an agent can perform and are described by the following tuple

```
action(Actor, Target, PreCondition, Effect)
```

The *printAPage* domain action can be described as

```
printAPage(X, hpLaitPrinter,
    (numPages(hpLaitPrinter, N), N>0),
    (numPages(hpLaitPrinter, N-1)))
```

- Deontic concepts of permissions, prohibitions (negative permissions), obligations and dispensations (waiver from an obligation) are used to describe the behavior of the agent.

```
deontic(Actor, Action, Constraint)
or
deontic(Actor, Action, StartingConstraint, EndingConstraint)
```

Consider the permission of an agent to perform an AGREE speech act to any agent regarding for the estimated cost of the Medicare prescription bill. This is considered a policy as it includes domain knowledge of the proposition used to model the cost of the bill.

```
permission(X, agree(X, Y, estimatedCostOfBill(Cost)), _)
```

We model four deontic objects: permission, prohibition, obligation and dispensation. Permissions and prohibitions are used to describe positive/ negative authorizations whereas obligations and dispensations describe positive/negative responsibilities. All these objects could be represented in terms of a single concept, either permission or obligation, but we use different terms for simplicity.

Associated with each deontic object is either *constraint*, which defines the conditions under which the deontic object is applicable, or *startingConstraint* and *endingConstraint* that define the window within which the deontic object is applicable. These constraints could also include conditions on time providing time validity to the deontic object. Obligations and dispensations have an additional field, obligedTo, which describes whom the agent is obliged to. Another property called sanctions is associated with both obligations and prohibitions and is used to describe the penalties imposed on the agent if it fails to fulfill the obligation or violates the prohibition. Consider a policy of a graduate assistant that obliges him to turn in a weekly status report to his advisor or risk missing a pay check.

```
obligation(X, inform(X, Y, weeklyStatus(X, W, Status)),
           (advisor(Y, X), endOfWeek(W)), Y, missPayCheck(X, W))
```

A *permission* allows an agent to perform the associated action as long as the constraint is true or the startingConstraint is true and the endingConstraint is false. A *prohibition* prevents an agent from performing the associated action as long as the constraint is true or during the time when the startingConstraint is true and the endingConstraint is false. An agent must perform an *obligation* sometime before the *endingConstraint* is false and after the *startingConstraint* is true. An agent is no longer obliged to fulfill an obligation if there is an associated dispensation freeing the agent from the obligation.

- Conflicts can occur between permissions and prohibitions, obligations and prohibitions, and obligations and dispensations. In order to resolve conflicts, meta-policies that are used to correctly interpret policies. There are two kinds of meta-policies namely setting the modality precedence (negative over positive or vice versa) or stating the priority between rules within a policy or between policies [8].

  In a multi-policy environment, it is possible to state that one policy overrides another. For example, it is possible to say that in case of conflict the CS department policy always overrides the Lait lab policy. As another example, consider the CS department policy. Students are prohibited from using the faculty printer but research assistants are permitted to. There is a potential conflict if a student is a research assistant and needs to use the faculty printer. This can be solved by setting the priority between the rules and stating that the permission overrides the prohibition.

```
rule1 : prohibition(X, print(X, facultyPrinter), student(X))
rule2 : permission(X, print(X, facultyPrinter),
researchAssistant(X)) overrides(rule2, rule1)
```

On the other hand, if a certain modality precedence is used, then when a conflict occurs the rule with the preferred modality overrides the other. For example, if positive modality is preferred then in case of conflict, permissions and obligations will override prohibitions and obligations will override dispensations. The conflict in the CS department policy in the earlier example can also be resolved if positive modality is given precedence.

```
precedence(positive-modality)
```

- We also use some additional expressions to describe the sequence of message that have been exchanged so far in an actual dialogue. The expression

```
received(X)
```

states that X was a message received and

```
sent(X)
```

states that X was a message that was sent.

2.2   Conversation Specifications

Using the semantics of the deontic objects and domain actions and the syntax of speech acts, we can model conversation specifications in agent communication languages like Knowledge Query and Manipulation Language (KQML) [9] or Foundation for Intelligent Physical Agents (FIPA) [5] as a set of permissions and obligations on the sender or the receiver depending on the performatives used thus far in the conversation.

As an example, we describe the QUERY-REF specification in FIPA.

- Speech acts used : QUERY-REF, REFUSE, AGREE, FAILURE, INFORM
- Sequence of messages : An agent sends a QUERY-REF message to another agent. The latter can reply either with a REFUSE or an AGREE stating its intent to either provide an answer or refuse to answer. Once an agent has sent an AGREE, it is obliged to send an INFORM providing the information required.
  - Every agent has the permission to perform a QUERY-REF performative

    ```
    permission(X, query-ref(X, Y, Proposition),_)
    ```

    In the above expression, the constraint field is left empty to specify that there are no constraints on the performing of a QUERY-REF performative.
  - On receiving a QUERY-REF, the recipient has the permission to either REFUSE the query or AGREE to provide the answer

    ```
    permission(Y, refuse(Y, X, Proposition),
               received(query-ref(X,Y, Proposition)))
    permission(Y, agree(Y, X, Proposition),
               received(query-ref(X,Y, Proposition)))
    ```

    The constraint here is that the agent has received a QUERY-REF speech act.
  - Once an agent has accepted a QUERY-REF, it is obliged to answer to it either with a FAILURE or with an INFORM and the agent is obligated to the recipient of the agree message.

    ```
    obligation(Y, failure(Y, X, Proposition),
               sent(agree(Y, X, Proposition)), X, _)
    obligation(Y, inform(Y, X, Proposition),
               sent(agree(Y, X, Proposition)), X, _)
    ```

Other specifications are simpler like the FIPA PROPOSE interaction protocol.

- Speech acts used : PROPOSE, REJECT-PROPOSAL, ACCEPT-PROPOSAL
- Sequence of messages : An agent sends a PROPOSAL message to another agent. The recipient can either use the REJECT-PROPOSAL or the ACCEPT-PROPOSAL.

- Every agent has the permission to perform a PROPOSAL performative
  permission(X, proposal(X, Y, Proposition), _)
- On receiving a PROPOSAL, the recipient has the permission to either reject the proposal or accept it.
  permission(Y, accept-proposal(Y, X, Proposition),
             received(proposal(X,Y, Proposition)))
  permission(Y, reject-proposal(Y, X, Proposition),
             received(proposal(X,Y, Proposition)))

The constraint here is that the agent has received a proposal speech act.

2.3   Policies

Policies like conversation, social, and privacy add restrictions on the performatives that can be used, the content of the speech act, the receiver, time of the message, etc. based on current attributes of the sender, receiver, content and all other context of the conversation. They narrow what is allowed by and broaden what is required by the conversation specifications. Policies can be defined at two levels; one that is independent of the syntax and semantics of the communication language and the second that is tightly integrated with them. In the latter case, the policies use the semantics of the performative and define constraints on how performatives can be used and under what conditions. Though this may be true in the case of conversation policies, we generally assume that policies like privacy, and social norms define restrictions at the higher level of abstraction and provide restrictions on the general behavior of the agent. Whenever these policies deal with information flow between agents, they need to be translated into lower level policies using the semantics of the communication language. For example, an agent's privacy policy might state that the SSN must not be disclosed. This is irrespective of the agent communication language being used or the specific performative. If FIPA is being used, the privacy policy could be translated in our framework as 'The agent is prohibited from sending an INFORM communicative act to any agent when the content involves SSN of the agent'. However, if KQML is the language being used for communication, the semantics specify that only the TELL is the only assertive performative that causes the agent to reveal its belief about a proposition. In this case, the policy could translate to 'The agent is prohibited from sending a TELL communicative act to any agent when the content involves SSN of the agent'. Similarly, a social policy can specify that an agent should not be rude. However, what it means to be rude and how it translates into speech acts and their content depends on the application domain. The agent would have to ensure that the effect of any speech act does not violate this social policy.

Following from the first example dealing with the Medicare bill, it is evident that there are several policies acting on an agent. This could lead to *conflicts* between policies. Foster's conversation specifications gave him the permission to reply to requests, however, the agency head prohibited him from replying to queries about the estimated cost of the Medicare bill. In Foster's case, Scully's policy would be enforced if it was of higher priority than Foster's other policies.

2.4   Specification Language

Our policy language, Rei, is represented in OWL [7], which is a ontology language. It includes logic-like variables to describe constraints over different aspects of deontic objects, actions and policies. The use of variables allows Rei to represent a wider range of constraints than would be possible in OWL. We used logic to describe the examples for ease of explanation and for conciseness. By using OWL, Rei gains extensibility as different kinds of domain-specific knowledge in RDF and OWL can be used for describing policies and specifications.

Our policy language is modeled on deontic concepts of permissions, prohibitions, obligations and dispensations [10, 11]. We believe that most policies can be expressed as what an entity can/cannot do and what it should/should not do in terms of actions, services, and conversations, making our language capable of describing a large variety of policies ranging from security policies to conversation and behavior policies. The policy language has some domain independent ontologies but will also require specific domain ontologies. The former includes concepts for permissions, obligations, actions, speech acts, etc. The latter is a set of ontologies, used by the entities in the system, which defines domain classes (person, file, deleteAFile, readBook) etc. and properties associated with the classes (age, num-pages, email).

The language includes two constructs for specifying meta-policies that are invoked to resolve conflicts; setting the modality precedence (negative over positive or vice versa) or stating the priority between policies [12, 13]. As an example of using priority consider a meta policy that states that in case of conflict the Federal policy always overrides the State policy. When modality precedences are used to resolve a conflict, the rule of the preferred modality overrides the other.

Another important aspect of the language is that it models speech acts like delegation, revocation, request and cancel for modifying existing policies dynamically. Delegations and revocations cause the permissions of agents to be modified, whereas requests and cancels affect the obligations. A delegation speech act, if valid, causes a permission to be created. A revocation speech act nullifies an existing permission (whether policy based or delegation based) of an agent. An agent can request another agent for a permission or to perform an action on its behalf. The former if accepted causes a delegation and the latter leads to an obligation. An agent can also cancel any previously made request causing a dispensation.

2.5   Policy Enforcement

Along with the specification of Rei, we have also developed a reasoning engine in Flora[1], which is an F-logic extension of XSB. The engine is built over F-OWL [14], a reasoner for OWL and RDF, enabling Rei to understand and reason over ontologies in both OWL and RDF. The engine reasons over policies, meta policies, history of speech acts, and domain information to answer the following types of questions :

---

[1] http://flora.sourceforge.net.

- What are the current permissions of X ?

  The engine looks for all those permissions whose actor property unifies with X and whose constraints are satisfied. If there is a conflicting prohibition or revocation, the engine uses the meta policies to decide whether the permission overrides the prohibition/revocation or vice versa. If the latter case is true, the permission is not valid. If the permission is valid, the policy engine checks the preconditions associated with the action over which the permission is specified. The permission is returned only if the precondition is satisfied.

  The engine also looks for valid delegations from any agent to X. The delegation is valid if the delegatee has the permission to make the delegation or has been delegated the permission to make the delegation. The entire delegation chain is checked by policy engine. At every level, the engine also checks that there is no conflicting prohibition or revocation.

- What are the current obligations of Y ?

  The engine locates all obligations whose actor property unifies with Y and whose startingConstraint is satisfied but whose endingConstraint is false. The engine ensures that there is no conflicting dispensation.

- Does X have the permission to perform action A or speech act S ?

  This is similar to the first case, but in this case, the policy engine also checks the action property of the permission and verifies that it unifies with A or S.

- Does X have any permissions on a resource R ?

  This is similar to the first case, but the policy engine also tries to unify the target property of the action associated with the permission with R.

- When policy P is deleted, does agent X still retain the permission to use the QUERY speech act for Proposition P ?

  This is part of the policy analysis provided by Rei. The policy engine deletes P but stores it in a temporary list. It then tries to verify that X has the permission to use QUERY speech act over P. It returns the answer and then restores P.

We envision that the reasoning engine will be used together with domain knowledge like the mental state of the agents, the history of the speech acts performed and other context by either a planning component or a workflow component to enable enforcement of policies over agent communication.

Using the policy engine, our earlier example of the Medicare bill would be inferred by Foster as

1. Received QUERY-REF from congressional Democrat enquiring about the cost of the Medicare bill
2. What are my current obligations ? I am obliged to AGREE to answer by my conversation work policy. I am also obliged to REFUSE the query that deal with the cost of the bill by Scully's policy.
3. As the meta policy states that Scully's policy has the highest priority, I use it.

4. So, I REFUSE the query.
5. However, Do I have the permission to REFUSE a query ? Yes, from the conversation specifications.

3 Example

We now walk through the Medicare bill example. We assume that the agent communication language used is FIPA and both Foster and Scully share the same conversation specifications. These specifications include the QUERY-REF specification described in section 2.2.

– Foster has a work conversation policy that specifies that all government employees should agree to all queries from congressional Democrats.

```
ConvPolicy :
obligation(X, agree(X, Y, Proposition),
        (received(query-if(Y, X, Proposition)),
         governmentEmployee(X),
         congressionalDemocrat(Y)),
        X, _)
obligation(X, agree(X, Y, Proposition),
        (received(query-ref(Y, X, Proposition)),
         governmentEmployee(X),
         congressionalDemocrat(Y)),
        X, _)
```

– Scully decides that Foster should not answer any queries from congressional Democrats that ask about the estimated cost of the Medicare prescription bill. This is a high level policy and could be translated in two ways; either as an obligation to use REFUSE or a prohibition on INFORM.

1. It can be translated based on the syntax and semantics the FIPA ACL as an obligation to refuse all queries about the estimated cost of the bill from congressional Democrats.

```
TempPolicy :
obligation(foster, refuse(foster, Y,
        estimatedCostOfBill(Cost)),
        (received(query-ref(Y, foster,
        estimatedCostOfBill(Cost))),
         congressionalDemocrat(Y)),
        scully, loseJob(foster))
```

2. It can also be translated as a prohibition from informing any congressional Democrat about the estimated cost of the bill.

```
TempPolicy :
prohibition(foster, inform(foster, Y,
        estimatedCostOfBill(Cost)),
```

```
(received(query-ref(Y, foster,
estimatedCostOfBill(Cost))),
congressionalDemocrat(Y)))
```

However, we believe that the former interpretation matches the statement made by Foster more closely, so we use it through the rest of the example.

– Scully gives this obligation policy higher priority than the existing conversation policy.

```
overrides(TempPolicy, ConvPolicy)
```

– At some point of time, a congressional Democrat, Walter, sends a query to Foster asking about the estimated cost of Medicare bill.

```
query-ref(walter, foster, estimatedCostOfBill(Cost))
```

– On receiving this speech act, Foster looks up the conversation specifications for QUERY-REF, and finds that he can respond either with an AGREE or REFUSE.
– Foster checks his work conversation policy, which states that he is obliged to answer all QUERY-IF and QUERY-REF speech acts from congressional Democrats with an AGREE.
– Foster then reasons over Scully's policy that is of higher priority than his work conversation policy. Scully's policy states that Foster is obliged to refuse all queries from congressional Democrats about the estimated cost of the bill. As Scully's policy is of higher priority and as the cost of violating the policy involves Foster losing his job, Foster uses Scully's policy and sends a REFUSE to Walter.

```
refuse(foster, walter, estimatedCostOfBill(Cost))
```

4   Related Work

Cohen and Levesque model the cognitive state of agents and base allowable speech acts on the cognitive states of collaborating agents [15]. In his earlier work, Singh provides semantics for speech acts in terms of beliefs and intentions of the agents [16, 17]. Fornara and Colombetti [18] describe an approach based on the notion of social commitment. Labrou and Finin also describe the semantics of KQML based on the beliefs and desires of agents [9]. These models are very tightly coupled to the mental states of agents and the semantics of the language that makes it difficult to extend them to work in different environments and with different agent communication languages. Cost et al. [19] develop a model using colored petri nets that can take into account various contextual properties and attributes. Greaves et al. define conversation policies as restrictions on how the agent communication language is used [2]. Though the last approach is similar to ours, we believe that conversation policies should be at a higher level of abstraction and should not involve specifics of the communication language.

We also propose that policies related to communication be translated into permissions and obligations that the agent has on specific speech acts supported by the communication language being used.

Kollingbaum et al. discuss how normative agents estimate the effect of adopting a new norm[20]. The current beliefs, norms and the selected plan are taken into consideration while estimating the level of consistency that will be brought about by the adopted norm. This work approaches the adoption of norms (or what we call policies) under the assumption that the agent can decide whether or not to accept a norm. Though this is advisable for contracting agents, we believe that certain policies are enforced by the environment and must be accepted by the agent irrespective of whether they cause conflicts or inconsistencies in the agent's current state. Also, Kollingbaum's approach does not try to resolve conflicts, it only categorizes the type of conflict in terms of consistency and uses this information to decide whether or not to accept a new norm.

Broersen et al. use agent types to resolve conflicts between beliefs, obligations, intentions and desires [21]. The agent types are determined by their characteristics namely social (obligations overrule desires), selfish (desires overrule obligations), realistic (beliefs overrule everything else) and simple-minded (intentions overrule obligations and desires). In our framework, conflicts basically occur between permissions and prohibitions, obligations and prohibitions, and obligations and dispensations. In order to resolve conflicts, our framework includes meta-policies namely setting the modality precedence (negative over positive or vice versa) or stating the priority between rules within a policy or between policies. Broersen et al. approach conflict resolution from the agent's point of view whereas we try to resolve conflicts in policies within the environment and not within agents themselves. We believe that Broersen's approach could be used by agents after conflict resolution is provided by our framework as the enforced policies may conflict with the agent's internal beliefs, desires, intentions, obligations, prohibitions, and permissions.

5   Summary

The main goal of our work is to provide flexible and integrated control over agent communication. Conversation specifications and policies are described as permissions and obligations over different agent communication languages like KQML and FIPA and different domain-specific information. Our framework allows specifications to be described as a sequence of permitted and obligated speech acts. Policies are described at a high level of abstraction and are translated into positive and negative permissions and obligations over speech acts using the syntax and semantics of the agent communication language. These permissions and obligations establish restrictions over performatives that can or must be performed in terms of attributes of the sender, receiver, content and other context of the conversation like time, and location.

Though we described all our examples in logic, our actual specification language is in OWL, a web ontology language. Our language can be used to describe positive and negative permissions and obligations over speech acts in terms of domain-specific information. We have developed a reasoning engine for our language that reasons over domain knowledge, speech act semantics, protocols, policies, and meta policies to answer questions about the actions and speech acts that an agent can/must perform. We envision that this reasoning engine will be integrated into the planning/workflow component of an agent to provide policy enforcement over agent communication. As part of our future work, we are looking into automating the translation process from high level policies to performative-specific permissions and obligations. We are also interested in integrating work on commitments like that by Mallya et al. [22], which involves reasoning over the status of obligations of agents, into our framework to provide greater obligation management.

References

1. Flores, R., Kremer, R.: A Model for Flexible Composition of Conversations: How a Simple Conversation got so Complicated. In: 3rd Workshop on Agent Communication Languages and Conversation Policies, M.P. Huget, F. Dignum and J.L. Koning (Eds.), First International Joint Conference on Autonomous Agents and Multiagent Systems (AAMAS 2002), Bologna, Italy, July 15-19, 2002. (2002)
2. Greaves, M., Holmback, H., Bradshaw, J.: What is a conversation policy? In: Autonomous Agents '99 Workshop on Specifying and Implementing Conversation Policies. (1999)
3. Phillips, L.R., Link, H.E. In: The Role of Conversation Policy in Carrying Out Agent Conversations. Volume 1916 of Lecture Notes in Computer Science. Springer (2000)
4. Kagal, L., Finin, T., Joshi, A.: Declarative Policies for Describing Web Service Capabilities and Constraints. In: W3C Workshop on Constraints and Capabilities for Web Services, Oracle Conference Center, Redwood Shores, CA, USA, W3C (2004)
5. FIPA: Foundation for Intelligent Physical Agents Specifications. (http://www.fipa.org)
6. Cable News Network (CNN): Probe under way on Medicare cost. http://www.cnn.com/2004/ALLPOLITICS/03/17/medicare.investigation/ (2004)
7. W3C: OWL Web Ontology Language. http://www.w3.org/2001/sw/WebOnt/ (2004)
8. Moffett, J., Sloman, M.: Policy Conflict Analysis in Distributed Systems Management. Journal of Organizational Computing (1993)
9. Labrou, Y., Finin, T.: A semantics approach for KQML – a general purpose communication language for software agents. In: Third International Conference on Information and Knowledge Management (CIKM'94). (1994)
10. Kagal, L., Finin, T., Joshi, A.: A Policy Language for Pervasive Systems. In: Fourth IEEE International Workshop on Policies for Distributed Systems and Networks. (2003)
11. Kagal, L., Finin, T., Joshi, A.: A Policy Based Approach to Security for the Semantic Web. In: 2nd International Semantic Web Conference (ISWC2003), September 2003. (2003)
12. Lupu, E.C., Sloman, M.: Conflicts in Policy-Based Distributed Systems Management. IEEE Transactions on Software Engineering (1999)

13. Lupu, E.C., Sloman, M.: Towards a Role Based Framework for Distributed Systems Management. Journal of Networks and Systemss Management, Plenum Press (1996)

14. Zou, Y., Chan, H., Finin, T.: F-OWL: an Inference Engine for Semantic Web. In: Third NASA-Goddard/IEEE Workshop on Formal Approaches to Agent-Based Systems (FAABS III), 26-28 April 2004, Greenbelt MD. (2004)

15. Cohen, P.R., Levesque, H.J.: Intention is choice with commitment. In: Artificial Intelligence. (1990)

16. Singh, M.: Towards a formal theory of communication for multiagent systems. In: International Joint Conference on Artificial Intelligence. (1991)

17. Singh, M.: A semantics for speech acts. Annals of Mathematics and Artificial Intelligence (1992)

18. Fornara, N., Colombetti, M.: Defining interaction protocols using a commitment-based agent communication language. In: Second international joint conference on Autonomous agents and multiagent systems, Melbourne, Australia pp 520-527, 2003, ACM Press. (2003)

19. Cost, R.S., Chen, Y., Finin, T., Labrou, Y., Peng, Y.: Using Colored Petri Nets for Conversation Modeling. In: Agent Communication Languages, Frank Dignum and Mark Greaves (editors), Springer-Verlag, Lecture Notes in AI, 2000. (2000)

20. Kollingbaum, M.J., Norman, T.: Norm consistency in practical reasoning agents. (2003)

21. Broersen, J., Dastani, M., Hulstijn, J., Huang, Z., van der Torre, L.: The BOID Architecture Conflicts Between Beliefs, Obligations, Intentions and Desire. (2001)

22. Mallya, A.U., Yolum, P., Singh, M.P.: Resolving Commitments Among Autonomous Agents. In: International Workshop on Agent Communication Languages and Conversation Policies (ACL), Melbourne, July 2003, Springer. (2003)

Coherence Constraints for Agent Interaction

Joris Hulstijn[1],[**], Frank Dignum[2], and Mehdi Dastani[2]

[1] Vrije Universiteit, Amsterdam
jhulstijn@feweb.vu.nl
[2] Utrecht University,
{mehdi, dignum}@cs.uu.nl

Abstract. This paper describes the use of coherence constraints as a means to regulate agent interaction. Coherence constraints describe relationships between the content of utterances, and the context. They can be used for example to express that an answer must refer back in a meaningful way to the question that it answers. We also discuss several possible ways in which the enforcement of coherence constraints can be implemented in a multiagent system. Finally we describe a possible implementation in the 3APL platform, which shows the feasibility of this form of interaction regulation.

1 Introduction

In the field of agent communication languages we observe a trend from specifying small dedicated interaction protocols towards specifications of flexible or open protocols [12, 41, 29], which are more widely usable. Moreover, interaction protocols tend to be viewed more as resources provided by an electronic institution in which the agents interact, than as fixed specifications attached to the agents. One of the reasons for this last trend is that protocols are increasingly studied in conjunction with the social organization that enforces them, and the software infrastructure that enables them [14].

Most agent communication infrastructures are based on the standards developed by FIPA. FIPA has provided a standard for structuring messages [15] and for simple interaction protocols [17]. The backbone of these standards is based on speech act theory [3, 37]. Like other actions, speech acts can be combined into protocols or plans to achieve a goal. The semantics of a speech act is commonly given by the preconditions and intended effect on the mental state of an agent, expressed using modal operators for belief and intention.

The FIPA standardization effort has been a relative success, although it has been criticized heavily, e.g. [34, 40]. Here are two points of criticism.

1. It is impossible to verify the correct usage of a speech act, since for most realistic multiagent settings the mental state of an agent is inaccessible.

[**] This research was conducted while the first author was at Utrecht University.

R.M. van Eijk et al. (Eds.): AC 2004, LNAI 3396, pp. 134–152, 2005.

Agents may well be lying. This makes it impossible to verify protocols under common assumptions regarding multiagent systems [40]. What is needed instead is a semantics that is based on *public information* about what agents are committed to, on the basis of what they have said.

2. Policies and protocols are often only defined in terms of speech act types, like request, accept or reject. Protocol definitions are thus mainly concerned with the form of interaction; nothing much is said about the content and function of the messages. Thus agents may conform to the 'letter' of the protocol, while not being coherent. What is needed is a way to extend protocols with so called *coherence constraints* on the content of messages.

The second criticism can be countered by stating that constraints on the coherence of messages can only be given if a certain representation language for the content of the messages is assumed. Because FIPA tries to remain as general as possible it abstracts over the content language and thus the coherence constraints cannot be expressed. Although this is true, we think that in many cases the platform in which the agents interact can in fact put constraints on the content of messages.

In general, interaction behavior is determined by a public protocol that offers a repertoire of messages and rules to define what sequences of messages are well-formed, and the strategy of individual participants to generate messages and accept or reject messages from other participants. A protocol formalizes conventional interaction patterns based on the underlying activity or application. We believe that for many applications, coherence constraints are an essential component of the protocol; they are conventional, just like the message order.

What we mean by coherence is illustrated by the following examples.

(1) propose$(s, b, 40)$; propose$(b, s, 30)$; propose$(s, b, 35)$; propose$(b, s, 20)$

(2) cfp$(a, b,$price_quote(shoes,x)); bid$(b, a,$price_quote(soles,80))

Example (1) shows a simple type of concessive negotiation, loosely inspired by the monotonic concession protocol [36]. Participants are supposed to make concessions, until they reach agreement. The last bid of buyer b is incoherent, because it is not a concession with respect to the previous bid. Note that what counts as a concession, depends on the content of the message, on the previous messages and on the role of the participant. Example (2) concerns a call for proposals. The example shows that coherence crucially depends on the background knowledge that can be assumed for participants. The bid by b seems incoherent, because it does not match the price quote for shoes that was called for. However, if we suppose that it is commonly known that soles are parts of shoes, and that therefore the price of shoes is partly determined by the price of soles, the bid does count as a coherent, though partial, response.

First, we investigate in this paper the use of coherence constraints as a part of the protocol definition. Because coherence constraints are a very general notion, they can be used to define the order of message types as well as constraints on the content of messages. One might thus use them both in addition to a traditional protocol, and to replace it. In the second case the order of messages can be left more open. Similar to other declarative formulations, like commitments [41] or landmarks, coherence constraints may specify the motivation behind a message sequence. This produces more flexible protocols, that leave more decisions to the strategies of the individual agents. Note however, that the issue of flexible protocols is orthogonal to the use of coherence constraints.

Second, we investigate multiagent architectures to verify coherence constraints. If the constraints are incorporated in the agents, compliance checking can be done by the agents themselves. The interactions can also be verified by the platform through which the communication takes place. The first option will, in general, be more efficient, but places a heavy burden on the agents. The second option is less efficient, but does not require agents to have additional reasoning capabilities. We will discuss a number of solutions to this trade-off, and show how they can be implemented using the 3APL platform [11], which provides a development platform for the 3APL agent programming language [21].

The rest of the paper is structured as follows. In section 2 we introduce the notion of coherence more fully. In section 3 we show how coherence constraints can be used in combination with existing protocol descriptions. In section 4 we describe a number of alternatives for the implementation of coherence checking in the communication infrastructure, and illustrate it using the 3APL platform.

2   Coherence

We review the notion of coherence as used in linguistics. Intuitively, a discourse (text or dialogue) can be called coherent when its parts 'belong together'. Coherence has been studied in natural language semantics and pragmatics under the header of discourse structure. There are many approaches, e.g. [10, 19, 39, 2].

Aspects of coherence that have to do with form are also called *cohesion* [20]. In natural language, cohesion shows by the use of a consistent vocabulary, a consistent style and parallel syntactic constructions. The use of anaphora and ellipsis to refer to objects mentioned earlier gives the impression of a coherent discourse. Coherence is strongly related to topic structure. A discourse of which the topics of the utterances are related, for example because they are subtopics, makes a more coherent impression than a text with frequent topic shifts.

A common approach to analyze coherence is rhetorical structure theory [28]. The content expressed by an utterance is related to the previous discourse, by a rhetorical relation, such as elaboration, explanation or contrast. Rhetorical relations are also called *coherence relations*. They are typically marked by adverbs like 'because' (explanation), or 'however' (contrast). If no explicit or implicit coherence relation can be found to link an utterance to the context, not even the 'neutral' elaboration relation, the discourse can be said to be incoherent. Coherence also relates to the purpose of utterances. For goal-directed discourse, whenever an utterance contributes to the underlying goal of the discourse, for example to convince the reader or explain something, this will increase the impression of coherence. Goal-based notions of coherence are prominent in models of misunderstanding [1].

A so called discourse context is used to record the contributions of each of the utterances to the over-all meaning of a discourse. We say that the context is *updated with* the content of an utterance. Coherence relations help to determine how the context must be updated with the content of an utterance. For example, the content of an elaboration can be added straightaway, provided it is logically consistent and does not already follow. But a contrast relation suggests that there is a conflict with a previous utterance, and an explanation induces a causal relation with an unexplained event.

Using a representation of the discourse context 'C' and a notion of update '$+$', the global notion of coherence can be reduced to a local notion of coherence, made relative to the context. Although this simplification does not hold for discourse in general, it does hold for the applications of multiagent interaction that we have in mind.

1. An utterance U is coherent with context C iff a coherence relation $R(U',U)$ can be found that connects U with some existing part U' of C.
2. In this case, a new context $C' = C + U$ is created which adds the content of U to C in a way that depends on $R(U,U')$.
3. A sequence of utterances $U_1, ..., U_n$ is called coherent, iff each U_k is coherent with context C_{k-1}, which represents the content of $U_1, ..., U_{k-1}$.

This analysis also applies to dialogue. Coherence relations for dialogue are based on the dialogue genre, like negotiation, persuasion or information exchange. For example, Asher and Lascarides [2] analyze question-answer sequences in terms of two coherence relations: IQAP (indirect question answer pair) and Q-ELAB (question elaboration). The IQAP relation expresses answerhood. Two utterance representations U_1 and U_2 stand in relation IQAP when U_1 somehow triggers a question, and U_2 conveys information that counts as an answer to that question. The Q-ELAB relation expresses that asking a question should contribute to the goals of the asker. So, two utterances U_1 and U_2 stand in relation Q-ELAB when U_2 is a question of which the answers will help to achieve part of the apparent goal suggested by U_1.

For human dialogue, this pattern can be illustrated by the following exchange. The response by B to the question in (3) is coherent, in case the asker is a traveler with the apparent goal of catching a train to London. The utterances by a and b stand in the IQAP relation. Note that the additional information about the platform is coherent too, even though it has not been asked explicitly. The apparent goal of the asker can be inferred from the circumstances.

(3) a: When does the train for London leave?
    b: in 2 minutes, platform 4.

The pattern seems to generalize to other goal-directed types of dialogue. An initiative is coherent when the expected responses to that kind of initiative would contribute to the apparent goal of the initiator, where the goal may be induced from previous utterances, from the dialogue setting, or from the initiative itself. A response is coherent when it contributes to resolving the problem or goal that is suggested by the initiative.

In computational linguistics, such reasoning about goals and ways to achieve them has been formalized. Just like other actions, speech acts can be combined into plans to achieve a goal. For dialogue, such plans are necessarily joint plans, that involve contributions from various participants. Thus, Lochbaum [26] applies a theory of joint planning and action [18] to explain the structure of goal-directed dialogues. An important aspect of such theories of joint planning and action is the notion of a recipe. A recipe is a partial plan, known to the participants by convention. Recipes are basic building blocks, that help to coordinate the actions in a joint plan. In records of natural language dialogue, we find frequently re-occurring patterns of interaction, such as questions followed by answers, or statements followed by acknowledgements. Such interaction patterns can be analyzed as dialogue games [7]. Elsewhere we have argued that dialogue games are a kind of recipes for joint action [23]. It is this kind of goal-based analysis that inspires our account of coherence.

3   Protocol Definitions

In this section we demonstrate the possibility of expressing coherence constraints as part of an agent communication protocol. Our protocol definitions are based on the idea of a dialogue game as expressed by Mann [27] and McBurney and Parsons [32], although we use a simplified terminology. Based on the notions discussed so far we show how to define two simple dialogue games: information exchange and concessive negotiation. These dialogue games are merely meant to illustrate aspects of multiagent interaction. Although inspired by linguistics, they are bound to over-simplify the complex aspects of coherence found in natural language.

3.1   Dialogue Game Rules

Each dialogue game is defined by five sets of rules.

1. The *initial context* defines the circumstances under which the dialogue game begins, including the expectations and commitments of the dialogue participants upon entering the game.
2. The *dialogue acts* define the repertoire of messages. A dialogue act consist of a dialogue act type (called performative by FIPA), a speaker, an addressee and an expression that represents the content. For example, in dialogues for information exchange we find $\mathbf{inform}(i, j, \varphi)$ and $\mathbf{question}(i, j, \psi)$. Here i is the speaker, j is the addressee, φ is a proposition and ψ is an expression that represents an issue: the semantic content of a question. In concessive negotiation we find $\mathbf{propose}(i, j, \varphi)$ where φ represents an offer, for example to about the price of a previously selected object.
3. *Combination rules* define under what circumstances a dialogue act is permitted or not, or obligatory or not. These rules incorporate the feasibility and sincerity preconditions of speech act theory. Combination rules implement conventional interaction patterns. For example, questions must be followed

by inform acts that count as answers. The combination rules also incorporate coherence constraints that specify, for example, that an answer must be relevant to some question.

4. *Update rules* define the meaning of the content of each dialogue act in terms of the changes to the commitment states of the participants. We write $C_i + \varphi$ to describe the result of updating agent i's commitments with φ, where φ may represent a proposition, an issue or an offer.

5. The *end contexts* define the circumstances under which a dialogue may end successfully or unsuccessfully.

Note that the approach is similar to the levels distinguished by Prakken and Sartor [35]. The *logical level* is concerned with the logical relations between the content of messages, such as consistency or relevance, or the attack relation between arguments in a dispute [13]. The *dialectical level* determines how moves affect the commitments of the participants. At this level we put our update rules. The *procedural level* is concerned with the way in which moves can be phrased, and in what order. At this level we find the dialogue acts, and combination rules. Coherence constraints are also placed at this level, but make use of the logical level. Finally, there is a fourth orthogonal *strategic* or *heuristic level*, which is concerned with the motivations of the agents themselves. Only in conjunction with individual strategies does a protocol determine the course of interaction.

Our example dialogue games are interpreted relative to a dialogue context $C = \langle C_1, ..., C_n, H, E \rangle$. A dialogue context consists of the commitments C_i of all participating agents i, along with a history H of all the acts that were uttered, and an environment model E, that contains basic facts about the dialogue situation, such as time, location and information about the roles of the participants.

$$\circ \qquad -\mathtt{inform}(i,j,\varphi); \mathtt{ack}(j,i,\varphi) \rightarrow \qquad \circ$$
$$\vert \qquad\qquad\qquad\qquad\qquad\qquad\qquad\qquad\qquad \vert$$
$$\langle C_i, C_j, H, E \rangle \qquad\qquad \langle C_i + \varphi, C_j + \varphi, H; \mathtt{inform}(i,j,\varphi); \mathtt{ack}(j,i,\varphi), E \rangle$$

Fig. 1. Accepted inform act and corresponding update

Now consider for example an $\mathtt{inform}(i, j, \psi)$ act (Figure 1). By the principle of sincerity, the inform commits the speaker to believing φ, so we must update C_i. The actual beliefs of i are irrelevant; what matters are the beliefs that i is committed to uphold on the basis of what was said. In other words: the speaker must appear to be sincere. If we suppose that addressee j accepts the information that φ, j is also committed to believe φ, so in that case we must also update C_j. Else we leave C_j as it is. Acceptance can be signalled explicitly by acknowledgement $\mathtt{ack}(j, i, \psi)$, or implicitly by a coherent continuation. More about acknowledgements below. After any accepted utterance, the history H is updated too.

The contents of a message are expressed in a first order language L. Based on this content language, we define a dialogue language L_d. Note that the definition of L_d is dependent on the specific dialogue game d.

Definition 1 (Language). Let $A = \{i, j, \ldots\}$ be the set of agent names, P_d be a set of dialogue act types for some dialogue game d, with $\alpha \in P_d$ and $\varphi \in L$. Then L_d is defined as follows:

$$\pi ::= \alpha(i, j, \varphi) \mid \pi; \pi' \mid \epsilon.$$

Intuitively, $\alpha(i, j, \varphi)$ means that agent i performs a dialogue act of type α towards agent j with semantic content φ. Sequence $\pi; \pi'$ means that first π and then π' should be done. Notation ϵ represents the empty sequence. The language can be further extended to a full protocol definition language, with for example if-then-else constructs, while-loops, or deadlines. An example of such constructs can be found in AUML [4]. For multiparty dialogue, j can be replaced with a set of addressees.

3.2 Information Exchange

Current theories of information exchange in natural language semantics assume that a dialogue context involves the *issues under discussion* [23, 25], in addition to the factual information being exchanged. Therefore, for each agent we record the issues it is apparently interested in, as well as the information it is committed to uphold, based on what has been said.

Definition 2 (Dialogue Context - Information Exchange). For each agent $i \in A$, let the *commitment state* be a tuple $C_i = \langle S_i, I_i \rangle$, where S_i is a set of closed formulae representing the information to which i is committed, and I_i is a set of formulae representing the issues to which i is committed.

Let *history* H be a sequence of dialogue acts, represented by a formula from L_p.

Let *environment* E be a set of ground formulae (no variables), representing basic facts about the dialogue situation. We can demand $E \subseteq S_i$ for all agents i, in which case the environment is part of the common ground of the agents, but this assumption is not necessary.

Now a *dialogue context* between agents $A = \{1, \ldots, n\}$, denoted as C, is an n-tuple consisting of the commitment states of the individual agents, the history, and the environment: $C = \langle C_1, \ldots, C_n, H, E \rangle$.

The following update definitions are rather straightforward. We restrict ourselves to $P_{\text{inf\_ex}} = \{\text{inform}, \text{question}\}$. Since π can be a complex expression, we define $C + \pi$ in a compositional way.

Definition 3 (Update - Information Exchange). Let $C = \langle C_1, \ldots, C_n, H, E \rangle$, $i, j \in A$, $\varphi \in L$ and $\pi, \pi_1, \pi_2 \in L_{\text{inf\_ex}}$. Then an update $C + \pi$ is defined as follows:

$$
\begin{aligned}
C + \text{inform}(i, j, \varphi) &= \langle\langle S_i \cup \{\varphi\}, I_i \rangle, \langle S_j \cup \{\varphi\}, I_j \rangle, H; \text{inform}(i, j, \varphi), E \rangle \\
C + \text{question}(i, j, \psi) &= \langle\langle S_i, I_i \cup \{\psi\} \rangle, \langle S_j, I_j \cup \{\psi\} \rangle, H; \text{question}(i, j, \varphi), E \rangle \\
C + \pi_1; \pi_2 &= (C + \pi_1) + \pi_2 \\
C + \epsilon &= C
\end{aligned}
$$

Relative to the issues recorded in the commitment states of an agent, a restricted notion of relevance can be defined [23]. A proposition is relevant when it partly resolves one of the issues in the context. Issues are represented here by first order formulas, possibly containing free variables, similar to Prolog queries. We say a formula φ *resolves* an issue ψ relative to a set of formulas S, in case there exists an assignment θ of variables to constants, such that $S, \varphi \models \psi\theta$. An issue ψ itself is relevant$_I$, whenever its resolution will resolve some other, more embedded, issue χ. Other definitions are quite possible. For example, we may stipulate that all questions are relevant. Note that we can not define relevance of questions by referring to the goals of the asker, since we only have access to what was said.

In our restricted version of information exchange, we demand that a contribution to an information exchange must also be informative and consistent. Consistency is the usual notion. A proposition is considered informative, when it is not already derivable from previous commitments; likewise for an issue. A fourth restriction, that information should not be over-informative, is left out for simplicity. Although these constraints roughly correspond to the maximes of Grice, they do not necessarily assume that agents are cooperative; they just require that agents behave as if they are cooperative.

In general we use notation $\texttt{coherent}(d, C, \pi)$ to denote that dialogue π of type d is coherent in dialogue context C. Again, it is defined compositionally.

Definition 4 (Coherence - Information Exchange). Let C be a dialogue context, $\pi_1, \pi_2 \in L_{\texttt{inf\_ex}}$ and $i, j \in A$ and $\varphi \in L$. Then, $\texttt{coherent}(\texttt{inf\_ex}, C, \pi)$ is defined as follows:

$\texttt{coherent}(\texttt{inf\_ex}, C, \texttt{inform}(i,j,\varphi)) \Leftrightarrow$
  $\texttt{consistent}(C_i, \varphi) \ \&$ (consistent for speaker)
  $\texttt{relevant}(C_j, \varphi) \ \&$ (relevant for addressee)
  $\texttt{informative}(C_i, \varphi), \&$ (informative for both)
  $\texttt{informative}(C_j, \varphi),$

$\texttt{coherent}(\texttt{inf\_ex}, C, \texttt{question}(i,j,\psi)) \Leftrightarrow$
  $\texttt{relevant}_I(C_i, \psi) \ \&$ (relevant for speaker)
  $\texttt{informative}_I(C_i, \psi), \&$ (informative for both)
  $\texttt{informative}_I(C_j, \psi),$

where for $x \in \{i, j\}$
  $\texttt{consistent}(\langle S_x, I_x \rangle, \varphi)$ iff $S_x, \varphi \not\models \bot$
  $\texttt{relevant}(\langle S_x, I_x \rangle, \varphi)$ iff there is a $\psi \in I_x$ and $S_x, \varphi \models \psi\theta$, for some θ
  $\texttt{relevant}_I(\langle S_x, I_x \rangle, \psi)$ iff there is a $\chi \in I_x$ and $S_x, \psi \models \chi$ i.e. for all θ
  $\texttt{informative}(\langle S_x, I_x \rangle, \varphi)$ iff $S_x \not\models \varphi$
  $\texttt{informative}_I(\langle S_x, I_x \rangle, \psi)$ iff $I_x \not\models \psi$

$\texttt{coherent}(\texttt{inf\_ex}, C, \pi_1; \pi_2) \Leftrightarrow \texttt{coherent}(\texttt{inf\_ex}, C, \pi_1) \ \&$
  $\texttt{coherent}(\texttt{inf\_ex}, C + \pi_1, \pi_2)$
$\texttt{coherent}(\texttt{inf\_ex}, C, \epsilon) \quad \Leftrightarrow \top$

An information exchange presupposes a so called *information potential*: there is some issue that the 'novice' is interested in, and that it expects to be known by the 'expert'. Unfortunately, we can only use public commitments; not the real interests of the agents, so we cannot express this constraint in the initial context. Therefore we have the following rather weak definition of an initial context.

Definition 5 (Initial Context - Information Exchange). Let $A = \{i, j\}$ be the participants. Let ϵ be the empty formula and E_0 the initial environment, then $C^0 = \langle \langle \emptyset, \emptyset \rangle, \langle \emptyset, \emptyset \rangle, E_0, \epsilon \rangle$ is the initial state of an information exchange.

Termination of an information exchange means that all issues are resolved.

Definition 6 (End context - Information Exchange). Let $A = \{i, j\}$ be the participants, then $C^+ = \langle \langle S_i, I_i \rangle, \langle S_j, I_j \rangle, E, H \rangle$ is a successful end context of an information exchange, iff $C^0 + H = C^+$, and $\texttt{coherent}(\texttt{inf\_ex}, C^0, H)$ and for all $\psi \in I_i \cup I_j$, $S_j \models \psi\theta$ or $S_i \models \psi\theta$, for some assignment θ.

3.3   Information Exchange with Grounding

The definitions above do not account for the fact that the speaker's commitments may differ from the addressee's commitments, for example in case the addressee does not accept some information. Let us try to take 'grounding' into account [9]. Grounding is the process of acknowledgement by which the content of utterances is added to the common ground. An update by the addressee will only take place after an utterance has been accepted. Acceptance is either signalled explicitly by an acknowledgement, or implicitly by a coherent continuation. Although in general the grounding process is very complex, both for human and artificial languages[1], our model can account for a simplified version of it. The trick it is to put constraints on the latest contribution to the dialogue history.

Suppose that acceptance of an inform act $\texttt{inform}(i, j, \varphi)$ is expressed by an acknowledgement $\texttt{ack}(j, i, \varphi)$. An inform act that is not (yet) acknowledged is added to the speaker's commitments and to the history, but not (yet) to the addressee's commitments. Note that inform acts also function as a kind of acknowledgement to a question.

Definition 7 (Update - Information Exchange with Grounding). Let $C = \langle C_1, ..., C_n, H, E \rangle$, $i, j \in A$, $\varphi \in L$ and $\pi, \pi_1, \pi_2 \in L_{\texttt{inf-ex}'}$. Then an update $C + \pi$ is defined as follows:

$$\langle \langle S_i, I_i \rangle, \langle S_j, I_j \rangle, H, E \rangle + \texttt{inform}(i, j, \varphi) =$$
$$\langle \langle S_i \cup \{\varphi\}, I_i \rangle, \langle S_j, I_j \rangle, H; \texttt{inform}(i, j, \varphi), E \rangle$$
$$\langle \langle S_i, I_i \rangle, \langle S_j, I_j \rangle, H; \texttt{inform}(i, j, \varphi), E \rangle + \texttt{ack}(i, j, \varphi) =$$
$$\langle \langle S_i, I_i \rangle, \langle S_j \cup \{\varphi\}, I_j \rangle, H; \texttt{inform}(i, j, \varphi); \texttt{ack}(i, j, \varphi), E \rangle$$
$$\langle \langle S_i, I_i \rangle, \langle S_j, I_j \rangle, H, E \rangle + \texttt{question}(i, j, \varphi) =$$
$$\langle \langle S_i, I_i \cup \{\varphi\} \rangle, \langle S_j, I_j \rangle, H; \texttt{question}(i, j, \varphi), E \rangle$$
$$\langle \langle S_i, I_i \rangle, \langle S_j, I_j \rangle, H; \texttt{question}(i, j, \varphi), E \rangle + \texttt{inform}(i, j, \psi) =$$
$$\langle \langle S_i, I_i \rangle, \langle S_j \cup \{\psi\}, I_j \cup \{\varphi\} \rangle, H; \texttt{question}(i, j, \varphi)\texttt{inform}(i, j, \varphi), E \rangle$$
$$C + \pi_1; \pi_2 = (C + \pi_1) + \pi_2$$
$$C + \epsilon = C$$

---

[1] Think of the handshake logic in internet protocols like TCP.

Obviously, the definition of coherence would have to be extended in a similar way to accommodate interaction patterns for acknowledgement. This is an issue for further research.

3.4   Concessive Negotiation

A concessive negotiation is a rather restricted type of dialogue. It is inspired by the *monotonic concession protocol*, which has been studied extensively, see for example [36]. We assume that participants are making bids that refer to an object, of which it has previously been decided that one agent, the buyer, wants to buy it and that the other agent, the seller, wants to sell it. In this version, we let $P_{co\_neg} = \{\texttt{propose}\}$ and we require that the content of all messages is of the form $\texttt{price}(x)$ where x is a positive amount.

For the dialogue contexts, we just re-use definition 2, although we do not use the issues. Note that we could have left out the commitment states altogether; all work can be done by the history. That would also remove the need for update rules. But as soon as we allow versions of the protocol with exceptions, or decommitment, we must record commitments separate from history.

Definition 8 (Dialogue Context - Concessive Negotiation).
Identical to definition 2.

The main coherence relation is that of a bid being a concession. In this restricted version, a concession means a lower price for the seller, and a higher price for the buyer. Obviously more interesting definitions of a concession exist for less well-defined domains, such as tasks in a household:

(4) A. Can you put the garbage out?
     B. Only if you will do the dishes.

In both cases, a concession means that a proposal is made which is less preferred than the previously made proposals, where the preference order is partly related to the role (buyer, seller) and partly to personal preferences. So to be coherent, an offer must fit the expected preferences belonging to the role of the speaker.

Note that unlike information exchange, negotiation does not involve logical consistency of commitments, since each price is strictly speaking inconsistent with previously mentioned prices. Informativeness follows from concession, which is a much stronger notion. Relevance would also follow from concession, if each agent were interested in the issue $\texttt{price}(x)$, i.e. what price is going to be paid.

Definition 9 (Coherence - Concessive Negotiation). Let $A = \{b, s\}$ with x, y variables ranging over A and $C = \langle C_b, C_s, H, E \rangle$, such that $E \models \texttt{buyer}(b) \land \texttt{seller}(s)$, then define:

$$\texttt{coherent}(\texttt{co\_neg}, C, \texttt{propose}(x, y, \texttt{price}(u))) \Leftrightarrow$$
$$\texttt{fits\_role}(C, x, \texttt{price}(u)) \ \&$$
$$\texttt{concession}(C, x, \texttt{price}(u)).$$
$$\texttt{coherent}(\texttt{co\_neg}, C, \pi_1; \pi_2) \Leftrightarrow \texttt{coherent}(\texttt{co\_neg}, C, \pi_1) \ \&$$
$$\texttt{coherent}(\texttt{co\_neg}, C + \pi_1, \pi_2)$$
$$\texttt{coherent}(\texttt{co\_neg}, C, \epsilon) \qquad \Leftrightarrow \top$$

where
$$\texttt{fits\_role}(\langle C_x, C_y, \epsilon, E\rangle, x, \texttt{price}(u)) \Leftarrow \top$$
$$\texttt{fits\_role}(\langle C_x, C_y, \pi, E\rangle, x, \texttt{price}(u)) \Leftarrow$$
$$\quad E \models \texttt{buyer}(x) \wedge \texttt{seller}(y) \;\&\; C_y \models \texttt{price}(v) \;\&\; u \leq v.$$
$$\texttt{fits\_role}(\langle C_x, C_y, \pi, E\rangle, y, \texttt{price}(v)) \Leftarrow$$
$$\quad E \models \texttt{buyer}(x) \wedge \texttt{seller}(y) \;\&\; C_x \models \texttt{price}(u) \;\&\; u \leq v.$$
and
$$\texttt{concession}(\langle C_x, C_y, \epsilon, E\rangle, x, \texttt{price}(u)) \Leftarrow \top$$
$$\texttt{concession}(\langle C_x, C_y, \pi, E\rangle, x, \texttt{price}(u)) \Leftarrow$$
$$\quad E \models \texttt{buyer}(x) \;\&\; C_x \models \texttt{price}(u') \;\&\; u' < u.$$
$$\texttt{concession}(\langle C_x, C_y, \pi, E\rangle, y, \texttt{price}(v)) \Leftarrow$$
$$\quad E \models \texttt{seller}(y) \;\&\; C_y \models \texttt{price}(v') \;\&\; v < v'.$$

The update rules are again rather straightforward. Each bid replaces the previous ones. This illustrates that updates do not have to be monotonic.

Definition 10 (Update - Concessive Negotiation). Let $A = \{b, s\}$, with x, y variables ranging over A, and $C = \langle C_b, C_s, H, E\rangle$, then define

$$C + \texttt{propose}(x, y, \texttt{price}(v)) =$$
$$\quad \langle\langle (S_x \setminus \{\texttt{price}(u)\}) \cup \{\texttt{price}(v)\}, I_x\rangle, H; \texttt{propose}(x, y, \texttt{price}(v)), E\rangle$$
$$C + \pi_1; \pi_2 \;=\; (C + \pi_1) + \pi_2$$
$$C + \epsilon \qquad = \; C$$

In the initial context, no agent has made a bid yet.

Definition 11 (Initial Context - Concessive Negotiation). Let $A = \{b, s\}$ and $E_0 \models \texttt{buyer}(b) \wedge \texttt{seller}(s)$, then $C^0 = \langle\langle\emptyset, \emptyset\rangle, \langle\emptyset, \emptyset\rangle, \epsilon, E_0\rangle$ is an initial state of a concessive negotiation.

At the end contexts, an agreement about the price must have been reached.

Definition 12 (End Context - Concessive Negotiation).
$C^+ = \langle\langle\{\texttt{price}(u)\}, \emptyset\rangle, \langle\{\texttt{price}(v)\}, \emptyset\rangle, H, E\rangle$ is a successful end state of a concessive negotiation, iff $u = v$, $C^0 + H = C^+$, and $\texttt{coherent}(\texttt{co\_neg}, C^0, H)$.

3.5   Dispute and Commissive Dialogues

The approach can be extended to dispute. In that case, the semantic *attack* relation [13] is the main ingredient used in coherence constraints.

Although we believe the approach would also work for dialogues that produce commitments, i.e. accepted requests, accepted proposals, and closed negotiations and deliberation in general, it is currently an open problem how to formalize the *fulfillment* relation for commitments, that would be the main candidate as a semantic relation underlying coherence for such dialogues. Under what conditions can we say a commitment has been fulfilled, or a promise has been kept? This will be left for further research.

4   Coherence in Agent Interaction

Several communication infrastructures for multiagent systems have become available [11, 5, 22], some of which conform to the FIPA recommendations [16]. Many of these systems provide a message passing mechanism that ensures messages are delivered, provided they are addressed using the right identifier. Alternatively, we may assume a shared data space with coordination mechanisms to regulate communication [8, 33].

4.1   Approaches to Coherence Validation

Given an agent communication platform, how can violations of coherence constraints be detected and reported? We discuss some possible architectures.

1. By a central *director* agent, that controls the interaction. An example is the role of an auctioneer in an auction. The auctioneer will only recognize well-formed and coherent bids. Another example is the role of a chairman in a meeting, that assigns turns, manages speaking time and sets the topic for each speaker. In case of violations, a director has the authority to sanction the violator, for example by banishment from the group.
2. By connecting each agent to an individual *governor* agent, as in ISLANDER [14]. The governor provides an API-like interface that allows an external agent to interact with other agents in the system and with the environment. The interface works as a filter: potential violations are simply blocked.
3. By getting each *participant* individually to play the role of a governor, and decide whether or not to accept messages. Incoherent or non well-formed messages are either ignored or explicitly rejected. One might say that in this case the protocol has been reduced to the message layer, and that all the work is now done by the strategy of the individual agents. In other words: rejecting a message has become a strategic action. Note that this solution puts a heavy requirement on the knowledge and reasoning capabilities of an agent. Each agent should know the protocol, be able to detect violations, and decide whether it is more beneficial to reject a message, or leave incoherencies unnoticed and maintain good relations with the speaker.
4. By means of a hybrid approach, in which a *mediator* agent monitors the interactions to detect and report violations as they occur. Such a mediator agent can have the same knowledge and reasoning capacities as other agents in the environment; it needs no special privileges except for access to the messages. The protocol can be made accessible on the platform, so all agents know how to behave. The advantage of having a mediator, is that the agents do not require a complex violation detection mechanism. With respect to violations, several different sanction policies can be devised. For example, the mediator can suffice with sending all affected agents a violation report. Agents can then decide a sanction for themselves, e.g., to abandon the interaction, put the violator on a black list, or continue after all. Alternatively, the mediator might request the agent management system to have the agent removed from the platform, or be banned for future occasions.

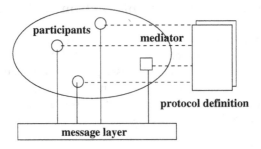

Fig. 2. Incoherence detection through a mediator on the platform

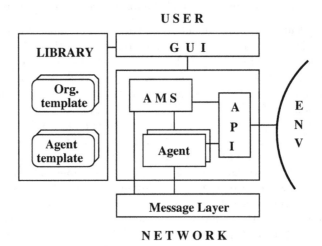

Fig. 3. Agent Platform

In the remainder of this section we explore the last option. The general set up of a mediator in a platform, is depicted in figure 2.

But before we can explain the implementation of a mediator, we first need to be more specific about the agent platform. We take the 3APL agent platform as an example; the approach is also possible in other platforms.

4.2   Agent Platform

Figure 3 shows an overview of the 3APL agent platform, which follows FIPA recommendations [16] and is therefore rather general. Such a platform provides communication and coordination facilities, access to knowledge sources, and a way of mediating between different agents. Many of these facilities are accessed through the *agent management system* (AMS) which also controls entry and exit of agents on the platform.

In the case of 3APL, the platform can also be used to assist programmers during development. A graphical user interface (GUI) enables the programmer to load agents from a library, implement and execute them, and observe their behavior.

Individual Agents. Figure 4 shows an example of a 3APL agent program. 3APL closely follows the BDI paradigm. It contains a *goal base*, and a *belief base*. These constructs together represent an agent's mental state throughout the execution of the program. The belief base is currently implemented using a Prolog interpreter. It allows one to reason, and match queries to beliefs. The agents *capabilities* are of the form {`Pre`}`Capability`{`Post`}, where both `Pre` and `Post` are formulas representing beliefs. A program transforms the mental state by means of a number of *practical reasoning rules*. These rules generally are of the form `Goal` ← `Guard` | `Body`, where the guard is a test on the belief base. The body contains goals, capabilities or combinations of these using sequence, while, if-then-else or a test. A test succeeds if a Prolog query to the belief base succeeds. By sending and receiving messages, facts of the form `sent` or `received` are added to the belief base.

Shared Knowledge File. For some applications, an agent needs general background knowledge or skills. Therefore an external Prolog file can be loaded. The agent behaves as if the clauses in the Prolog file are part of its personal belief base. This facility is used to distribute the protocol and make the coherence relations accessible to all agents, including the mediator.

Communication Management. The 3APL agent platform provides communication by means of message passing. A message will be delivered by the message layer, provided the agent management system knows the identifier of the agent being addressed. The messages themselves have the structure of speech acts, with a sender, receiver and a content, which is compliant with the FIPA standards for agent communication [15].

4.3   Mediator

A 3APL template for a mediator agent is shown in figure 4. This version applies a simple message driven monitor-detect-report loop. For each message that is sent on the platform, a copy is sent to the mediator. The mediator maintains a list of interaction sessions, containing a representation of the context with a message history, the particular dialogue game, the participating agents and their roles. The session list is matched against the incoming message. Based on a classification procedure, the mediator decides which protocol may be applicable. The classification is based on the set of dialogue acts that may occur in a certain dialogue game, but also takes the current participants into account. Because one dialogue act type can occur in several protocols, there may be a list of several candidate sessions. When possible, the message identifier and the session identifiers are used to speed up this matching process.

   If the mediator can match the incoming message to one of the candidate sessions such that it makes a coherent contribution, the message is stored as part

```
PROGRAM "mediator"

LOAD "H:\protocol.pl" \\ classify\2, update\2, coherent\3, sanction\3

CAPABILITIES: {session(SID, DialGame, As, C)} Store(C1)
   {NOT session(SID, DialGame, As, C), session(SID, DialGame, As, C1)},
   {} StoreViolation(Message,Session) { violation(Message, Session) }
   \\ ...

BELIEFBASE:
\\ example of a session fact, with (C_harry, C_sally, Hist, Env)
\\ session(023,info_exch,[harry,sally],
\\   c(c_harry([],[dep_time(kl108,?Time)]),c_sally([],[])),
\\   [m(023,harry,[sally],question,dep_time(kl108,?Time))],[ams, 9:34]))

GOALBASE: monitor_detect_report(),sanction()

RULEBASE: monitor_detect_report() <- received(Id,Sender,Addrs,Perf,Phi) |
    BEGIN                                             // monitor
        classify( m(Id,Sender,Addrs,Perf,Phi), DialGames)?;
        member(DialGame, DialGames)?;
        session(SID, DialGame, As, C)?;
        IF  member(Sender,As) AND subset(Addrs, As) AND   // detect
            coherent(DialGame, C, m(Id,Sender,Addrs,Perf, Phi))
        THEN
            BEGIN
                update(DialGame, m(Id,Sender,Addrs,Perf,Phi), C, C1)?;
                Store( C1 );
            END
        ELSE
            BEGIN                                         // report
                Send(99, [Sender|Addrs], announce,
                    violation( m(Id,Sender,Addrs,Perf,Phi),
                               session(SID, DialGame, As, C)));
                StoreViolation( m(Id,Sender,Addrs,Perf,Phi),
                               session(SID, DialGame, As, C))
            END
    END,

sanction() <-  violation(Message,Session) |
    BEGIN
        sanction_policy(Message, Session, Sanction)?;
        execute(Sanction)                    // to be filled in
    END.
```

Fig. 4. 3APL template for a mediator agent

of that session. If no such match can be made, the message is deemed incoherent. In that case the mediator sends a so called *violation report* to all participants involved: the violator and the addressees of the message. The violation report contains references to the message and the session. Violations are also stored for later reference. Based on a sanctioning policy, further action may be initiated. A slot for such action is indicated in the template.

5   Related Research

The idea that a protocol should be seen as a resource, rather than as a fixed given entity, is implicit in work on *skeleton programming* [38]. Here, agents are generated on the basis of protocol definitions, using so called skeleton programs. Only agent specific details, such as the strategy, will need to be filled in by the programmer. Architectures that allow validation of protocols are becoming more and more common. See for example [29] for an approach that uses open protocols, expressed in Petri Nets. As far as we know, we are the first to propose protocol validation as a service provided by the communication platform.

With respect to coherence conditions, work from linguistics lies outside the scope of this paper. We refer to our favorite information state approach [2, 25] for more information. There is little work on semantic relations in the context of agent communication. An interesting exception is the work by McBurney and Parsons [31] on scientific investigation. They describe a risk agora, as they call it, that allows the storage of multiple arguments for and against some claim. Another example is their recent work on deliberation dialogues [30].

Finally, the different ways in which protocols can be enforced, is reminiscent of work on normative systems and the enforcement of policies [6]. A recent and very interesting development, is the design of specific *policy languages*. The idea is that the behavior of agents is influenced by a myriad of policies, based on the various groups and social contexts that they are part of. These policies may concern interactive behavior, as in our dialogue games, but they may also relate to other kinds of norms, permissions or expectations. Because policies may conflict, specific meta policies exist to resolve such conflicts. This requires that agents reason about policies, which must therefore be expressed in some declarative form [24].

6   Conclusion

We have proposed a way to formulate coherence constraints on the content of messages in agent communication protocols, in addition to the usual syntactic constraints. The notion is inspired by linguistic research. Protocols of two kinds of dialogue types, information exchange and concessive negotiation, can be reformulated in terms of coherence constraints.

We have discussed several ways in which coherence checks can be implemented in an agent communication infrastructure: using a central director, a governor for each individual agent, by the agents themselves or by means of a mediation service provided by the platform. An architecture using a mediator, is presented in detail. The approach is illustrated using the the 3APL communication infrastructure.

The design is currently being implemented in the 3APL platform. Experiments for empirical evaluation of the approach are envisioned.

With respect to the two criticisms raised against the FIPA approach in the introduction, we may conclude the following.

1. A mediator agent with similar capabilities and privileges as other agents, turns the semantics of the speech acts and protocol into a public affair, and removes the necessity of accessing the mental states of agents.
2. Coherence constraints make it possible to specify protocols in terms of the content and semantics of messages, and not just their syntax.

The proposals in this paper must be seen as extensions to the FIPA standards, which can be incorporated in an agent communication infrastructure that allows the kinds of reasoning needed. The article is not meant to criticize the FIPA standards as such.

References

1. Liliana Ardissono, Guido Boella, and Rossana Damiano. A plan-based model of misunderstandings in cooperative dialogue. *Human Computer Studies*, 48:649–679, 1998.
2. Nicholas Asher and Alex Lascarides. *Logics of Conversation*. Cambridge University Press, 2003.
3. J.L. Austin. *How to do things with words*. Harvard University Press, Cambridge Mass., 1962.
4. Bernhard Bauer, Jörg P. Müller, and James Odell. Agent UML: A formalism for specifying multiagent interaction. In M. Wooldridge, P. Ciancarini, and G. Weiss, editors, *Prodeedings of the 2nd International Workshop on Agent-Oriented Software Engineering (AOSE'01)*, LNCS, pages 91–103. Springer Verlag, 2001.
5. Fabio Bellifemine, Agostino Poggi, and Giovanni Rimassa. JADE: a FIPA2000 compliant agent development environment. In *Proceedings of the fifth international conference on autonomous agents (Agents'01)*, pages 216–217. ACM, 2001.
6. G. Boella, J. Hulstijn, and L. van der Torre. Virtual organizations as normative multiagent systems. In *Proceedings of the Hawaii International Conference on System Sciences (HICSS'05)*, to appear.
7. Jean Carletta, Amy Isard, Stephen Isard, Jacqueline C. Kowtko, Gwyneth Doherty-Sneddon, and Anne H. Anderson. The reliability of a dialogue structure coding scheme. *Computational linguistics*, 23(1):13–32, 1997.
8. N. Carriero and D. Gelernter. Linda in context. *Communications of the ACM*, 32:444–458, 1989.
9. H.H. Clark and S. A. Brennan. Grounding in communication. In L.B. Resnick, J.M. Levine, and S.D. Teasley, editors, *Perspecives on socially shared cognition*, pages 127–149. APA BOOKs, Waskington, D.C., 1991.
10. Robert T. Craig and Karen Tracy, editors. *Conversational Coherence: Form, Structure and Strategy*. Sage Publications, Beverly Hills, 1983.

11. M. Dastani, J. Hulstijn, Dignum, and J-J. Ch F. Meyer. Issues in multiagent system development. In *Third International Joint Conference on Autonomous Agents and Multi-Agent Systems (AAMAS'04)*, to appear.

12. M. Dastani, J. Hulstijn, and L. van der Torre. Dialogue games and negotiation. In *Proceedings of the Fifth International Conference on Autonomous Agents (AA'2001)*, pages 180–181. ACM Press, 2001.

13. P. M. Dung. On the acceptability of arguments and its fundamental role in nonmonotonic reasoning, logic programming and *n*-person games. *Artificial Intelligence*, 77:321–357, 1995.

14. M. Esteva, D. de la Cruz, and C. Sierra. ISLANDER: an electronic institutions editor. In *First Interantional Joint Conference on Autonoumous Agents and Multiagent Systems (AAMAS'02)*, pages 1045 – 1052. ACM Press, 2002.

15. FIPA. FIPA ACL message structure specification. Technical Report XC00061, Foundation for Intelligent Physical Agents, 2001.

16. FIPA. FIPA agent management specification. Sc0023j, Foundation for Intelligent Physical Agents, 2002.

17. FIPA. FIPA interaction protocol specifications. Technical Report SC00026 – SC00036, Foundation for Intelligent Physical Agents, 2002.

18. Barabara J. Grosz and Sarit Kraus. Collaborative plans for complex group action. *Artificial Intelligence*, 86(2):269–357, 1996.

19. Barbara J. Grosz and Candace L. Sidner. Attentions, intentions and the structure of discourse. *Computational Linguistics*, 12:175–204, 1986.

20. M.A.K. Halliday and R. Hasan. *Cohesion in English*. Longman, New York, 1976.

21. K.V. Hindriks, F.S. de Boer, W. van der Hoek, and J.-J.Ch. Meyer. Agent programming in 3APL. *Autonomous Agents and Multi-Agent Systems*, 2(4):357–401, 1999.

22. Nick Howden, Ralph Ronnquist, Andrew Hodgson, and Andrew Lucas. Jack summary of an agent infrastructure. In *5th International Conference on Autonomous Agents*. 2001.

23. Joris Hulstijn. *Dialogue Models for Inquiry and Transaction*. PhD thesis, University of Twente, Enschede, 2000.

24. Lalana Kagal and Tim Finin. Modeling conversation policies using permissions and obligations. In Frank Dignum, Rogier van Eijk, and Marc-Philippe Huget, editors, *Developments in Agent Communication (this volume), Proceedings of the AAMAS'04 workshop on Agent Communbication, July, New York*, volume LNCS XXXX. Springer Verlag, Berlin, 2005.

25. Stafan Larsson and David Traum. Information state and dialogue management in the TRINDI dialogue move engine toolkit. *Natural Language Engineering*, 6(3-4):323 – 340, 2000.

26. Karen E. Lochbaum. A collaborative planning model of intentional structure. *Computational Linguistics*, 24(4):525–572, 1998.

27. William C. Mann. Dialogue games: Conventions of human interaction. *Argumentation*, 2:511–532, 1988.

28. William C. Mann and Sandra A. Thompson. Rhetorical structure theory: Towards a functional theory of text organization. *Text*, 8(3):243–281, 1988.

29. Hamza Mazouzi, Amal El Fallah Seghrouchni, and Serge Haddad. Open protocol design for complex interactions in multi-agent systems. In *Proceedings of the 1st international joint conference on Autonomous agents and multiagent systems (AAMAS'02)*, pages 517 – 526. ACM Press, 2002.

30. P. McBurney and S. Parsons. A denotational semantics for deliberation dialogues. In N.R. Jennings, C. Sierra, L. Sonenberg, and M. Tambe, editors, *Proceedings of the third International Joint Conference on Autonomous Agents and Multiagent Systems (AAMAS'04)*, pages 86–93. ACM Press, 2004.
31. Peter McBurney and Simon Parsons. Representing epistemic uncertainty by means of dialectical argumentation. *Annals of Mathematics and Artificial Intelligence*, 32(1):125–169, 2001.
32. Peter McBurney and Simon Parsons. Games that agents play: A formal framework for dialogues between autonomous agents. *Journal of Logic, Language and Information*, 11(3):315–334, 2002.
33. Andrea Omicini. Towards a notion of agent coordination context. In D. Marinescu and C. Lee, editors, *Process Coordination and Ubiquitous Computing*, page 187200. CRC Press, 2002.
34. Jeremy Pitt and Abe Mamdani. Some remarks on the semantics of FIPA's agent communication language. *Autonomous Agents and Multi-Agent Systems*, 2(4):333–356, 1999.
35. H. Prakken and G. Sartor. Modelling reasoning with precedents in a formal dialogue game. *Artificial Intelligence and Law*, 6:231–287, 1998.
36. Jeffrey S. Rosenschein and Gilad Zlotkin. *Rules of Encounter: designing conventions for automated negotiation among computers*. MIT Press, Cambridge Mass., 1994.
37. John R. Searle. *Speech acts: an Essay in the Philosophy of Language*. Cambridge University Press, Cambridge, 1969.
38. Wamberto W. Vasconcelos, Jordi Sabater, Carlos Sierra, and Joaquim Querol. Skeleton-based agent development for electronic institutions. In *First Interantional Joint Conference on Autonoumous Agents and Multiagent Systems (AAMAS'02)*, pages 696–703. ACM Press, 2002.
39. Bonnie Webber. Computational perspectives on discourse and dialogue. In Deborah Schiffrin, Deborah Tannen, and Heidi Hamilton, editors, *The Handbook of Discourse Analysis*. Blackwell Publishers Ltd., 2001.
40. Michael. J. Wooldridge. Semantic issues in the verification of agent communication languages. *Journal of Autonomous Agents and Multi-Agent Systems*, 3(1):9–31, 2000.
41. P. Yolum and M. P. Singh. Flexible protocol specification and execution: Applying event calculus planning using commitments. In *Proceedings of the 1st International Joint Conference on Autonomous Agents and MultiAgent Systems (AAMAS'02)*, pages 527–534. ACM Press, 2002.

Formulating Agent Communication Semantics and Pragmatics as Behavioral Expectations*

Matthias Nickles, Michael Rovatsos, and Gerhard Weiss

AI/Cognition group, Department of Informatics, Technical University Munich (TUM)
D-85748 Garching bei München, Germany
{nickles, rovatsos, weissg}@cs.tum.edu

Abstract. Although several approaches to the semantics of agent communication have been proposed, none of them is really suitable for dealing with agent
autonomy, which is a decisive property of artificial agents. This paper introduces
an observation-based approach to the semantics of agent communication, which
combines benefits of the two most influential traditional approaches to agent communication semantics, namely the *mentalistic* (agent-centric) and the *objectivist*
(i.e., commitment- or protocol-oriented) approach. Our model makes use of the
fact that the most general meaning of agent utterances lays in their expectable *consequences* in terms of agent actions, and that communications result from hidden
but nevertheless rational and to some extent reliable agent intentions. In this work,
we present a formal framework which enables the empirical derivation of communication meanings from the observation of rational agent utterances, and introduce
thereby a probabilistic and utility-oriented perspective of social commitments.

Keywords: Agent Communication Languages, Open Multiagent Systems, Computational Autonomy, Stochastic Processes, Artificial Sociality.

1 Introduction

Currently, two major approaches to the meaning of agent communication in a broader
sense, covering both traditional sentence-level semantics and pragmatics, exist. The
mentalistic approach (e.g. [5, 6]) specifies the meaning of utterances by means of a description of the mental states of the respective agents (i.e., their beliefs and intentions,
and thus indirectly their behavior), while the more recent commitment-based *objectivist*
approaches (e.g. [3, 15], also called *social semantics*) try to determine communication
from an external point of view, focussing on public rules and inter-agent contracts. The
former approach has some well-known shortcomings, which eventually led to the development of the latter: Especially in *open* multiagent systems, agents appear more or
less as black boxes, which makes it in general impossible to impose and verify a semantics described in terms of agent cognition. They could only be put into practice
making simplifying but unrealistic assumptions to ensure mental homogeneity among
the agents, for example that the interacting agents were benevolent and sincere, and it

---

* This article is an extended and revised version of [12].

R.M. van Eijk et al. (Eds.): AC 2004, LNAI 3396, pp. 153–172, 2005.
© Springer-Verlag Berlin Heidelberg 2005

neglects the social context of utterances. Objectivist semantics in contrast is fully verifiable, it achieves a big deal of complexity reduction through limiting itself to a small set of normative rules, and has therefore been a significant step ahead. But it oversimplifies social processes, and it doesn't have a concept of meaning indefiniteness, rational attitude (but see [4] for an objectivist approach to modeling the "intuitive" meaning of speech acts) and agent malevolence. In contrast to these approaches, we propose a semantics which is based on the assumption that the meaning of utterances lies basically in their *consequences* in terms of *expectable* future agent actions and other events which can be continuously learned and adapted from observed communications [8, 9]. These consequences are represented as probabilistic *Social Interaction Structures*, which are a variant of *Expectation Networks* [8, 11], and they are learned from ongoing communication processes by a *semantics observer* that can be either an agent participating in the communication himself, or an external agent (e.g., a special middle agent, or a supervision facility [13] of the system designer or application users). This learning task puts two general assumptions about agent communication into practice: i) observed agent interactions within a certain social context are likely to reoccur in similar situations in the future (empirical stationarity assumption), and ii) agents act individually but more or less rationally towards their communicated goals within a *limited sphere of communication* (limiting their commitments' trustability and the predictability of other behavioral characteristics). Therefore, the semantics observer deals with the "intentional stances" [2] of otherwise opaque agents towards their communicated goals and believes (learned empirically from observed utterances) rather than with real "cognitive agents". From these assumptions, we retrieve the following replacements for traditional semantical concepts:

- Verification of semantics according to normative rules as in social semantics $\rightarrow$ Verification regarding a learned empirical model of observed agent communication processes
- Assumption of a certain mental agent architecture and cognition $\rightarrow$ revisable, probabilistic expectation of bounded rational behavior (the so called *rational hulls* of communications)
- Social commitments and agent sincerity $\rightarrow$ revisable, probabilistic expectation of the limited maintenance of communicated goals by the uttering agents

For lack of space, and in order to provide a general, flexible approach, we do not make use of a concrete ACL in this work. Instead, we propose the dynamic semantics of so-called *Elementary Communication Acts* (ECAs) which obtain their concrete meaning not from some pre-defined speech-act typology as usual, but from their usage context. The theoretical assumption behind ECAs is that all kinds of speech acts can be translated into one or more demands to act in pragmatical conformance with a declared course of events (a certain probability distribution of events in the future), in which each ECA can be contextualized with companion social structures resulting from other ECAs to clarify and get accepted the demand (e.g. sanctions). E.g., an assertive act is the request to communicate in conformance with the expressed belief from now on, a command is a request to perform the described actions in order to reach the declared future world state, accompanied with norms and the threatening with sanctions, and the utterance of a performative sentence is also an assertive act which demands to communicate *as if* the proposed (social) consequences this act "makes true" were/would become true in fact. ECAs are represented as pointers to demanded and otherwise rather unlikely world states within some assumably shared world knowledge represented as a so-called *Expectation Network*. Thus, the abstract a priory semantics of ECAs (in contrast to their full meaning which is derived empirically at run-time) can be considered to be the low-level replacement of both traditional a priory sentence semantics (concerned with the propositional content of messages, based on an assumably shared ontology with a semantics given as truth-conditions) and speech act types. In contrast, the "full semantics" of an actually uttered ECA is the probability distribution of expected future events triggered by this utterance.

The remainder of this paper is organized as follows: The next section introduces our novel approach to ACL semantics and pragmatics. Section 3 defines *Expectation Networks* as the data structure used to describe agent communication semantics empirically. Section 4 provides a formal learning and adaptation framework for social (i.e., communication) structures, and finally, section 5 draws some conclusions regarding current limitations of our approach and future work.

2 A Novel Approach to the Modeling of Communication

In this section, we provide an informal overview of our approaches called *Empirical Agent Communication Semantics* [8, 9, 10] and *Empirical-Rational Agent Communication Semantics* [12] in order to motivate the formal framework presented in the following sections.

In its most general sense, the *semantics*[1] of agent communication describes the effect a single communication has in the context of / on its environment. Both the context and the effect can include / affect every changeable aspect of the uttering agents' environment and the agent itself, e.g. agent cognition, other communications, social structures, the "physical" environment, the mental dispositions of the uttering and other agents. Having knowledge about the semantics of agent communication has several obvious advantages, both for the agents (active and passive) and the designer of the agent-based application. Since for truly autonomous black-box agents, every kind of meaningful interaction can be expressed in terms of symbolic, rejectable communications *only* [1, 8] (in contrast to the direct influencing of agents through physical actions or commands), agent communication semantics covers *every* aspect of socially relevant behavior, from social mechanism design (e.g. auctions) and game theory to large artificial societies.

2.1 Demands and Issues

Traditionally, the comprehensive semantics mentioned above is assumed to have two dimensions that need to be covered by a comprehensive approach to the semantics of agent communication: First, the *sentence level*, which is the aspect of meaning that is

---

[1] If not stated otherwise, we use the term "semantics" in the computer scientific sense, not as a linguistic term. Linguists would talk about "meaning" instead, covering both linguistic sentence semantics and pragmatics.

traditionally subject of linguistical semantics. This aspect of meaning is contextualized with an environmental description in the form of an *assumably* (not necessarily actually) shared *ontology* (maybe requiring the alignment of individual ontologies [14]). In addition, a calculus to describe objects and events within the environment the respective utterance refers to has to be provided, for example predicate logic and temporal modalities. The second dimension of meaning is its *pragmatics*, i.e., the actual use and effect of utterances in social encounters. Contemporary approaches to agent communication language (ACL) semantics go pretty far in their claimed area of coverage, since they attach either far-reaching mentalistic or social-normative assumptions to single ACL sentences. This leads to a mixture of traditional sentence-level semantics and pragmatics. Even though also sentence-level semantics largely depends from use-dependant contextual information, required e.g. for the resolution of anaphora, most linguists carefully prevent the mixing of (socio-)pragmatic issues and sentence-level semantics. In contrast, most approaches to ACL semantics are in fact "pragsemantics" since they include elements which traditionally belong to pragmatics, mostly borrowed from speech-act theory and socio-normative theories. In principle, there is nothing wrong with such an hybrid approach (at least for the case of formal languages, where things are less complicated than with human languages), and our approach follows this direction too. But there are several problems with the mentioned mentalistic and objectivist approaches to put "pragsemantics" into action, as discussed now.

Following [9], we have identified the following demands and issues for ACL semantics, for which we aim to provide a basic approach:

Expressibility. Communications are basically (possibly false) demands directed to other agents to bring about or to act in accordance with a certain projected (respectively asserted) world state (respectively point of view), in which a "world state" is a expected course of events or a proposed view of history. Thus, the means in order to bring these states about, possible reactions from other agents (including bystanders) and other aspects and implications of the initial and resulting states need to be modeled. In our opinion, neither the notation of social commitment nor the specification of mental agent properties are adequate order to do so. The former not, because it essentially reduces interaction meaning to contracting protocol semantics (leaving the term "commitment" itself rather under-specified [16]), the latter not also, because communication meaning external to the agents' minds can be modeled only indirectly.

Verifiability. Whereas most approaches to ACL semantics use this term in order to check if normatively imposed regulations are observed (i.e., if agents think and behave "correctly"), we use the term "verifiability" in a model-theoretical sense to express that a model of agent communication corresponds with observable processes of agent interactions, in which this model is to its largest part learned from observations itself, and only to a small, abstract part imposed normatively.

Flexibility and Support for Meaning Indifference, Emergence and Change. Current approaches to ACL semantics work if the set of speech act types is known a-priori and each locution denotes a fixed and known illocutionary act. Tackling these issues, Empirical-Rational Semantics restricts itself to a very small predefined core part, decomposes all kinds of communication acts into a single type of elementary act, and determines much of the actual semantics empirically at run-time.

Consideration of Heterogeneous Agent Architectures and Agent Insincerity. If the semantics of utterances is given in terms of mental agent states, it can either not be validated (from an agent-external point of view, e.g. of the responding agent, or of the system designer), or requires the restriction of agent autonomy (e.g. demanding sincerity). The latter also affects some "objectivist" approaches, if these require norm fulfilling, or make additional mentalistic assumptions (e.g. "whole-hearted satisfaction" [17]).

Consideration of Agent Intentionality and Rational Attitude. Communication has an unique property: It constructs a social situation, which is inherently consistent and reasonable, even if it opposes the "real world" outside communication and the cognitive beliefs of the agents: 1) Communicated information is supposed to be consistent with information previously communicated by the same agent, or this agent at least justifies his change of mind, 2) the agent defends and asserts his utterances by means of argumentation or other rational means like rewards and sanctions, and 3) information not expressed explicitly can be deduced from information communicated before and background knowledge. If, for example, in an open auction on the internet some agent a asserts "I will deliver the goods if you win the auction.", an observer does not need to believe him. But the observer believes that the further communication of a complies with this assertion. To make communication work, this belief is to some extent independent from reasoning about the true motives "within the agents mind". Agent a is supposed to act at least for some time in a rational manner in accordance with the social image that he *projects* for himself by means of communication (e.g., a sanctions the denial of his proposal, rewards its acceptance etc). The information about such (bounded-)rational attitude is implicitly associated with each communication of a self-interested agent, and is thus part of communication semantics. Commitment-based approaches largely neglect this kind of intentionality, moving ACL semantics towards contract making instead.

Interaction Process Generalization and Social Structures. Social structures like norms strongly influence the semantics of communications. If for example an agent appoints another agent to be group leader, an explicit acceptance by other agents is not necessary (in contrast to the joint acceptance of a commitment as in commitment-based semantics) if the appointing agent already has the necessary power granted by existing social structures. Empirical-Rational semantics supports such pre-structuring, and the extrapolation of past interaction experiences (if, e.g., the appointing agent has been successful in the past, it becomes more likely he also will with his new appointment, even before this proposal has been accepted explicitly).

Support for Agent Generalizations and Mass Communication. Current approaches to ACL semantics are intended primarily for dyadic situations. Some of them allow for message broadcasts, but they lack a concept for unification and weighting of multiple messages or, respectively, responses, to reflect a (possibly inconsistent) common point of view of multiple agents, or to enable collaboration in joint communicative action. It is hardly imaginable, how thousands or even millions of agents shall contribute to, e.g., the Semantic Web, if social agents are unable to generalize upon their communications by means of statistical evaluation. Whereas our current formal framework still focusses on

1:1 communication, and does not yet support generalization, it allows for the stochastic representation of communication processes, providing a basis for the future inclusion of the described features.

2.2   Empirical-Rational Semantics

The three central assumptions underlying our approach are that 1) the meaning of communications lies primarily in their expectable, observable consequences, that 2) these consequences can be learned from the observation and as extrapolations of past communication processes (without too much reasoning about what is "inside the agents heads", which significantly reduces the complexity of the learning task), and that 3) the meaning of communications might evolve during the interaction processes. Please refer to [1, 8, 9] for theoretical justifications of these assumptions. The basic requirements in order to put these assumptions into practice are the presence of a *semantics observer* which derives communication semantics from observations, and a knowledge medium which represents the assumably shared semantics among the agents as interrelated stochastic expectations (*Expectation Network*).

In our communication model (which does not follow speech act theory), a single communication can be seen as a request to act in conformance with a desired state declared by its utterance, in which this state is given as a probability distribution of future events, and the meaning of the utterance is the probability distribution of expected events subsequent to the utterance. If one agent e.g. utters "Close the door" to another agent, the desired world state is the door being closed by the addressed agent, and the meaning of that utterance is if and how the addressed agent works towards this state, possibly together with side-effect as the sanctioning in case of non-compliance. As another example, if an agent performs the act "You are the group leader now", then this act demands that other agents act as if the addressed agent would perform like a group leader from now on. In a strict sense, even this performative act will become successful only a posteriori, but if the nominating agent has been assigned the necessary social power in the past, its success can be derived immediately from past successes empirically.

In contrast to non-communicative events, an utterance has no (significant) direct impact on the physical environment. Instead, its physical consequences are achieved socially and indirectly, and, most important, the addressee is free to deny the communicated proposition. Since an utterance is always explicitly produced by a self-interested agent to influence the addressee which is not already convinced from the necessity of the proposal, communicated content will very likely not "believed" immediately, but needs to be accompanied with communicated reasons given to the addressee to increase the probability of an acceptance of the communicated content. This can be done either explicitly by previous or subsequent communications (especially *reciprocally*: "If you comply, I'll comply too"), or implicitly by means of generalizations from past events (e.g., trust) or given social structures. The whole of the expectations which are triggered by a communication in the context of the preceding communication process we call its *rational hull*. The rational hull specifies the rational social relationships which steer the acceptance or denial of communicated content according the rational attitude the agents exhibit. Typically, a rational hull is initially very indefinite and becomes increasingly definite in the course of interaction, provided that the agents work towards

Table 1. A grammar for event nodes of ENs, generating the language $\mathcal{M}$ (the language of concrete actions and events, with $Action$ as the start symbol)

$$
\begin{aligned}
Expect &\in [0;1] \\
Agent &\rightarrow agent\_1 \quad | \quad \ldots \quad | \quad agent\_n \\
PhysicalAction &\rightarrow move\_object \quad | \quad touch\_agent \quad | \quad \ldots \\
Action &\rightarrow ECA(Agent, Projection) \\
&\quad | \quad do(Agent, PhysicalAction) \\
&\quad | \quad UnpersonalizedEvent \\
ActionPattern &\rightarrow Action \quad | \quad ? \\
Projections &\rightarrow (Conditions, GoalStates) \\
Conditions &\rightarrow SimplePath \\
GoalStates &\rightarrow SimplePath \\
SimplePath &\rightarrow Action\ SimplePath \quad | \quad \varepsilon
\end{aligned}
$$

mutual understanding. The utterances themselves are modeled as pointers pointing to the desired/proposed states within the Expectation Network (thus denoting subjective expectation directed to other agents in contrast to the objective expectations maintained by the semantics observer).

3 Expectation Networks

Expectation Networks (ENs) are the graphical data structures we want to use for the stochastical modeling of Social Interaction Structures, which in turn represent the semantics of utterances in the form of EN branches. The formal EN definition we present in this work is an improved yet simplified version of the definition presented in [11].

The central assumption that is made in ENs is that observed events like agent actions (especially symbolic agent messages) may be categorized as expected continuations of other observed event sequences. An edge leading from event m to event m' is thought to reflect the probability of m and m' being correlated from the observer's point of view (the descriptive power of ENs is thus similar to Markov processes, but in contrast edges in ENs relate events, not states).

As for $\mathcal{M}$, this is a formal language that defines the events used for labeling nodes in expectation networks. Its syntax is given by the grammar in table 1. Actions observed in the system can be either "physical" actions of the format (a, ac) where a is the executing agent, and ac is an domain-dependent symbol used for a physical action, or symbolic elementary communication acts $ECA(a, c)$ sent from a to another agent with content c, or an arbitrary "physical" event ($UnpersonalizedEvent$, considered to be communicated implicitly to all agents). We do not talk about "utterances" or "messages" here, because a single utterance might need to be decomposed into multiple ECAs. The symbols used in the $Agent$ and $PhysicalAction$ rules might be domain-dependent symbols the existence of which we take for granted. For convenience, $agent(eca)$ shall retrieve the acting agent of an ECA eca.

In addition to normal node labels, we use the symbol ($\triangleright_{EN}$) to denote the root node of an specific EN. The special symbol ? marks pseudo-nodes which are just graphical abbreviations for the so-called *completeEN* which models the uniform distribution of *all* possible combinations and sequences of observable events (see below). A "node" labeled with ? thus stands for a branch with infinite depth. The content c of a non-physical action is given by type *Projections*. The meaning of *Projections* will be described later.

Syntactically, expectation networks are here represented as lists of edges (m, p, n) where m and n are actions, and p is a transition probability (*expectability*) from m to n. We use functions $in : V \rightarrow 2^C$, $out : V \rightarrow 2^C$, $source : C \rightarrow V$ and $target : C \rightarrow V$ which return the ingoing and outgoing edges of a node and the source and target node of an edge, respectively. $children : V \rightarrow 2^V$ returns the set of children of a node, with $children(v) = \emptyset$ in case v is a leaf. $\prec : V \times V \rightarrow \{true, false\}$ returns *true* iff there is a path leading from the first argument node to the second and the event associated with the second node is expected to occur after the event of the first node. C is the set of all edges, V the set of all nodes in the EN. Edges denote correlations in observed communication sequences. Each cognitive edge is associated with an expectability (returned by $Expect : C \rightarrow [0; 1]$) which reflects the probability of $target(e)$ occurring after $source(e)$ in the same communicative context (i.e. in spatial proximity, between the same agents, etc.).

Sometimes we denote a path p in an EN leading from $v_0 \in V$ to $v_n \in V$ as concatenations of message labels (ECAs) $Label(v_0) \sqcup ... \sqcup Label(v_n)$. The $\sqcup$ are sometimes omitted for shortness. $|p| := n$. $Node : SimplePath_{EN} \rightarrow V$ results in the last node of a certain path given as a string of labels. Nodes or corresponding messages along a path p will be denoted as p_i. $\mathcal{EN}(\mathcal{M})$ is the set of all possible expectation networks over $\mathcal{M}$.

Definition 1. An *Expectation Network* is a structure

$$EN = (V, C, \mathcal{M}, Label, Expect) \in \mathcal{EN}(\mathcal{M})$$

where

- V with $|V| > 1$ is the set of nodes,
- $C \subseteq V \times V$ are the edges of EN. (V, C) is a tree called *expectation tree*. (V, C) shall have a unique root node called $\triangleright_{EN} \in V$ which corresponds to the first ever observed action[2]. The following condition should hold:

$$\forall v \sum_{e \in out(v)} Expect(e) = 1$$

- $\mathcal{M}$ is the *action language*. As defined in table 1, actions can be symbolic actions ($ECA(...)$), other agent actions or other physical events. While we take the existence and the meaning of the latter in terms of resulting observer expectations as granted and domain-depended, the former will be described in detail later.

---

[2] Of course, there are semantics observers imaginable which maintain multiple ENs to model different social systems, states of knowledge or environmental domains at the same time.

- $Label : V \rightarrow \mathcal{M}$ is the *action label* function for nodes, with $\forall v \in V : \forall e, f \in children(v)$:
  $\neg unify(Label(e), Label(f))$ (where $unify$ shall be $true$ iff its arguments are syntactically unifiable. Cf. [11] for the use of variables in ENs),
- $Expect : C \rightarrow [0; 1]$ returns the edges' expectabilities. For convenience, we define $Expect(label|path) = Expect(in(v))$ if $Node(path \sqcup label) = v$.

Paths starting with $\triangleright$ are called *states* (of communication)[3]

4   Social Interaction Structures

Based on the definition of ENs, we can now define *Social Interaction Structures* as a special kind of communication structures. Social Interaction Structures capture the regularities of externally observed communication processes and other assumably publicly observable events (the latter can be considered as being communicated "by doing", or as projected information). The basic ideas behind this concept are that 1) agent sociality emerges from agent communication, and that 2) communications form a so-called *social system* which is closed in the sense that, to some degree, communication regularities come into being from communications themselves [1], such that the semantics observer does not need to have to "look inside the agents' heads" to derive these structures. Because of that, communication structures can meaningfully be learned from observations. Nevertheless, this learning process needs to be continuously repeated to adapt the EN to new perceptions (since open systems with truly autonomous agents with unknown life spans have no final state), and does always imply the possibility of failure of its prediction task (yet the term "expectation"). The Social Interaction Structures (respectively the probabilistic distribution it represents, as, e.g., an EN branch) following an utterance (the node denoting the ECA which is part of this utterance, to be precise) [4] is called the *semantics* of this utterance.

4.1   Social Interaction Systems

In [11], we've introduced *Communication Systems* as a universal means for the description of social dynamics of multiagent systems. The two main purposes of a Communication System are i) to capture the social expectations (represented as an EN) in the current state of a multiagent system under observation, and ii) to capture changes to these expectations. Whereas the EN models the meaning of communicative action sequences at a certain time (i.e., their expected, generalized continuations in a certain context of previous events), the communication system models the way the EN is build up, and, if necessary, adapted according to new observations of events. We introduce now *Social Interaction Systems* (SIS) as a concrete kind of general Communication Systems. The

---

[3] Actually, two different paths can have the same semantics in terms of their expected continuations, a fact which could be used to reduce the size of the EN by making them directed graphs with more than one path leading to a node instead of trees as in this work.

[4] Usually, this context is build up from previous events, but it would also be possible that utterances become contextualized (e.g., more specific) by *succeeding* utterances.

difference between general Communication Systems and Social Interaction Systems is that the latter come with a concrete EN learning algorithm, whereas for general Communication Systems we just demand unspecifically that the expectations within learned ENs shall reflect the expectation of the semantics observer regarding the future course of events [11], not specifically taking into account agent rationality and social commitment. The term "interaction system" comes from social systems theory [1], where it denotes the most basic kind of communication (=social) system.

As seen in Table 1, we also allow purely physical, non-symbolic events to be contained, like agent actions, but without projections. So the EN of an SIS comprises physical states of the domain too, as far as these are visible for the semantics observer, and of course physical events projected by ECAs.

The SIS maintained by the semantics observer is also the *assumably* shared world knowledge the agents use as the common ground for their uttered ECAs. Social Interaction Systems are thus two dimensional, in the sense that they do not only contain expectations regarding actual agent behavior including utterances (first dimension), but also descriptions of the imaginative behavior which the uttering agents tries to bring about or demand, i.e., which they expect other agents to do.

Definition 2. A *Social Interaction System* at time t is a structure

$$SIS_t = (\mathcal{M}, f, \varpi_t, \rho)$$

where

- $\mathcal{M}$ is the formal language used for agent actions (according to table 1),
- $f : \mathcal{EN}(\mathcal{M}) \times \mathcal{M} \to \mathcal{EN}(\mathcal{M})$ is the *expectations update function* that transforms any expectation network EN to a new network upon experience of an action $m \in \mathcal{M}$. $f(\perp, m)$ returns the so-called *initial EN*, transformed by the observation of m. This initial EN can be used for the pre-structuring of the social system using given e.g. social norms or other a-priori knowledge which can not be learned using f. Any ENs resulting from an application of f are called *Social Interaction Structures*. As a non-incremental variant we define $f : \mathcal{M}^+ \to \mathcal{EN}(\mathcal{M})$ to be $f(m_0 \sqcup m_1 ... \sqcup m_t) = f(...(f(f(\perp, m_0), m_1)...), m_t)$,
- $\varpi_t = m_0 \sqcup m_1 ... \sqcup m_t \in \mathcal{M}^*$ is the list of all actions observed until time t. The subindexes of the m_i impose a linear order on the actions corresponding to the times they have been observed[5],
- $\rho \in \mathbf{N}$ is a time greater of equal the expected life time of the SIS. We require this to calculate the so-called *spheres of communication* (see below). If the life time is unknown, we set $\rho = \infty$.

We refer to events and EN nodes as *past*, *current* or *future* depending on their timely position (or the timely position of their corresponding node, respectively) before, at or after t. We refer to $EN_t = f(\varpi_t)$ as the *current EN* from the semantics observer's

---

[5] For simplicity, we assume a discrete time scale with $t \in \mathbb{N}$, and that no pair of actions can be performed at the same time, and that the *expected* action time corresponds with the depth of the respective node.

point of view, if the semantics observer has observed exactly the sequence $m_0 m_1 ... m_t$ of events so far.

The intuition behind our definition of SIS_t is that a social interaction system can be characterized by how it would update an existing expectation network upon newly observed actions $m \in \mathcal{M}$. The EN within SIS_t can thus be computed through the sequential application of the structures update function f for each action within ϖ, starting with a given expectation network which models the observers' a-priori knowledge. ϖ_{t-1} is called the *context* (or *precondition*) of the action observed at time t.

To simplify the following formalism, we demand that an EN ought to be implicitly complete, i.e., to contain *all* possible paths, representing all possible event sequences (thus the EN within a social interaction system is always infinite and represents all possible world states, even extremely unlikely ones). If the semantics observer has no a-priori knowledge about a certain branch, we assume this branch to represent uniform distribution and thus a very low probability for every future decision alternative ($\frac{1}{|M|}$), if the action language is not trivially small.

Note that any part of an EN of an SIS does describe exactly one time period, i.e., each node within the respective EN corresponds to exactly one moment on the time scale in the past or the future of observation or prediction, respectively, whereas this is not necessarily true for ENs in general. For simplicity, and to express the definiteness of the past, we will define the update function f such that the a-posteriori expectabilities of past events (i.e., observations) become 1 (admittedly leading to problems if the past is unknown or contested, or we would like to allow contested assertive ECAs *about* the past). There shall be exactly one path pc in the current EN leading from start node $\triangleright_{en_t}$ leading to a node pc_t such that $|pc| = t$ and $\forall i, 0 \leq i \leq t : Label(pc_i) = m_i$. The node pc_i and the ECA m_i are called *corresponding*.

The *semantics* of ϖ_t (i.e. m_t within context ϖ_{t-1}) is defined as the probability distribution Δ_{EN_t, ϖ_t} represented by the branch starting with the node within EN_t that corresponds to ϖ_t:

$$\Delta_{EN_t, \varpi_t}(w') = \frac{\prod\limits_{i, 1 \leq i \leq |w'|} Expect(w'_i | \varpi_t w'_1 ... w'_{i-1})}{\sum\limits_{m \in M^+} \prod\limits_{i, 1 \leq i \leq |m|} Expect(m_i | \varpi_t m_1 ... m_{i-1})}$$

for all $w' :\Leftrightarrow \varpi_t \sqcup w' \in M^+$. The w'_i denote single event labels along w'.

4.2   Projections

As defined in table 1, ECAs consist of two parts: The uttering agent, and the ECA content (*projections*). Each projection is a set of EN node pairs which are derived from the following two syntactical elements (cf. table 1)[6].

- *Conditions* chooses, using an EN path (without expectabilities), a possibly infinite set of EN states which have to become reality in order to make the uttering agent

---

[6] Future version of our framework might allow the utterance of whole ENs as projections, in order to freely project new expectabilities or even introduce novel event types not found in the current EN.

start to act towards its uttered goal (e.g. in "*If I deliver the goods*, you must pay me the money"). As shown in table 1, conditions are given as a linear list of node labels. This path must match with paths in the current EN, either absolutely beginning with ▷, or starting at nodes after the node which corresponds to the ECA. The end nodes of all matches in EN are called the *condition nodes* of the ECA projections. So, if the node list is empty, the only condition node is the node corresponding to the ECA. The path matching is always successful, since in our model, an EN implicitly contains all possible paths, although with a probability near zero for most of them.

– *GoalStates* chooses, using an EN path (without expectabilities), the (possibly infinite) set of states of the expectation network the uttering agent is expected to strive for. The uttered *GoalStates* path must match with a set of paths within the EN such that the last node of each match is a node of an EN branch that has a condition node from *Conditions* as its root. Both in Conditions and GoalStates paths, wildcards "?" for single actions are allowed.

For the purpose of this paper, we demand that the projections either refer to future interactions or be semantically inactive (i.e., they already failed or have been successful). Theoretically, we could also imagine projections regarding the past. In this case the respective ECA would express that the uttering agent will likely try to change the way other agents communicate about the past, but we do not consider this difficult and rather unusual case here for simplicity.

Note also that projected goal states possibly describe actions the uttering agent announces to perform *himself*, not just explicit demands directed to other agents. In this case, the rational hull for this goal consists of behavior which likely increases the support from other agents in order to make the goal state come true.

In the context of an EN, every projection implicitly refers to previous or future projections which announce *reasons* or positive or negative *sanctions* the uttering agent would impose on the ECA receiver in case of a positive or negative response to the ECA. So, in our model, sanctions and argumentative reasons are projections also, in order to support the realization of other projections (of course, this can be continued recursively, e.g. projections in order to support sanctions), and learned from previous processes as anticipations of future reasons and sanctions[7]. The projection of accompanying reasons and sanctions is an inevitable part of every elementary communication act, since among self-interested agents it would be unreasonable to make propositions without providing any reciprocative utility to the receiver, with the exception of implicit reasons and sanctions given as pre-existing social structures social structures like social power, laws or other norms (which we do not consider in this work). Such supporting projections can be either unspecified, to be specified later, or already be specified by means of previous events. Of course, like any other kinds of projections, they need not to be "honest", or put into action, or be effective.

Because the projections set can represent arbitrary probability distributions, it is possible for multiple ECAs to express disjunctive statements like "I want you to do either

---

[7] In order to model explicit argumentation or social reasoning systems as special cases of Social Interaction Systems, we would additionally need to provide an explicit logical interpretation of ENs, which our framework does not yet accomplishes.

a *or* b", if a and b are inconsistent events (i.e., events which cannot occur both in the same context). Since consistent ECAs uttered by the same agent are interpreted as conjunctively related, and ECAs with redundant projections are allowed (which increases its impact of these projections on the social structures), one can project arbitrary probability distributions using multiple ECAs. The following functions returns the set of projections of a single ECA $ECA(condition, goal) \in M$ with paths $condition \in Conditions$ and $goal \in GoalStates$:

$$projections_{\mathcal{EN}(\mathcal{M})} : M \rightarrow V \times V$$
$$projections_{(V,C,M,Label,E)}(ECA(ce_1...ce_n, ge_1...ge_m)) =$$
$$\{(v_n, v_m) : \{(v_i, v_{i+1}) : 1 \leq i \leq n - 1\} \subseteq C$$
$$\wedge\ unify(Label(v_i), ce_i)$$
$$\wedge\ \{(v_i, v_{i+1}) : n + 1 \leq i \leq n + m - 1\} \subseteq C$$
$$\wedge\ unify(Label(v_i), ge_i)$$
$$\wedge\ v_n \prec v_{n+m} \wedge unify(Label(v_n), ce_n)$$
$$\wedge\ unify(Label(v_{n+m}), ge_m)\}$$

$unify(?, l)$ and $unify(l, ?)$ shall always be true. For convenience, we write $Goal((c, g)) = g$ and $Condition((c, g)) = c$.

4.3   Rational Hulls

Per se, a projection has no power to make its goal states become true. In fact, projections don't have to be rational at all. But we consider it to be rational that the uttering agent will act towards the projected events *at least for some significant amount of time* [8]. This time span and the events within, starting directly after the projecting utterance event, are called *sphere of communication* (cf. figure 1). Theoretically, each ECA could have its own sphere of communication. For simplicity, in this work we assume that the sphere of communication of any ECA *eca* is simply $\rho - time(eca)$, where the first operand is the expected time of the last observed utterance within the SIS, and the second is the utterance time of the projecting ECA. This setting is assumable realistic for small and simple interaction systems, where the interacting agents likely stick to their opinions and desires for the whole and usually short duration of the SIS (like auctions). For other domains we would have to determine the spheres of communication *a posteriori* from empirical observations.

The actions the uttering agents is expected to perform within the respective sphere of communication in order to make his projections come true is called the *rational hull* of the ECA. Thus, the determination of the rational hulls of observed ECAs constitutes the crucial part of the determination of ACL semantics. The rational hull can be seen as the actual pragmatics and meaning "behind" the more normative and idealistic concept of social commitments.

We assume the manifestation of the following attitudes by means of ECAs *within the respective spheres of communication* and contextualized by means of other ECAs:

– *Information of other agents about desired states of communication.* This information is given as projections as described above.

---

[8] This time span of projection trustability can be very short though - think of *joke questions*.

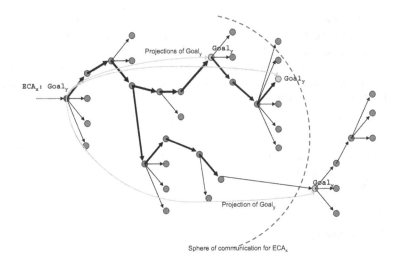

Fig. 1. An EN with projections and a sphere of communication

- *Support of other communicated goals.* The supportive functionality communication has regarding other communications is defined by the rational hulls of the supported elementary communication acts, which will become implicitly more expectable too if supporting rational hulls increase their own expectabilities.
- *Manifestation of understanding.* In case the agents "understand" each other, ECAs cannot express contradiction to the fact that other ECAs pursue the two previous intentions (i.e., Agent 1 does not need to believe Agent 2 is right, but she needs to believe at least that Agent 1 *wants* to be right in a specific case). We do not consider misunderstanding in this work.

Capturing these intentions, and given the set of projections for each ECA *eca* uttered by an agent *a*, we calculate the rational hull of a certain ECA using the following two principles.

4.3.1   Bounded Rational Choice

After uttering *eca*, an agent *a* is expected to choose an action policy such that, within the respective sphere of communication, his actions maximize the probability of the projected state(-s). Let $p \in projections(eca, EN_t)$ be a projection. Then, considered that p would be a useful state for the uttering agent to be in, the rule of rational choice proposes that for every node v_d with $agent(v_d) = a$ along the path $v_t...p$ leading from the current node v_t to p, $Expect(in(v_d)) = 1$ for the incoming edge of v_d, and that the expectabilities of the reminding outgoing edges of the predecessor of v_d are reduced to 0 appropriately (if no other goals have to be considered). To reduce the complexity of applying this general rule on the possibly infinite projections set, and to observe the bounds of observer rationality, we propose the following constraints:

- Expectabilities will be adapted within the respective sphere of communication of *eca* only, even if the goal state p is located beyond this sphere.
- Expectabilities will be adapted only for parts of the current EN with a significant evidence regarding actions performed by other agents. Since we represent missing knowledge as uniform distribution, we put this rule into practice by demanding that at decision nodes of other agents (i.e., nodes with children representing actions of agents other than the agent which uttered *eca*) the *expectabilities entropy* $entropy_{EN} : V \to \mathbb{R}$ should be below some given limit.

$$entropy_{EN}(v) =$$
$$\sum_{v' \in children(v)} -Expect(in(v'))log_2 Expect(in(v'))$$

- If multiple elements in *projections* are identical apart from their context, and the paths leading to these projections overlap, priority is given to those projections with a higher cumulative expectability. Finding the right paths is a markovian multiple-decision problem from the perspective of the uttering agent a (and thus from the perspective of the semantics observer which models the behavior of a also), which in general cannot simply be solved by pairwise comparison of paths leading from the current node to the competitive projections regarding their maximum expected utilities, if $projections(eca, EN_t) = \{p_1, ..., p_n\}$ contains more than two elements.
- The projections of previously uttered ECAs have to be maintained, so the rule of rational choice needs to do a weighting assessment of previously calculated rational hulls instead of simply outdating them.

We use the following function $u_{\mathcal{EN}(\mathcal{M})} : \mathcal{M} \times V \to [0;1]$ to calculate the *utility* of an arbitrary node v regarding its supporting function for a specific elementary communication act *eca*.

$$u_{EN}(eca, v) = \begin{cases} 0 \text{ if } \forall i, 1 \leq i \leq n: \\ \quad \neg v \prec Goal(p_i) \lor \neg Condition(p_i) \prec v \\ 0 \text{ if } entropy_{en}(v) > \kappa, \text{ or else:} \\ 1 \text{ if } \exists i : v = Goal(p_i) \\ \max_{j, 1 \leq j \leq c} u_{EN}(eca, vc_j) \\ \quad \text{if } agent(Label(vc_j)) = agent(eca) \\ \max_{j, 1 \leq j \leq c} Expect(in(vc_j))u_{EN}(eca, vc_j) \\ \quad \text{otherwise} \end{cases}$$

with $\{p_1, ..., p_n\} = projections(eca)$, $\{vc_1, ..., vc_c\} = children(v)$, and κ being some predefined entropy maximum.
$\max(...)$ could be replaced with $(\sum_{j, 1 \leq j \leq c} ...)/c$ to prefer a high number of paths leading to a goal instead of the highest expectability for one goal node.

Figure 1 shows an EN modeling the future of some communication process. ECA_X is an utterance which encodes $Goal_Y$. This goal itself stands for several (seemingly) desired states of the EN (yellow nodes). Since within the so-called *sphere of communication* of ECA_X (see below) it is expected that the uttering agent rationally strives for these states, certain EN paths leading to these states become more likely (bold edges). Such behavior paths need to be (more or less) rational in terms of their expected utility (e.g. in comparison with competing goal states), and they need to reflect experiences from analogous agent behavior in the past.

4.3.2   Empirical Stationarity Assumption

If we would use the previous rule as the only EN updating mechanism, we would face at least three problems: 1) Predicting agent actions according to the rule of rational choice requires some given evidence about subsequent actions of other agents. In case this previous evidence is missing, the rule of rational choice would just "convert" uniform distribution into unform distribution. Therefore, we have to provide an initial probability distribution the rule can be applied on[9]. 2) the set of projections for a single ECA might be infinite. Most of the expectabilities along the paths leading from the current node to these EN branches sum up to very low probabilities for the respective projection. Thus, a pre-selection of likely paths will be necessary. And most important 3), the rule of rational choice does not consider individual behavioral characteristics like (initially opaque) goal preferences of the agents, but treats all projections uniformly. Goal hierarchies need thus to be obtained from past agent practice as well as individual strategies towards these projections. For these reasons, we combine the application of the rule of rational choice with the assumption of some stationarity of past event trajectories, i.e., the assumption that previously observed action sequences repeat themselves in the future in a similar context. We use this assumption to retrieve a probability distribution the rule of rational choice can be applied on and weighted with subsequently.

In order to learn EN stationarity from previous observations, we follow the so-called *variable-memory approach* to higher-order Markov chains using *Probabilistic Suffix Automata* (PSA) introduced for *L-predictable* observation sequences [7]. This approach efficiently models Markov chains of order L (i.e., with a model memory size of L), allowing for rich stochastical models of observed sequences. The applicability of this approach to our scenario is based on the heuristical assumption that many Social Interaction Systems are *short-memory systems*, which allow the empirical prediction of social behavior from a relatively short preceding event sequence (assumedly pre-structuring using social norms, constraints from rational choice etc is done properly). The main characteristic of the PSA-based approach is its straightforward learning method, with expressiveness and prediction capabilities comparable with the more common *Hidden Markov Models* [7].

For the calculation of the PSA from a set of sample agent action sequences, we use an algorithm introduced in [7], originally coming from *PAC-learning*, in a slightly modified version. It constructs a so-called *Prediction Suffix Tree* (PST) (sometimes called *Probabilistic Suffix Tree*) from the samples, which is roughly equivalent to the target PSA, but

---

[9] This probability distribution must also cover projected events and assign them a (however low) probability even if these events are beyond the spheres of communication, because otherwise it would be impossible to calculate the rational hull.

easier to build up. Its only disadvantage in comparison to the corresponding full PSA is that the time complexity for the predicting task is higher approximately by the factor L.

Definition 3. A *Prediction Suffix Tree* with memory size L over the language of concrete agent actions M is a structure $PST_L(M) = (V, C, Label, \gamma)$ where

- (V, C) defines a tree graph consisting of a set of nodes V, $|V| > 0$ and a set of edges $C \subseteq V \times V$,
- $Label : V \rightarrow M^+$ returns for a node its label (with maximum length L),
- $\gamma : V \rightarrow \{(d_1, ..., d_{|M|}) : d_i \in \mathbb{R}\}$ returns for each node a vector which defines the probability distribution associated with this node. Each element $\gamma_\sigma(v)$ of the resulting vector corresponds to the conditional probability of the particular message σ in M.
  $\sum_{\sigma \in M} \gamma_\sigma(v) = 1$ should hold - nevertheless, vector elements with a very low probability are omitted.

A PST is able to predict the probability of sequences using a tree traversal up to the root, as γ returns for a specific message its conditional occurrence probability given that the largest *suffix* ν, $|\nu| \leq L$, of the message sequence observed before matches with the label of this node. L should depend from the available memory resources, the length of the samples and the expected spheres of communication.

In order to build up the PST from the empirical observations, we need to define the conditional empirical probability within a set of sample action sequences (where actions are either ECA utterances or physical actions). As input we us the set $samples_{SIS_t} = \{m_0 m_1..., m_t\} \cup \{r_1^1...r_1^{l_1}, ..., r_n^1...r_n^{l_n}\}$, where $m_0 m_1..., m_t$ is the sequence of events observed so far for SIS_t until time t, and the reminder of this set consists of additional samples to improve prediction accuracy. The $r_i^1 r_i^{l_i}$ are optional; we can omit these additional samples and learn the PSA from the single sequence $m_0 m_1..., m_t$ only. But as a rule of thumb, the lengths of the sample sequences should be at least polynomial in L[7]. If an a-priori EN is given for pre-structuring, the r_i could be obtained from a frequency sampling of sequences from this EN, which is straightforward and thus omitted here. For lack of space, we also omit the detailed PST-learning algorithm, which can be found in [7].

The probability for the PST-generation of an event sequence $m = m_1...m_n \in (M)^n$ is

$$P_{PST}(m) = \prod_{i=1}^{n} \gamma_{m_i}(v^{i-1})$$

where v^0 is the (unlabeled) root node of the PST and for $1 \leq i \leq n-1$ v^i is the deepest node reachable by a tree traversal corresponding to a prefix of $m_i m_{i-1}...m_1$, starting at the root node.

From the probability distribution obtained from P_{PST}, we derive the corresponding EN using the function $\delta : M^+ \rightarrow \mathcal{EN}(\mathcal{M})$:

$$\delta(m_0 m_1..., m_t) = (V, C, M, Label, Expect)$$

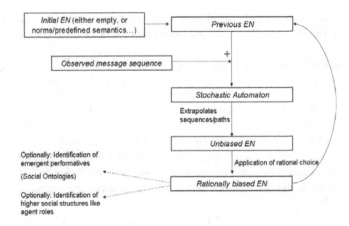

Fig. 2. Iterative version of the algorithm (outline)

with
$$V = \{\triangleright\} \cup \{v_p : p \in paths\},$$
$$Label = \{v_{p_1...p_n} \mapsto p_n : p_1 \sqcup ... \sqcup p_n \in paths\},$$
$$C = \{(\triangleright, v_p) : |p| = 1, v_p \in V\}$$
$$\cup \{(v_{p_1...p_{n-1}}, v_{p_1...p_n}) : v_{p_1...p_{n-1}} \in V \wedge v_{p_1...p_n} \in V\},$$
$$Expect =$$
$$\{in(v_{p_1...p_n}) \mapsto \frac{P_{PST}(p_1...p_n)}{P_{PST}(p_1...p_{n-1})}, v_{p_1...p_n} \in V\}, \text{ and}$$
$$paths = \{p : p \in M^+ \wedge P_{PST}(p) > P_{min}\}, \text{ where } P_{min} \text{ is a predefined lower bound}$$
for significant expectabilities.

4.3.3   Rationality-Biased Empirics

Putting together the rule of rational choice and the assumption of empirical stationarity, we gain the following (non-iterative) definition for the Social Interaction Structures update function f of an SIS. Figure 2 outlines the iterative counterpart not described here.

$$f(m_0 m_1 ... m_t) = \varrho(EN_{stat}, \triangleright_{EN_{stat}})$$

with $EN_{stat} =$
$(V_{EN_{stat}}, C_{EN_{stat}}, \mathcal{M}, Label_{EN_{stat}}, Expect_{EN_{stat}})$ such that
$V_{EN_{stat}} = \{v_{m_0}, ..., v_{m_t}\} \cup V_\delta,$
$C_{EN_{stat}} =$
$C_\delta \cup \{(\triangleright_{EN_{stat}} = v_{m_0}, v_{m_1}), ..., (v_{m_{t-1}}, v_{m_t}), (v_{m_t}, \triangleright_\delta)\}$
and $\forall i, 1 \leq i \leq t:$
$Expect(in(v_{m_i})) = 1, \forall i, 0 \leq i \leq t : Label(v_{m_i}) = m_i,$ with
$(V_\delta, C_\delta, \mathcal{M}, Label_\delta, Expect_\delta) = \delta(m_0 m_1 ... m_t).$

$Expect(in(v_{m_i})) = 1$ reflects the definiteness of already observed events.

Above, $\varrho : \mathcal{EN}(\mathcal{M}) \times SimplePath \rightarrow \mathcal{EN}(\mathcal{M})$ applies the results of the calculation of rational hulls to the entire EN resulting from the PST by means of a recursive top-down tree traversal which is limited by the maximum search depth maxdepth (alternatively, we could apply a entropy-based search limitation criterion similar to the criterion used in 4.3.1).

$\varrho((V, C, M, Label, Expect), path) =$

$$\begin{cases} (V, C, M, Label, Expect) \text{ if } |path| > \text{maxdepth} \\ (V, C, M, Label, Expect_{|children(v)|}) \text{ otherwise} \end{cases}$$

using $v = Node(path)$, $\Delta U(v) = \{(v_j, u(Label(v), v_j)) :$
$v_j \in V, agent(Label(v_j)) = agent(Label(v))\}$,

$\forall v_j \in V : Expect_0(in(v_j)) =$
$$\begin{cases} \dfrac{Expect(in(v_j)) + \Delta U(v)[v_j]}{2} \\ \text{if } Time(v_j) < \rho \wedge agent(Label(v_j)) = agent(Label(v)) \quad \text{and} \\ Expect(in(v_j)) \text{ otherwise} \end{cases}$$
$\forall n, 1 \leq n \leq |children(v)| :$
$\quad Expect_n :\Leftrightarrow (V, C, M, Label, Expect_n) =$
$\quad \varrho((V, C, M, Label, Expect_{n-1}),$
$\quad path \sqcup Label(children(v)_n)).$

Here, $\Delta U(v)$ assigns every node v_j its utility regarding the ECA $Label(v)$, if the acting agent is the same for v and v_j. $Expect_0(in(v_j))$ assigns the node its new expectability (equally weighted with its previous expectability, which might be already be utility biased from another ECA), and $Time(v_j) < \rho$ limits the application to nodes within the sphere of communication. $\Delta U(v)[v_j]$ denotes the utility for reaching v assigned to v_j.

5   Conclusions

We have introduced an approach to the semantics of agent communication which combines features from traditional mentalistic and objectivist approaches. Being a novel and very basic proposal, several important things remain to do:

- ECAs and ENs do not explicitly model logical propositions and their relationships (e.g., in an EN, a low probability for uttering "no" does not automatically increase the probability for uttering "yes", as it should, and one can express logical statements only indirectly by stating their pragmatical consequences in terms of events).
- To be of practical use with common ACLs, ECAs also need to be obtainable from conventional speech acts, which requires a translation of speech act types into ECA patterns within the EN (and vice versa, in order to learn new speech act types from emergent ENs).
- Related to the previous issue, the explicit emergence of communication symbols as "shortcuts" for combinations of ECA patterns is not yet supported.
- Meta-communication (communication about communication) is not yet supported, and also not different spheres of communications and the empirical derivation of the

boundaries of spheres (required e.g. in order to model multiple coexistent, inconsistent opinions of a certain agent).

- The EN learning algorithm does not yet make use of generalizable behavior patterns that *different* agents have in common (like agent roles).

Acknowledgements. This work has been supported by DFG (German National Science Foundation) under contracts no. BR609/11-2 and MA759/4-2.

References

1. N. Luhmann. Social Systems. Stanford University Press, Palo Alto, CA, 1995.
2. D. C. Dennett. The Intentional Stance. MIT Press, 1989.
3. M. P. Singh. A Social Semantics for Agent Communication Languages. In Procs. of the IJCAI Workshop on Agent Communication Languages, 2000.
4. F. Guerin, J. Pitt. Denotational Semantics for Agent Communication Languages. In Procs. of the 5th International Conference on Autonomous Agents (Agents'01), 2001.
5. P. R. Cohen, H. J. Levesque. Performatives in a Rationally Based Speech Act Theory. In Procs. 28th Annual Meeting of the ACL, 1990.
6. P. R. Cohen, H. J. Levesque. Communicative Actions for Artificial Agents. In Procs. of the First International Conference on Multiagent Systems (ICMAS-95), 1995.
7. D. Ron, Y. Singer, N. Tishby. The Power of Amnesia - Learning Probabilistic Automata with Variable Memory Length. In Machine Learning Vol. 25, p. 117–149, 1996
8. K. F. Lorentzen, M. Nickles. Ordnung aus Chaos – Prolegomena zu einer Luhmann'schen Modellierung deentropisierender Strukturbildung in Multiagentensystemen. In T. Kron (Ed.), Luhmann modelliert. Ansätze zur Simulation von Kommunikationssystemen, Leske & Budrich, 2002.
9. M. Nickles, G. Weiss. Empirical Semantics of Agent Communication in Open Systems. In Procs. of the 2nd International Workshop on Challenges in Open Agent Environments. 2003
10. M. Rovatsos, M. Nickles, G. Weiß. Interaction is Meaning: A New Model for Communication in Open Systems. In Procs. of the Second International Joint Conference on Autonomous Agents and Multiagent Systems (AAMAS-03), 2003.
11. M. Nickles, M. Rovatsos, W. Brauer, G. Weiss. Communication Systems: A Unified Model of Socially Intelligent Systems. In K. Fischer, M. Florian (Eds.): Socionics: Its Contributions to the Scalability of Complex Social Systems. Springer LNAI, 2004. To appear.
12. M. Nickles, M. Rovatsos, G. Weiss. Empirical-Rational Semantics of Agent Communication. In Procs. of the Third International Joint Conference on Autonomous Agents and Multiagent Systems (AAMAS-04), 2004.
13. W. Brauer, M. Nickles, M. Rovatsos, G. Weiss, K. F. Lorentzen. Expectation-Oriented Analysis and Design. In Procs. of The Second International Workshop on Agent-Oriented Software Engineering (AOSE-01), 2001.
14. R.-J. Beun, R. M. van Eijk, H. Prust. Ontological Feedback in Multiagent Systems. In Procs. of the Third International Joint Conference on Autonomous Agents and Multiagent Systems (AAMAS-04), 2004.
15. R. A. Flores, P. Pasquier, B. Chaib-draa. Conversational Semantics with Social Commitments. In Procs. AAMAS-04 Workshop on Agent Communication (AC-2004), 2004.
16. M. Colombetti, M. Verdicchio. An analysis of agent speech acts as institutional actions. In Procs. of the First International Joint Conference on Autonomous Agents and Multiagent Systems (AAMAS-02), 2002.
17. M. P. Singh. Multiagent Systems - A Theoretical Framework for Intentions, Know-How, and Communications. Springer LNCS 799, 1994.

Agent Interaction Semantics by Timed Operating Instructions

Mirko Viroli and Alessandro Ricci

DEIS, Università di Bologna in Cesena,
via Venezia 52, FC, Italy
{mviroli, aricci}@deis.unibo.it

Abstract. Contrasting the standard framework based on agent-to-agent direct communication, in this paper we focus on agent interaction with the environment. In particular, the environment is seen as populated by *coordination artifacts* [1], automatising coordination tasks and mediating agent interaction.

As a semantic framework for this context we propose operating instructions, which the agent reads and interprets to become aware of the allowed actions and perceptions at a given time, and the MAS infrastructure can exploit to enforce correct agent behaviours and detect wrong ones. This allows us to conceptually handle a number of crucial aspects related to agent interaction, including interaction protocols, timing properties — such as delays and timeouts —, and a notion of contract featuring violation and guarantees.

Formally, our framework is based on a process algebra featuring *(i)* explicit connection between action and its related perceptions, *(ii)* a time-based branch operator, *(iii)* violation and guarantee deadlock states, and *(iv)* association of mental properties to interactions.

1 Introduction

The semantic study of agent interaction is a key topic of the Multi-Agent Systems (MAS) research field. A basic goal of this line of research is to define a standard approach for interaction, enabling heterogeneous agents to collaborate, to semantically interoperate by understanding not only the content but also the "rational meaning" of their interaction. This study has mainly focussed on direct communication between agents, namely by considering Agent Communication Languages (ACLs) based on speech-act theory — examples of such semantics include mentalistic [2], protocol-oriented [3], and social commitments [4, 5] approaches. However, mediated forms of interaction have been increasingly considered as an interesting, plausible alternative to direct interaction, in particular in scenarios like environment-based coordination, such as stigmergy [6] and coordination infrastructures [7]. Even following the frequently exploited connection between agent and human behaviour, one observes — inspired e.g. by Activity Theory [8] — that humans very often do not collaborate by direct speaking, but through *mediating artifacts* of various kinds, such as blackboards, semaphores, signs, and the like, which are all constructed with the specific aim of simplifying interaction. Such artifacts are not suitably modelled as agents, because agent peculiarities such as autonomy, proactiveness, and rationality simply do not apply for them — we stress this difference by referring to an artifact by "it" and to an agent by "he".

R.M. van Eijk et al. (Eds.): AC 2004, LNAI 3396, pp. 173–192, 2005.

In spite of the emergence of these new scenarios, however, the very issue of semantics for mediated interaction has still to be understood and studied in detail. As a reference case we consider the framework of *coordination artifacts* introduced in [9, 1] and inspired by Activity Theory. Coordination artifacts are abstractions provided by the MAS infrastructure so as to embody a mediating artifact: their role is to mediate the interactions of a group of agents by realising a given coordination task. An agent sees a coordination artifact as an entity of the environment, and interacts with it by executing actions that the artifact is designed to support: from this viewpoint such interactions are more similar in nature to *physical acts* rather than to *communicative acts* [10].

Conceptually inspired by the way humans exploit electronics-based physical devices, our semantic approach to the interaction of agents with coordination artifacts is based on the notion of *operating instructions*, namely, instructions operationally describing how an agent has to use a coordination artifact. As such, operating instructions specify the protocol of actions and perceptions which are step-by-step allowed to the agent by the artifact, also including timing properties and constraints related to the occurrence of these interactions. In particular, operating instructions can also serve as a tool to support a notion of *contract*: they can specify which interaction paths are considered wrong agent behaviour or wrong artifact behaviour, identifying situations of agent *violation* or agent *guarantee* that the MAS infrastructure is in charge of properly handling.

From the agent viewpoint, operating instructions can be seen as a model for the agent plan concerning the exploitation of the coordination artifact (similarly to e.g. [11]): agent intentions can be suitably set by simply considering the operating instructions, which are to be executed on a step-by-step basis. Moreover, operating instructions can also come with the specification of preconditions for actions and effects to perceptions, both formulated in terms of mental properties. This information can be leveraged by the agent to relate interaction to his mental state, enabling interaction protocols to be carried on by means of rationality.

Elaborating on [12], in this paper we provide the formal description of a language for operating instructions, which is a key ingredient of our methodology, crucially affecting not only the design of coordination artifacts, but most importantly here the way agents interpret them. This is developed using an algebraic approach: like in calculi such as CCS [13], operating instructions are seen as elements of a process algebra, describing the allowed agent interactive behaviour. The process algebra we introduce to this end features common operators such as action prefix, choice and parallel composition, and recursive definitions. Nevertheless, new mechanisms have been introduced to fit the aims of our context: *(i)* connection of actions and perceptions through matching identifiers, inspired by the name restriction operator of CCS; *(ii)* violation and guarantee deadlock states, modelled as absorbing elements of the algebra with different priority; *(iii)* a time branch operator inspired and adapted from [14], allowing a number of properties such as deadlines and delays to be specified. The operational semantics we provide for this process algebra serves not only as a specification tool, but is actually the abstract design of the agent part in charge of interpreting operating instructions.

The remainder of the paper is organised as follows. Section 2 introduces the notion of coordination artifact and its main properties; Section 3 describes the formal framework behind our semantic approach, and provides a number of useful examples; Section 4 deepens the relationship between operating instructions and agent rationality; Section 5 shows an application based on the Contract-Net protocol; Section 6 discusses related work in the context of ACL semantics; and finally Section 7 concludes providing final remarks.

2   Environment and Coordination Artifacts

The MAS scenario we consider in this paper is based on the notion of coordination artifact [9, 1]. This is conceived by adapting to the MAS field the concept of mediating artifact introduced in the Activity Theory [8], where it is used to model those entities and abstractions that humans construct and then use to coordinate one to each other. Coordination artifacts are abstractions provided by the MAS infrastructure, and embodying some coordination laws designed to mediate the interaction of a group of agents. An example of coordination infrastructure that supports this notion is TuCSoN [7], where *tuple centres* play the role of coordination artifacts for agents. In spite of an existing implementation, the remainder of the paper remains completely independent of it, for we intend to focus on semantics aspects.

A coordination artifact is characterised by a *usage interface*, which is a set of operations allowed to agents, such as requesting information, notifying results, providing replies, issuing broadcasts, and so on. A coordination service is provided to agents by allowing them to execute actions over the coordination artifact, each specifying an operation of the usage interface. Hence, from the agent viewpoint coordination artifacts are very much like physical resources living in the agent environment: the agent can act on them by executing actions, and sense them by eventually perceiving the outcomes of such actions — also called action *completions*. In particular, action execution is used when some information has to flow from an agent to a coordination artifact, with the corresponding perceptions carrying information about a related flow from the coordination artifact to the agent. These two kinds of interaction are modelled in a combined way by the action/perceptions schema, so as to support and stress the idea that the agent acts upon the coordination artifact, and never the opposite — since the artifact, differently from an agent, is not a proactive component.

Connected to this notion of usage interface, coordination artifacts are also characterised by the idea of *operating instructions* — sometimes only instructions for brevity. An agent interacting with a coordination artifact is given operating instructions that specify the precise procedure by which the coordination artifact is to be exploited, and that characterise the role — in the broader acceptation of the term — the agent is playing in the collaborating group. These not merely define the operations allowed — which are in general a subset of all the operations supported by the artifact — but rather the protocol to be used, the allowed sequences of actions and completions. Instructions can describe a non-deterministic agent behaviour, in the sense that at a given time the agent might be allowed to execute more actions or obtain more perceptions, each possibly involving a different protocol continuation. Also, instructions can describe an unbounded protocol, e.g. because the number of interacting agents is not fixed a priori, so that the number of necessary interactions can dynamically change. Moreover, when specifying some instructions, actions and perceptions can come equipped by preconditions and effects, respectively, which are expressed in terms of agent beliefs. In the end, as described in detail in [15] and in next sections, the instructions along with these preconditions and effects provide an effective means by which rational agents can carry on the interaction protocol in a meaningful way.

Developing the work in [1], in this paper we add other features to operating instructions, so as to make them a more powerful tool for the semantic interaction between agents. We first add the notion of violation. Operating instructions can be seen as a contract between the agent and the coordination artifact, which the MAS infrastructure is in charge of enforcing. In particular, instructions are the suitable place where specify wrong paths of interaction that can be ascribable to either the agent or the coordination artifact. From the viewpoint of the agent playing the instructions, they are respectively seen as *violations* and *guarantees*. In either case, the operating instructions should become invalid, prevent any further interaction, and be in a state distinguishing between the two possibilities. In this way, by making some entity of the MAS infrastructure reify the instructions state on a step-by-step basis, it is possible to intercept wrong behaviour, and e.g. legally address them by charging the agent (in case of violation) of refunding its expenses (in case of guarantee).

We then add timing properties to operating instructions. This feature, which allow us to specify deadlines and delays, is particularly useful to flexibly express violations. In fact, as far as openness and high dynamism are concerned, it is crucial to prevent agents to either fail to timely respond to a protocol, or conversely to act too frequently over a coordination artifact. Similar arguments hold from the agent viewpoint, as he may require a certain level of quality of service from a coordination artifact.

In this paper, we suppose that an agent is aware of the instructions he is currently following, and can then reason about them. This can be obtained in several ways: *(i)* by hard-coding this information in the agent, *(ii)* by including it in the domain ontology description, *(iii)* by allowing the agent to inspect the artifact, or *(iv)* by some infrastructural support (such as the notion of Agent Coordination Context [16]), depending on the application scenario. We abstract away from this issue, and make non further hypothesis on the negotiation phase leading to agents agreeing on exploiting a given artifact — called the *co-operation phase* in Activity Theory. In this paper we instead concentrate on the run-time aspects of an agent playing given operating instructions.

Coordination artifacts feature other key properties, such as malleability and inspectability of behaviour, which are less relevant in the context of this paper, but are rather fundamental in making them engineering abstractions effectively and efficiently supporting coordination tasks. The details of all these aspects, which the interested reader can find in [9, 1], make coordination artifacts abstractions for which the agent model is not particularly suitable, and which provide an interesting case for studying the semantics of mediated interaction.

3   Formal Framework

A general picture of the whole formal framework of coordination artifacts is presented in [1], based on coordination artifact behaviour (implementing given coordination rules), an abstract architecture for agents (dealing with internal agent details), and an operational semantics for operating instructions. As far as interaction semantics is concerned, we here focus on formalising operating instructions — the other aspects being less relevant.

Operating instructions are here described in terms of a language. Syntax is provided as usual with a BNF grammar, expressing the shape of allowed instructions. Semantics is represented operationally, through a labelled transition system specifying how instructions evolve as agent interactions occur or as time passes (similarly to the approach in [17]). Indeed, this semantics is particularly useful as it specifies how the agent should interpret instructions, namely, which actions/perceptions are allowed at a given time.

In this paper we adopt the notion of meta-variables — see [18] for a formal discussion on this widely exploited notion. Given a meta-variable x, we denote by $Set(x)$ the set of elements over which it ranges, we consider it as a non-terminal symbol in grammars, and see its decorations x', x'', x_0, x_1, and the like as ranging over the same set.

In the specific scope of this paper, we let meta-variable α range over agent actions, π over agent perceptions, $\mathcal{N}$ over the names of operating instructions definitions, i over interaction identifiers, and consider their sets as disjunct. Then, α, π, and $\mathcal{N}$ denote terms whose syntax is abstracted away here, but which can be subject to substitutions $\sigma \in \Sigma$ (partial functions from terms to terms). We write σt for the substitution σ applied to term t, say that term t is more general than t' (and that t' is more specific than t) if for at least one substitution we have $\sigma t = t'$, and denoted by $\{t/t'\}$ the most general substitution (if present) such that $\{t/t'\}t' = t$.

3.1   Actions and Violations

We start presenting a subset of the language for operating instructions, neglecting timing aspects. What we obtain is a language able to express protocols of actions and perceptions, along with notions of agent and coordination artifact violations.

Meta-variable ω ranges over agent interactions, and is expressed by the syntax:

$$\omega ::= !^{(i)}\alpha \mid ?^i\pi$$

$!^{(i)}\alpha$ represents an action α tagged by the identifier i, while $?^i\pi$ a perception π corresponding to a previous action with identifier i. In order for a trace (or sequence) of interactions to be well-formed, any interaction $?^i\pi$ must be preceded by an interaction $!^{(i)}\alpha$, that is, featuring the same identifier i — the action could occur several interactions before a related perception. This is compatible with the idea that in our framework agent perceptions only represent the outcomes of an action the agent has previously executed.

To the end of this language presentation, actions and perceptions are seen as abstract terms without any further hypothesis on their content. However, in real cases they can carry some information about their nature, including their source and target, the time at which they occurred, as well as ontological aspects such as the mental preconditions and effects they are equipped with — as described in previous section.

The abstract syntax of operating instructions, ranged over by I and L, is expressed by the following grammar:

$$I, L ::= 0 \mid \epsilon \mid \gamma \mid \omega.I \mid I + L \mid I \| L \mid \mathcal{N}$$

Term 0 represents the terminated instructions, in that state the agent cannot execute actions. ϵ is the state of instructions representing agent violation, and dually, γ the state of instructions representing a violation by the coordination artifact (also called, an agent guarantee). $\omega.I$ denotes the instructions allowing interaction ω (or any more specific one) followed by instructions I. Then, as in more standard process algebras (e.g. CCS [13]) $I + I'$ is the choice between I and I', $I||I'$ the parallel (interleaved) composition between I and I', and finally $\mathcal{N}$ is the invocation of an instructions definition of the kind $\mathcal{N} := I$, which should be specified along with the instructions where $\mathcal{N}$ occurs.

When parenthesis are not specified, we assume operator $+$ to have priority over $||$. The prefix action operator $\omega.I$ allows us to express sequences of interactions, choice $+$ to define instructions featuring more possible interaction histories, parallel composition $||$ for specifying concurrent instructions, and finally $\mathcal{N}$ to recursively define instructions so as to enable infinite behaviours. In a sequence of interactions $\omega_1.\omega_2.\ldots.\omega_n.0$ we often avoid reporting the concluding ".0" notation.

We introduce an equivalence relation defining instructions that should be considered syntactically identical. This is defined as the smallest congruence relation satisfying the rules:

$$0 + I \equiv I \qquad I + L \equiv L + I \qquad (I + L) + I' \equiv I + (L + I') \qquad \text{[C-CHO]}$$
$$0||I \equiv I \qquad I||L \equiv L||I \qquad (I||L)||I' \equiv I||(L||I') \qquad \text{[C-PAR]}$$
$$\mathcal{N}' \equiv \{\mathcal{N}'/\mathcal{N}\}I \text{ if } \mathcal{N} := I \qquad \text{[C-DEF]}$$
$$\epsilon + I \equiv \epsilon \qquad \epsilon||I \equiv \epsilon \qquad \text{[C-VIO]}$$
$$\gamma + (\omega.I||L) \equiv \gamma + L \qquad \gamma + \gamma \equiv \gamma \qquad \text{[C-GUA1]}$$
$$\gamma||(\omega.I + L) \equiv \gamma||L \qquad \gamma||\gamma \equiv \gamma \qquad \text{[C-GUA2]}$$

Rules [C-CHO] and [C-PAR] define choice and parallel composition as commutative and associative operators absorbing instructions 0. Rule [C-DEF] states that an invocation $\mathcal{N}$ to some instructions definition $\mathcal{N} := I$ behaves like the associated instructions I, modulo the necessary substitution. That is, if a more specific name $\mathcal{N}'$ is actually invoked, substitution $\{\mathcal{N}'/\mathcal{N}\}$ is applied to I as well. In particular, this rule features overloading of the substitution operator, which is applied to instructions other than to terms: in this case substitution is to be applied to any term (action, perception, instruction names) inside the instructions. Rules [C-VIO] are used to make ϵ absorbing any instructions through operators $+$ and/or $||$ — namely, a violation gets propagated to the composed instructions. Similarly, rules [C-GUA1] and [C-GUA2] propagates a guarantee state γ, with the only difference that such a propagation has lower priority than ϵ, in that e.g. $\epsilon||\gamma \equiv \epsilon$.

In the following, we assume the specification of some operating instructions to be well-formed, in the sense that in any instructions (or sub-instructions) of the kind $!^{(i)}\alpha.I$ the identifier i never occurs in another action in I or in definitions in I — this prevents clash of action identifiers.

Operational semantics is defined by a transition system specified by tuple $\langle Set(I), \rightarrow , \rightarrow_\delta, Set(\omega) \rangle$. Labelled transition relation $\rightarrow$ is of the kind $\rightarrow \subseteq Set(I) \times Set(\omega) \times Set(I)$: when $\langle I, \omega, L \rangle \in \rightarrow$, also written $I \xrightarrow{\omega} L$, we mean that (i) instructions I allow the agent to execute ω (action or perception), and that correspondingly (ii) instructions I move to state L. Notation $I \xrightarrow{\omega}\!\!\!\!\!/\,\,$ means that for no L we have $I \xrightarrow{\omega} L$. Predicate $\rightarrow_\delta \subseteq Set(I)$ over instructions is used instead for identifying *deadlock* states: when

$I \in \to_\delta$, also written $I \to_\delta$, we mean that I is a deadlock state (an agent or coordination artifact violation); $I \not\to_\delta$ denotes the opposite case.[1]

Deadlock predicate $\to_\delta$ is defined by rules

$$\epsilon \to_\delta \quad [\text{VIO}] \qquad\qquad \frac{}{\gamma \to_\delta} \quad [\text{GUA}]$$

$$\frac{I \to_\delta}{I + L \to_\delta} \quad [\text{V-CHO}] \qquad\qquad \frac{I \to_\delta}{I \| L \to_\delta} \quad [\text{V-PAR}]$$

which simply state that ϵ and γ are deadlocked along with any parallel or choice composition involving them. The transition relation $\to$ is instead defined by rules:

$$\frac{I \xrightarrow{\omega} I' \quad L \not\to_\delta}{I + L \xrightarrow{\omega} I'} \quad [\text{O-CHO}] \qquad\qquad \frac{I \xrightarrow{\omega} I' \quad L \not\to_\delta}{I \| L \xrightarrow{\omega} I' + L} \quad [\text{O-PAR}]$$

$$!^{(i)}\alpha.I \xrightarrow{!^{(i)}\alpha'} \{\alpha'/\alpha\}I \quad [\text{ACT}] \qquad\qquad ?^i\pi.I \xrightarrow{?^i\pi'} \{\pi'/\pi\}I \quad [\text{PER}]$$

Rule [O-CHO] says that among two (or more) choices, only one is allowed to proceed, as long as the others are not deadlocked. Conversely, rule [O-PAR] says that in a parallel composition, any instruction is allowed to proceed, as long as the others are not deadlocked. Finally, rule [ACT] says that in instructions $!^{(i)}\alpha.I$, any more specific action α' can be executed, and the corresponding substitution is applied to the continuation I; similarly for rule [PER], handling perceptions.

The computational model induced is as follows. Following the idea in [19], we denote by "completed trace of execution" an evolution of instructions I (along with the involved interactions ω) reaching a final point where no more interactions can occur. Then, given an initial state of instructions I, a completed trace of execution is of one of the two kinds:

– Finished instructions:

$$I \xrightarrow{\omega_1} I_1 \xrightarrow{\omega_2} I_2 \xrightarrow{\omega_3} \ldots \xrightarrow{\omega_n} I_n \equiv 0$$

The agent executes actions and obtain perceptions as allowed by the instructions, until reaching the terminated instructions.

– Violation:

$$I \xrightarrow{\omega_1} I_1 \xrightarrow{\omega_2} I_2 \xrightarrow{\omega_3} \ldots \xrightarrow{\omega_n} I_n \not\to_\delta$$

As interactions occur, the agent reaches a deadlocked state I_n, in this case we have $I_n \not\xrightarrow{\omega}$ for any ω, and either $I_n \equiv \gamma$ or $I_n \equiv \epsilon$.

3.2 Examples

We here report some remarkable example of operating instructions along with their intuitions. Elements written in typetext font are considered variables possibly subject to substitution.

---

[1] Differently from more common interpretations of the term "deadlock", here we do not intend a synchronisation fault between a composition of processes, but rather, a single abstraction — operating instructions — getting stuck because of a wrong interaction path.

Actions, Perceptions, and Substitutions. Consider the following operating instructions definition:

$$N := !^{(i)} ask(\text{query}).?^i reply(\text{query}, \text{res})$$

They state that the agent may first execute an action of the kind $ask(\text{query})$, and then perceive a corresponding perception $reply(\text{query}, \text{res})$. The link between action and perception is set by the same identifier i in them. Then, because of substitutions ([ACT]), if the agent executes an actual action $ask(q_0)$, he will later obtain a perception $reply(q_0, r_0)$ (with same query specification q_0). This simple protocol can be executed indefinitely as follows:

$$N := !^{(i)} ask(\text{query}).?^i reply(\text{query}, \text{res}).(N + !^{(i')} stop)$$

In this case, the protocol can terminate after any number of queries, by executing action *stop*. Finally, due to the substitution mechanism again, we can force the agent to ask for the same query all the times by the specification:

$$N := !^{(i)} ask(\text{query}).?^i reply(\text{query}, \text{res}).(N(\text{query}) + !^{(i')} stop)$$
$$N(\text{query}) := !^{(i)} ask(\text{query}).?^i reply(\text{query}, \text{res}).(N(\text{query}) + !^{(i')} stop)$$

In fact, after the first action, the query value is substituted in all the following actions through the instructions name $N(\text{query})$.

Linking Actions and Perceptions. In our framework it is crucial for an agent to relate a perception to an action previously executed. Consider the case where an agent executes two actions α and α' and then obtains the corresponding perceptions π and π'. This can be modelled in any of the following ways:

$$N := !^{(i)}\alpha.!^{(i')}\alpha'.?^i\pi.?^{i'}\pi'$$
$$N' := !^{(i)}\alpha.!^{(i')}\alpha'.(?^i\pi || ?^{i'}\pi')$$
$$N'' := (!^{(i)}\alpha.?^i\pi) || (!^{(i')}\alpha'.?^{i'}\pi')$$

In the first case, the order of actions and corresponding perceptions is completely determined; in the second case, the agent executes action α, then α', then he waits for the two perceptions concurrently; in the third case the two couples action/perception are handled separately and concurrently.

Also, we can model the situation where more perceptions result from a single action, which is simply obtained through the proper identifiers. The following specification models the case of two perceptions related to the same action

$$N := !^{(i)}\alpha.?^i\pi.?^i\pi'$$

whereas an unbound number of perceptions can be modelled as:

$$N := !^{(i)}\alpha.N'$$
$$N' := ?^i\pi^{last} + ?^i\pi.N'$$

Protocols. Choice composition operator along with sequential composition allows the specification of any protocol of actions and perceptions. A paradigmatic example is the following:

$$N := !^{(i)}\alpha.(?^i\pi_1.I_1 + \ldots + ?^i\pi_n.I_n)$$

As action α is executed, the agent can distinguish between n perceptions $\pi_1, \ldots, \pi_n$: depending on which one is received a different continuation is considered (either $I_1, \ldots, I_n$), that is, different operating instructions are to be followed next.

Violations. Operating instructions endorse a notion of contract between the agent and the coordination artifact involved. As such, they may specify sequences of interactions interpreted as agent violations, or others as coordination artifact violations. As a first example, at a given time an agent may be required to execute a given action α and not another α^v; this is realised as follows:

$$N := !^{(i)}\alpha.I + !^{(i')}\alpha'.\epsilon$$

If action α is executed, continuation I is allowed to carry on; if action α' is executed instead, the instructions move to state ϵ representing an agent violation, where no other interactions can occur.

Conversely, as an agent executes an action α, he might be guaranteed to obtain perception π instead of π^g — the latter may e.g. represent a failure or a not-understood message. This is represented as:

$$N := !^{(i)}\alpha.(?^i\pi.I + ?^i\pi^g.\gamma)$$

If perception π^g occurs, the instructions move to state γ, representing a violation by the coordination artifact.

3.3   Timed Properties

We add to the framework developed so far the notion of time passing, by which we aim to handle interesting aspects such as delays and deadlines. The general approach we follow is that of timed process algebras — see [20] for a general framework and further references. In particular, our timed extension is inspired by the branch operator in [14], though its integration with violation states is novel.

Let k and h range over non negative integer values. The syntax of the language is extended with a time-based operator as follows:

$$I, L ::= 0 \mid \epsilon \mid \gamma \mid \omega.I \mid \lfloor I \rfloor_k L \mid I + L \mid I \| L \mid \mathcal{N}$$

Informally, instructions $\lfloor I \rfloor_k L$ means that instructions I are allowed, but if the agent does not starting executing I within k units of time this possibility disappears, and the agent should proceed with instructions L. Accordingly we add to the transition relation labels of the kind $\tau(k)$ ($k > 0$): we write $I \xrightarrow{\tau(k)} L$ to say that instructions I may move to state L as k units of time have passed. While predicate $\to_\delta$ is unchanged, the following rules are to be added that extend the semantics of transition relation $\to$:

$$\omega.I \xrightarrow{\tau(k)} \omega.I \quad \text{[T-ACT]} \qquad\qquad \lfloor I \rfloor_k L \xrightarrow{\tau(k-h)} \lfloor I \rfloor_h L \quad \text{[TIME]}$$

$$\frac{L \xrightarrow{\tau(h)} L'}{\lfloor I \rfloor_k L \xrightarrow{\tau(k+h)} L'} \quad \text{[DEAD]} \qquad\qquad \frac{I \xrightarrow{\omega} I'}{\lfloor I \rfloor_k L \xrightarrow{\omega} I'} \quad \text{[BRANCH]}$$

$$\frac{I \xrightarrow{\tau(k)} I' \quad L \xrightarrow{\tau(k)} L'}{I||L \xrightarrow{\tau(k)} I'||L'} \quad \text{[T-PAR]} \qquad\qquad \frac{I \xrightarrow{\tau(k)} I' \quad L \xrightarrow{\tau(k)} L'}{I + L \xrightarrow{\tau(k)} I' + L'} \quad \text{[T-CHO]}$$

Rule [ACT] says that prefix interaction $\omega.I$ is not affected by time passing. Rule [TIME] states that if time passes (of $k - h$ units of time) but the branch deadline k does not expire (note that $k > h$ by construction), then the left possibility (I) remains open, but the deadline is to be updated (to h). Due to rule [DEAD], if on the other hand the deadline expires (of h units of time), the right instructions L proceed, after applying to them h units of time. Rule [BRANCH] is used to state that if prior to the deadline the left instructions I move due to an interaction ω, then the right instructions J are excluded. Finally, rules [T-PAR] and [T-CHO] say that time passing propagates to both parallel and choice composition. The computational model we obtain is similar to the previous one: interactions and type passing occur evolving the operating instructions, until either the state 0 or a violation (ϵ or γ) is reached.

3.4   Examples

The branch operator introduced allows for a number of interesting time-based constructs, as shown in the following examples.

Actions with Deadline. A first, remarkable example of exploitation of timing properties is the case where operating instructions specify that an agent must execute a given action within k time units. This is obtained as follows:

$$N := \lfloor !^{(i)} \alpha.I \rfloor_k \epsilon$$

If the agent executes action α within k time units, then continuation I is allowed to carry on, otherwise, after $k + 1$ time units instructions will move to the violation state ϵ. Thanks to parallel compositions, then, a deadline to an action is compatible with other behaviours carrying on independently. For instance, int the following schema

$$N := I || \lfloor !^{(i)} \alpha.L \rfloor_k \epsilon$$

instructions I can be executed as usual: however, if after k time units action α is not executed, then the right hand side moves to ϵ, making the whole instructions to being violated. This idea can be useful to impose global deadlines to some instructions.

Action deadline can be simply extended to the case of more actions featuring different deadlines. First, write $[I]_k J$ as a shorthand for $\lfloor I + J \rfloor_k J$, meaning that the agent can execute either I or J, but the possibility of executing I disappears after k time units. Notice that this new operator could be added to an actual implementation of our language for operating instructions. Suppose that $k_1 < k_2 < \ldots < k_n$: we may require an agent to execute any action α_j $(1 \leq j \leq n)$, but each within its own deadline k_j. This is expressed by the instructions:

$$N := [!^{(i1)}\alpha_1.I_1]_{k_1}[!^{(i2)}\alpha_2.I_2]_{k_2-k_1} \ldots \lfloor !^{(in)}\alpha_n.I_n \rfloor_{k_n-k_{n-1}}\epsilon$$

Notice that, differently from the others, the last branch construct is the standard one $\lfloor I \rfloor_k L$: this is to prevent ϵ to be a possibility before k_n expires.

Perceptions with Deadline. Conversely, it might be interesting to guarantee an agent to obtain a perception within a certain amount fo time. By the instructions

$$N := !^{(i)}\alpha.\lfloor ?^i\pi.I \rfloor_k \gamma$$

if the agent perceives π within k time units then the continuation I can carry on, otherwise the deadlock state γ is reached. Multiple deadlines for more perceptions can be expressed similarly to the case of actions, as follows:

$$N := !^{(i)}\alpha.[?^i\pi_1.I_1]_{k_1}[?^i\pi_2.I_2]_{k_2-k_1} \ldots \lfloor ?^i\pi_n.I_n \rfloor_{k_n-k_{n-1}}\gamma$$

Waiting and Expiring Actions. Our approach allows for describing even more timing properties. In some scenario, it may be crucial to allow a coordination artifact to require a maximum frequency of interactions, e.g. in order to guarantee a certain quality of service. For instance, it may force an agent to wait k time units before executing an action. This is obtained by the definition:

$$N := \lfloor !^{(i)}\alpha.\epsilon \rfloor_k !^{(i)}\alpha.I$$

if the agent executes α within k time units then the deadlock ϵ is reached, otherwise the continuation I can carry on.

For similar reasons, an artifact may guarantee a service to an agent only for few time units, if the agent does not exploit it the possibility disappears. By the instructions:

$$N := \lfloor !^{(i)}\alpha.I \rfloor_k I$$

the possibility of executing α disappears after k time units, if this is not exploited the continuation I carries on.

4   Relation to Agent Rationality

As most ACL semantics, our semantic framework for mediated interaction does not require any specific agent architecture, but can leverage agent intelligence to enable dynamically emerging cooperations. This is achieved by means of the operating instructions, by the joint exploitation of interaction protocols and mentalistic (belief-based) semantics to actions and perceptions. We here briefly review this aspect, which is amenable to a formal model following the approach in [15].

Preconditions and Effects. First of all, we assume that actions α and perceptions π are equipped by information about their impact on the agent mental state. In particular, denote $Pre(\alpha)$ preconditions to the execution of α expressed as agent beliefs: only if that preconditions hold the agent *should* execute α. Similarly, denote $Eff(\pi)$ effects to the perception π expressed as changes to agent beliefs: as the agent perceives π the changes *should* be applied to his beliefs. Let $\mathcal{B}$ the set of all possibile agent belief states, for simplicity we simply suppose that $Pre(\alpha)$ is a predicate over $\mathcal{B}$, and $Eff(\pi)$ is a function $\mathcal{B} \mapsto \mathcal{B}$.

As described in detail in Section 6, by the terms "should" above we do not mean that validity of preconditions and application of effects are mandatory for the agent complying to the interaction semantics. Rather, they are just to be interpreted as a means to exploit agent rationality to maximise his benefits when using the coordination artifact — e.g. to decide which of the allowed actions to execute, and how the agent knowledge should update due to perceptions.

Agent Perception of Time. In order to correctly reason about operating instructions with timing properties, the agent should be aware of time passing. Write $B\,pass(k)$ for the agent getting aware about the fact that k units of time passed. We distinguish two basic cases.

If the coordination artifact and the agent reside in the same physical place, it is reasonable to assume they have a common and uniform perception of time passing. In this case, the way they track time passing in operating instructions is equal.

However, it can be the case that they stay in different nodes of a network, so that it is impossible to enforce a completely synchronised notion of time. Notice that this problem is general, and would hold in any protocol over a distributed system. In this situation, we first assume that time passing is always relative to the coordination artifact, which is in fact the entity that should mediate between different agents and is in charge of keeping a consistent state of shared data and of providing a quality coordination service. Then, we assume that the agent perceives time passing directly from the coordination artifact, that is, $B\,pass(k)$ is the result of an implicit interaction between the agent and the artifact. If ordering of interactions is guaranteed, this should at least allow the agent to recognise whether the execution of an action has occurred before a deadline expired.

Notice that in order to overcome this partial solution to the problem, in [21] we proposed the notion of Agent Coordination Context (ACC), which is an infrastructure abstraction local to the agent site, and in charge of enabling and enforcing its correct behaviour. The ACC appears to be the right place where timing properties must be controlled and enforced.

Agent Abstract Behaviour. Following the discussion in Section 2, we assume that before actually interacting with the coordination artifact, each agent is aware of the operating instructions he has to follow — namely, he has a correct believe about the current state of the protocol, about preconditions to actions, and effects to perceptions. Most likely, the agent contracted with the MAS infrastructure the operating instructions to use to interact with a coordination artifact, and thus downloaded the corresponding specification.

Write $B\,instr(I)$ for the fact that the agent believes that I is the current state of the instructions he has to follow, briefly referred to as the *current instructions* — expressed using the algebraic notation of previous section or an equivalent one.

The key point of our semantic approach is that an agent meaning to follow the operating instructions simply intends to execute the prescribed actions (and gets aware of the corresponding perceptions) on a step-by-step basis, keeping track of how instructions correspondingly evolve. More precisely:

– At any point of the interaction protocol, among the available actions the agent should intend to execute any of those allowed by the current instructions *and* satisfying the preconditions $Pre(\alpha)$: that is, the agent intends to execute α if, given $B\,instr(I)$, we have $I \xrightarrow{!^{(i)}\alpha}_\mathcal{T} I'$ for some I' and i, and $Pre(\alpha)$ holds in current agent beliefs $\mathcal{B}$. From the point of view of our interaction semantics, the agent could choose any of such actions: if many of them exist, a decision can be taken by reasoning on the effects that can be obtained later by following a given choice. As one action is chosen, say α_0 (and i_0), this can be executed — it is allowed by the coordination artifact by construction —, and correspondingly the current instructions of the agent will move to the state I_0 such that $I \xrightarrow{!^{(i_0)}\alpha_0} I_0$.

– Eventually, a perception π of a previously executed action α will also be received, which the agent gets aware of due to the occurrence of $B\,done(?^{i_0}\pi)$ in the beliefs. Given the current instructions I, by construction there is some I' such that $I \xrightarrow{?^{i_0}\pi} I'$: so I' will be the next state of the instructions, and the effects $Eff(\pi)$ will be applied to the beliefs.

– Moreover, as the agent perceives the passage of k units of time, he will update its current instructions from I to I' if and only if $I \xrightarrow{\tau(k)} I'$.

– If the agent instructions reach state 0, the agent knows he finished to play them. If they reach ϵ or γ the agent stops playing instructions, e.g. waiting for the MAS infrastructure to legally proceed against the violator.

This schema, combining the intentions set by the current state of instructions and the beliefs affected by action and perception semantics, ensures a good support for semantic interoperability, as discussed in [15].

5   A Contract-Net Case

In this section we show the operating instructions of a Contract-Net scenario [22], where a coordination artifact mediates the interactions between an initiator and a number of participants. We assume that, at the beginning, the initiator and the participants negotiate with the infrastructure for a coordination artifact realising the Contract-Net protocol with given features, including e.g. all the related timeouts. Therefore, agents receive information about the instructions they have to use, and then simply start following them.

The initiator issues call for proposals (CFP) by specifying an action he wants to be executed. To simplify our discussion without loss of generality, we suppose that such an action is a term with two variables: *(i)* one is bounded by the participant with information about his proposal, and is used by the initiator to evaluate which proposals have to be accepted; *(ii)* the other is bounded by the participant after executing the action, and will contain the result of the execution. For instance, suppose a participant gets aware of a CFP for buying goods, due to the perception of term $newCFP(buy(good\_name, \mathtt{v\_prize}, \mathtt{v\_qty}))$; he makes a proposal (with 1000 as prize) by action $propose(buy(good\_name, 1000, \mathtt{v\_qty}))$, and later notifies the result of buying 5 items by $result(buy(good\_name, 1000, 5))$. This allows us to specify instructions for the participant with the general schema:

$$\ldots ?newCFP(v).\ldots !propose(v).\ldots !result(v).\ldots$$

as the variable v can get specialised further by substitution of variables to terms at each step, thanks to the operational rules [ACT] and [PER].

5.1   Instructions for the Participant

Instructions for participants are described by definition Np as follows:

$$
\begin{aligned}
Np(v) := {}& !^{(1)}getCFP(v).(\\
& ?^1finished+ \\
& ?^1newCFP(v).(\\
& \quad !^{(2)}refuse(v).Np(v)+ \\
& \quad !^{(2)}propose.(v).(\\
& \qquad ?^2rejected.Np(v)+ \\
& \qquad ?^2accepted.\lfloor !^{(3)}fail.Np(v)+!^{(3)}result(v).Np(v)\rfloor_{k_P}\epsilon \\
&)\quad)\quad)
\end{aligned}
$$

The participant first executes action *getCFP*, in order to receive information about a currently pending CFP. By completion *finished*, he perceives the fact that his participation to the collaboration is over, because e.g. the initiator has terminated his work, or the participant is banned from the collaboration by the artifact. Alternatively, the completion *newCFP* is perceived meaning that a CFP has been raised: its actual content — the requested proposal — is stored in variable v. As the CFP has been received, the agent can either refuse the CFP by action *refuse* (and then recursively invoke the instructions in order to participate to a new CFP), or make a proposal through action *propose*. If a proposal is made, it can be either accepted or rejected by the artifact, represented by perceptions *accepted* and *rejected*. In the case of acceptance, the participant is meant to execute the requested action, eventually notifying the result by action *result* or a failure by *fail*. In particular, these two actions are associated with a timeout of k_P time units. If this expires, instructions are violated (ϵ), otherwise the action is executed and the whole protocol is executed again by the recursive invocation to Np.

5.2   Instructions for the Initiator

Instructions for the initiator are described by definition Ni as follows:

$$Ni(v) \quad := !^{(1)}CFP(v).($$
$$Ni\_reply(v)||$$
$$\lfloor ?^1finished.Ni(v)\rfloor_{k_{IF}}\epsilon$$
$$)$$

$$Ni\_reply(v) \quad := \lfloor ?^1new\_prop(v).(Ni\_reply(v)||Ni\_handler(v))\rfloor_{k_{IN}}\epsilon$$

$$Ni\_handler(v) := !^{(3)}reject(v)+$$
$$!^{(2)}accept(v).[?^2fail]_{k_{IF}}\lfloor ?^2result(v)\rfloor_{k_{IR}}\gamma$$

The initiator first issues a CFP by executing action $CFP(v)$, specifying the requested proposal. Then he spawns two parallel sub-instructions: *(i)* he invokes Ni_reply that will handle all the replies to the CFP; and *(ii)* waits for perception *finished*, meaning no other proposals will be available, with a deadline of k_{IF} time units: if the deadline expires the whole instructions will be considered violated (ϵ). Definition Ni_reply waits for a proposal *new_prop* to be perceived, guaranteeing (γ) the agent to receive one within k_{IN} time units. As the proposal is perceived the agent spawns two sub-instructions again: *(i)* he recursively invoke Ni_reply to obtain new perceptions, and *(ii)* he invokes instructions Ni_handler to handle the proposal just arrived. This basically rejects or accepts the proposal: in the case this is accepted, it waits for the result or a perception about a failure with a deadline of k_{IR} time units.

5.3   Mentalistic Semantics to Actions and Perceptions

The execution of actions by participants and initiator is not only guided by the requirement to follow the operating instructions — which would hardly be sufficient to make the agent meaningfully carry on the protocol — but also leverages preconditions and effects, shown as follows:

ACTION	Precondition	PERCEPTION	Effect
$getCFP$	-	$newCFP(v)$	-
		$finished$	-
$refuse(v)$	$B \neg feasible(v)$	$none$	
$propose(v)$	$B\ feasible(v)$	$rejected$	-
		$accepted$	-
$fail$	$\neg B\ feasible(v)$	$none$	
$result(v)$	$B\ done(v)$	$none$	
$CFP(v)$	$\neg B\ done(v)$	$finished$	-
		$new\_prop(v)$	-
$accept(v)$	-	$fail$	-
		$result(v)$	$B(v)$
$reject(v)$	-	$none$	

Notice that in our approach, since intentions are driven by operating instructions and preconditions/effects relate interactions only to agent beliefs, then such preconditions and effects are sensibly simpler and cleaner than e.g. the semantics of FIPA performatives involved in the Contract Net protocol [2].

More specifically, an action is attached a precondition only if it involves the communication of some information from the agent to the coordination artifact, in which case it should be properly connected to the agent beliefs. For simplicity, we denote by $B\ done(a)$ the fact that the agent believes action a has already been executed, and by $B\ feasible(a)$ that he might be able to execute action a. In our case of the Contract-Net protocol, a participant *(i)* refuses to make a proposal if he believes he cannot execute the action $(B\neg feasible(v))$, *(ii)* makes a proposal if he believes he can execute its action $(B\ feasible(v))$, *(iii)* produces a failure message if he no longer believes the action can be executed $(\neg B\ feasible(v))$, and finally *(iv)* he provides a result only if he believes the resulting action has been executed $(B\ done(v))$. Notice e.g. that without this last precondition, it would have been impossible for the agent to understand from the operating instructions what to inform, which is now instead clear from the conjunction of preconditions, effects, and operating instructions.

Analogously, effects have to be specified only when the interaction protocol reaches a point where the agent is receiving some information that should change his perception of the world — not all the times he changes his assumptions about the protocol state as e.g. in FIPA ACL. Therefore, for the Contract-Net protocol case, effects have to be specified only when the initiator perceives the positive completion to the *accept*: in this case the instructions tell him to believe the result. Notice that we never consider preconditions and effects as prescriptive, but rather as suggestions for agents to act in meaningful way, to maximise the benefits when using the artifact: each aspect that should be checked against violations have to be addressed at the level of interaction protocol.

5.4   The Role of the Coordination Artifact

Finally, it is interesting to point out the role played by the coordination artifact in this coordination scenario. As far as providing a coordination task is concerned, the coordination artifact can be understood in terms of an interactive behaviour [23], namely allowing agents to execute actions and providing the proper perceptions consistently with respect to the operating instructions of each agent. This is obtained by means of the proper coordination rules stored and realised in the artifact. Provided that such coordination rules are quite fundamental to implement an effective and efficient Contract-Net protocol scenario, one should notice that they do not make into our semantics of interaction, since the agent only perceives their effect through the operating instructions. In particular, in our framework agents participate in a collaboration without a necessary knowledge about the identity (and even the presence) of other agents: their viewpoint over coordination is rather subjective, for the artifact has the burden of the objective part of coordination [9].

This is not a limitation bur rather a feature of our approach, for the artifact encapsulates and hides a significant coordination burden that would otherwise charge each involved agent. In general, the artifact should be able to satisfy the timing guarantees of all the agents even though one or more of them violate their own part of the contract.

Since handling this aspect can be considered a purely coordination task, it is reasonable to realise it by an ad-hoc policy within the coordination artifact, instead of tackling it through a complex deliberation inside an agent.

Other nice features of the coordination artifact for the Contract-Net protocol include its intrinsic decoupling properties. On the one hand, it decouples the information flow from participants and initiator, e.g. the initiator could handle a large amount of participants without significant design changes: indeed, our approach scales better with the size of the collaborating group. On the other hand, the initiator is not required to initially know the identity (and even the number) of participants, the coordination artifact is in charge of making participants perceiving CFPs, allowing the initiator to perceive only meaningful proposals — e.g. automatically refusing late ones, bad ones, proposals from agents with bad reputation, etcetera.

The interested reader can refer to [9, 15, 1, 12] for further details on the conceptual and engineering approach promoted by coordination artifacts.

6   Related Works in ACL Semantics

Our semantic approach is not a competitor of other semantics proposed for MAS in current and past research. First of all, the motivation goal of our study is different: our interaction semantics is meant to support an engineering methodology for environment-based coordination, rather than to define a standardised approach for interoperability of heterogeneous agents as for ACL semantics. Then, technically our approach applies to the scenario where interactions are not communications sent and received by agents, but are related to the execution of actions over coordination artifacts. So, a basic difference is that our agents are required the ability to follow some specific operating instructions, rather than a general, standardised ACL.

Nevertheless, our approach tackles some issues raised in the context of existing proposals for ACL semantics. From mentalistic semantics such as those of FIPA ACL [2] and KQML [24], we inherited the very idea of connecting an agent rationality with his interactions by preconditions and effects over the agent mental state. Thanks to the support of operating instructions, however, we can tackle the main drawbacks of purely mentalistic approaches — as remarked in the following — while retaining their advantages in a simple and effective way.

Protocol-based semantics have been proposed to provide a better support to interaction protocols, which can in fact be only indirectly expressed by mentalistic approaches — as argued in detail in [25, 26]. In [3, 27], the ACL semantics is equipped by a function associating to each incoming communicative act the set of possible outgoing replies. From this viewpoint, our methodology based on process algebras is much more expressive, since it not only supports the above mechanism, but flexibly allows to exploit in a compositional way the operators for choice, sequential composition, parallel composition, and recursive definitions, as well as including timing aspects. A crucial role is here played by the framework of process algebras, which is a standard approach to describe interaction protocols in the distributed systems field.

Another limit of mentalistic approaches is the non-observability of mental properties (and thus of the outcomes of preconditions and effects to interactions), which makes impossible e.g. to check an agent for compliance. This issue is addressed by commitment-based semantics [4, 5], which interpret communicative acts as manipulations (creation, deletion,..) of commitments, each made by an agent relative to another agent. Since communications are observable, also commitments are: so they can be tracked by some institutional abstraction, which is then in charge of intercepting agent violations.

To a certain extent, a notion of observable commitment is supported in our framework as well. As agents accept to interact with a coordination artifact they commit, relative to the artifact, to follow the associated operating instructions, executing actions in the right sequence and with the required timing. Moreover, each choice made by an agent when more actions are allowed can be interpreted as the commitment to follow the corresponding continuation – in the Contract-Net example, accepting a proposal implies that either a failure notification or the result will be provided. In the case some of these conditions are violated, the MAS infrastructure can intercept them, and support e.g. legal addressing.

Finally, our approach has also some relationship with dialogue games [28, 29], where direct interaction between agents is meant to be ruled by some institutional abstraction — e.g. by commencement, locution, combination, commitment, and termination rules. The notion of coordination artifact could be in principle exploited to support the enforcement of these rules. However, it is worth noting that our approach is here indeed different, for we consider agents as perceiving the coordination artifact as the abstraction they interact with.

7   Conclusions

In this paper we addressed the issue of interaction semantics in the framework of co-ordination artifacts for MAS, which enables an engineering methodology for mediated interaction significantly different from standard MAS approaches. Our semantics tackles some of the most relevant issues raised in the context of ACL semantics, such as connection with agent rationality, support for protocols and for social commitments. Also, the formal framework of process algebras is here used for the first time in the context of interaction semantics for MAS. This is thanks to the peculiar aspects of coordination artifacts, which, differently from agents, can be characterised in terms of coordination rules and operating instructions [1] — i.e. in an operational way.

Future works of this line of research are on implementation in the TuCSoN infrastructure [7], where integration with the Agent Coordination Context notion is concerned [30], and on evaluating the applicability of operating instructions to the conception of a new approach to ACL semantics as well.

References

1. Omicini, A., Ricci, A., Viroli, M., Castelfranchi, C., Tummolini, L.: Coordination artifacts: Environment-based coordination for intelligent agents. In Jennings, N.R., Sierra, C., Sonenberg, L., Tambe, M., eds.: 3rd international Joint Conference on Autonomous Agents and Multiagent Systems (AAMAS 2004). Volume 1., New York, USA, ACM (2004) 286–293

2. FIPA: FIPA communicative act library specification. `http://www.fipa.org` (2000) Doc. XC00037H.
3. Pitt, J., Mamdani, E.: A protocol-based semantics for an agent communication language. In: IJCAI '99. (1999) 486–491
4. Verdicchio, M., Colombetti, M.: A logical model of social commitment for agent communication. In: Proceedings of AAMAS 2003, ACM Press (2003) 528–535
5. Singh, M.P.: A social semantics for agent communication languages. In: Issues in Agent Communication. Volume 1916 of LNCS., Springer (2000) 31–45
6. Parunak, V.D.: 'Go To The Ant': Engineering principles from natural agent systems. Annals of Operations Research **75** (1997) 69–101
7. Omicini, A., Zambonelli, F.: Coordination for Internet application development. Journal of Autonomous Agents and Multi-Agent Systems **2** (1999) 251–269
8. Nardi, B.A.: Context and Consciousness: Activity Theory and Human-Computer Interaction. MIT Press (1996)
9. Ricci, A., Omicini, A., Denti, E.: Activity Theory as a framework for MAS coordination. In: ESAW III. Volume 2577 of LNCS. Springer-Verlag (2003)
10. Omicini, A., Ricci, A., Viroli, M., Cioffi, M., Rimassa, G.: Multi-agent infrastructures for objective and subjective coordination. Applied Artificial Intelligence **18** (2004) 815–831 Special Issue: Best papers from EUMAS 2003: The 1st European Workshop on Multi-agent Systems.
11. Khan, S.M., Lesp´erance, Y.: A model of rational agency for communicating agents. In: This volume. (2005)
12. Viroli, M., Ricci, A.: Instructions-based semantics of agent mediated interaction. In Jennings, N.R., Sierra, C., Sonenberg, L., Tambe, M., eds.: 3rd international Joint Conference on Autonomous Agents and Multiagent Systems (AAMAS 2004). Volume 1., New York, USA, ACM (2004) 102–110
13. Milner, R.: Communication and Concurrency. Prentice Hall (1989)
14. Hennessy, M., Regan, T.: A dialogue game protocol for agent purchase negotiations. A Process Algebra for Timed Systems **117** (1995) 221–239
15. Viroli, M., Ricci, A., Omicini, A.: A semantics for the interaction of agents with coordination artifacts. In: Cybernetics and Systems 2004. Volume 2. (2004) 564–569 Workshop AT2AI 2004.
16. Ricci, A., Viroli, M., Omicini, A.: Agent coordination context: From theory to practice. In: Cybernetics and Systems 2004. Volume 2., Austrian Society for Cybernetic Studies (2004) 618–623 Workshop AT2AI 2004.
17. McBurney, P., Parsons, S.: Locutions for argumentation in agent interaction protocols. In: This volume. (2005)
18. Sato, M., Sakurai, T., Kameyama, Y., Igarashi, A.: Calculi of meta-variables. In Baaz, M., Makowsky, J.A., eds.: Computer Science Logic, 17th International Workshop, CSL 2003, 12th Annual Conference of the EACSL, and 8th Kurt Gödel Colloquium, KGC 2003, Vienna, Austria, August 25-30, 2003, Proceedings. Volume 2803 of LNCS. Springer-Verlag (2003)
19. Glabbeek, R.v.: The linear time – branching time spectrum I. The semantics of concrete, sequential processes. In: Handbook of Process Algebra. North-Holland (2001) 3–100
20. Baetene, J., Middleburg, C.: Process algebra with timing: Real time and discrete time. In: Handbook of Process Algebra. North-Holland (2001) 3–100
21. Ricci, A., Viroli, M., Omicini, A.: Agent coordination context: From theory to practice. In Trappl, R., ed.: Cybernetics and Systems 2004. Volume 2., Vienna, Austria, Austrian Society for Cybernetic Studies (2004) 618–623 17th European Meeting on Cybernetics and Systems Research (EMCSR 2004), Vienna, Austria, 13–16 April 2004. Proceedings.

22. Smith, R.G.: The contract net protocol: High-level communication and control in a distributed problem solver. In: Proceedings of the 1st International Conference on Distributed Computing Systems, Washington D.C., IEEE Computer Society (1979) 186–192

23. Viroli, M., Omicini, A.: Coordination as a service: Ontological and formal foundation. In: Proceedings of FOCLASA '02. Volume 68(3) of ENTCS. Elsevier Science B. V. (2003)

24. Labrou, Y., Finin, T.: Semantics and conversation for an agent communication language. In: 15th International Joint Conference on Artificial Intelligence. (1997)

25. Colombetti, M.: A commitment-based approach to agent speech acts and conversations. In: Workshop on Agent Languages and Conversation Policies. (2000)

26. Singh, M.P.: Agent communication languages: Rethinking the principles. IEEE Computer **31** (1998) 40–47

27. Pitt, J., Kamara, L., Artikis, A.: Interaction patterns and observable commitments in a multi-agent trading scenario. In: Internation Conference on Autonomous Agents, ACM Press (2001) 481–488

28. Parsons, S., Wooldridge, M., Amgoud, L.: Properties and complexity of some formal inter-agent dialogues. Journal of Logic Computation **13** (2003) 347–376

29. McBurney, P., van Eijk, R.M., Parsons, S., Amgoud, L.: A dialogue game protocol for agent purchase negotiations. Journal of Autonomous Agents and Multi-Agent Systems **7** (2003) 235–273

30. Omicini, A., Ricci, A., Viroli, M.: Formal specification and enactment of security policies through Agent Coordination Contexts. In: Proceedings of SecCo'03. Volume 85(3) of ENTCS. Elsevier Science B. V. (2003)

Dialogization and Implicit Information in an Agent Communicational Model

Karim Bouzouba[1], Jamal Bentahar[2], and Bernard Moulin[2]

[1] IERA, Mohamed V Souissi University,
BP 6216, Rabat, Morocco
karim.bouzoubaa@iera.ac.ma

[2] Laval University, Department of Computer Science and Software Engineering,
Ste-Foy, QC, G1K 7P4, Canada
jamal.bentahar.1@ulaval.ca
bernard.moulin@ift.ulaval.ca

Abstract. In this paper we propose a computational model for human-agent and agent-agent conversation. This model has two fundamental characteristics: (1) it takes into account the implicit aspects of conversations by dealing with the non literal level of speech acts; (2) it models the dialogization process. Theoretically, our model uses a public approach based on social commitments and on what we call communicational states. In addition, we consider communication as a negotiation process formed by a set of initiative/reactive dialogue games. The paper also presents an implementation of our model in a multi-agent system called POSTAGE.

1   Introduction

For almost a decade, industry and researchers have been seriously considering applications involving "conversational interfaces" instead of the classical graphical user interfaces [18, 22]. A conversational interface attempts to leverage natural aspects of human dialogue and social interaction, and makes user interfaces more appealing and approachable for a wide variety of users. Although the current conversational interfaces are still simple, we can expect that they will integrate several features of human conversations in the future.

On the other hand, in multi-agent systems, it is widely recognized that communication between autonomous agents is a challenging research area [9, 13]. In this domain, in order to enable agents to negotiate, to solve conflicts of interest, to cooperate, to find proofs, etc., they have to be able not only to exchange single messages, but also to take part and to engage in coherent conversations with other agents as well as with human users.

In the last few years, different research works on agent communicational models based on commitments [2, 3, 10, 15, 19, 24, 25, 30] and dialogue games [12, 20, 21] seem to offer an interesting direction. However, not only the semantics of such models are not yet standardized but also to our knowledge, none of them integrate features found in human conversations.

R.M. van Eijk et al. (Eds.): AC 2004, LNAI 3396, pp. 193–208, 2005.
© Springer-Verlag Berlin Heidelberg 2005

The phenomena of human conversations we are interested in are those proposed as an enrichment of the traditional version of speech act theory: (1) Taking into account the non literal level of speech acts [8, 11, 28]; (2) Modeling the dialogization process (or conversational sequencing) [8, 26, 29] and (3) Taking into account the influence of social relationships [5].

More specifically, we think that future agent/user and agent/agent interactions should allow the manipulation of *indirect speech* acts that are commonly used in human conversations. In addition, agents involved in such conversations should also be able to take into account the *conversational sequencing* and *the influence of social relationships*.

To illustrate the problem, let us consider the following dialogue between a human user and his conversational agent.

(1)   User: Agent!
(2)   Agent: Yes, sir
(3)   User: Can you send an email to Paul to let him know that I won't come for lunch and can you please also search the best price on internet for a Pentium V
(4)   Agent: OK
(5)   User: It's necessary to contact Adam also
(6)   Agent: What should I tell him?
(7)   User: No, no, I will contact Adam myself

It is easily observed from this simple dialogue that an agent involved in agent/user conversation should reason on:

1. The indirectness of speech acts: can you send an email to Paul?
2. The dialogization process: the utterance "it's necessary to contact Adam" is interpreted first by the agent as a directive until the user corrects this situation later in the conversation by telling "no, no, I will contact Adam myself"[1].

This paper is a continuation of our prior research [1, 2, 3, 6, 7] that deals with the automation of conversations between human agents and software agents as well as between software agents. In this paper, we focus on two conversational phenomena: indirect speech acts and the dialogization process. More specifically, our aim is to propose an agent communicational model with its specific semantics that integrates these two phenomena of human conversations. The purpose is to show that our formal framework for social commitments can be used as a theoretical background for this model.

The paper is organized as follows. Section 2 presents the theoretical background of our approach. Section 3 introduces our communicational model. In Section 4, we see how this model deals with and manages indirect speech acts. Section 5 concerns the dialogization process. In Section 6 we describe the POSTAGE prototype. Finally, we conclude the paper and present some directions for future research.

---

[1] Simply speaking, dialogization concerns the understanding of the communicative intention between the interlocutors during the dialogue.

2   Theoretical Background

2.1   Social Commitments

Our communication model is based on the notion of social commitments. A social commitment is a commitment made by an agent (the *debtor*), that some fact is true or to do something. This commitment is directed to a set of agents (*creditors*) [24]. Social commitments are a kind of deontic concept. They can be viewed as a generalization of obligations as studied in deontic logic [25]. Indeed, considering their deontic nature, these commitments define constraints on the agents' behavior. The agent must behave in accordance to its commitments. For example, by committing towards other agents that a certain fact is true, the agent is compelled not to contradict itself during the conversation. It must also be able to explain, argue, justify and defend itself if another participant contradicts it. In fact, we do not speak here about the expression of a belief, but rather about a particular relationship between a participant and a statement.

In our framework, the *commitment content* is characterized by time t_φ, which is different from the utterance time denoted t_u and from the time associated with the commitment and denoted t_{sc}. Time t_{sc} refers to the time during which the commitment holds. Fig. 1 illustrates the relation between t_φ, t_u, t_{sc}.

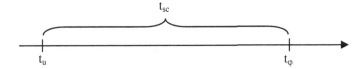

Fig. 1. Times tu, tsc and tφ

We denote a social commitment: $SC(Ag_1, A^*, t_{sc}, \varphi, t_\varphi)$ where Ag_1 the debtor, A^* the set of the creditors $(A^*=A/\{Ag_1\})$, where A is the set of participants), t_{sc} is the time associated with the commitment, φ its content and t_φ the time associated with the content φ. To simplify the notation, we suppose throughout this paper that $A=\{Ag_1, Ag_2\}$.

In our approach we interpret a speech act as an action performed by an agent on a commitment in order to model the dynamics of conversations. This interpretation is denoted:

Definition 1. $SA(Ag_1, Ag_2, t_u, U) =_{def} Act(Ag_1, t_u, SC(Ag_1, Ag_2, t_{sc}, \varphi, t_\varphi))$

where $=_{def}$ means "is interpreted by definition as", *SA* is the abbreviation of "Speech Act", and *Act* indicates the action performed by the debtor on the commitment. The definiendum ($SA(Ag_1, Ag_2, t_u, U)$) is defined by the definiens ($Act(Ag_1, t_u, SC(Ag_1, Ag_2, t_{sc}, \varphi, t_\varphi))$) as an action performed on a commitment. The agent that performs the speech act is the same agent that performs the action Act. Act can take one of four values: Create, Withdraw, Violate and Fulfill. These four actions are the actions that the debtor can apply to a commitment. This reflects only the debtor's point of view. However, we must also take into account the creditors when modeling a conversation which is, by definition, a joint activity. We thus propose modeling the creditors' actions which do not apply to the commitment, but to the content of this commitment. The semantics associated with this type of actions is expressed in a dynamic logic [3]. This semantics is different from the temporal semantics proposed in [19, 25 and 30] and from the operational specification proposed in [15]. Unlike these semantics, our semantic differentiates commitments as static structures from the operations applied to these commitments as dynamic structures. In our framework, all communicative acts are actions that agents apply to commitments. This enables us to describe more naturally the evolution of the conversations as a system of states / transitions which reflects the interaction dynamics. Hence we redefine a speech act as follows:

Definition 2. $SA(Ag_1, Ag_2, t_u, U) =_{def}$
$\qquad Act(Ag_1, t_u, SC(Ag_1, Ag_2, t_{sc}, \varphi, t_\varphi))$
$\qquad | Act\text{-}content(Ag_k, t_u, SC(Ag_i, Ag_j, t_{sc}, \varphi, t_\varphi))$

where $i, j \in \{1, 2\}$ and $(k=i$ or $k=j)$. Agent Ag_k can thus act on the content of its own commitment (in this case we get $k=i$) or on the content of the commitment of another agent (in this case we get $k=j$).
For example, the utterance:

$\qquad U: \text{"I met agent } Ag_3 \text{ on MSN one hour ago"}$

leads to the creation of the commitment:

$\qquad SC(Ag_1, Ag_2, t_{sc}, Meet(Ag_1, Ag_3, MSN), t_{sc} - 1h).$

The creation of such a commitment is an *action* denoted:

$\qquad Create(Ag_1, t_u, SC(Ag_1, Ag_2, t_{sc}, Meet(Ag_1, Ag_3, MSN), t_{sc}-1h)).$

2.2 Taxonomy

In this section, we explain the various types of social commitments we use in our model:

A. Absolute Commitments (ABC): They are commitments whose fulfillment does not depend on any particular condition. Two types can be distinguished:
A1. Propositional Commitments (PCs): They are related to the state of the world and expressed by assertives.
A2. Action Commitments (AC): They are always directed towards the future and are related to actions that the debtor is committed to carrying out. This type of commitments is typically conveyed by promises.

B. Conditional Commitments (CC): In several cases, agents need to make commitments not in absolute terms but under given conditions. Conditional commitments allow us to express that if a condition β is true, then the creditor will be committed towards the debtor to making γ or that γ is true.

C. Commitment Attempts (CT): The social commitments described so far directly concern the debtor who commits either that a certain fact is true or that a certain action will be carried out. These commitments do not allow us to explain the fact that an agent asks another one to be committed to carrying out an action. To solve this problem, we propose the concept of commitment attempt. We consider a commitment attempt as a request made by a debtor to push a creditor to be committed.

3   The Communicational Model

Computationally speaking, a conversational model should possess a communicational model to which we integrate the phenomena we are interested in. Our communication model is based on the following fundamental principles:

- Communication is considered as a negotiation process [17, 23]. This process is formed by a set of initiative/reactive dialogue games [12, 21].
- Communication results in a manipulation of social commitments [1, 10, 20, 24].
- Agents use their private mental states to manipulate social commitments.

We adopt these principles in our approach and we consider agents' communication as actions applied on commitments and as exchanges of what we call *communicational states*[2] (CS). Fig. 2 illustrates our communication model.

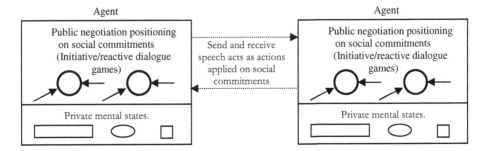

Fig. 2. The communicational model

A CS is characterized by one of five types, each type corresponding to a performative type as defined by Vanderveken [27]. Since we consider that agents communicate by conversing, a CS is similar to a speech act and is used by an agent to express its communicative intentions. However, a CS differs from a speech act in the sense that (1) a CS is associated to a negotiation positioning and (2) a CS is not composed of seven components as it is the case for a speech act [27]. A CS is also expressed in terms of social commitments.

A directive CS performed by an agent Ag_1 toward an agent Ag_2 at time t concerning the propositional content p has the following form[3]: $DIR(Ag_1, Ag_2, t, p, t_p)$ where t_p is the time associated to the content p. A directive CS is defined as a commitment attempt:

Definition 3. $DIR(Ag_1, Ag_2, t, p, t_p) =_{def} CT(Ag_1, Ag_2, t_{ct}, p, t_p)$

where $t = t_{ct}$.

The other types of CS are *ASS* for an assertive, *DECL* for a declarative, *COMMIT* for a commissive and *EXPR* for an expressive. To represent explicitly the conditional aspect of assertives and commissives, we add two other types of CS: *CON-ASS* for

---

[2] We chose the term "Communicational State" analogously to the term "Mental State".
[3] For the formalization of communicational states, we have been inspired by the work of [13].

conditional assertives and *CON-COMMIT* for conditional commissives. An assertive CS is defined as a propositional commitment and a conditional assertive is defined as a conditional commitment about a proposition (**Definition 4**). A declarative and an expressive CS are defined as propositional commitments (**Definitions 5** and **6**). Finally, a commissive CS is defined as an action commitment and a conditional commissive is defined as a conditional commitment about an action (**Definition 7**).

Definition 4. $ASS(Ag_1, Ag_2, t, p) =_{def} PC(Ag_1, Ag_2, t_{pc}, p, t_p)$
$\qquad CON\text{-}ASS(Ag_1, Ag_2, t, p_1, t_{p1}, p_2, t_{p2}) =_{def} CC(Ag_1, Ag_2, t_{cc}, p_1, t_{p1}, p_2, t_{p2})$

Definition 5. $DECL(Ag_1, Ag_2, t, p, t_p) =_{def} PC(Ag_1, Ag_2, t_{pc}, p, t_p)$

Definition 6. $EXPR(Ag_1, Ag_2, t, p, t_p) =_{def} PC(Ag_1, Ag_2, t_{pc}, p, t_p)$

Definition 7. $COMMIT(Ag_1, Ag_2, t, \alpha, t_\alpha) =_{def} AC(Ag_1, Ag_2, t_{ac}, \alpha, t_\alpha)$
$\qquad CON\text{-}COMMIT(Ag_1, Ag_2, t, p, t_p, \alpha, t_\alpha) =_{def} CC(Ag_1, Ag_2, t_{cc}, p, t_p, \alpha, t_\alpha)$

where p is a propositional formula and α is an action symbol.

Communication is considered as a set of initiative/reactive dialogue games in which agents negotiate about CSs. In other words, agents negotiate the acceptance or the refusal of CSs. An agent proposes a CS (initiative dialogue game) and other agents react to this proposal by accepting, rejecting the proposed CS, asking for further information, etc. (reactive dialogue game). Thus, a negotiation positioning is associated to a CS. Since finding a settlement is not the main goal of our negotiation process, this process is different from the negotiation dialogue defined in Walton and Krabbe's typology [31]. On the other hand, this process is similar to the persuasion dialogue that arises from a conflict of opinions and whose goal is to solve the conflict. In our framework, a positioning takes the following form:

$$POSIT(Ag_1, Ag_2, t, CS(Ag_1, Ag_2, t, \varphi, t_\varphi))$$

where $CS \in \{DIR, ASS, DECL, EXPR, COMMIT, COND\text{-}COMMIT\}$
which represents the positioning of agent Ag_1 toward agent Ag_2 at time t with respect to a communicational state CS.

The positionings we consider are the proposition *PROPOSE*, the acceptance *ACCEPT* and the refusal *REFUSE* of a CS. We also add the special *INQUIRE* positioning for asking questions. We distinguish two types of *INQUIRE*. The first type requires a *Yes/No* answer. The second type requires an answer substituting a set of free variables X in the propositional content by a certain valuation. We denote a formula φ in which appears a sequence of free variables X by $?X\varphi$. These two types of *INQUIRE* are denoted as follows:

$$INQUIRE(Ag_1, Ag_2, t, CS(Ag_1, Ag_2, t, p, t_p), Yes/No?)$$
$$INQUIRE(Ag_1, Ag_2, t, CS(Ag_i, Ag_j, t, ?X\varphi, t_\varphi))$$

where $i, j \in \{1, 2\}$ and $i \neq j$.

A positioning with respect to a communicational state CS is defined as an action applied by an agent on a social commitment SC or on the content of a social commitment:

Definition 8. $POSIT(Ag_1, Ag_2, t, CS(Ag_1, Ag_2, t, \varphi, t_\varphi)) =_{def}$

$$Act(Ag_1, t_u, SC(Ag_1, Ag_2, t_{sc}, \varphi, t_\varphi))$$
$$| Act\text{-}content(Ag_k, t_u, SC(Ag_i, Ag_j, t_{sc}, \varphi, t_\varphi))$$

where $i, j \in \{1, 2\}$ and ($k=i$ or $k=j$).

For example, the proposition of a CS is defined as a creation action of a commitment (**Definition 9**). The commitment type depends on the type of the CS as specified by **Definitions 4, 5, 6** and **7**.

Definition 9. $POSIT(Ag_1, Ag_2, t_u, CS(Ag_1, Ag_2, t, \varphi, t_\varphi)) =_{def}$

$$Create(Ag_1, t_u, SC(Ag_1, Ag_2, t_{sc}, \varphi, t_\varphi))$$

Let us take the following simple dialogue between agents Ag_1 and Ag_2.

(SA₁)	*Ag₁:*	*Print the document number 5*
(SA₂)	*Ag₂:*	*Ok!*

The speech act SA_1 is represented by the proposal of a directive:

$$PROPOSE(Ag_1, Ag_2, t_1, CS_1)$$

where CS_1 represents $DIR(Ag_1, Ag_2, t_1, print(AGT(Ag_2), OBJ(document\text{-}5)))$

Ag_1 is proposing to Ag_2, at time t_1, a directive in which Ag_1 is asking Ag_2 at time t_1 that agent Ag_2 print the object document 5. The speech act SA_2 is represented by the acceptance of the first directive:

$$ACCEPT(Ag_2, Ag_1, t_2, CS_1)$$

Ag_2 is accepting, at time t_2, the directive proposed at time t_1 where Ag_1 is asking Ag_2 to print the document 5.

Furthermore, it is easy to notice that usually human conversants are able to recall the utterances (at least the most important ones) that have been exchanged during a conversation along with the locutors' positionings. In our approach, we consider that the exchanged CSs are recorded into a conceptual structure called the *conversational trace*. Using the conversational traces of both agents, this dialogue is represented in Fig. 3. It is important to mention that each agent possesses its own conversational trace and thus its own viewpoint of the communication. This assumption of no central agent (called also external observer) is considered in other agent models. It is the case

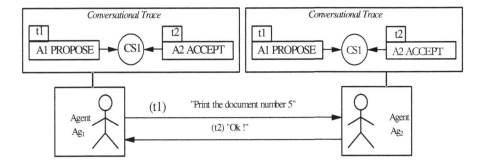

Fig. 3. Conversational traces of agents Ag_1 and Ag_2

for [4] where agents detect ontological discrepancies during communication on the basis of their own subjective view on the world.

Our communicational model is based on a negotiation process in which agents (human or artificial) are negotiating on CSs. Agents record all the negotiation positionings as well as the CSs during the conversation process. Let us see now how this model can be used in order to deal with the non-literal level of speech acts.

4   Implicit Information

It is easily observed that human locutors use indirect speech acts more frequently than direct speech acts. For instance, when a manager says to his secretary "Can you print the document number 5?", his utterance should be interpreted as a polite way of ordering her to print the document (non literal interpretation) and not as a question about her ability to print (literal interpretation). Also, the question asked by the user to his agent (in the first dialogue) "Can you send an email to Paul?" should be interpreted too as a directive speech act.

In order to take into account this conversational phenomenon, we suggested to model implicit information conveyed by speech acts [6]. Given a speech act SA performed by locutor L_1 and directed to locutor L_2, we define the *implicit information* conveyed by SA as the information that L_1 intends to transfer to L_2 and which is different from SA's propositional content. For example, the implicit information associated with the question "Can you send an email to Paul?" is the request to send the email. To our knowledge, no current implementation of software agents integrates this aspect in its communicational model. Implicit information can be compared to presuppositions that Beun et al. [4] are using in their model. Indeed, in that model, agents extract presuppositions from incoming messages on the basis of the pragmatics of the communication language.

In order to provide a mapping between implicit and explicit information, we use knowledge structures called *conversational schemas* that are similar to conversational postulates that Gordon and Lakoff proposed to interpret indirect speech acts [16]. Conversational schemas specify conversational conventions that apply in a given socio-organizational context. A conversational schema can be used by an agent either for choosing a speech act that reflects its communicative intention, or for interpreting other agents' speech acts. For example, the conversational schema of the above example could be formulated by the following definition:

Definition 10: *INQUIRE(Ag₁, Ag₂, t, CS(Ag₁, Ag₂, t,*
$\quad\quad$ *HAS-CAPACITY(AGT(Ag₂),OBJ(Prop)), Yes/No?)*$=_{def}$
$\quad\quad\quad$ *PROPOSE(Ag₁, Ag₂,t, DIR(Ag₁, Ag₂, t, Prop))*

A conversational schema has the following form:

CONV-SCH "ident"
$\quad\quad$ *Context*
$\quad\quad$ *Characteristics*
$\quad\quad$ *Communicative intention*
$\quad\quad$ *Explicit information*
$\quad\quad$ *Communicative Expectation*

Each agent possesses a set of conversational schemas. This set represents its knowledge of the conversational practices of the society to which it belongs. The set of conversational schemas that agents share could be considered as part of the common conversational ground of these agents. The *Characteristics* slot has two components. The first component concerns the illocutionary strength, which is quantitative, and allows the agent to have different formulations for the same communicative intention. The second component is the refusal option that indicates if the agent can refuse a given directive. When an agent wants to express a certain *Communicative intention*, it chooses a conversational schema depending on the social and personality context. This conversational schema gives it the corresponding formulation in the *Explicit information* slot. The slot *Communicative Expectation* will be explained in the next section.

For example, the corresponding conversational schema for a *"polite request"* is formulated as follows:

CONV-SCH "polite request"
    Characteristics: illoc-strength(0), refusal-option(yes)
    Communicative intention:
        PROPOSE(Ag₁, Ag₂ t, DIR(Ag₁, Ag₂, t, Prop))
    Explicit information:
        INQUIRE(Ag₁, Ag₂,t, CS(Ag₁, Ag₂, t,
            HAS-CAPACITY(AGT(Ag₂),OBJ(Prop)), Yes/No?)

The above *"polite request"* conversational schema is used by an agent Ag_1 toward an agent Ag_2.. This conversational schema has *illocutionary strength* of 0 and it concerns a directive CS (*DIR*), which gives a *refusal option* to the interlocutor. In this CS, agent Ag_1 has the intention to propose a directive to agent Ag_2 and for this purpose, it will publicly perform an inquire (*INQUIRE*) asking agent Ag_2 about its capacity to do the needed action expressed by *Prop*. Indeed, explicit information indicates the action applied by the agent on a social commitment.

In order to take into account the explicit and implicit information managed by an agent during a dialogue, we divided the conversation trace into two categories: an *explicit conversational trace* in which it records the public utterances and an *implicit conversational trace* in which it records the intentional utterances. This aspect is detailed in the next section. Let us mention that we plan to extend our approach in order to take into account the influence of social relationships during the interaction. Indeed, according to [5], there is little doubt that social relationships influence the way people interpret indirect speech acts. Some preliminary results of this extension could be found in [6].

5   Dialogization

Dialogization is based on the understanding of the communicative intention between interlocutors during the dialogue. In other agent frameworks [4], this phenomenon is called feedback. The schema of the dialogization process is shown in Fig. 4. During the first stage, an initiator agent Ag_1 makes an initial proposal corresponding to its communicative intention. It waits for the positioning of its interlocutor agent Ag_2

regarding this proposal. If Ag_2's positioning matches what Ag_1 was expecting as an answer, then it concludes that Ag_2 understood its communicative intention and in this case it can go ahead and make another proposal. In the case in which Ag_2's positioning doesn't match what Ag_1 is expecting, then it concludes that Ag_2 didn't understand its communicative intention and reacts by expressing its communicative intention more explicitly. This is done by the choice of a different conversational schema in which the communicational intention and explicit information slots are almost the same.

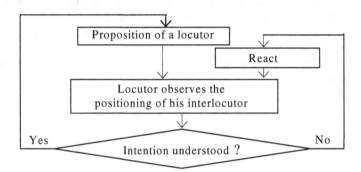

Fig. 4. The dialogization process

We still need to provide a way to determine if the agent's intention has been understood or not by its interlocutor. This is the role of the *Communicative Expectation* slot of a conversational schema. In our approach, an agent Ag_1 determines if the intention corresponding to its initial speech act has been recognized by the interlocutor agent Ag_2, if Ag_2's speech act matches the *Communicative Expectation*. For instance, the actual "polite request" conversation schema is:
CONV-SCH "polite request"

> *Characteristics: illoc-strength(0), refusal-option(yes)*
> *Communicative intention:*
> > $PROPOSE(Ag_1, Ag_2, t_1, DIR(Ag_1, Ag_2, t_1, Prop))$
> *Explicit information:*
> > $INQUIRE(Ag_1, Ag_2, t_1, CS(Ag_1, Ag_2, t_1,$
> > > $HAS\text{-}CAPACITY(AGT(Ag_2),OBJ(Prop)), Yes/No?)$
> *Communicative Expectation:*
> > $ACCEPT(Ag_2, Ag_1, t_2, DIR(Ag_1, Ag_2, t_1, Prop))$

This conversational schema states that Ag_1 will expect Ag_2 to accept its proposal of the implicit directive even if Ag_1 publicly asks Ag_2 about its capacity of doing the needed action (represented by *Prop*).

Let us take as an example the following dialogue illustrating the dialogization phenomenon.

(1)   User: It's necessary to contact Adam
(2)   Agent: What should I tell him?
(3)   User: No, no, I will contact Adam myself
(4)   Agent: OK!

The agent interpreted the first user's utterance as a directive, while the user actually intended only to express an assertive. The agent responded to the directive by asking information about the way to execute it. The user expecting an acceptance of the assertive, reacts to this question, and expresses his assertive more explicitly. The corresponding conversational traces - both implicit and explicit - of the user are illustrated in Fig. 5. An oval shape represents a CS. Using a plain line,

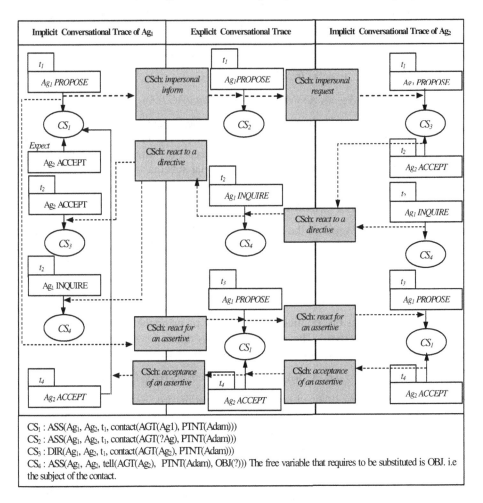

CS_1 : ASS(Ag_1, Ag_2, t_1, contact(AGT(Ag_1), PTNT(Adam)))
CS_2 : ASS(Ag_1, Ag_2, t_1, contact(AGT(?Ag), PTNT(Adam)))
CS_3 : DIR(Ag_1, Ag_2, t_1, contact(AGT(Ag_2), PTNT(Adam)))
CS_4 : ASS(Ag_1, Ag_2, tell(AGT(Ag_2), PTNT(Adam), OBJ(?))) The free variable that requires to be substituted is OBJ. i.e the subject of the contact.

Fig. 5. Implicit and explicit conversational traces of agents Ag_1 and Ag_2

each CS is associated to a rectangular shape representing a given position with its time point (e.g. Ag_1 PROPOSE CS_1 at t_1). Using dashed lines, the negotiation positioning (position and CS) are associated to gray background rectangles that represent the Conversational Schema the user is using to interpret the negotiation positioning (e.g. Ag_1 PROPOSE CS_2 at $t_1 \rightarrow$ use of ConvSc (impersonal inform) $\rightarrow Ag_1$ PROPOSE CS_1 at t_1).

At time t_1, Ag_1 wants, at the implicit level, to propose an assertive ASS CS_1 consisting of contacting Adam. This is represented by the structure:

$$PROPOSE(Ag_1, Ag_2, t_1,\ ASS(Ag_1, Ag_2, t_1, contact(AGT(Ag_1), PTNT(Adam))))$$

Using the conversational schema 'impersonal inform', the user Ag_1 translates the proposition of CS_1 to a proposition of another assertive CS_2 in which the agent is unknown. This assertive that becomes public has the structure:

$$PROPOSE(Ag_1, Ag_2, t_1, ASS(Ag_1, Ag_2, t_1, contact(AGT(?A), PTNT(Adam))))$$

At the same time, Ag_1 expects from Ag_2 to accept CS_1:

$$ACCEPT(Ag_2, Ag_1, t_2, ASS(Ag_1, Ag_2, t_1, contact(AGT(Ag_1),PTNT(Adam))))$$

Using the conversational schema 'impersonal request', agent Ag_2 who receives this proposition determines in its implicit conversational trace that Ag_1 is requesting it to contact Adam (CS_3). At time t_2, Ag_2 implicitly accepts the directive and publicly asks Ag_1 how to do that action, using the conversational schema 'react to a directive'. At this time, Ag_1 observes that Ag_2 is accepting a directive but not an assertive:

$$ACCEPT(Ag_2, Ag_1, t_2, DIR(Ag_1, Ag_2, t_1, contact(AGT(Ag_2), PTNT(Adam))))$$

Ag_1 understands that Ag_2 used the conversational schema 'impersonal request' to infer CS_3 from CS_2. Thus, what Ag_1 is expecting does not match the answer of Ag_2. This leads Ag_1 to react in order to state his first communicative intention. He uses for this purpose, at time t_3, a more explicit conversational schema 'react for an assertive':

$$PROPOSE(Ag_1, Ag_2, t_3, ASS(Ag_1, Ag_2, t_3, contact(AGT(Ag_1), PTNT(Adam))))$$

At time t_4, Ag_2 accepts CS_1 implicitly and publicly by using the conversational schema 'acceptance of an assertive'. The acceptance of Ag_2 means for Ag_1 that Ag_2 understood the intention since the answer matches the communicative expectation:

$$ACCEPT(Ag_2, Ag_1, t_4, ASS(Ag_1, Ag_2, t_3, contact(AGT(Ag_1), PTNT(Adam))))$$

In this section, we explained how the dialogization process can be modeled using our model. Indeed, adding a communicative expectation to a conversational schema allows agents to reason on that process: they compare their interlocutors' positioning with their expectation and react accordingly.

The time complexity of the algorithm implementing this process is linear in the size of the communicative intention bases $|CB_{Ag1} + CB_{Ag2}|$ that are a kind of knowledge bases of the two agents. It is also linear with the number $NCS_{Ag1} + NCSAg_2$ of the conversational schemas that the two agents can use. Because we associate to each communicative intention n conversational schemas ($n \geq 1$), the time complexity is only linear in the number of the conversational schemas, i.e. $O(max(NCS_{Ag1}, NCS_{Ag2}))$.

6   The POSTAGE Prototype

In large and small organizations, correspondence between users exists in various forms: formal and informal letters, memos, notices, etc. Developing a software agent taking care of the administrative correspondence would greatly benefit to the user: (1) the user is not obliged to remember all the formulations used in his/her organization thanks to the use of conversational schemas; (2) The user can be informed about the different interpretations of a message thanks to the dialogization process done by the agent.

The POSTAGE (POSTman AGEnt) agent can formulate a user's message in an informal way which agrees with (1) the user communicative intention and (2) the formulation rules used in a particular organization. For example, the informal message "You are laid off" would be transformed into "As general manager, I deeply regret having to announce your dismissal from our company". For the present work, we have chosen the university organization as an example for the development of the prototype. A POSTAGE agent has a specific architecture that allows it to perform the correspondence task (Fig. 6). This architecture is divided into two parts. The first part includes four knowledge models and the second one three execution modules. The user's model contains knowledge concerning the user such as his/her preferences and his/her social relationships with other users. The static knowledge contains plans and specific formulation schemas. A formulation schema is used by the agent to find a natural language expression for a given conversational schema.

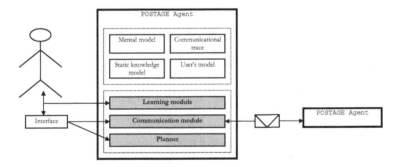

Fig. 6. Architecture of a POSTAGE agent

The other modules are the communicational trace and the mental model. The planning module allows the agent to create messages on the basis of the elements selected by the user. The task of the learning module is to learn new knowledge such as user's preferences or formulations used in a given organization. The communication module receives a request from the planning module and determines the corresponding negotiation positionings.

Let us show an example using the conversational sequencing reasoning of the POSTAGE agent (Fig. 7). Consider two users Viviane and Brigitte with their corresponding agents. Viviane sends a first message to Brigitte by selecting as a subject "Update of web pages". Viviane clicks on the generate button and the agent proposes the text "Can you please update the web pages?". When Brigitte's agent receives the message, it notices that this text has two possible interpretations, and asks Brigitte the interpretation she prefers. In this example, Brigitte takes the literal interpretation. When Viviane's agent receives the answer, it automatically understands that the answer does not correspond to Viviane expectation, informs her, and proposes her to re-express her intention more explicitly. In this case, Viviane's agent proposes the text "No, I am asking you to update the web pages".

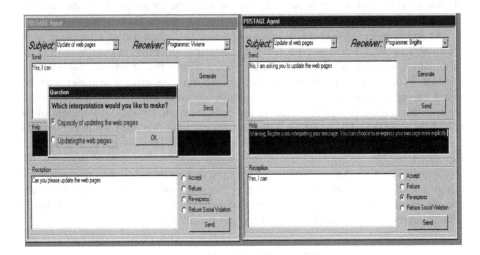

Fig. 7. The conversational sequencing

7   Conclusion and Future Work

In this paper we proposed a computational model for human-agent and agent-agent conversation. This model deals with the implicit aspects of conversations and the dialogization process. The implicit aspects is captured by taking into account the non literal level of speech acts. The dialogization process is treated by considering communication as a negotiation process of social commitments. This process is formed by a set of initiative/reactive dialogue games.

As future work, we intend to integrate the influence of social relationships in our framework and to improve our prototype by using real corpora. We also intend to integrate argumentation issues to capture the reasoning aspect of agents.

References

1. Bentahar, J., Moulin, B., and Chaib-draa, B.: Vers une approche à base d'engagements et d'arguments pour la modélisation du dialogue. Modèles Formels de l'Interaction (2003) 19-28.
2. Bentahar, J., Moulin, B., and Chaib-draa, B.: Commitment and Argument Network: a New Formalism for Agent Communication. In: F. Dignum (Ed.) Advances in Agent Communication. LNAI 2922. Springer (2004) 146-165.

3. Bentahar, J., Moulin, B., Meyer, J-J. Ch., and Chaib-draa, B.: A logical model for commitment and argument network for agent communication. In: Proc. Of the 3rd Int. J. Conf. On AAMAS (2004) 792-799.
4. Beun, R.J., Van Eijk, R.M., Prüst, H., Ontological Feedback in Multiagent Systems, In: Proc. Of the 3rd Int. J. Conf. On AAMAS (2004), 110-117.
5. Boden, D., and Zimmerman, D.H.: Talk and social structures. Berkley: University of California Press (1991).
6. Bouzouba, K., Moulin, B.: KQML+: An extension of KQML in order to deal with implicit information and social relationships. In: Proc. of FLAIRS'98 Sanibel Island (1998) 289-293.
7. Bouzouba, K., Moulin, B., and Kabbaj, A.: CG-KQML+: An Agent Communication Language and its use in a Multi-Agent System. In: Proc of the 9th Int. Conf. on Conceptual Structures (2001) 1-14.
8. Brassac, C.: Speech acts and conversational sequencing. Pragmatics and cognition. Vol. 2(1) (1994) 191-205.
9. Chaib-draa, B. and Dignum, F.: Trends in agent communication language. In: Computational Intelligence. Vol. 18(2) (2002) 1-14.
10. Colombetti, M.: A commitment-based approach to agent speech acts and conversations. In: the Autonomous Agent Workshop on Conversational Policies. 4th Int. Conf. on Autonomous Agent (2000) 21-29.
11. Dascal, M.: On the pragmatic structure of conversation. In: J.R. Searle et al. (On) Searle on Conversation, compiled and introduced by H. Parret and J. Verschueren. Amsterdam: John Benjamins (1992) 35-56.
12. Dastani, M., Hulstijn, J., and van der Torre, L.: Negotiation protocols and dialogue games. In: Proc. of the Belgium/Dutch AI Conf. (BNAIC'2000) Kaatsheuvel (2000) 13-20.
13. Dignum, F. and Greaves, M.: Issues in agent communication: an introduction. In: F. Dignum, and M. Greaves (Eds.). Issues in Agent Communication. LNAI 1916. Springer (2000) 1-16.
14. Dignum, F. and van Linder, B.: Modelling social agents: Communication as actions. In: M. Wooldridge, J. Muller, and N. Jennings (Eds.). Intelligent Agents III. LNAI 1193. Springer (1997) 205-218.
15. Fornara, N. and Colombetti, M.: Operational specification of a commitment-based agent communication language. In: Proc. of the First Int. J. Conf. on AAMAS (2002) 536- 542.
16. Gordon, D. and Lakoff, G.: Conversational postulates. In: P. Cole & J.L. Morgan (Eds.). Syntax and semantics: Vol. 3. Speech acts. Seminar Press (1975) 83-106.
17. Haddadi, A. Communication and Cooperation in Agent Systems. A Pragmatic Theory. Springer (1995).
18. Hayes-Roth, B., van Gent, R., Hubert, D.: Acting in Character. Technical Report KSL 96-13. Knowledge Systems Laboratory (1996).
19. Mallya, A.U., Yolum, P., and Singh, M.: Resolving commitments among autonomous agents. In: Dignum, F. (ed.). Advances in Agent Communication. Springer (2003) 166-182.
20. Maudet, N. and Chaib-draa, B.: Commitment-based and dialogue-game based protocols, new trends in agent communication languages. In: Knowledge Engineering Review. Vol. 17(2) Cambridge University Press (2002) 157- 179.
21. McBurney, P.J. and Parsons, S.: Games that agents play: A formal framework for dialogues between autonomous agents. In: Journal of Logic, Language, and Information. 11(3) (2002) 1-22.
22. Microsoft, ActiveXTM Technology for interactive Software Agents.
23. ttp://www.microsoft.com/intdev/agent/.

24. Rousseau, D., Moulin, B., and Lapalme, G.: A multiagent approach for modelling conversations. In: Proc. of the Int. conference AI'94. Sub-Conf. on Natural Language (1994) 35-50.
25. Singh, M.P.: Agent communication languages: rethinking the principles. IEEE Computer (1998) 40-47.
26. Singh, M.P.: A social semantics for agent communication language. In F. Dignum and M. Greaves (Eds.). Issues in Agent Communication. Springer (2000) 31-45.
27. Van Rees, M.A.: The adequacy of speech act theory for explaining conversational phenomena: a response to some conversation analytical critics. Journal of Pragmatics. 17 (1992) 31-47.
28. Vanderveken, D.: Meaning and speech acts. Vol.1 Principles of language use. Cambridge University Press (1990).
29. Vanderveken, D.: Formal Pragmatics of Non Literal Meaning. In: the Special Issue (edited by E. Rolf) Pragmatik de Linguistische Berichte. Vol 8 (1997) 324-341.
30. Vanderveken, D.: Illocutionary Logic and Discourse Typology. In: Special Issue 216 (edited by D. Vanderveken) Searle with his Replies of Revue Internationale de Philosophie (2001) 243-255.
31. Verdicchio, M. and Colombetti, M.: A logical model of social commitment for agent communication. The Second Int.. Conf. on AA MAS (2003) 528-535.
32. Walton, D.N. and Krabbe, E.C.W. Commitment in dialogue: basic concepts of interpersonal reasoning. State Univ. of New York Press, Albany, NY (1995).

Locutions for Argumentation in Agent Interaction Protocols

Peter McBurney[1] and Simon Parsons[2]

[1] Department of Computer Science,
University of Liverpool,
Liverpool L69 7ZF UK
`p.j.mcburney@csc.liv.ac.uk`
[2] Department of Computer and Information Science,
Brooklyn College,
City University of New York,
Brooklyn NY 11210 USA
`parsons@sci.brooklyn.cuny.edu`

Abstract. Recent work in the design of agent interaction protocols has focused on applications involving dialectical argumentation — the giving and receiving of reasons for statements. Yet the most widely-known language for agent communications — the *FIPA ACL* — lacks locutions for such argument. Drawing on both speech act theory and the philosophy of communicative action, we first present a novel typology of speech acts for agent communications. We use this as the basis for proposing an interaction protocol, called *Fatio*, comprising five locutions we consider necessary for argumentation, and which may be added to the *FIPA ACL*. Both an axiomatic and an operational semantics for the *Fatio* Protocol are given.

1   Introduction

The last decade has seen considerable attention devoted to designing generic communication languages for agent interactions. The most widely-known of these languages is the Foundation for Intelligent Physical Agents' Agent Communication Language (*FIPA ACL*) [7]. Although the leading standard, *FIPA ACL* has been criticized on several grounds, for example: that it requires co-operative agents and sincerity [20]; that its axiomatic semantics *SL* cannot be verified in open systems [28]; that specific locutions have inappropriate semantics [20]; and that it does not readily facilitate the expression of *self-transformation*, the process by which agents change their beliefs, preferences or intentions as a result of their interactions with one another [17].

This paper will address another criticism previously made of the *FIPA ACL*: that it encodes an impoverished theory of argumentation [17]. Agents participating in a dialogue using *FIPA ACL* have only limited means to question or contest information given to them by others; indeed, there are even limitations on what information may be confirmed [20]. Moreover, the semantics defines the post-conditions of utterances only in terms of their effects on the mental states of hearers; there are no rules concerning combinations of locutions, or the dialectical obligations of the participants, such as requiring questions to

R.M. van Eijk et al. (Eds.): AC 2004, LNAI 3396, pp. 209–225, 2005.
© Springer-Verlag Berlin Heidelberg 2005

be answered, or requiring that assertive statements be justified when challenged. In part, this weakness is due to the implicit assumption of the participants being co-operative; fully co-operating agents, presumably, do not lie, obfuscate or prevaricate. In part also, the lack of a rich argumentation structure is due to a semantics defined without reference to time and only in terms of single locutions, rather than in terms of conversations or protocols [20, 26].

From the perspective of a designer of an open agent system comprising intelligent, autonomous and self-interested agents the absence of a sophisticated and explicit argumentation theory for the agent interaction protocol is a serious obstacle. In open systems, the beliefs of agents may not coincide, and so their interactions will require dialogues involving information seeking, information provision, mutual inquiry and persuasion; similarly, their intentions may also not coincide, and so their interactions will require dialogues involving persuasion, commands, negotiation and deliberation [27]. This need explains the recent attention given in the multi-agent systems literature to the design of protocols for argument-based interaction, eg, [1, 13, 14]. Indeed, even in models of decision-making by a single agent the essential role of argument-based reflection and evaluation has recently been emphasized, e.g., [23].

But no widely-accepted locutions or protocols yet exist for the requesting and providing of reasons for beliefs and intentions between software agents. The main contribution of this paper is to propose a set of locutions which serve precisely this purpose. These locutions are presented in the form of an interaction protocol, the *Fatio* protocol (Section 3), which may be used by a system designer as a stand-alone protocol or may be incorporated into other protocols and ACLs, such as *FIPA ACL*. The definition of the protocol is undertaken within a novel typology of speech acts, which we propose in Section 2. An axiomatic and an operational semantics for the protocol are given in Section 4. An example application is presented in Section 5, and the paper concludes with a discussion in Section 6.

2   Types of Speech Acts

Before presenting our argumentation protocol, we first present a syntactic classification of agent speech acts, based on the earlier classifications of John Austin [2], John Searle [22] and Jürgen Habermas [10]. Both Austin and Searle developed their classifications at a time when the prevailing approach to the semantics of propositions in the philosophy of (human) language was truth-conditional. Under this semantics, due originally to Gottlob Frege and Alfred Tarski, if an agent A claims to believe some proposition P, then the relevant semantic question is: *"Is P true?"* This view of meaning has been criticized, most prominently by Michael Dummett [5] and Crispin Wright [29], on the basis that for most assertive statements we cannot answer this question definitively; for example, almost all propositions about the past or the future have an inherent uncertainty. At best, we can find evidence for believing P rather than for holding some contrary belief. A better question, therefore, would be: *"Can agent A justify his belief in P?"* This is the essence of verificationist semantics.

Habermas, in his philosophy of communicative action, extended verificationist ideas to statements other than those concerning factual propositions [10], for example, to expressions of preference and to imperative statements. In doing so, he asked how such statements may be justified. One may justify a command, for example, by reference to some social relationship in which the speaker is superior to the hearer. This viewpoint led Habermas to revise Searle's typology of speech acts [10–pp. 325–326], and we have used this revised typology as the basis for our own classification. Our typology is based on, firstly, the entities referenced by the utterance, for example: states of the real-world, internal mental states of the speaker, or the social relationships between participants; and secondly, on the nature of attacks which may be made on an utterance of each type. These attributes are described below and summarized in Table 1.

Table 1. Typology of Speech Acts

No.	Type	Referants	Basis of Attack
1	Factual Statements	Real-world states	Verifiability
2	Expressive Statements	Internal mental states of Speaker	Sincerity
3	Social Connection Statements	Social relations	Normative rightness
4	Commissives	Social relations Internal mental states of Speaker	Sincerity Feasibility Consequences Efficacy Etc
5	Directives	Social relations Internal mental states of Speaker Internal mental states of Hearer	Normative rightness Feasibility Consequences Efficacy Etc
6	Inferences	Consequences of earlier utterances	Inferential validity
7	Argumentation Statements	Content of utterances	Dialogical rightness
8	Control Statements	Form of utterances	

1. **Factual Statements:** These are statements which claim to represent the state of the external world, and so may be objectively-verified. Examples are statements of belief about factual matters. For these statements, reasons for belief may be requested and provided. Contesting such a statement means denying that it is a true description of the reality external to the dialogue. Defending such a statement involves providing objective verification for it, or the provision of means by which it may be objectively verified.

2. **Expressive Statements:** These are statements which seek to represent the state of the internal world of the speaker, i.e., they aim to reveal publicly a subjective preference, a value assignment, or an intention. As with factual statements, the reasons for a speaker having the mental states revealed by a value statement may be requested and provided. However, value statements cannot be objectively verified or refuted; instead, only the sincerity of the speaker may be challenged. Sincerity of a speaker's internal states may be assessed, for example, by the consistency of these; if a speaker knowingly expresses conflicting intentions, a hearer would be entitled to conclude

that the speaker is not sincere about one or more intentions. Similarly, assessment of a speaker's sincerity may involve issues of trust and reputation, as perceived by the hearer.

3. **Social Connection Statements:** These are statements which assert some social or other relationship between different participants. Examples of such relationships include: employer and employee; customer and supplier; peers; etc. Again, the reasons for a speaker asserting a particular connection may be requested and provided; contestation of these utterances takes the form of challenging the normative rightness of the relationship.

4. **Commissive Statements:** Here, the speaker desires that the world be in a particular state, and so commits to the hearer to undertake some action or course of action to establish or maintain this world state. Promises and vows are examples. They are stronger than merely expressive statements because, if accepted, they create obligations on the speaker in the world beyond the dialogue. Accordingly, they make reference to both the internal mental states (eg, desires, intentions) of the speaker and to the social relations existing between speaker and hearers. Because they refer to internal states, they may be challenged on the grounds of sincerity. They may also be challenged on substantive grounds, eg: their direct or indirect costs and benefits; their opportunity costs; their consequences; their practical feasibility; etc.

5. **Directive Statements:** Here, the speaker desires that the world be in a particular state, and so seeks that the hearer commits to undertaking some action or course of action to establish or maintain this world state. Requests, commands, warnings and entreaties are examples of these statements. As with commissives, they are stronger than merely expressive statements because, if accepted, they create obligations on the hearer to the speaker in the world beyond the dialogue. They make reference to the internal mental states of both the speaker (eg, desires) and the hearers (eg, intentions) and to the social relations existing between speaker and hearers. They may be challenged on all the substantive grounds for which commissives may be challenged, in addition to contestation of the normative rightness of the social connections required for their valid utterance.

6. **Inference Statements:** These are statements which refer to the content of earlier statements in a dialogue, drawing inferences from them or assessing their implications. Contestation of such statements can take the form of questioning the appropriateness or the validity of the inferences made.

7. **Argumentation Statements:** These are statements which refer to the contents of prior speech acts, for example, questions, challenges, and requests for justification. These acts may be attacked on the basis of inappropriateness, timing or dialectical validity. They may also create dialectical obligations on the part of the speaker and/or the hearers.

8. **Control Statements:** These are statements which refer to speech itself, aiming to synchronize communication. Examples of such statements are requests to repeat an utterance, or acknowledgments that an utterance was received.

Both commissive and directive statements concern commitments to undertake an action (or a course of action) to create or maintain a state of the world in which specified propositions are true. Because of these commitments, the allowable attacks for these statements are stronger than are those for expressive statements. Thus, for example, promising someone undertake a specific action is a stronger statement than expressing an intention to undertake it. It is for this reason that we consider commissives as a separate class of speech act, rather than being considered as a subclass of expressive statements.

Table 2. Classification of FIPA ACL locutions

Locution Type	FIPA ACL Locutions
Factual Statements	confirm
	disconfirm
	failure
	inform
	inform-if
	inform-ref
	query-if
	query-ref
Expressive Statements	inform
Social Connection Statements	inform
Commissives	accept-proposal
	agree
	propose
	refuse
	reject-proposal
Directives	cancel
	cfp
	request
	request-when
	request-whenever
Inferences	inform
Argumentation Statements	
Control Statements	not-understood
	propagate
	proxy
	subscribe

Does the *FIPA ACL* support all types of statements? To answer this question, we classified the 22 locutions of *FIPA ACL* according to our typology (Table 2). As can be seen, making expressive statements, social connection statements or inferences requires use of the *inform* illocution, the same illocution used to make factual statements. This conflation creates problems for the designer of argumentation-theoretic combination rules for locutions, for such rules would need to examine the content of an *inform* utterance to determine what locutions are valid in response. Moreover, Table 2 also shows that none of the *FIPA ACL* locutions relate to argumentation; this supports the criticism, made in [17], of an impoverished argumentation theory underlying *FIPA ACL*.

It would be possible to design a new generic Agent Communications Language using this typology. In doing so, it would be sensible to build on the *FIPA ACL*, which (one might argue) is strong in illocutions for factual statements, for commissives and for directives. A new generic ACL could also build on the recent work in the agent communications literature on social semantics, which considers utterances in a dialogue as means to manipulate inter-participant commitments in some wider social institution [3, 24]. The work on social semantics therefore provides illocutions by which commissives and directives may be uttered, responded to, and modified, and a framework for viewing these illocutions. Finally, recent research has also considered illocutions for inter-participant synchronization, the category of acts we have termed Control Statements [19]. Combining all this prior work to design a new generic ACL would be very ambitious, and so for this paper, we consider only illocutions for argumentation.

3   Protocol Syntax

We now present a protocol for undertaking arguments over statements in a dialogue. The statements made in the argument may be any of the first six types of illocutions: factual statements, expressive statements, social connection statements, commissives, directives, and inferences. Our aim here is to define a concise, generic protocol which can be used on its own, or incorporated into other interaction protocols or ACLs (including *FIPA ACL*).[1] For ease of reference, we name the protocol *Fatio*.[2]

Our syntax for utterances will be:

$$illocution(P_i, \phi) \text{ or } illocution(P_i, P_j, \phi)$$

where *illocution* is an illocution, P_i is an identifier for the agent making the utterance (the speaker), $P_j \neq P_i$ denotes an agent at whom the utterance is directed, and ϕ is the content of the utterance. It would also be possible to have an identifier for the intended recipient (the hearer) of the utterance, but for simplicity we assume all utterances are made to the entire group involved in the dialogue. For the content of the utterance, any agreed formal language may be used. We will assume the content layer is represented in a propositional language, with lower-case Greek letters as propositions. We denote the set of these well-formed content formulae, closed under the usual connectives, as C. These propositions may represent objectively-verifiable statements about the world, or internal preferences, or intentions, or commitments, etc. Because we wish to use the protocol to exchange justifications for claims, some utterances will also have content comprising arguments (eg, premises and inference-rules), which will be represented by upper-case Greek letters. We denote the set of these well-formed argument formulae, closed under the usual connectives, as A. Note that C is a proper subset of A. If $\phi \in C$ is a proposition in the content language and $\Phi \in A$ is a justification, we will write $\Phi \vdash^+ \phi$ to indicate that Φ is an argument in support of ϕ, and $\Phi \vdash^- \phi$ to indicate that Φ is an argument against ϕ. Finally, we assume that time is discrete and may be represented by the natural numbers, and that precisely one utterance occurs on each time-step. The first

---

[1] If used as a stand-alone protocol, additional locutions for entry to, withdrawal from, and termination of the dialogue would be necessary [15]. These could be taken from another protocol, eg, [13].

[2] After Nicolas Fatio de Duillier (1664–1753), a Swiss mathematician and polymath, and famous disputant, on Newton's behalf, with Leibniz over who had invented the differential calculus [4]. Fatio was also the originator of the *"Push"* theory of gravity [12].

utterance of each dialogue is made at time-step 1. For simplicity, we do not include a time stamp in the syntax.

Before proceeding, we note the differing usages of the word "commitment" in the agent communications and argumentation literatures.[3] In the early dialogue game literature in philosophy, commitments refer to dialectical obligations incurred by participants inside a dialogue, and may have no relationship to the true beliefs or actions of the participants [11]. More recently, philosophers of argumentation have defined commitments more broadly, to include actions intended to establish or maintain a particular state of the world, including states of the dialogue [27]. Commitments as actions external to the dialogue is closer to usage in agent communications literature, eg, [24].

For the *Fatio* protocol, we reserve the word *commitment* to refer only to actions external to the dialogue: in other words, only commissive and directive statements make reference to commitments. We use the term *dialectical obligations* to refer to commitments inside the dialogue, for example, an obligation within a dialogue to defend an assertion against attack by another participant.

We now define the five legal locutions in *Fatio*:

F1: assert(P_i, ϕ): A speaker P_i asserts a statement $\phi \in C$ (a belief, an intention, a social connection, an external commitment, etc). In doing so, P_i creates a dialectical obligation within the dialogue to provide justification for ϕ if required subsequently by another participant.

F2: question(P_j, P_i, ϕ): A speaker P_j questions a prior utterance of *assert(P_i, ϕ)* by another participant P_i, and seeks a justification for ϕ. The speaker P_j of the question creates no dialectical obligations on himself by the question utterance.

F3: challenge(P_j, P_i, ϕ): A speaker P_j challenges a prior utterance of *assert(P_i, ϕ)* by another participant P_i, and seeks a justification for ϕ. In contrast to a question, with this locution, P_j also creates a dialectical obligation on himself to provide a justification for not asserting ϕ, for example an argument against ϕ, if questioned or challenged. Thus, *challenge(P_j, P_i, ϕ)* is a stronger utterance than *question(P_j, P_i, ϕ)*.

F4: justify($P_i, \Phi \vdash^+ \phi$): A speaker P_i who had uttered *assert(P_i, ϕ)*, and was then questioned or challenged by another speaker, is able to provide a justification $\Phi \in \mathcal{A}$ for the initial statement ϕ by means of this locution. The utterance *justify($P_i, \Phi \vdash^- \phi$)* is similarly defined.

F5: retract(P_i, ϕ): A speaker P_i who had uttered *assert(P_i, ϕ)* or *justify($P_i, \Phi \vdash^+ \phi$)* can withdraw this statement with the utterance of *retract(P_i, ϕ)* or the utterance of *retract($P_i, \Phi \vdash^+ \phi$)*, respectively. This removes the earlier dialectical obligation on P_i to justify ϕ or Φ if questioned or challenged.

As part of the protocol, these locutions are subject to several combination rules [15]:

CR1: The utterance *assert(P_i, ϕ)* may be made at any time.

CR2: The utterances *question(P_j, P_i, ϕ)* and *challenge(P_j, P_i, ϕ)* may be made at any time following an utterance of *assert(P_i, ϕ)*. Similarly, the utterances

---

[3] Note that we are not using the word in the sense of an agent's persistent intentions.

$question(P_j, P_i, \Phi)$ and $challenge(P_j, P_i, \Phi)$ may be made at any time following an utterance of $justify(P_i, \Phi \vdash^+ \phi)$.

CR3: Immediately following an utterance of $question(P_j, P_i, \phi)$ or $challenge(P_j, P_i, \phi)$, the speaker P_i of $assert(P_i, \phi)$ must reply with $justify(P_i, \Phi \vdash^+ \phi)$, for some $\Phi \in \mathcal{A}$.

CR4: The utterances $question(P_k, P_j, \phi)$ and $challenge(P_k, P_j, \phi)$ may be made at any time following an utterance of $challenge(P_j, \phi)$.

CR5: Following an utterance of $question(P_k, P_j, \phi)$ or $challenge(P_k, P_j, \phi)$, the speaker P_j of $challenge(P_j, \phi)$ must reply immediately with $justify(P_j, \Delta \vdash^- \phi)$, for $\Delta \in \mathcal{A}$.

CR6: The utterance $retract(P_i, \phi)$ may be made at any time following an utterance of $assert(P_i, \phi)$. The utterance $retract(P_i, \Phi)$ may be made at any time following an utterance of $justify(P_i, \Phi \vdash^+ \phi)$.

We may ask why each locution is needed. $assert(.)$ is necessary in order that some assertion be made explicitly which can form the basis of argument. If these locutions are added to an existing ACL, then an existing illocution could be used for $assert(.)$, provided it is given an appropriate semantics. For instance, in *FIPA ACL*, *inform(.)* could be used, so long as it given the semantics assigned to $assert(.)$ in Section 4. Then, given a claim, other participants need illocutions to request justifications for the claim from the original speaker. Both $question(.)$ and $challenge(.)$ enable this. Once questioned or challenged, an illocution is needed to enable the original speaker to present her justification for the claim; this is made possible with $justify(.)$. In the course of an argument, a rational speaker may change her view on the matter under discussion, and therefore an illocution is needed to enable the speaker to express this *self-transformation* [17]; the illocution $retract(.)$ enables this.

Another question here is why both $question(.)$ and $challenge(.)$ are needed. The answer lies in the semantics of the two locutions. On the basis of the informal definitions above (and ignoring any complications due to the timing of utterances), one could say that the utterance:

$challenge(P_j, P_i, \phi)$

is equivalent in effect to the sequence of two utterances:

$question(P_j, P_i, \phi)$

$assert(P_j, \neg\phi)$.

However, this equivalence only holds if the propositions concern beliefs and the Law of Excluded Middle (LEM) is assumed. Participant P_j may have an argument against ϕ, but no argument in favor of $\neg\phi$; if LEM is not assumed, then having a negative argument against one is not necessarily the same as having a positive argument for the other. Similarly, if, for example, the propositions concern intended actions, then attacking a proposed action ϕ is not at all the same as supporting a conflicting action included in $\neg\phi$. Moreover, one may agree with a proposed action, and yet feel required to challenge it because one disagrees with the reasons advanced for it, as in [9]. Accordingly, we retain both $question(.)$ and $challenge(.)$.

Another question is whether these locutions and combination rules are sufficient for argumentation-based interactions. An obvious absence is a specific illocution to enable a hearer P_j to endorse or support an earlier utterance of $assert(P_i, \phi)$ by a speaker P_j. For some application domains, such as the scientific inquiries of [14], hearers may desire to indicate partial or qualified acceptance, and so specific locutions are valuable. However, for the generic protocol, participant P_j can indicate acceptance with an utterance of $assert(P_j, \phi)$. Another absence are specific rules regarding termination. We have not included these in keeping with the absence of commencement and termination rules in *FIPA ACL*. For the same reason, we have not included combination rules to preclude malevolent, capricious or badly-coded agents from making repeated or meaningless utterances.

4   Protocol Semantics

4.1   Axiomatic Semantics

An **axiomatic semantics** for a programming language defines a set of axioms which the language obeys, such as the pre-conditions and post-conditions for each command [25]. We give a formal, axiomatic semantics for the locutions of *Fatio* in terms of the beliefs and desires of the participating agents, when the content of utterances under the protocol refer to beliefs. This approach could equally well apply for other types of utterance content, such as intentions, social connections, commitments, etc. We provide such a mentalistic semantics in order to facilitate the use of these locutions alongside those of the *FIPA ACL*, which locutions have been given such a semantics [7]. Our choice of agent beliefs and desires as the basis for the semantics ensures consistency with the axiomatic semantics SL of *FIPA ACL*. The classes $\mathcal{C}, \mathcal{A}$ are as before.

Central to the axiomatic semantics are publicly-viewable stores to record dialectical obligations of the participants. Following [11], we define a private-write, public-read store for each participant P_i in the dialogue, called a *dialectical obligations store*, $DOS(P_i)$, and containing the dialectical obligations currently incurred by P_i. All participants can view this store, but only P_i may write to it (by means of the appropriate utterances). We denote the contents of $DOS(P_i)$ by triples, (P_i, X, Y), where P_i is a participant, where $X \in \mathcal{C}$ is a well-formed formula in the content language (here a proposition about the world), or $X \in \mathcal{A}$ is a well-formed formula in the argument language, and $Y \in \{+, -\}$. The triple $(P_i, \phi, +) \in DOS(P_i)$ denotes that participant P_i has a dialectical obligation to provide justification or argument in support for the proposition ϕ, while the triple $(P_i, \phi, -) \in DOS(P_i)$ denotes that participant P_i has a dialectical obligation to provide justification or argument against the proposition ϕ.

Our semantics is specified in terms of two classes of modal operators, $\{B_i, D_i\}$, where i is an agent identifier. Other symbols have the same definitions as in Section 4.1. These classes have the following intended interpretations:[4]

$B_i\phi$: "Agent i believes that ϕ is true."
$D_i\phi$: "Agent i desires that ϕ be true."

---

[4] Beliefs and desires are time-dependent. Because we are ignoring time in the locution syntax, we also ignore it here. Note that the semantics SL of the *FIPA ACL* also ignores time [7].

We also use simplified elements of FIPA's action language [7–Annex A]; in particular, we let

Done [illocution(P_i, ϕ), pre-con]

indicate that *illocution(P_i, ϕ)* has been uttered by participant P_i with content ϕ, and with pre-conditions *pre-con* true just before the utterance. These operators may be embedded to any depth. Accordingly, we can now define the locutions of *Fatio* in terms of these modal operators and the *done* operator, presenting pre- and post-conditions for each instantiated locution.

– *assert(P_i, ϕ)*
   Pre-conditions: A speaker P_i desires that each participant $P_j(j \neq i)$, believes that P_i believes the proposition $\phi \in \mathcal{C}$.
   $((P_i, \phi, +) \notin DOS(P_i)) \wedge (\forall j \neq i)(D_i B_j B_i \phi)$.

   Post-conditions: Each participant $P_k(k \neq i)$, believes that participant P_i desires that each participant $P_j(j \neq i)$, believe that P_i believes ϕ.
   $(P_i, \phi, +) \in DOS(P_i) \wedge (\forall k \neq i)(\forall j \neq i)(B_k D_i B_j B_i \phi)$.

   Dialectical Obligations: $(P_i, \phi, +)$ is added to $DOS(P_i)$, the Dialectical Obligations Store of speaker P_i.

– *question(P_j, P_i, ϕ)*
   Pre-conditions: Some participant $P_i(i \neq j)$ has a dialectical obligation to support ϕ and participant P_j desires that each other participant $P_k(k \neq j)$, believe that P_j desires that P_i utter a *justify(P_i, ϕ, .)* locution.
   $\exists i(i \neq j)(((P_i, \phi, +) \in DOS(P_i)) \wedge (\forall k \neq j)D_j B_k D_j(\exists \Delta \in \mathcal{A})$
   *Done [justify(P_i, $\Delta \vdash^+ \phi$), $((P_i, \phi, +) \in DOS(P_i))]))$.

   Post-conditions: Participant P_i must utter a *justify* locution.
   $(\exists \Delta \in \mathcal{A})$ *Done (justify(P_i, $\Delta \vdash^+ \phi$), Done [question(P_j, P_i, ϕ), $((P_i, \phi, +) \in DOS(P_i))])$.*

   Dialectical Obligations: No effect.

– *justify(P_i, $\Phi \vdash^+ \phi$)*
   Pre-conditions: A speaker P_i has a dialectical obligation to support $\phi \in \mathcal{C}$, another speaker $P_j(j \neq i)$ has uttered a *question(P_j, P_i, ϕ)* or a *challenge(P_j, P_i, ϕ)* locution, and P_i desires that each participant $P_k(k \neq i)$ believes that P_i believes that $\Phi \in \mathcal{A}$ is an argument for ϕ.
   $((P_i, \phi, +) \in DOS(P_i)) \wedge (Done [question(P_j, P_i, \phi), ((P_i, \phi, +) \in DOS(P_i))] \vee$
   Done [challenge(P_j, P_i, ϕ), $((P_i, \phi, +) \in DOS(P_i))]) \wedge$
   $(\exists \Phi \in \mathcal{A})(\forall k \neq i)(D_i B_k B_i(\Phi \vdash^+ \phi))$.

   Post-conditions: Each participant $P_k(k \neq i)$ believes that P_i desires that each participant $P_j(j \neq i)$ believes that P_i believes that $\Phi \in \mathcal{A}$ is an argument for ϕ.
   $((P_i, \phi, +) \in DOS(P_i)) \wedge ((P_i, \Phi, +) \in DOS(P_i)) \wedge$
   $(\forall k \neq i)(\forall j \neq i)(B_k D_i B_j B_i(\Phi \vdash^+ \phi))$.

Dialectical Obligations: $(P_i, \Phi, +)$ is added to $DOS(P_i)$, the Dialectical Obligations Store of speaker P_i.

– *challenge(P_j, P_i, ϕ)*
Pre-conditions: Some participant $P_i (i \neq j)$ has a dialectical obligation to support ϕ and participant P_j desires that each other participant $P_k (k \neq j)$, believe both that P_j desires that P_i utter a *justify($P_i, \Delta \vdash^+ \phi$)* locution for some $\Delta \in \mathcal{A}$ and that P_j does not believe ϕ.
$\exists i (i \neq j)(((P_i, \phi, +) \in DOS(P_i)) \wedge (\forall k \neq j)(D_j B_k \neg B_j \phi)$
$\wedge (\forall k \neq j) D_j B_k D_j (\exists \Delta \in \mathcal{A})$
Done $[justify(P_i, \Delta \vdash^+ \phi), ((P_i, \phi, +) \in DOS(P_i))]))$.

Post-conditions: Participant P_i must utter a *justify* locution and speaker P_j becomes dialectically obligated to provide an argument against ϕ if questioned or challenged.
$((P_j, \phi, -) \in DOS(P_j) \wedge (\exists \Delta \in \mathcal{A})$ *Done* $[justify(P_i, \Delta \vdash^+ \phi),$
Done $[question(P_j, P_i, \phi), ((P_i, \phi, +) \in DOS(P_i))]]$.

Dialectical Obligations: $(P_j, \phi, -)$ is added to $DOS(P_j)$, the Dialectical Obligations Store of speaker P_j.

– *retract(P_i, ϕ)*
Pre-conditions: For proposition $\phi \in \mathcal{C}$, with $(P_i, \phi, +) \in DOS(P_i)$, P_i desires that each participant $P_j (j \neq i)$ believes that P_i no longer believes ϕ. For proposition $\phi \in \mathcal{C}$, with $(P_i, \phi, -) \in DOS(P_i)$, P_i desires that each participant $P_j (j \neq i)$ believes that P_i no longer does not believe ϕ.
$((P_i, \phi, +) \in DOS(P_i) \wedge (\forall j \neq i)(D_i B_j \neg B_i \phi))$
$\vee$
$(((P_i, \phi, -) \in DOS(P_i)) \wedge (\forall j \neq i)(D_i B_j \neg \neg B_i \phi))$.

Post-conditions: Depending on the two cases in the pre-conditions, either each participant $P_k (k \neq i)$, believes that participant P_i desires that each participant $P_j (j \neq i)$, believe that P_i no longer believes ϕ, or each participant $P_k (k \neq i)$, believes that participant P_i desires that each participant $P_j (j \neq i)$, believe that P_i no longer does not believe ϕ.
$((P_i, \phi, +) \notin DOS(P_i) \wedge (\forall k \neq i)(\forall j \neq i)(B_k D_i B_j \neg B_i \phi))$
$\vee$
$((P_i, \phi, -) \notin DOS(P_i) \wedge (\forall k \neq i)(\forall j \neq i)(B_k D_i B_j \neg \neg B_i \phi))$.

Dialectical Obligations: Either $(P_i, \phi, +)$ or $(P_i, \phi, -)$ is removed from $DOS(P_i)$, the Dialectical Obligations Store of speaker P_i.

The illocutions *justify($P_i, \Phi \vdash^- \phi$)* and *retract(P_i, Φ)* have similar semantics to that for *justify($P_i, \Phi \vdash^+ \phi$)* and *retract(P_i, ϕ)*, respectively. Because $\mathcal{C}$ is a proper subset of $\mathcal{A}$, this semantics permits a speaker to use proposition ϕ as a justification for itself. Whether or not this is acceptable to the other participants in a dialogue depends on their attitudes at the time [18].

4.2   Operational Semantics

We also present an operational semantics for the *Fatio* protocol. An operational semantics indicates how the states of a system change as a result of execution of the commands in a programming language [25]. In this case, the commands in question are the locutions in an argumentation dialogue conducted according the rules of the protocol.[5]

Our definition of the protocol in Section 3 was deliberately exclusively syntactical: we made no assumptions regarding the decision-making architectures or the mental states of the participants before, during or after the dialogue in which they engage. Consequently, any agent willing to submit to the defined rules of the argumentation dialogue may participate in it, regardless of the meaning(s) the agent may place on the utterances made. We believe this property ensures wide applicability. However, the rules for *Fatio* are not sufficient to ensure the automatic generation of agent dialogues. To achieve this, the individual participants need to be vested with mechanisms which will invoke particular utterances at particular points in the dialogue, responding to past and anticipated future utterances. We call these mechanisms *agent decision mechanisms*, although they still may be simulated by the participants, and thus bear little or no relationship to the true decision-making processes or associated "mental states" of the participants.

Agent Decision Mechanisms. We present a portfolio of internal agent decision mechanisms. Although defined here at a high level, each mechanism is readily implementable using argumentation reasoning methods (**D1–D4**) or meta reasoning methods (**D5**).

D1(ϕ): Claim or Not: A procedure, for each statement ϕ, to enable an agent P_i to decide to utter an *assert(P_i, ϕ)* locution. If the agent is vested with a reasoning process using argumentation, as in [1, 18], then this procedure may operate by assessing the arguments for and against ϕ, and then deciding to speak or not on the basis of the agent's *argument assertion attitudes* [18]. The two outputs of this mechanism are: *listen* and *utter-assert(ϕ)*.

D2: React or Not: A procedure to enable an agent P_j to decide to utter a *question(P_j, P_i, ϕ)* or a *challenge(P_j, P_i, ϕ)* locution, following an *assert(P_i, ϕ)* utterance. As with mechanism **D1**, an agent using argumentation-based reasoning may decide to speak on the basis of the agent's *argument acceptance attitudes* [18]. The three outputs of this mechanism are: *listen*, *utter-question(P_i, ϕ)* and *utter-challenge(P_i, ϕ)*.

D3(ϕ): Defend or Not: A procedure to enable an agent P_i with a dialectical obligation to provide justification for some statement or argument to utter a *justify(.)* locution to meet this obligation. This procedure could include, as a sub-procedure, the identification of the best justification for the statement at this time in the dialogue. The two outputs of this mechanism are: *listen* and *utter-justify(.)*.

D4(ϕ): Fold or Not: A procedure to enable an agent P_i with a dialectical obligation to provide justification for some statement or argument to utter a *retract(.)* locution. The two outputs of this mechanism are: *listen* and *utter-retract(.)*.

---

[5] Other agent communications protocols for which operational semantics have been defined include the negotiation dialogue protocol of [13].

D5: Listen or Do: A procedure to await a new utterance from other participants, and, upon its receipt, to decide which of the four classes of mechanisms **D1–D4** to execute. The five outcomes are: *listen* and *do-mech(Di)*, for $i = 1, 2, 3, 4$.

Note that mechanism **D5** is a meta-level decision mechanism, and may include procedures for intention-reconsideration, as in [21].

Transition System. We now present the transition rules of the operational semantics for *Fatio*. We assume the participating agents are imbued with the decision mechanisms above, enabling them to initiate utterances and to respond to utterances in the dialogue, and so the states we will take to be the inputs and outputs of these decision mechanisms. The locutions uttered in the dialogue effect transitions between states of the decision mechanisms, as utterances serve as inputs to one or more of the mechanisms of the participating agents, and then these mechanisms in turn produce outputs causing further utterances in the dialogue. Thus, our operational semantics provides a formal linkage between the dialogue utterances and agent decision mechanisms.

To define these links, we let the triple $\langle P_i, \mathbf{K}, s \rangle$ denote the mechanism with number **K** and with an output s of participant P_i. For ease of presentation, where a transition is invoked by or invokes a particular output of a mechanism **K** this is denoted by the specific output s in the third place of the triple; where no specific output is invoked, we denote this by a period in the third place, $\langle P_i, \mathbf{K}, . \rangle$. Some transitions occur between mechanisms of different agents by means of dialogue locutions; these are denoted by arrows, labelled by the relevant locution number (**F1–F5**) from Section 3. Other transitions occur between the mechanisms of a single agent; these are denoted by unlabelled arrows. Where different agent subscripts appear in the same transition rule, they refer to distinct agents. The rules are defined as follows, for any statement ϕ, and for any agents P_i, P_j and P_k:

TR1: $\langle P_i, \mathbf{D1}(\phi), \textit{listen} \rangle \rightarrow \langle P_i, \mathbf{D5}, . \rangle$

TR2: $\langle P_i, \mathbf{D1}, \textit{utter-assert}(\phi) \rangle \overset{\mathbf{F1}}{\rightarrow} \langle P_i, \mathbf{D5}, \textit{listen} \rangle$

TR3: $\langle P_i, \mathbf{D1}, \textit{utter-assert}(\phi) \rangle \overset{\mathbf{F1}}{\rightarrow} \langle P_j, \mathbf{D5}, \textit{do-mech(D2)} \rangle$

TR4: $\langle P_j, \mathbf{D2}, \textit{listen} \rangle \rightarrow \langle P_j, \mathbf{D5}, . \rangle$

TR5: $\langle P_j, \mathbf{D2}, \textit{utter-question}(P_i, \phi) \rangle \overset{\mathbf{F2}}{\rightarrow} \langle P_j, \mathbf{D5}, \textit{listen} \rangle$

TR6: $\langle P_j, \mathbf{D2}, \textit{utter-question}(P_i, \phi) \rangle \overset{\mathbf{F2}}{\rightarrow} \langle P_i, \mathbf{D5}, \textit{do-mech(D3}(\phi)) \rangle$

TR7: $\langle P_j, \mathbf{D2}, \textit{utter-question}(P_i, \phi) \rangle \overset{\mathbf{F2}}{\rightarrow} \langle P_k, \mathbf{D5}, \textit{listen} \rangle$

TR8: $\langle P_j, \mathbf{D2}, \textit{utter-challenge}(P_i, \phi) \rangle \overset{\mathbf{F3}}{\rightarrow} \langle P_j, \mathbf{D5}, \textit{listen} \rangle$

TR9: $\langle P_j, \mathbf{D2}, \textit{utter-challenge}(P_i, \phi) \rangle \overset{\mathbf{F3}}{\rightarrow} \langle P_i, \mathbf{D5}, \textit{do-mech(D3}(\phi)) \rangle$

TR10: $\langle P_j, \mathbf{D2}, \textit{utter-challenge}(P_i, \phi) \rangle \overset{\mathbf{F3}}{\rightarrow} \langle P_k, \mathbf{D5}, \textit{listen} \rangle$

TR11: $\langle P_i, \mathbf{D3}(\phi), \textit{listen} \rangle \rightarrow \langle P_i, \mathbf{D5}, . \rangle$

TR12: $\langle P_i, \mathbf{D3}(\phi), \textit{utter-justify}(\phi) \rangle \overset{\mathbf{F4}}{\rightarrow} \langle P_i, \mathbf{D5}, \textit{listen} \rangle$

TR13: $\langle P_i, \mathbf{D3}(\phi), \textit{utter-justify}(\phi) \rangle \overset{\mathbf{F4}}{\rightarrow} \langle P_k, \mathbf{D5}, . \rangle$

TR14: $\langle P_i, \mathbf{D4}(\phi), \textit{listen} \rangle \rightarrow \langle P_i, \mathbf{D5}, . \rangle$

TR15: $\langle P_i, \mathbf{D4}(\phi), \textit{utter-retract}(\phi) \rangle \overset{\mathbf{F5}}{\rightarrow} \langle P_i, \mathbf{D5}, \textit{listen} \rangle$

TR16: $\langle P_i, \mathbf{D4}(\phi), \textit{utter-retract}(\phi) \rangle \overset{\mathbf{F5}}{\rightarrow} \langle P_k, \mathbf{D5}, . \rangle$

TR17: $\langle P_i, \mathbf{D5}, \textit{listen} \rangle \rightarrow \langle P_i, \mathbf{D5}, . \rangle$

TR18: $\langle P_i, \mathbf{D5}, \textit{do-mech}(D1(\phi)) \rangle \rightarrow \langle P_i, \mathbf{D1}(\phi), . \rangle$
TR19: $\langle P_i, \mathbf{D5}, \textit{do-mech}(D2) \rangle \rightarrow \langle P_i, \mathbf{D2}, . \rangle$
TR20: $\langle P_i, \mathbf{D5}, \textit{do-mech}(D3(\phi)) \rangle \rightarrow \langle P_i, \mathbf{D3}(\phi), . \rangle$
TR21: $\langle P_i, \mathbf{D5}, \textit{do-mech}(D4(\phi)) \rangle \rightarrow \langle P_i, \mathbf{D4}(\phi), . \rangle$

To illustrate the meaning of these rules, consider rule **TR6**, which indicates that when agent P_j utters locution **F2** — $\textit{question}(P_j, P_i, \phi)$ — to agent P_i, then P_i initiates mechanism **D5** with output mechanism **D3(ϕ): Defend or Not**. Transition Rules **TR11**–**TR13** show the possible transitions on from agent P_i's execution of mechanism **D3**.

5   Example

We give a brief example of a dialogue conducted under the *Fatio* protocol, between participants labelled *A, B* and *C*. The argument uses four propositions relating to a fictional restaurant, the Brigade Brigade:

   R: The Brigade Restaurant is excellent.
   P: I had a great meal at the Brigade.
   Q: I am vegetarian.
   S: Vegetarian food at the Brigade is awful.

The dialogue proceeds as follows, with utterances numbered in bold, and annotation following each utterance:

1: *assert(A, R)*
Agent A asserts that the Brigade Restaurant is excellent.

2: *challenge(B, A, R)*
Agent B challenges agent A's assertion, and creates a dialectical obligation to defend a contrary claim.

3: *justify(A, P $\vdash^+$ R)*
Agent A justifies his assertion by stating he had a great meal at the Brigade.

4: *question(C, B, R)*
Agent C asks B to provide an argument for his claim, implicit in utterance 2, that it is not the case that the Brigade Restaurant is excellent.

5: *justify(B, Q & S $\vdash^-$ R)*
Agent B respond's to C's question, by claiming that the vegetarian food at the Brigade is awful.

6: *retract(A, R)*
Agent A retracts his claim that the Brigade Restaurant is excellent.

7: *question(C, B, Q)*
Agent C questions B's claim that that the vegetarian food at the Brigade is awful.

$\vdots$

etc.

Although only a simple example, this illustrates the use of the *Fatio* protocol for argument-based interaction. Because *FIPA ACL* has no illocutions for argumentation, such a dialogue is not possible using only the 22 illocutions of that language defined as in the *FIPA* modal semantics.

6   Conclusions

The primary contribution of this paper has been to define a new protocol for argument-based dialogue between autonomous, intelligent agents. The protocol, *Fatio*, allows participants to make assertions, request justifications for assertions, make challenges to assertions, provide justifications (or arguments) for assertions, and retract prior assertions. The content of dialogues conducted under the protocol may range over any domain: objectively-verifiable beliefs about the world beyond the dialogue; internal mental states of the participants, such as their preferences and intentions; statements about the social relationships between the participants; commitments of the participants to actions in the world beyond the dialogue; even dialectical obligations of the participants to one another.

In this paper, we also presented a novel classification of illocutions in agent interactions, drawing on speech act theory and the philosophy of communicative action. The definition of the *Fatio* protocol presented illocutions in the class of Argumentation Statements, namely utterances questioning, challenging and defending the contents of other speech acts. As our work shows, this is a class of statements ignored by the *FIPA ACL* agent communications language. We also presented both an axiomatic semantics and an operational semantics for the *Fatio* protocol. The axiomatic semantics was defined for the case where the content of utterances concerns the beliefs of the participants and in terms of modal operators representing the beliefs and desires of the participants. The basis of this semantics is similar to the semantic language defined for the *FIPA ACL*. Thus, the five *Fatio* locutions could readily be added to the 22 standard *FIPA ACL* locutions should an agent system designer so wish. Such addition would help to overcome the impoverished argumentation theory of *FIPA ACL*. The *Fatio* protocol could also be used on a stand-alone basis, or as an addition to other agent interaction protocols.

It is well-known that the axiomatic semantics of the *FIPA ACL* is not verifiable in general [28]. To seek to ameliorate this, in other work we have defined the notion of a *contestability semantics* [16], in which claims made by agents in a dialogue are contestable by other participants, who can question or challenge the claims, and seek justifications for them. In this manner, agent claims may be assessed, for example, for correspondence to the truth; for consistency; for sincerity; and so on. Such assessments take place at run-time, in the dialogue itself, by the other participants as and when required, rather than being undertaken by the design teams in some conformance testing process before any dialogue commences. The *Fatio* Protocol provides the means to undertake such run-time assessments, and therefore is an operationalization of our notion of contestability semantics.

In this paper, we articulated the syntax, an axiomatic semantics and an operational semantics for the locutions of the *Fatio* Protocol. It should also be possible to define a denotational semantics for the protocol, linking utterances made under the protocol to the nodes and edges of a graph representing the arguments created by the participants in course of a dialogue together. Such a graph would be similar in spirit to the argumentation graph constructed by the participants in Thomas Gordon's *Pleadings Game* [8]. We hope to explore these ideas in future work.

Acknowledgments. We are grateful for comments received from Michael Wooldridge, from the anonymous referees, and from the participants at the *Agent Communications Workshop* in New York City in July 2004.

References

1. L. Amgoud, S. Parsons, and N. Maudet. Arguments, dialogue, and negotiation. In W. Horn, editor, *Proceedings of the Fourteenth European Conference on Artificial Intelligence (ECAI 2000)*, pages 338–342, Berlin, Germany, 2000. IOS Press.
2. J. L. Austin. *How To Do Things with Words.* Oxford University Press, Oxford, 1962.
3. M. Colombetti and M. Verdicchio. An analysis of agent speech acts as institutional actions. In C. Castelfranchi and W. L. Johnson, editors, *Proceedings of the First International Joint Conference on Autonomous Agents and Multi-Agent Systems (AAMAS 2002), Bologna, Italy,* pages 1157–1164, New York City, NY, USA, 2002. ACM Press.
4. C. A. Domson. *Nicolas Fatio de Duillier and the Prophets of London: An Essay in the Historical Interaction of Natural Philosophy and Millennial Belief in the Age of Newton.* Arno Press, New York, NY, USA, 1981. Reprint of PhD Thesis awarded at Yale University, 1972.
5. M. Dummett. What is a Theory of Meaning? (II). In *The Seas of Language*, pages 34–93. Clarendon, Oxford, 1993.
6. M. R. Edwards, editor. *Pushing Gravity: New Perspectives on Le Sage's Theory of Gravitation.* Apeiron, Montreal, Quebec, Canada, 2002.
7. FIPA. Communicative Act Library Specification. Standard SC00037J, Foundation for Intelligent Physical Agents, 2002.
8. T. F. Gordon. The Pleadings Game: An exercise in computational dialectics. *Artificial Intelligence and Law,* 2:239–292, 1994.
9. K. Greenwood, T. Bench-Capon, and P. McBurney. Towards a computational account of persuasion in law. In G. Sartor, editor, *Proceedings of the Ninth International Conference on AI and Law (ICAIL 2003)*, pages 22–31, New York, 2003. ACM Press.
10. J. Habermas. *The Theory of Communicative Action: Volume 1: Reason and the Rationalization of Society.* Heinemann, London, 1984. Translation by T. McCarthy of: *Theorie des Kommunikativen Handelns, Band I, Handlungsrationalitat und gesellschaftliche Rationalisierung.* Suhrkamp, Frankfurt, Germany. 1981.
11. C. L. Hamblin. *Fallacies.* Methuen, London, 1970.
12. F. van Lunteren. *Nicolas Fatio de Duillier on the mechanical cause of universal gravitation.* 2002. In [6].
13. P. McBurney, R. M. van Eijk, S. Parsons, and L. Amgoud. A dialogue-game protocol for agent purchase negotiations. *Journal of Autonomous Agents and Multi-Agent Systems,* 7(3):235–273, 2003.
14. P. McBurney and S. Parsons. Representing epistemic uncertainty by means of dialectical argumentation. *Annals of Mathematics and AI,* 32:125–169, 2001.
15. P. McBurney and S. Parsons. Games that agents play: A formal framework for dialogues between autonomous agents. *Journal of Logic, Language and Information,* 11(3):315–334, 2002.

16. P. McBurney and S. Parsons. Engineering democracy in open agent systems. In A. Omicini, P. Petta, and J. Pitt, editors, *Engineering Societies in the Agents World (ESAW-2003): Post-Proceedings*, Lecture Notes in Artificial Intelligence, Berlin, Germany, 2004. Springer.

17. P. McBurney, S. Parsons, and M. Wooldridge. Desiderata for agent argumentation protocols. In C. Castelfranchi and W. L. Johnson, editors, *Proceedings of the First International Joint Conference on Autonomous Agents and Multi-Agent Systems (AAMAS 2002), Bologna, Italy*, pages 402–409, New York City, NY, USA, 2002. ACM Press.

18. S. Parsons, M. Wooldridge, and L. Amgoud. An analysis of formal interagent dialogues. In C. Castelfranchi and W. L. Johnson, editors, *Proceedings of the First International Joint Conference on Autonomous Agents and Multi-Agent Systems (AAMAS 2002)*, pages 394–401, New York, NY, USA, 2002. ACM Press.

19. S. Paurobally, J. Cunningham, and N. R. Jennings. Ensuring consistency in the joint beliefs of interacting agents. In M. Wooldridge J. S. Rosenschein, T. Sandholm and M. Yokoo, editors, *Proceedings of the Second International Joint Conference on Autonomous Agents and Multi-Agent Systems (AAMAS 2003), Melbourne, Australia*, pages 662–669, New York City, NY, USA, 2003. ACM Press.

20. J. Pitt and A. Mamdani. Some remarks on the semantics of FIPA's Agent Communications Language. *Journal of Autonomous Agents and Multi-Agent Systems*, 2:333–356, 1999.

21. M. Schut and M. Wooldridge. The control of reasoning in resource-bounded agents. *Knowledge Engineering Review*, 16(3):215–240, 2001.

22. J. Searle. *Speech Acts: An Essay in the Philosophy of Language*. Cambridge University Press, UK, 1969.

23. A. Sen. *Rationality and Freedom*. Harvard University Press, Cambridge, MA, 2002.

24. M. P. Singh. An ontology for commitments in multiagent systems: toward a unification of normative concepts. *Artificial Intelligence and Law*, 7:97–113, 1999.

25. R. D. Tennent. *Semantics of Programming Languages*. Prentice-Hall, Hemel Hempstead, UK, 1991.

26. M. Verdicchio and M. Colombetti. Dealing with time in content language expressions. In R. M. van Eijk, M-P. Huget, and F. Dignum, editors, *Proceedings of the International Workshop on Agent Communication (AC 2004)*, pages 90–104, New York City, NY, USA, 2004. AAMAS 2004.

27. D. N. Walton and E. C. W. Krabbe. *Commitment in Dialogue: Basic Concepts of Interpersonal Reasoning*. State University of New York Press, Albany, NY, USA, 1995.

28. M. J. Wooldridge. Semantic issues in the verification of agent communication languages. *Journal of Autonomous Agents and Multi-Agent Systems*, 3(1):9–31, 2000.

29. C. Wright. Strict finitism. In *Realism, Meaning and Truth*, pages 107–175. Blackwell, Oxford, 1993.

Toward a Suite of Performatives Based Upon Joint Intention Theory

Marcus J. Huber[1], Sanjeev Kumar[2], and David McGee[3]

[1] Intelligent Reasoning Systems, San Diego, CA
marcush@marcush.net
[2] Oregon Health and Science University, Beaverton, OR
skumar@cse.ogi.edu
[3] Natural Interaction Systems, Portland, OR
dmcgee@naturalinteraction.com

Abstract. Agent communication languages defined using joint intention theory have enjoyed a long research history. A number of performatives have been defined and refined in this literature with particular emphasis on the basic performatives of REQUEST and INFORM, which subsequently have many subtle versions. Even these less common performatives have been extended and refined multiple times. In many cases the underlying definitions upon which the various performatives are based have been modified as well. While working toward implementing a multi-agent system with communications based upon joint intention semantics, it quickly became apparent that it was going to be difficult to identify a single set of performatives with correct and compatible definitions. We also realized that a set of performatives with enough breadth to cover the needs of real fielded multi-agent systems has not yet been defined. We intend this paper to provide in a single place a broadly applicable set of compatible performatives defined using joint intention semantics. Many of the performatives previously defined in the literature have been brought to the same semantic basis while we have also defined a number of new performatives to increase the breadth of performatives available to agent developers.

1 Introduction

This paper defines a broad range of Agent Communication Language (ACL) performatives based upon the semantics of joint intention (JI) theory [2,4,5,6,7,10,11,13,14,15,20,25]. A great deal of prior research on specifying "speech acts" [27] for agent communication languages based on joint intention theory has already been performed [2,4,5,6,7,12,16,17,20,28,29].

Researchers fielding multi-agent systems using joint intention theory and performatives based upon it [13,14,15,24,31,33] run into several issues however, due primarily because joint intention theory has such a rich research history:

- Performative definitions are spread throughout the literature, with no single paper to refer to.
- Base-level semantic definitions related to joint intentions have changed slowly over time in the research, both in its semantics and in its notation (as limitations are eliminated or extensions made).

R.M. van Eijk et al. (Eds.): AC 2004, LNAI 3396, pp. 226–241, 2005.

- Performative definitions have changed to match changes in these basic definitions, but not all performatives previously defined are updated with each underlying definition change.
- Performative definitions have been modified over time even when the underlying semantic definitions have remained constant (again, ostensibly to remove limitations, make extensions, etc.)
- The complexity of the definitions may sometimes cause confusion when selecting the correct performative in multi-message exchanges.
- Not all of the performatives that might be considered necessary for fielding a multi-agent system have been defined, notably "utility" performatives, both those implicitly required by joint intention theory and those not so required but found to be useful when fielding systems based on ACLs with other semantics [8,19,34].

To address these issues, we extensively reviewed the semantic definitions of performatives based on Joint Intention theory, particularly those based on the work of Cohen and Levesque, and defined a broad range of performatives with a single, consistent, unified semantic basis with more explicit historical context. This has the benefit of 1) a single semantic basis for all of the performatives, 2) a single place to refer to performative definitions, 3) a much broader selection of performatives than has been specified to date, and 4) more direct and clearer applicability to a much broader set of singe and multi-message interactions than the performatives defined to date.

The performative defined in the paper fall into the following general categories:

- Core: INFORM, REQUEST, SHOUT
- Specialized Core: SUBSCRIBE, QUERY, PROXY, PROXY-WEAK, STANDINGOFFER
- Team-oriented: AGREE, REFUSE, CANCEL, FAILURE, ACCEPT, REJECT, WITHDRAW, ORDER
- Utility: IMPOSSIBLE, RELFAIL, SUCCESS, ACKNOWLEDGE, NOTUNDERSTOOD

Core performatives are the most basic performatives, defined directly using the basic definition of ATTEMPT. The Core performatives are those that all of the other performatives are based, either using specialization or composition. The Specialized Core performatives are Core performatives that have particular message content expressions. Team-oriented performatives exploit the semantics of Joint Intention theory to form and dissolve teams of agents under various circumstances. Utility performatives are also specializations of Core performatives, but are in general used in service of the semantic ramifications of the other performatives. This categorization of the performatives is arbitrary to some extent and we could have categorized them differently. For example, the performatives in the Utility category could be considered Specialized or Team-oriented. Nevertheless, we have found it useful to group them as shown above.

2 Agent Communication Language Components

2.1 Basic Semantic Notation and Definitions

A summary of the basic notation and definitions follows. Full details of this modal language, including formal models, are beyond the scope of this paper, but can be found in [3] and [4].

e, e′, etc. are events
a, a′, etc. are actions (complex event expressions)
p, q, etc. are propositions (where q, q′, etc. are used as relativizing conditions)
t, t′, t_1, t_2, etc. are time points
x, y, z are agents
□ = always
◊ = eventually
e < e′ says that e occurs before e′
(BEL x p) say that p follows from x's beliefs.
(GOAL x p) say that p follows from x's choices.
(HAPPENS a), (HAPPENED a), and (DONE a) say that a sequence of actions described by the action expression a will happen next, happened sometime in the past, or has just happened, respectively. (HAPPENS x a) and (DONE x a) also specify the agent for the action sequence that is going to happen or has just happened.
(UNTIL p q) says that q holds up to the time that p becomes true.
BEFORE and AFTER are defined using HAPPENS and DONE.
(EARLIER p) ≡ ¬p ∧ ∃e (HAPPENED p?;e)

An action expression is built from variables ranging over sequences of events using constructs of dynamic logic: a;b is action composition, p? is a test action, | specifies non-deterministic choice, and ‖ indicates concurrent actions. Mutual belief is defined in terms of unilateral mutual belief (BMB) [16].

In some of the definitions to follow, we need to specify how rewriting occurs for embedded speech. We use a parameter substitution function $subst_{perf}$ such that $subst_{perf}$(param/val) replaces all occurrences of the schematic variable param representing a specified parameter of performative *perf* by the given value val. For the speech acts defined within this paper, we use the following abbreviations for speech act parameters: speech act (*sa*), sender (*s*), intended-recipient (*i*), distribution (final) recipient (*d*), event (*e*), action (*a*), proposition (*p*), constraint condition (*c*), relativizing condition (*q*), and time (*t*). All unreferenced speech act parameters are left unchanged.

For example, if sact = (INFORM x y e on-vacation(x) t), a fully specified speech act, we can specify a new speech act sact' using our substitution function

$$sact' = subst_{sact}(s/y \ i/z \ e/e' \ t/t')$$

which represents an INFORM speech act with all occurrences of the sender parameter replaced by y, all occurrences of the intended recipient parameter replaced by z, etc.

Definition: HAPPENING

(HAPPENING a) ≡ (DONE a) ∨ (HAPPENS a) ∨
    [∃e.(e ≤ a) ∧ (DONE e) ∧ ¬(DONE a)]

An action expression a is happening if one of the following is true (1) a has just been done, or (2) a is going to happen next (i.e. a is just starting), or (3) there exists some initial subsequence of a (represented by e) that has just been done but a is not yet done [13].

Definition: PGOAL (Persistent Goal)

(PGOAL x p q) ≡ (BEL x ¬p) ∧ (GOAL x ◊p) ∧
            (UNTIL [(BEL x p) ∨
                (BEL x □¬p) ∨
                (BEL x ¬q)]
            GOAL x ◊p)

A persistent relativized goal formalizes the notion of commitment. An agent x having a persistent goal p is committed to that goal. The agent x cannot give up the goal that p is true in the future, at least until it believes that one of the following is true: p is accomplished, is impossible, or the relativizing condition q is untrue [3]. Note that we assume that agents are competent with respect to their commitments [18].

Definition: INTEND (An Action)

(INTEND x a q) ≡ (PGOAL x
            [HAPPENS x
            (BEL x (HAPPENS a))?;a] q)

Intention to do an action a is a commitment to do the action knowingly. The agent x is committed to being in a mental state in which it has done the action a and, just prior to which, it believed that it was about to do the intended action next [3].

Definition: ATTEMPT

(ATTEMPT x e   t) ≡
    t?;[(BEL x ¬) ∧
        (GOAL x (HAPPENS e;• ?)) ∧
        (INTEND x t?;e; ?(GOAL x (HAPPENS e;• ?)))]?;e

An attempt to achieve   via   is a complex action expression in which the agent x is the actor of event e at time t and, just prior to e, the actor chooses that   should eventually become true and intends that e should produce   relative to that choice. So   represents some ultimate goal that may or may not be achieved by the attempt, while   represents what it takes to make an honest effort [4].

Definition: PWAG (Persistent Weak Achievement Goal)

(PWAG x y p q) ≡
    [¬(BEL x p) ∧ (PGOAL x p q)] ∨
    [(BEL x p) ∧ (PGOAL x (MB x y p) q)] ∨
    [(BEL x □¬p) ∧ (PGOAL x (MB x y □¬p) q)] ∨
    [(BEL x ¬q) ∧ (PGOAL x (MB x y ¬q))]

This definition, recently revised in [17], states that an agent x has a PWAG with respect to another agent y when the following holds: (1) if agent x believes that p is not currently true, it will have a persistent goal to achieve p, (2) if it believes p to be either true, or to be impossible, or if it believes the relativizing condition q to be false, then it will adopt a persistent goal to bring about the corresponding mutual belief with agent y. A PWAG expression is often used in the performatives below that are intended to create a joint, or social, commitment.

2.2   ACL Performative Semantics and Descriptions

Definition: Inform

(INFORM x y e p t) ≡ (ATTEMPT x e   t)
  where
    = (BMB y x p)
  and
    = (BMB y x
          (BEFORE e
          [GOAL x
            (AFTER e
            (BEL y
              [BEFORE e
              (BEL x p)
              ]))
          ]))

In this performative, the sender x has the goal that the intended recipient y come to believe that there is mutual belief that y believes p. The intention of INFORM is that the y comes to believe there is a mutual belief between the y and x that before sending the INFORM, x had a goal that after sending the INFORM the intended recipient y would believe that, before sending the INFORM, x believed proposition p (most recently from [17]).

The INFORM performative is a general-purpose speech act suitable for any communication related to propositional belief. Many of the following speech acts specialize this speech act or us it in more complex action expressions.

Definition: Request

(REQUEST x y e a q t) ≡ (ATTEMPT x e   t)
  where
    = (DONE y a) ∧ [PWAG y x (DONE y a)
                              (PWAG x y (DONE y a) q)∧q]
  and
    = (BMB y x (BEFORE e
              [GOAL x
                (AFTER e
                (BEL y [PWAG x y   q]))]))

We use the single-agent version of the definition of the REQUEST performative that is defined in [16] and later refined in [17]. Intuitively, this definition says that in making a request of addressee y, the requestor x is trying to get y to do the action a, and to form the commitment to do a relative to the context q and the requester's commitment that it do it.

The goal of the requester is that the intended actor y eventually do the action a and have a PWAG with respect to the requester x to do a. The intended actor's PWAG is with respect to (i.e., relativized to) the requester's PWAG (towards y) that y does the action a and also with respect to q. The requester's PWAG is itself relative to some higher-level goal q.

The intention of REQUEST is that the recipient y believe there is a mutual belief between the recipient and the requester that before performing the REQUEST, the requester x had a goal that after performing it, the requester x will have a PWAG with respect to the intended actor y about the goal φ of the request.

The REQUEST performative is a general-purpose speech act useful whenever one agent wants another agent to do something. Many of the following speech acts specialize this speech act or us it in more complex action expressions.

Definition: Subscribe

(SUBSCRIBE x y e $\prod$ q t) $\equiv$ (REQUEST x y e α q t)

where,

$\alpha = \Diamond(\forall t_1,t_2,t_3.(t < t_1 < t_2 < t_3).\forall e',\forall \tau.$

$\quad$ (DONE $(t_1?;\neg\prod(\tau)?;t_2?;\prod(\tau)?;$(INFORM y x e' $\prod(\tau)$ t$_3$) |

$\qquad$ t$_1$?; $\prod(\tau)?;t_2?;\neg\prod(\tau)?;$(INFORM y x e' $\neg\prod(\tau)$ t$_3$))))?

$\quad$ where τ represents a grounded object and

$\quad$ $\prod$ is a unary predicate, indicating the information of interest to the sender, that evaluates to true or false for objects (τ):

A new JI performative, a SUBSCRIBE is a REQUEST for the sender to INFORM the recipient whenever the indicated predicate changes state for any objects known to y that satisfy $\prod$. Unless initially REFUSEd or subsequently CANCELed (see below), the recipient y should INFORM $\prod(\tau)$ or $\neg\prod(\tau)$ whenever the truth value of the predicate changes from false to true or true to false, respectively.

The SUBSCRIBE performative is useful in situations where an agent needs to be kept up to date on another agent's beliefs over an extended period of time. For example, $\prod$=OnTable, y might come to inform x that OnTable(blockA), another message to inform x that ¬OnTable(blockB), etc. In the CIANC project, in which autonomous vehicles might be used for surveillance [33], $\prod$ can be the predicate HostileWithinRange(), such that an agent subscribing to a surveillance agent using that predicate will be kept advised on hostile units that come into and leave weapons range.

Definition: Query

(QUERY x y e p q t) $\equiv$ (REQUEST x y e α q t)

$\quad$ where

$\quad$ $\alpha = \Diamond(\exists e',t', t'>t, e'>e.$(DONE (INFORM y x e' p t') |

$\qquad\qquad\qquad$ (INFORM y x e' ¬p t')))?

In this performative, the sender asks the recipient about their belief in the truth value of a particular proposition (similar to the "yes-no question" performative in [7]).

In other words, y is requested to INFORM x, at some future time with a distinct event, of its belief in the value of p. The QUERY performative is useful in situations when only the current belief value of a single proposition is required by the querying agent.

Definition: Proxy

(PROXY x y z e c sact q t) $\equiv$
  (REQUEST x y e
          (c?;$\Diamond$[$\exists$e',t'.(DONE $subst_{sact}(s/y\ i/z\ e/e'\ t/t')$))]?) q t)

PROXY is defined as a request by the sender x for an intermediary agent y to perform a specified speech act, sact, to a final target agent z if the condition c is met (modified from the [12], which gives details of this speech acts' 3rd party semantics). sact can be any fully-specified speech act, but the sender of sact (performed as a distinct event at a future time) will be y and the final recipient will be z. With the PROXY performative, the "middle agent" y assumes all responsibility associated with uttering the proxied performative sact to z. The PROXY performative provides agents the important capability of using intermediary agents [8,9,19,21,30,34] to do speech acts on its behalf.

Definition: Proxy-Weak

(PROXY-WEAK x y z e c sact q t) $\equiv$
  (REQUEST x y e
          (c?;$\Diamond$[$\exists$e',t'.(DONE (INFORM y z e' θ t')))]?) q t)
  where
    θ = (HAPPENING $subt_{sact}(s/y\ i/z\ e/e;e'\ t/t')$)

This performative is a weaker version than PROXY, where the middle agent y sends an INFORM message about sact rather than perform sact itself. This protects the middle agent from bearing the obligations associated with performing sact directly and at the same time results in a state *as if* x had performed sact directly to z (modified from [10], which gives details of this speech acts' 3rd party semantics). The PROXY-WEAK performative provides agents the important capability of using intermediary agents [8,9,19,21,30,34] to pass on requests or information to third agents.

Definition: Shout

Given that Π is a unary group membership predicate indicating who the intended recipients are,

(SHOUT x e p t) $\equiv$ (ATTEMPT x e ϕ ψ t)
  where
    = $\forall$y. (y) [BMB y x p]
  and
    = $\forall$y. (y). [BMB y x
                (BEFORE e
                  [GOAL x
                    (AFTER e
                      [BEL y
                        (BEFORE e
                          [BEL x p]
)])])]

The sending agent x holds that some proposition is true and intends that the receiving agents, specified as those satisfying the predicate , also come to believe that the proposition is true. This is an extended form of INFORM to support making an utterance to multiple, incompletely-specified recipients, a capability not supported by the ACLs of KQML, Singh, FIPA, and others [8,19,27,34]. In this SHOUT performative, the sending agent is essentially performing an INFORM to each of the agents satisfying . Examples of in real applications might be of the form contractors() (to represent all agents the sending agent has contracts with), inferiors() (to represent all agents that the agent considers as inferiors), platoon-members() (to represent all agents that are associated with supporting a platoon), etc.

A group-theoretic version of this performative based on [16] would provide more flexible semantics (in that the speaker would not have to know anything about the recipients beliefs, unlike in this definition in which it eventually does) but creating a complete suite of performatives with the group-theoretic work remains for future work.

Definition: StandingOffer

(STANDINGOFFER x y e a q t) ≡ (INFORM x y e θ t)
where
$$\theta = \forall e'.(\text{DONE}$$
$$(\text{INFORM y x e' (PWAG y x (DONE x a) q)))} \supset$$
$$(\text{DONE e';(PWAG x y (DONE x a)}$$
$$(\text{PWAG y x (DONE x a) q)} \wedge q)?)$$

In this performative (most recently from [17]), the sender x is making a standing offer to the recipient y to form a commitment (PWAG) to do something for the recipient in the future. This obligation on x's part will only arise, however, when y sends it an INFORM message saying that it has a commitment and wants x to adopt the commitment relative to y's. As shown in [18], the STANDINGOFFER followed by the definition's INFORM results in a Joint Intention team just as if y had sent a REQUEST and x had replied with an AGREE.

Definition: Order

Within the confines of this paper, we define the following relationship definitions for use in the ORDER performative:

OBEDIENT-TO
(OBEDIENT-TO x y a q) ≡
    $\forall$e,t.[(DONE y (REQUEST y x e a q t)) $\supset$
        (PWAG y x (DONE x a) q) $\wedge$
        (PWAG x y (DONE x a)
            [PWAG y x (DONE x a) q] $\wedge$q)]

Agent x is obedient to y with respect to action a and relativizing condition q when for every REQUEST by y, x will always adopt a PWAG to do a with respect to y's PWAG that x do a. A synonym to OBEDIENT-TO is INFERIOR (i.e., if y is OBEDIENT-TO x, then y is INFERIOR to x).

AUTHORITY-OVER

(AUTHORITY-OVER x y a q) ≡ (OBEDIENT-TO y x a q)

Agent x has authority over agent y with respect to a and q. A synonym to AUTHORITY-OVER is SUPERIOR (i.e., if x has AUTHORITY-OVER y, then x is SUPERIOR to y).

Then, the definition of ORDER is:

$$(ORDER\ x\ y\ e\ a\ q\ t) \equiv (SUPERIOR\ x\ y\ a\ q)?;(REQUEST\ x\ y\ e\ a\ q\ t)$$

In this new performative, we extended the single-agent version of the definition of the REQUEST performative to support authority relationships, wherein the sender has some recognized authority to unilaterally task the recipient. Here, x is the agent performing the ORDER, y is the intended recipient (the intended actor), e is the event of performing the ORDER, a is the action to be done, q is a relativizing condition, and t is the time point of the utterance. An ORDER with the appropriate SUPERIOR relationship automatically results in nested persistent goals (PWAGs) as if an explicit AGREE (see below) had been performed by the recipient.

Definition: Agree

(AGREE x y e a q t) ≡
　(∃e', t'.(EARLIER (DONE (REQUEST y x e' a q t'))))?;
　(INFORM x y e (PWAG x y (DONE x a)
　　　　　　　　(PWAG y x (DONE x a) q)∧q))

This performative is an agreement to perform an action requested by another agent. This is similar to the CONFIRM performative of [29] and [17], but revised extensively to require the historical context (i.e., an earlier REQUEST). As shown in [17], this performative is sufficient to create a team with interlocking PWAGs when in response to a prior REQUEST.

Definition: Refuse

(REFUSE x y e a q t) ≡
　(∃e', t'.[EARLIER
　　　　　(DONE (REQUEST y x e' a q t'))])?;
　(INFORM x y e ¬[PWAG x y (DONE x a)
　　　　　　　　(PWAG y x (DONE x a) q)∧q])

The sender will NOT adopt the recipient's goal to do an action from a prior request. This is similar in some respect to that of the REFUSE performative of [29] and [17]. Our formulation is more specific in the context term (a REQUEST compared to a more general PWAG expression). In addition, their formulation uses □¬[PWAG...], indicating that the refusing agent would never perform the action for the other agent. However, we feel that this is not desirable as the agent that is currently refusing might accept to do the action at a later time. The definition of [28] has the same ¬[PWAG ...] semantics but does not include the historical context (i.e., the EARLIER term).

Definition: Cancel

(CANCEL x y e a q t) ≡
  (∃e′,t′.[EARLIER
            (DONE (REQUEST x y e′ a q t′))])?;
  (INFORM x y e ¬(PWAG x y (DONE y a) q))

In the CANCEL performative, the sender no longer has the goal that the recipient perform an action (accepted in response to a prior REQUEST by the sender). This has been revised from [17] to specify REQUEST in the context rather than a PWAG expression. Not that this performative can also be used to dissolve a team in certain circumstances, such as when a REQUEST/AGREE performative sequence was performed between x and y.

Definition: Failure

(FAILURE x y e a q t) ≡
  (∃e′,t′.(EARLIER [DONE (REQUEST y x e′ a q t′)]))?;
  (INFORM x y e
        (DONE x (¬p ∧ (INTEND x ¬p?;a;p?);a;¬p?)?))

In this new performative, the sender tells the recipient that the action a was attempted but was not successfully completed. The DONE expression indicates that the sender intended that the action would have certain expected results but that after performing the action the results were not what was expected. This is not sufficient to terminate a team of agents; if the sender is part of a team with respect to performing action a, it will persist in pursuing the action until the team's PWAG is eventually satisfied. Even without the power to dissolve a team, this message is often useful as a status message between agents in fielded multi-agent systems.

Definition: Accept

(ACCEPT x y e a q t) ≡
  (∃e′,t′.(EARLIER [DONE (STANDINGOFFER y x e′ a q t′)]))?;
  (INFORM x y e (PWAG x y (DONE y a) q))

This performative is an acceptance of the other agent standing offer to perform action a (significantly modified from [17] by adding the explicit historical context term). Note that an additional difference between ACCEPT and AGREE is that the ACCEPT's PWAG is only relative to q while the AGREE's PWAG is relative to the other agent's PWAG and q.

Definition: Reject

(REJECT x y e a q t) ≡
  (∃e′,t′.(EARLIER
            [DONE (STANDINGOFFER y x e′ a q t′)]))?;
  (INFORM x y e ¬(PWAG x y (DONE y a) q))

This performative is the opposite of an ACCEPT, in that the sending agent tells the recipient that it will not be taking up the standing offer for y to perform action a. This has been modified significantly from [17] by adding the explicit historical context term and using ¬(PWAG...) rather than □¬(PWAG ...). Note that the difference between REFUSE and REJECT is that the REJECT's PWAG is only relative to q while the REFUSE's PWAG is relative to the other agent's PWAG *and* q.

Definition: Withdraw

(WITHDRAW x y e a q t) ≡
  (∃e′,t′.(EARLIER [DONE (STANDINGOFFER x y e′ a q t′)]))?;
  (INFORM x y e ¬θ t)

where

  θ = ∀e″.t″.(DONE (INFORM y x e″ (PWAG y x (DONE x a) q)) t″) ⊃
        (DONE e″;(PWAG x y (DONE x a)
                (PWAG y x (DONE x a) q)∧q)?)

This performative provides the means by which an agent can remove its STANDINGOFFER (the semantics of which is represented by θ) to do an action for another agent (revised from [17]). Note that the recipient of a STANDINGOFFER need do nothing to "remove" itself from a STANDINGOFFER relationship, as it has no outstanding commitment to the original sender.

Definition: Impossible

(IMPOSSIBLE x y e a t) ≡
  (∃e′,t′.(EARLIER
        (DONE [(REQUEST x y e′ a q t′) |
                (REQUEST y x e′ a q t′)])))?;
  (INFORM x y e □¬(DONE a) t)

In this new performative, the sender tells the recipient that it is no longer possible to perform action a. Per the definition of PWAG, this is sufficient to dissolve a "team" of agents with interlocking PWAGs and will typically be used only (but often) for this purpose. Note that either agent involved in the team may send this message to satisfy the PWAG and thereby dissolve the team.

Definition: RelFail

(RELFAIL x y e q t) ≡
  (∃e′,t′.(EARLIER
        (DONE [(REQUEST x y e′ a q t′) |
                (REQUEST y x e′ a q t′)])))?;
  (INFORM x y e ¬q t)

In this new performative, the sender tells the recipient that the relativizing condition of an earlier REQUEST is no longer valid. Per the definition of PWAG, this is sufficient to dissolve a "team" of agents with interlocking PWAGs and will typically be used only (but often) for this purpose. Note that either agent involved in the team may send this message to satisfy the PWAG and thereby dissolve the team.

Definition: Success

(SUCCESS x y e a t) ≡ (INFORM x y e (DONE x a) t)

In this new performative, the sender tells the recipient that action a has been performed successfully. Per the definition of PWAG, this is sufficient to dissolve a "team" of agents with interlocking PWAGs (assuming such communication achieves a state of mutual belief). This is a very simple performative specialization, but since it is a very common message in fielded multi-agent systems, particularly those based upon joint intention theory, the resulting simplified parsing and interpretation will result in significant time and computational resources savings over time.

Definition: Acknowledge

(ACKNOWLEDGE x y e a q t) ≡
    (INFORM x y e
        (∃e′,t′.[EARLIER
            (DONE y
                (REQUEST y x e′ a q t′))]) t)

An agent will use this performative to acknowledge that a prior REQUEST has been made. Among other uses, this can act as a courtesy message between agents. Note that this is a new performative definition and is completely different than the ACKNOWLEDGE performative in [29]. This utility performative fills a vital role in fielded agent systems.

Definition: NotUnderstood

(NOTUNDERSTOOD x y e a p t) ≡ (INFORM x y e θ t)
  where
    θ = ∃e′,t′.(EARLIER (DONE (sact y x e′ t′)) ∧
            ¬*intentof*(sact y x e′ t′) ∧
            ¬*goalof*(sact y x e′ t′)
sact is any fully specified speech act,
intentof is an operator that extracts the goal portion of sact, and
goalof is an operator that extracts the intention portion of sact

In this new performative, the sender x informs y, the sender of an earlier message (sact), that it does not understand something about the message by expressing that it did receive the message but that neither the goal nor intention portion of the speaker's speech act was successful. Note that this performative is not yet semantically correct because, strictly speaking, the intention portion of our speech acts cannot be untrue (by definition of speech acts, they are automatically true by their utterance) but might be completed using 2nd-order logic. Even though the semantics of this performative remains an area of future work, we found it useful as agent implementers to include this performative in fielded multiagent applications.

3 Discussion

In this paper, we have defined a broad number of performatives based upon a single, coherent semantics of Joint Intention theory definitions. While we have based many of the performatives upon a variant found in prior literature, most of those have received an update to the latest semantics of this paper. Many of the other performatives in this paper are completely novel.

We recognize that agents will often interact in some form of typical or common pattern of performative exchange (so-called conversation policies or interaction protocols [1,8,17,29]) and many of the performatives have been designed with this in mind. However, a significant amount of communications will be performed outside of the auspices of any *explicit* interaction pattern. These "standalone" performatives, INFORM, REQUEST, SHOUT, and ORDER, will certainly be used within conversation policies, but are more likely than the other performatives here to be used alone.

Oftentimes an *implicit* protocol will be employed in practical, fielded, multiagent systems [15,31,33]. For example, the performatives NOTUNDERSTOOD might be returned after any utterance, and ACKNOWLEDGE might be returned after any REQUEST, irrespective of any explicit conversation policy. The REQUEST performative itself holds a special place in Joint Intention theory in that its utterance implies certain subsequent behavior (the establishment of mutual belief, in particular) on the part of the requesting and requested agent, much of which can be satisfied by messaging. We created the SUCCESS, RELFAIL, and IMPOSSIBLE performatives to fill the messaging needs of the agents involved in a REQUEST utterance, as each of these performatives can be used to establish mutual belief regarding one aspect of the PWAGs in the definition of REQUEST. So, while an explicit conversation policy may be in place upon the utterance of a REQUEST, the implicit messaging requirements can be satisfied by our suite of performatives.

The SUBSCRIBE and QUERY performatives also have a simple implicit protocol associated with them. By definition, utterance of a SUBSCRIBE will be followed by one or more INFORM messages should the recipient AGREE to the SUBSCRIBE request. To terminate a SUBSCRIBE performative, a CANCEL performative must be sent by the agent that performed the SUBSCRIBE. Similarly, the QUERY performative will be followed by one INFORM should the recipient of the QUERY decide to honor the request. Interaction protocols that make the messages subsequent to SUBSCRIBE and QUERY are certainly not prohibited.

The remaining performatives were defined with the expectation of using them primarily, if not solely, within interaction protocols. For example, we designed a number of other performatives to complement the REQUEST performative within an interaction protocol. These specifically are AGREE, REFUSE, CANCEL, SUCCESS, FAILURE, IMPOSSIBLE, and RELFAIL. AGREE and REFUSE can immediately follow a REQUEST in order to establish or prevent establishment of a Joint Intention team of agents, respectively. Following an AGREE message, the requesting agent can utter a CANCEL to dissolve the team. A FAILURE message, not strictly required by Joint Intention theory, can be used by the requested agent to indicate a particular state of progress toward performing the requested task; the FAILURE message indicates that the tasked agent is actively trying to do the task and is having some setbacks (but that the task might yet be performed, as otherwise it would have sent an

IMPOSSIBLE performative). A SUCCESS performative can be used to indicate that the action was completed successfully and will dissolve a JI team. The IMPOSSIBLE performative indicates from either requesting or requested agents that the task requested can never be accomplished and will result in dissolution of a JI team. RELFAIL, similarly, indicates that the context under which a REQUESTed task is relevant has become false and use of this performative will also result in the dissolution of a JI team.

With regards to the PROXY and PROXY-WEAK performatives, their utterance will be followed, by definition, by another speech act, assuming that the middle agent decided to honor the sender's request. Whether or not the PROXY and PROXY-WEAK performatives are included within explicit interaction protocols is a domain specific decision, but they will always engender the possibility of future speech acts due to their utterance.

The ACCEPT, REJECT, and WITHDRAW performatives are all designed to be complementary performatives to the STANDINGOFFER performative. Once an agent performs a STANDINGOFFER speech act, the recipient can perform and ACCEPT or REJECT performative to establish or prevent establishment of a JI team, respectively. Subsequent to an ACCEPT, the agent performing the STANDINGOFFER can utter a WITHDRAW to terminate the terms of the offer.

The ORDER performative stands out from the others defined in this paper due to its use of agent-to-agent relationships. Inclusion of this performative within the paper was motivated by the CIANC project [33], in which agents related to human operators interact with each other while controlling and interacting with agent-based autonomous robotic vehicles within a military environment. We have found the need to make explicit the authority relationships between agents as well as the "rules of engagement" (authorized to do a, prohibited from doing a, obliged to x to do a, etc. much like deontic logic relationships [32]) that the agents are constrained by. As such, we have subsequently found it useful to develop performatives specialized to these authority and deontic relationships. The ORDER primitive is just one example of a set of performatives that will be developed along these lines.

This paper presents significant progress towards our goals of a single semantic basis for all of the performatives, a single place to refer to performative definitions, a much broader selection of performatives than has been specified to date, and clearer applicability to a much broader set of single and multi-message interactions than has been previously defined.

Much remains to be done in the field of developing an ACL based on Joint Intention Theory, however. For example, the semantics of the NOTUNDERSTOOD performative, which is important in fielded systems, has yet to be correctly defined in JI semantics. Of even broader impact, we need to apply the developments of group-theoretic semantics of [16] to all of the performatives to provide the flexibility of groups of agents as senders and/or recipients. There are a large number of applications where this capability is useful in multiagent systems, when agents acting as representatives of institutions and organizations (e.g. sales and purchasing agents) interact with each other.

Acknowledgements

This report was prepared under a Department of the Army Small Business Innovation Research Program 2000.2 contract for topic A02-024 (contract #DASW01-03-c-0019). We gratefully acknowledge the sponsorship of this research by the United States Army Research Institute and thank ARI Contracting Officer's Representative (COR) Dr. Carl Lickteig for his guidance and support.

References

1. Bauer B.; Muller, J.P.; Odell, J. An Extension of UML by Protocols for Multiagent Interaction. In Proceedings of the Fourth International Conference on MultiAgent Systems (ICMAS'00), pages 207-214, Boston, Massachussetts, 2000.
2. Cohen, P.R.; Levesque, H.J. Rational Interaction as the Basis for Communication. In P.R. Cohen, J. Morgan, and M.E. Pollack, Eds. Intentions in Communication, System Development Foundation Benchmark Series, MIT Press, Cambridge, MA, 221-256, 1990.
3. Cohen, P.R.; Levesque, H.J. Intention is Choice with Commitment, Artificial Intelligence, 42(3):213-261, 1990.
4. Cohen, P.R.; Levesque, H.J. Performatives in a Rationally Based Speech Act Theory, In Proceedings of the 28th Annual Meeting of the Association for Computational Linguistics, Pittsburgh, Pennsylvania, 1990.
5. Cohen, P.R.; Levesque, H.J. Confirmations and Joint Action, In Proceedings of the 12th International Joint Conference on Artificial Intelligence, San Mateo, California, 1991.
6. Cohen, P.R.; Levesque, H.J. Teamwork. Nous, 25(4): 487-512. 1991.
7. Cohen, Philip; Levesque, Hector. Communicative Actions for Artificial Agents, in Proceedings of the First International Conference on Multi-Agent Systems, San Francisco, CA, 65-72, 1995.
8. Finin, T.; Labrou, Y.; Mayfield, J. KQML as an Agent Communication Language. Software Agents, Bradshaw ed., MIT Press, 1995.
9. Giampapa, J.; Paolucci, M.; Sycara, K. Agent Interoperation Across Multi-Agent System Boundaries, Proceedings of the Fourth International Conference on Autonomous Agents (Agents 2000), pgs 179-186, 2000.
10. Grosz, Barbara J.; Kraus, Sarit. Collaborative Plans for Complex Group Action. Artificial Intelligence 86(2):269-357. 1996.
11. Grosz, Barbara; Hunsberger, Luke; Kraus, Sarit. Planning and Acting Together, AI Magazine 20(4):23-34, Winter 1999.
12. Huber, Marcus; Kumar, Sanjeev; Cohen, Philip; McGee, David. A Formal Semantics for Proxy Communicative Acts, In Proceedings of Agent Theories, Architectures, and Languages (ATAL), 221-234. Seattle, WA, August, 2001.
13. Jennings, N. R. Commitments and Conventions: The Foundation of Coordination in Multi-Agent Systems, The Knowledge Engineering Review, 8(3):223-250. 1993.
14. Jennings, N.R. Specification and Implementation of a Belief-Desire-Joint-Intention Architecture for Collaborative Problem Solving, Intelligent and Cooperative Information Systems, 2(3):289-318. 1993.
15. Jenning, N.R. Controlling Cooperative Problem Solving in Industrial Multi-Agent Systems using Joint Intentions, Artificial Intelligence, 75(2):195-240. 1995.

16. Kumar, S.; Huber, M.J.; McGee D.R.; Cohen, P.R.; Levesque, H.J. Semantics of Agent Communication Languages for Group Interaction. In Proceedings of the 16th National Conference on Artificial Intelligence, 42-47, 2000.

17. Kumar, Sanjeev; Huber, Marcus; Cohen, Philip R. Representing and Executing Protocols as Joint Actions, In Proceedings of the First International Conference on Autonomous Agent and MultiAgent Systems, 543-550, Bologna, Italy, June, 2002.

18. Kumar, Sanjeev; Huber, Marcus; Cohen, Philip; McGee, David. Toward a Formalism for Conversational Protocols Using Joint Intention Theory, Journal of Computational Intelligence (Special Issue on Agent Communication Language), Brahim Chaib-draa and Frank Dignum (Guest Editors), 18(2):174-228, 2002.

19. Labrou, Y.; Finin, T. A Semantic Approach for KQML - A General Purpose Communication Language for Software Agents. In Proceedings of the Third International Conference on Information and Knowledge Management, 447-455. 1994.

20. Levesque, H.J.; Cohen, P.R.; Nunes, J.H.T. On Acting Together. In Proceedings of AAAI-90, Boston, 1990.

21. Martin, D.L., Cheyer, A.J., and Moran, D.B. The Open Agent Architecture: A Framework for Building Distributed Software Systems, Applied Artificial Intelligence, vol. 13, pages 91-128, 1999.

22. Pitt, J.; Kamara, L.; Artikis, A. Interaction Patterns and Observable Commitments in a Multi-Agent Trading Scenario. In Proceedings of Agents 2001, Montreal, 2001.

23. Pitt, J.; Mamdani, A. A Protocol-Based Semantics for an Agent Communication Language. In Proceedings of the Sixteenth International Joint Conference on Artificial Intelligence, Stockholm, Sweden, 486-491, 1999.

24. Pynadath, D.V.; Tambe, M.; Chauvat, N.; Cavedon, L. Toward Team-Oriented Programming. In Intelligent Agents VI: Agent Theories, Architectures and Languages, 233-247. N.R. Jennings and Y. Lespérance, eds., Springer-Verlag, 1999.

25. Rao, A.S.; Georgeff, M.P. Social plans: Preliminary report. In E. Werner and Y. Demazeau, editors, Decentralized AI 3. 57-76. Elsevier Science Publishers B.V. Amsterdam, Netherlands, 1992.

26. Searle J.R. Speech Acts. Cambridge University Press, 1969.

27. Singh, M.P. Agent Communication Languages: Rethinking the Principles, Computer 31(12):40-47, IEEE Computer Society, December 1998.

28. Smith, I.A., Cohen, P.R. Toward a Semantics for an Agent Communications Language based on Speech Acts. In Proceedings of AAAI-96, 24-31, Portland, Oregon, 1996.

29. Smith, I.A.; Cohen, P.R.; Bradshaw, J.M.; Greaves, M.; Holmback, H. Designing Conversation Policies using Joint Intention Theory. In Proceedings of the Third International Conference on MultiAgent Systems, 269-276, Paris, France, IEEE Press, 1998.

30. Sycara, K., Decker, K., and Williamson, M., Middle-Agents for the Internet, In Proceedings of the Fifteenth International Joint Conference on Artificial Intelligence, pgs 578-583, January, 1997.

31. Tambe, M., Towards Flexible Teamwork. Journal of Artificial Intelligence Research, 7:83-124. 1997.

32. von Wright, G.H. Deontic Logic, Mind. 60:1-15, 1951.

33. Wood S.; Zaientz J.; Beard J.; Frederiksen R.; Huber M. CIANC3: An Agent-Based Intelligent Interface for Future Combat Systems Command and Control, In Proceedings of the 2003 Conference on Behavior Representation in Modeling and Simulation, 2003.

34. www.fipa.org/specifications.

A Model of Rational Agency for Communicating Agents

Shakil M. Khan and Yves Lespérance

Dept. of Computer Science, York University,
Toronto, ON, Canada M3J 1P3
{skhan, lesperan}@cs.yorku.ca

Abstract. The Cognitive Agent Specification Language (CASL) is a framework for specifying and verifying complex communicating multiagent systems. In this paper, we extend CASL to incorporate a formal model of means-ends reasoning suitable for a multiagent context. In particular, we define a simple model of cooperative ability, give a definition of rational plans, and show how an agent's intentions play a role in determining her next actions. This bridges the gap between intentions to achieve a goal and intentions to act. We also define a notion of subjective plan execution and show that in the absence of interference, an agent that is able to achieve a goal, intends to do so, and is acting rationally will eventually achieve it.

1   Introduction

Most agent theories [1, 25] suffer from a similar problem: they axiomatize the relation between the different mental attitudes of the agents and the physical states of the world; but they do not account for how the agents will achieve their goals, how they plan and commit to plans. Ideally, an agent's intention to achieve a state of affairs in a situation should drive the agent to intend to execute a plan that she thinks is rational in that situation. In other words, an agent's future directed intentions should lead her to adopt rational plans and eventually achieve her intentions.

Another recent thread in agent theory introduces a procedural component to the framework in an attempt to close the gap between agents' intentions to achieve a state of affairs and their intentional actions, as well as to support the modeling of complex multiagent systems. One example of this is the Cognitive Agent Specification Language (CASL) [32, 33], which is a framework for specifying and verifying complex communicating multiagent systems. However, it is somewhat restricted in the sense that it requires the modeler to specify agent behavior explicitly, and the program that controls the agent's actions need not be consistent with the agent's intentions, or do anything to achieve them.

In this paper, we propose a solution to this problem by extending CASL. In particular, we define rational plans and ability in a multiagent context, and use these notions to link future and present directed intentions. We introduce a special action, the *commit* action, that makes the agent commit to a plan, and define a meta-controller *BehaveRationallyUntil* that has the agent act rationally

R.M. van Eijk et al. (Eds.): AC 2004, LNAI 3396, pp. 242–259, 2005.

to achieve a specific goal by choosing and committing to a rational plan, and carrying it out. We also define a notion of subjective execution of plans where the agent must have the required knowledge to execute the plan. Then we show that given that an agent has an intention, she will act to achieve it provided that she is able to do so.

The paper is organized as follows: in the next section, we outline previous work on CASL. In Section 3, we develop a simple formalization of cooperative ability for agents working in a multiagent setting. In Section 4, we define rational plans, relate future and present directed intentions, and discuss what it means for an agent to behave rationally and execute plans subjectively. We also state a theorem that links an agent's intentions and abilities to the eventual achievement of her intentions.

2   CASL

In CASL [32, 33], agents are viewed as entities with mental states, i.e., knowledge and goals, and the specifier can define the behavior of the agents in terms of these mental states. CASL combines a declarative action theory defined in the situation calculus with a rich programming/process language, ConGolog [5]. Domain dynamics and agents' mental states are specified declaratively in the theory, while system behavior is specified procedurally in ConGolog.

In CASL, a dynamic domain is represented using an action theory [27] formulated in the situation calculus [21], a second order language for representing dynamically changing worlds in which all changes are the result of named actions. CASL uses a theory that includes the following set of axioms:

- domain-independent foundational axioms describing the structure of situations [14],
- action precondition axioms, one per action,
- successor state axioms (SSA), one per fluent, that encode both effect and frame axioms and specify exactly when the fluent changes [26],
- initial state axioms describing what is true initially including the mental states of the agents,
- axioms identifying the agent of each action, and,
- unique name axioms for actions.

Within CASL, the behavior of agents is specified using the notation of the logic programming language ConGolog [5], the concurrent version of Golog [19]. A typical ConGolog program is composed of a sequence of procedure declarations, followed by a complex action. Complex actions can be composed using constructs that include the ones given in Table 1.[1] These constructs are mostly

---

[1] Since we have predicates that take programs as arguments, we need to encode programs as first-order terms as in [5]. For notational simplicity, we suppress this encoding and use formulae as terms directly. Also, here ϕ is used to denote a formula whose fluents may contain a placeholder now that stands for the situation in effect at the time that ϕ is tested. $\phi(s)$ is the formula that results from replacing now with s. Where the intended meaning is clear, we suppress the placeholder.

Table 1. Examples of ConGolog Constructs

a,	primitive action
$\phi?$,	wait for a condition
$(\delta_1; \delta_2)$,	sequence
$(\delta_1 \mid \delta_2)$,	nondeterministic choice
$\pi x.\delta$,	nondet. choice of argument
If ϕ Then δ_1 Else δ_2 EndIf,	conditional
While ϕ Do σ EndWhile,	while loop
$\beta(\overrightarrow{p})$,	procedure call.

self-explanatory. Intuitively, $\pi x.\delta$ nondeterministically picks a binding for the variable x and performs the program δ for this binding of x. ConGolog also supports nondeterministic iteration, concurrent execution with and without priorities, and interrupts. To deal with multiagent processes, primitive actions in CASL take the agent of the action as argument.

The semantics of the ConGolog process description language is defined in terms of *transitions*, in the style of structural operational semantics [24]. Two special predicates *Final* and *Trans* are introduced, and are characterized by defining axioms for each of the above constructs, where $Final(\delta, s)$ means that program δ may legally terminate in situation s, and where $Trans(\delta, s, \delta', s')$ means that program δ in situation s may legally execute one step, ending in situation s' with program δ' remaining. The overall semantics of a ConGolog program is specified by the Do relation:

$$Do(\delta, s, s') \doteq \exists \delta' \cdot (Trans^*(\delta, s, \delta', s') \wedge Final(\delta', s')).$$

$Do(\delta, s, s')$ holds if and only if s' can be reached by performing a sequence of transitions starting with program δ in s, and the remaining program δ' may legally terminate in s'. Here, $Trans^*$ is the reflexive transitive closure of the transition relation $Trans$.

CASL allows the specifier to model the agents in terms of their mental states by including operators to specify agents' information (i.e., their knowledge), and motivation (i.e., their goals or intentions). Following [22, 30], CASL models knowledge using a possible worlds account adapted to the situation calculus. $K(agt, s', s)$ is used to denote that in situation s, agt thinks that she could be in situation s'. s' is called a K-*alternative situation* for agt in s. Using K, the knowledge or belief of an agent, $Know(agt, \phi, s)$, is defined as $\forall s'(K(agt, s', s) \supset \phi(s'))$, i.e. agt knows ϕ in s if ϕ holds in all of agt's K-accessible situations in s. Two useful abbreviations are also defined: $KWhether(agt, \phi, s) \doteq Know(agt, \phi, s) \vee Know(agt, \neg\phi, s)$, i.e., agt knows whether ϕ holds in s, and $KRef(agt, \theta, s) \doteq \exists t.Know(agt, t = \theta, s)$, i.e., agt knows who/what θ is. In CASL, K is constrained to be reflexive, transitive, and euclidean in the initial situation to capture the fact that agents' knowledge is true, and that agents have positive and negative introspection. As shown in [30], these constraints then continue to hold after any sequence of actions since they are preserved by the successor state axiom for K.

Scherl and Levesque [30] showed how to capture the changes in beliefs of agents that result from actions in the successor state axiom for K. These include knowledge-producing actions that can be either binary sensing actions or non-binary sensing actions. Following [18], the information provided by a binary sensing action is specified using the predicate $SF(a, s)$, which holds if the action a returns the binary sensing result 1 in situation s. Similarly for non-binary sensing actions, the term $sff(a, s)$ is used to denote the sensing value returned by the action.

Lespérance [17] extends the SSA of K in [30] to support two variants of the *inform* communicative action, namely *informWhether* and *informRef*. Here, $inform(inf, agt, \phi)$, $informWhether(inf, agt, \psi)$, and $informRef(inf, agt, \theta)$ mean that *inf* informs *agt* that ϕ currently holds, *inf* informs *agt* about the current truth value of ψ, and *inf* informs *agt* of who/what θ is, respectively. The preconditions of these three actions are as follows:[2]

$Poss(inform(inf, agt, \phi), s) \equiv$
$\qquad$ Know$(inf, \phi, s) \wedge \neg$Know$(inf, $KWhether$(agt, \phi, now), s),$

$Poss(informWhether(inf, agt, \psi), s) \equiv$
$\qquad$ KWhether$(inf, \psi, s) \wedge \neg$Know$(inf, $KWhether$(agt, \psi, now), s),$

$Poss(informRef(inf, agt, \theta), s) \equiv$
$\qquad$ KRef$(inf, \theta, s) \wedge \neg$Know$(inf, $KRef$(agt, \theta, now), s).$

In other words, the agent *inf* can inform *agt* that ϕ, iff *inf* knows that ϕ currently holds, and does not believe that *agt* currently knows the truth value of ϕ, and similarly for *informWhether* and *informRef*. The SSA for K is defined as follows:

$K(agt, s^*, do(a, s)) \equiv \exists s'. [K(agt, s', s) \wedge s^* = do(a, s') \wedge Poss(a, s') \wedge$
$\quad ((BinarySensingAction(a) \wedge Agent(a) = agt) \supset (SF(a, s') \equiv SF(a, s))) \wedge$
$\quad ((NonBinarySensingAction(a) \wedge Agent(a) = agt) \supset$
$\qquad\qquad (sff(a, s') = sff(a, s))) \wedge$
$\quad \forall inf, \phi. (a = inform(inf, agt, \phi) \supset \phi(s')) \wedge$
$\quad \forall inf, \psi. (a = informWhether(inf, agt, \psi) \supset (\psi(s') \equiv \psi(s))) \wedge$
$\quad \forall inf, \theta. (a = informRef(inf, agt, \theta) \supset (\theta(s') = \theta(s)))].$

This says that after an action happens, every agent learns that it has happened. Moreover, if the action is a sensing action, the agent performing it acquires knowledge of the associated proposition or term. Furthermore, if the action involves someone informing *agt* that ϕ holds, then *agt* knows this afterwards, and

---

[2] We modified the preconditions given in CASL by adding the second clause on the right side. Also, the SSA for K presented here is a bit different from that of CASL, and similar to the one given by Lespérance [17].

similarly for *informWhether* and *informRef*. Note that since all agents are aware of all actions, with $inform(inf, agt, \phi)$, every agent learns that ϕ is true. However, with $informWhether(inf, agt, \psi)$ and $informRef(inf, agt, \theta)$, only the addressee learns the truth value/value of ψ/θ. So with the latter, there is some privacy in the communication.[3] Also note that this axiom only handles knowledge expansion, not revision.

CASL extends the framework described in [15] to incorporate goal expansion and a limited form of goal contraction. Goals or intentions are modeled using an accessibility relation W over possible worlds (situations, in this case). The W-accessible worlds for an agent are the ones where she thinks that all her goals are satisfied. W-accessible worlds may include worlds that the agent thinks are impossible, unlike Cohen and Levesque's [1] G-accessible worlds. But intentions are defined in terms of the more primitive W and K relations so that the intention accessible situations are W-accessible situations that are also compatible with what the agent knows, in the sense that there is a K-accessible situation in their history.[4] This guarantees that agents' intentions are realistic, that is, agents can only intend things that they believe are possible. Thus we have:

$Int(agt, \psi, s) \doteq$

$\forall now, then.[W(agt, then, s) \wedge K(agt, now, s) \wedge now \leq then] \supset \psi(now, then)$.

This means that the intentions of an agent in s are those formulas that are true for all intervals between situations *now* and *then* where the situations *then* are W-accessible from s and have a K-accessible situation in their history, namely *now*. Intentions are future oriented, and any goal formula will be evaluated with respect to a finite path defined by a pair of situations, a begining situation *now* and an ending situation *then*. This formalization of goals can deal with both achievement goals and maintenance goals. An achievement goal ψ is said to be eventually satisfied if ψ holds in some situation s' over the interval between *now* and *then*.[5] Eventually$(\psi, now, then)$ is defined as $\exists s'.(now \leq s' \leq then \wedge \psi(s'))$. In [31], Shapiro showed that positive and negative introspection of intentions can be modeled by placing the following constraints on K and W:

$a) \forall s_1, s_2, s. K(agt, s_1, s) \wedge G(agt, s_2, s) \supset G(agt, s_2, s_1)$,

$b) \forall s_1, s_2, s. K(agt, s_1, s) \wedge G(agt, s_2, s_1) \supset G(agt, s_2, s)$.

(a) yields positive introsepection of intentions, whereas (b) gives negative introspection. To make sure that agents' wishes and intentions are consistent, W is also constrained to be serial.

---

[3] In [13], we show how one can formalize *inform* actions to appear as *informWhether* actions to third parties, thus enhancing privacy.

[4] Intention accessible situations $G(agt, s', s)$ are defined using K and W as $W(agt, s', s) \wedge \exists s''. K(agt, s'', s) \wedge s'' \leq s'$, that is, a G-accessible situation is a W-accessible situation that has a K-accessible situation in its history.

[5] Once again, *now* and *then* are not actual situations, but placeholders for situations that are bound in the definition.

The SSA for W which handles intention change in CASL, has the same structure as a SSA for a domain dependent fluent. In the following, $W^+(agt, a, s', s)$ ($W^-(agt, a, s', s)$, respectively) denotes the conditions under which s' is added to (dropped from, respectively) W as a result of the action a:

$$W(agt, s', do(a, s)) \equiv [W^+(agt, a, s', s) \vee (W(agt, s', s) \wedge \neg W^-(agt, a, s', s))].$$

An agent's intentions are expanded when it is requested something by another agent. After the *request(req,agt,ψ)* action, *agt* adopts the goal that ψ, unless she has a conflicting goal or is not willing to serve *req* for ψ. Therefore, this action should cause *agt* to drop any paths in W where ψ does not hold. This is handled in W^-:

$$W^-(agt, a, s', s) \doteq IncompRequest(agt, a, s', s),$$

$$IncompRequest(agt, a, s', s) \doteq [\exists req, \psi. \, a = request(req, agt, \psi)$$
$$\wedge \, Serves(agt, req, \psi, s) \wedge \neg Int(agt, \neg\psi, s)$$
$$\wedge \, \exists now. \, K(agt, now, s) \wedge now \le s' \wedge \neg\psi(do(a, now), s')].$$

Here, the *request* action is considered a primitive action. The preconditions of request are:
$$Poss(request(req, agt, \phi), s) \equiv Int(req, \phi, s).$$

A limited form of intention contraction is also handled in CASL. Suppose that the agent *req* requests *agt* that ψ and later decides it no longer wants this. The requester *req* can perform the action *cancelRequest(req,agt,ψ)*. This action causes *agt* to drop the goal that ψ. *cancelRequest* actions are handled by determining what the W relation would have been if the corresponding *request* action had never happened. This type of goal contraction is handled in W^+, which can be defined as follows:

$$W^+(agt, a, s', s) \doteq \exists s_1. \, W(agt, s', s_1) \wedge \exists a_1. \, do(a_1, s_1) \le s \wedge Cancels(a, a_1)$$
$$\wedge \, (\forall a^*, s^*. \, do(a_1, s_1) < do(a^*, s^*) \le s \supset \neg W^-(agt, a^*, s', s^*)).$$

Suppose that a *cancelRequest* action occurs in situation s. The W relation is first restored to the way it was before the corresponding *request* action occured, i.e., in s_1. Then starting just after the *request*, all the actions a^* that occured in the history of s (say in situation s^*) are considered, and any situation s' in W that satisfies $W^-(agt, a^*, s', s^*)$ is removed from W. $Cancels(a, a_1)$ can be defined as follows:

$$Cancels(a, a') \doteq$$
$$[\exists req, \psi. \, a' = request(req, agt, \psi) \wedge a = cancelRequest(req, agt, \psi)].$$

A *cancelRequest* action can only be executed if a corresponding *request* action has occured in the past:

$$Poss(cancelRequest(req, agt, \phi), s) \equiv \exists s'. \, do(request(req, agt, \phi), s') \le s.$$

CASL has been encoded in the Prototype Verification System (PVS) [23] to form the basis of a verification environment for CASL, *CASLve* [33], that uses theorem proving. CASLve makes it possible to verify properties of multi-agent specifications and prove various types of results such as safety, liveness, termination, etc.

3   Simple Cooperative Ability

An agent cannot be expected to eventually achieve an intention just because she has that intention, and she is acting rationally. We also need to make sure that the agent is capable of achieving the goal in the current situation [16]. In a single agent domain, an agent's ability can roughly be defined as her knowledge of a plan that is physically and epistemically executable and whose execution achieves the goal. However, modeling multiagent ability is a more complex problem, since in this case we need to consider the agents' knowledge about each other's knowledge and intentions as well as how they choose actions, behave rationally, etc. In this section, we develop a simple model of cooperative ability of agents suitable for a limited multiagent context in the absence of exogenous actions, i.e., actions whose performance is not intended by the planning agent. In an open multiagent framework, agents' actions may interfere with each other, possibly perturbing their plans. In some cases, there are multiple strategies to achieve a common goal, and the agents may fail unless they coordinate their choice of strategy by reasoning about each other's knowledge, ability, and rational choice. Moreover, agents may have conflicting goals or intentions. To simplify, we restrict our framework by only allowing plans where the actions that the other agents must do are fully specified, i.e., action delegation is possible, but (sub)goal delegation is not. The primary agent, who is doing the planning, is constrained to know the whole plan in advance. Thus, the primary agent is allowed to get help from others, but she can only ask other agents to perform specific actions. As a consequence, we do not need to model the fact that the other agents behave rationally.

When dealing with ability, it is not enough to say that the agent is able to achieve a goal iff she has a physically executable plan, and any execution of this plan starting in the current situation achieves the goal. We should also take into account the epistemic and intentional feasibility of the plan. This is necessary as physical executability does not guarantee that the executor will not get stuck in a situation where it knows that some transition can be performed, but does not know which. For example, consider the plan $(a; \text{If } \phi \text{ Then } b \text{ Else } c \text{ EndIf}) \mid d$, where actions a, b, c and d are always possible, but where the agent does not know whether ϕ holds after a. If the agent follows the branch where the first action is a, she will get stuck due to incomplete knowledge. Hence, the result of deliberation should be a kind of plan where the executor will know what to do next at every step, a plan that does not itself require deliberation to interpret. To deal with this, De Giacomo *et al.* [4] defined the notion of *Epistemically Feasible Deterministic Programs* (EFDPs) for single agent plans and characterized deliberation in terms of it. Note that EFDPs are deterministic, since they are the result of deliberation and their execution should not require making further choices or deliberation.

Since we are dealing with cooperative multiagent ability, we also need to make sure that the cooperating agents intend to perform the requested actions when it is their turn to act. In our framework, we extend the notion of EFDP to handle simple multiagent plans. A program is called an *Epistemically and Intentionally Feasible Deterministic Program* (EIFDP) in situation s for agent agt, if at each step of the program starting at s, agt always has enough infomation to execute the next action in the program, or knows that the executor of the next action is another agent, and that this agent has enough information to execute this action and intends to do it. Put formally:

$$EIFDP(agt, \delta, s) \doteq \forall \delta', s'.\ Trans^*(\delta, s, \delta', s') \supset LEIFDP(agt, \delta', s'),$$

$$LEIFDP(agt, \delta, s) \doteq$$
$$\mathrm{Know}(agt, Final(\delta, now) \wedge \neg \exists \delta', s'.\ Trans(\delta, now, \delta', s'), s) \vee$$
$$\exists \delta'.\ \mathrm{Know}(agt, \neg Final(\delta, now) \wedge UTrans(\delta, now, \delta', now), s) \vee$$
$$\exists \delta', a.\ \mathrm{Know}(agt, \neg Final(\delta, now)$$
$$\wedge Agent(a) = agt \wedge UTrans(\delta, now, \delta', do(a, now)), s) \vee$$
$$\exists \delta', agt'.\ \mathrm{Know}(agt, \neg Final(\delta, now) \wedge \exists a.\ UTrans(\delta, now, \delta', do(a, now))$$
$$\wedge Agent(a) = agt' \neq agt$$
$$\wedge \mathrm{Int}(agt', \exists s'.\ s' \leq then \wedge Do(a, now, s'), now), s),$$

$$UTrans(\delta, s, \delta', s') \doteq Trans(\delta, s, \delta', s') \wedge$$
$$\forall \delta'', s''.\ Trans(\delta, s, \delta'', s'') \supset \delta'' = \delta' \wedge s'' = s'.$$

Thus to be an EIFDP, a program must be such that all configurations reachable from the initial program and situation, involve a *Locally Epistemically and Intentionally Feasible Deterministic Program* (LEIFDP). A program is a LEIFDP in a situation with respect to an agent, if the agent knows that the program is currently in its *Final* configuration and no further transitions are possible, or knows that she is the agent of the next action and knows what unique transition (with or without an action) it can perform next, or knows that someone else agt' is the agent of the next action, that agt' knows what the action is and intends to do it next, and knows what unique transition the program can perform next with this action. Here, $UTrans(\delta, s, \delta', s')$ means that the program δ in s can perform a unique transition, which takes the agent to s' with the remaining program δ'. Note that when it is the other agent's turn, agt does not have to know exactly what the next action is, i.e., she does not have to know all the parameters of the next action. However, at every step of the program, she must know what the remaining program is.

EIFDPs are suitable results for planning. They can always be executed successfully and since they are deterministic, they do not require further deliberation to execute. Using EIFDP, the ability of an agent can be defined as follows:[6]

$$Can(agt, \psi(now, then), s) \doteq \exists \delta. \, Know(agt, EIFDP(agt, \delta, now)$$
$$\wedge \, \exists s'. \, Do(\delta, now, s') \wedge \forall s'. \, (Do(\delta, now, s') \supset \psi(now, s')), s).$$

Thus, an agent can achieve a goal in situation s, iff she knows of a plan δ that is an EIFDP, is executable starting at s, and any possible execution of the plan starting in the current situation brings about the goal.

We use the following as our running example (adapted from [22]) throughout the paper. Consider a world in which there is a safe with a combination lock. If the safe is locked and the correct combination is dialed, then the safe becomes unlocked. However, dialing the incorrect combination will cause the safe to explode. The agent can only dial a combination if the safe is intact, and it is not possible to change the combination of the safe. Initially, the agent Agt_1 has the intention to open the safe, but does not know the combination. However, she knows that Agt_2 knows it. She also knows that Agt_2 is willing to serve her, and that Agt_2 does not have the intention of not informing her of the combination of the safe. Here are some of the axioms that we use to model this domain:

$sf_1)$ $Poss(a, s) \supset [Exploded(do(a, s)) \equiv$
$\qquad \exists c, agt. \, (a = dial(agt, c) \wedge Comb(s) \neq c) \vee Exploded(s)].$

$sf_2)$ $Poss(dial(agt, c), s) \equiv \neg Exploded(s).$

$sf_3)$ $Agent(dial(agt, c)) = agt.$

$sf_4)$ $\neg Exploded(S_0).$

$sf_5)$ $W(Agt_1, s, S_0) \equiv \neg Locked(s).$

The first axiom, a successor state axiom, states that the safe has exploded after doing action a iff a denotes the action of dialing the wrong combination, or if the safe has already exploded. The second axiom, a precondition axiom, states that it is possible to dial a combination for the safe in situation s iff the safe is intact in s. The third axiom is an agent axiom and defines the agent of the *dial* action. The last two axioms are initial situation axioms, and state that the safe is initially intact, and that Agt_1 initially only intends to open the safe, respectively. From now on, we will use D_{safe} to denote the set of axioms that we use to model this safe domain (see [13] for the complete axiomatization).

Now, consider the follwing plan:[7]

$$\sigma_{safe} = requestAct(Agt_1, Agt_2, informRef(Agt_2, Agt_1, Comb(s)));$$
$$informRef(Agt_2, Agt_1, Comb(s)); dial(Agt_1, Comb(s)).$$

---

[6] Note that this definition of *Can* handles non-achievement goals, as there are two situation placeholdes in ψ, i.e., *now* and *then*. An achievement goal $\psi(now)$ can be placed inside an Eventually block to provide both *now* and *then*.

[7] *requestAct* is an abbreviation introduced in the next section; it denotes a special kind of request, namely, the request to perform an action.

So, the plan is that Agt_1 will request Agt_2 to inform her of the combination of the safe, Agt_2 will inform Agt_1 of the combination of the safe, and finally, Agt_1 will dial the combination to open the safe. We claim that σ_{safe} is an EIFDP in the initial situation for Agt_1, and that Agt_1 is able to achieve her intention of opening the safe in the initial situation:

Theorem 1.

$$a.\ D_{safe} \models EIFDP(Agt_1, \sigma_{safe}, S_0).$$
$$b.\ D_{safe} \models Can(Agt_1, \text{Eventually}(\neg Locked), S_0).$$

(a) holds as all configurations reached by σ_{safe} starting in S_0 are LEIFDP. (b) holds as Agt_1 knows of a plan (i.e., σ_{safe}), which she knows is an EIFDP and is executable, and knows that any execution of this plan ends up in a situation where the safe is unlocked.

4   From Intentions That to Intentions to Act

In this section, we define rational plans and extend CASL to model the role of intention and rationality in determining an agent's actions. This bridges the gap between future directed intentions and present directed ones. We also discuss a notion of subjective plan execution and present a theorem that relates intention and ability to the eventual achievement of intended goals.

Before going further, let us discuss the communication actions that we will use in our framework. Like in CASL, we use three primitive informative communication actions, namely, *inform*, *informWhether*, and *informRef*. However, unlike in CASL, we provide two intention transfer communication actions, *request* and *requestAct*, and these are defined in terms of *inform*.[8] The *request* action can be used by an agent to request another agent to achieve some state of affairs, whereas *requestAct* involves an agent's request to another agent to perform some particular complex action starting in the next situation. Formally,

$$request(req, agt, \phi) \doteq inform(req, agt, \text{Int}(req, \phi, now)),$$

$$requestAct(req, agt, \delta) \doteq request(req, agt, \exists s'.\ a.\ Do(\delta, do(a, now), s')$$
$$\wedge\ now < s' \leq then \wedge Agent(\delta) = agt).$$

Here $Agent(\delta)=agt$ means that the agent of all actions in δ is agt. In our specification, we only allow sincere requests. That is, an agent can perform a request if the request is not contradictory to her current intentions. So defining requests as informing of intentions is reasonable. However, since requests are modeled in

---

[8] A similar account of request was presented by Herzig and Longin [9], where it is defined as inform about intentions, and the requested goals are adopted via cooperation principles.

terms of *inform*, and since we are using true belief, the usual preconditions of the *inform* action are relaxed:

$$Poss(inform(inf, agt, \phi), s) \equiv$$
$$\text{Know}(inf, \phi', s) \land \neg\text{Know}(inf, \text{KWhether}(agt, \phi', now), s),$$

where, ϕ' is ϕ with all $\text{Int}(inf, \phi'', now)$ are replaced by $\neg\text{Int}(inf, \neg\phi'', now)$. This axiom says that the agent *inf* can inform *agt* that ϕ, iff *inf* knows that ϕ' currently holds, and does not believe that *agt* currently knows the truth value of ϕ', where ϕ' is defined as above. Note that, if we use ϕ instead of ϕ' in the above axiom, the account would be overly strict. For instance, in the safe domain, σ_{safe} is a rational plan for Agt_1 in the initial situation. However, initially, Agt_1 does not have the intention that Agt_2 informs her the combination of the safe. So if we use ϕ instead of ϕ' in the axiom, we cannot show that σ_{safe} is rational, since it requires Agt_1 to know that she has the intention before she can inform about it. So we relax the requirements so that the agent only needs to know that she does not have the opposite intention.[9]

To facilitate the cancellation of requests, we also provide two actions, namely, *cancelRequest*, and *cancelReqAct*. Unlike CASL where *cancelRequest* is primitive, we define it using *inform*. These two actions are defined as follows:

$$cancelRequest(req, agt, \psi) \doteq inform(req, agt, \neg\text{Int}(req, \psi, now)),$$

$$cancelReqAct(req, agt, \delta) \doteq$$
$$cancelRequest(req, agt, \exists s^*, s^+, prev. \, prev = do(requestAct(req, agt, \delta), s^+)$$
$$\land s^+ < now \leq s^* \leq then \land Do(\delta, prev, s^*) \land Agent(\delta) = agt).$$

To keep the theory simple, we only use these aforementioned communicative acts (see [6] and [12] for definitions of a much richer array of speech acts).

Now let us look at what plans are rational for an agent. To keep the theory simple, we only consider conditional plans. An agent that is acting rationally, should prefer some plans to others. To this end, we define an ordering on plans:

$$\succeq (agt, \delta_1, \delta_2, s) \doteq \forall s'. \, K(agt, s', s) \land \exists s''. \, Do(\delta_2, s', s'') \land W(agt, s'', s)$$
$$\supset [\exists s''. \, Do(\delta_1, s', s'') \land W(agt, s'', s)].$$

That is, a plan δ_1 is as good as another plan δ_2 in situation s for an agent *agt* iff for all W-accessible situations that can be reached by following δ_2 from a situation that is K-accessible from s (say s'), there exists a W-accessible situation that can be reached from s' by following δ_1. In other words, δ_1 is at least as good as δ_2 if it achieves the agent's goals in all the possible situations where δ_2 does.

---

[9] In [13], we discuss a way to avoid this change in the usual preconditions of *inform* by building commitment into plans.

Using EIFDP and the $\succeq$ relation, we next define rational plans. A plan δ is said to be *rational* in situation s for an agent agt if the following holds:

$$Rational(agt, \delta, s) \doteq \forall \delta'. \succeq (agt, \delta', \delta, s) \supset \succeq (agt, \delta, \delta', s)$$
$$\land EIFDP(agt, \delta, s).$$

Thus, a rational plan in a situation s, is a plan that is as good as any other plan in s and is an EIFDP in s.

For example, consider the plan σ_{safe}. We claim that σ_{safe} is as good as any other plan available to Agt_1 in the initial situation, and that σ_{safe} is rational in the initial situation.

Theorem 2.

        a. $D_{safe} \models \forall \sigma. \succeq (Agt_1, \sigma_{safe}, \sigma, S_0).$

        b. $D_{safe} \models Rational(Agt_1, \sigma_{safe}, S_0).$

Since this plan achieves Agt_1's intention of opening the safe starting in any situation that is K-accessible to S_0, (a) holds. (b) follows from the fact that σ_{safe} is as good as any other plan in S_0 and is an EIFDP in S_0.

In most cases, there are many rational plans (i.e., ways of achieving as many goals as possible). The decision of which plan the agent commits to is made based on pragmatic/non-logical grounds. We do not model this here. Instead, we introduce a $commit(agt, \delta)$ action that will model the agent's commiting to a particular plan δ, more specifically, commiting to executing δ next. The action precondition axiom for the *commit* action is as follows:

$$Poss(commit(agt, \delta), s) \equiv \neg Int(agt, \neg \exists s^*. s \leq s^* \leq then \land Do(\delta, now, s^*), s).$$

That is, the agent agt can commit to a plan δ is situation s, iff the agent currently does not have the intention that the actions in the plan do not happen next.

Next, we extend the SSA for W to handle intention revision as a result of the agent's commitment to a rational plan, and also as a result of other agents' *requestAct* and *cancelReqAct* actions. This axiom has a similar structure to that of CASL; however, we modify W^- as follows:

$$W^-(agt, a, s', s) \doteq IncompRequest(agt, a, s', s) \lor IncompCommit(agt, a, s', s).$$

Here, *IncompCommit* handles the expansion of the agent's intentions that occur when a *commit* action occurs. We define *IncompCommit* as follows:

$$IncompCommit(agt, a, s', s) \doteq [\exists \delta. a = commit(agt, \delta) \land Rational(agt, \delta, s)$$
$$\land \exists s^*. s^* \leq s' \land K(agt, s^*, s)$$
$$\land \neg \exists s^{**}. (s^* < s^{**} \leq s' \land Do(\delta, do(a, s^*), s^{**}))].$$

So, after the performance of a *commit* action in s, a W-accessible situation s' in s will be dropped from agt's new set of W-accessible situations if the plan to which *agt* is commiting is rational, and the committed to action does not happen next over the interval between the W-accessible situation s' and its predecessor s^* that is K-accessible from the current situation s.

The definition of W^+ remains unchanged. Note that if exogenous actions are allowed, agents need to revise their commitments when an exogenous action occurs by uncommiting from the currently committed plan, and committing to a new rational plan. We return to this issue in Section 5.

We now show that our formalization of intentions has some desirable properties:

Theorem 3.

$a. \models \neg Int(agt, \neg\phi, s) \land Serves(agt, req, \phi, s) \supset$
$\quad\quad Int(agt, \phi, do(request(req, agt, \phi), s)).$

$b. \models \neg Int(agt, \neg\exists s'. Do(\delta, now, s') \land now \leq s' \leq then, s) \supset$
$\quad\quad Int(agt, \exists s'. Do(\delta, now, s') \land now \leq s' \leq then, do(commit(agt, \delta), s)).$

(*a*) says that if an agent *agt* does not have the intention that not ϕ in s, then she will have the intention that ϕ in the situation resulting from another agent *req*'s request to *agt* that ϕ in s, provided that she is willing to serve *req* on ϕ . (*b*) states that if an agent *agt* does not have the intention of not performing a complex action δ in s, then she will have the intention of performing it after she commits to it.

commit provides a way to link future directed intentions and present directed ones. We next specify a generic meta-controller for an agent that arbitrarily chooses a rational plan, commits to it, and executes it. Then we can prove a theorem about the relationship between intention, ability, and the eventual achievement of an intended goal. This theorem serves as a proof of soundness of our agent theory.

The following meta-controller allows us to refer to the future histories of actions that may occur for an agent who is behaving rationally until ψ holds. Rational behavior until ψ can be defined as follows (we assume that there are no exogenous actions):

$BehaveRationallyUntil(agt, \psi(now)) \doteq$
$\quad \pi\delta. \ Rational(agt, \delta, now)?; commit(agt, \delta);$
$\quad \text{While } \neg\psi(now) \text{ Do}$
$\quad\quad \text{If } \exists a. \ Int(agt, do(a, now) \leq then, now) \land Agent(a) = agt) \text{ Then}$
$\quad\quad\quad [\pi a. \ (Int(agt, do(a, now) \leq then, now) \land Agent(a) = agt)?; a]$
$\quad\quad \text{Else}$
$\quad\quad\quad \pi agt'. \ [\mathbf{Int}(agt, \exists a. \ do(a, now) \leq then$
$\quad\quad\quad\quad\quad\quad\quad\quad \land Agent(a) \neq agt \land Agent(a) = agt', now)?;$
$\quad\quad\quad\quad\quad\quad (\pi a'. \ \mathbf{Int}(agt', do(a', now) \leq then, now)?; a')]$
$\quad\quad \text{EndIf}$
$\quad \text{EndWhile.}$

That is, rational behavior until ψ can be defined as arbritarily choosing a rational plan, committing to it, and then executing it as long as ψ does not hold. A rational plan can have actions by the planning agent as well as actions by other agents. When it is the planning agent's turn to act, she should perform the action that she intends to perform next; otherwise, she should wait for the other agent to act. When it is the other agent's turn, it will perform the action that it is supposed to perform, because rational plans are EIFDP, and thus the other agent must intend to do the action required by the plan. Note that we only deal with achievement goals here.

One problem with CASL is that the execution of plans is viewed from the system's perspective rather than from the agents' perspective. So, although CASL includes operators that model agents' knowledge and goals, the system behavior is simply specified as a set of concurrent processes. These processes may refere to the agents' mental states, but they don't have to. To deal with this problem, Lespérance [17] proposed an account of subjective plan execution in CASL that ensures that plans can be executed by the relevant agents based on their knowledge state. Here we extend this to deal with multiagent plans (i.e. plans with actions by agents other than the executor) and to consider other agents' intentions. We define the subjective execution construct $\mathrm{Subj}(agt, \delta)$ as follows:

$$Trans(\mathrm{Subj}(agt, \delta), s, \gamma, s') \equiv \exists \delta'. \ (\gamma = \mathrm{Subj}(agt, \delta') \land$$
$$[\mathrm{Know}(agt, Trans(\delta, now, \delta', now), s) \land s = s' \lor$$
$$\exists a. \ (\mathrm{Know}(agt, Trans(\delta, now, \delta', do(a, now)) \land Agent(a) = agt, s)$$
$$\land s' = do(a, s)) \lor$$
$$\exists agt'. \ (\mathrm{Know}(agt, \exists a. \ Trans(\delta, now, \delta', do(a, now)) \land Agent(a) = agt'$$
$$\land \mathrm{Int}(agt', \exists s^*. \ s^* \leq then \land Do(a, now, s^*), now), s)$$
$$\land s' = do(a, s))]),$$

$$Final(\mathrm{Subj}(agt, \delta), s) \equiv \mathrm{Know}(agt, Final(\delta, now), s).$$

This means that when a program is executed subjectively by an agent agt, the system can make a transition only if agt knows that it can make this transition, and if the transition involves a primitive action by another agent, then the transition is possible provided that agt also knows that the other agent will intend to perform the action. A subjective execution may legally terminate only if the agent knows that it may.

Next, we present our "success theorem":[10]

Theorem 4 ((From Commitment and Ability to Eventuality)).

$$\models [\mathrm{OInt}(agt, \mathrm{Eventually}(\gamma, now, then), s)$$
$$\land Can(agt, \mathrm{Eventually}(\gamma, now, then), s)$$

---

[10] The construct $AllDo$ is a strict version of Do that requires that all possible executions of a program terminate successfully; see [17] for a formal definition.

$$\land \operatorname{Int}(agt, \operatorname{Eventually}(\psi, now, then), s)] \supset$$
$$AllDo(\operatorname{Subj}(agt, BehaveRationallyUntil(agt, \psi)), s).$$

Intuitively, if in some situation, an agent intends to achieve some goal and is able to achieve all its intentions, then the agent will eventually achieve the goal in all rational histories from that situation. $OInt(agt, \psi, s)$ means that ψ is all the intentions that agt has in s. This construct must be used as we have to assume that the agent is able to achieve all her intentions. If this is not the case, the agent may have to choose between some of its goals and the $BehaveRationallyUntil$ operator will not guarantee that a specific goal (i.e., ψ) will be achieved. If there are exogenous actions, then a more generic meta-controller can be defined. We discuss this in the next section.

We also have the following corrolary for the safe domain:

Theorem 5.

$$D_{safe} \models AllDo(\operatorname{Subj}(Agt_1, BehaveRationallyUntil(Agt_1, \neg Locked)), S_0).$$

We have shown in Theorem 1(b) that Agt_1 can achieve her intention of opening the safe in the initial situation. Moreover, by sf_5, the only intention of Agt_1 is to open the safe. It follows from Theorem 4 that Agt_1 will eventually open the safe if she behaves rationally starting in S_0 (see [13] for a complete proof).

5   Discussion and Future Work

In this paper, we have presented a formal theory of agency that deals with simple multiagent cooperation and shows how future directed intentions and present directed ones can be related. An agent's current rational plans depend on her current intentions. The *commit* action models how the agent's intentions can be updated to include a commitment to a rational plan. Using this, we have formulated a planning framework for multiple cooperating and communicating agents in CASL. We specified how an agent's future directed intentions will lead the agent to adopt a rational plan and then carry it out using the meta-controller *BehaveRationallyUntil*.

To relate agents' intentions with their actions, Cohen and Levesque [1, 2] required that agents eventually drop all their intentions either because they had been achieved or because they were viewed as impossible to achieve (AKA the *no infinite deferral* assumption). However, this assumption should follow from other axioms of the theory, rather than be imposed separatly. A similar account was presented by Rao and Georgeff [25]. A more intuitive account was presented in [35], where Singh showed that rather than having it as an assumption, the no infinite deferral principle can be derived from the theory. However, he does not explicitly address the interaction between knowledge and actions and its relationship with ability. Another account was presented by Sadek [28], where he incorporated a backward chaining planning mechanism in his framework. However, his account is limited in the sense that it uses hardcoded perlocutionary or rational effects of actions rather than actual effects. Although independently motivated, our account closely resembles the one in [20], where a similar notion of commitment to actions was introduced to relate intentions and actions. However, that framework does not model rationality and provide a success theorem. There has also been related work that tries to extend agent programming languages to support declarative goals [11, 3, 29].

It should be noted that our formalization views communication acts as actions that change the mental states of the participants, i.e. our semantics of communication acts is mentalistic in the tradition of [2, 6]. Recently, there have been many proposals for semantics of communication acts based on social commitments [7, 8]. The commitments associated with a conversation would be accessible to an observer and relevant social rules could be enforced. We think that it is very important to capture the social aspects of agent comunication, the obligations that go with membership in an agent society. Enforcing these could also be useful in certain contexts. But we think that communication cannot be reduced to this public social commitments level. The reason agents communicate is that this serves their private goals. One must usually reason about these goals and the associated beliefs to really understand the agents' behavior, for instance to provide cooperative answers to queries, or to deal with the duplicitous behavior of a competitor requesting a quote for a service in order to know the agent's price and make a lower bid. Thus, a mentalistic semantics is also essential. There has also been a suggestion that public social commitment semantics support more efficient reasoning and are more "tractable". We think that this is an orthogonal issue. The efficiency of reasoning about the content of communication depends on the expressiveness of the language used to represent this content. It is possible to reason about information/knowledge efficiently if one disallows incomplete knowledge (e.g. disjunctive information). This is independent of whether the content is the subject of a social commitment or of a private intention or belief.

The theory presented here is a part of our ongoing research on the semantics of speech acts and communication in the situation calculus. In [13], we present an extended version of our framework where we allow exogenous actions. To deal with these unintended actions, an agent needs to revise the plan it is committed to whenever an exogenous action occurs. In other words, she needs to un-commit from the previously committed plan, consider the new set of rational plans, and commit to one of them. We handle the un-commiting part in the SSA for W. The agents' commitment to a new rational plan is handled using a more general meta-controller. This controller iterates the *BehaveRationallyUntil* program as long as the goal remains un-achieved and there is a plan that is rational in the current situation. In [13], we also define a notion of conditional commitment, and model some simple communication protocols using it.

Our current agent theory is overly simplistic in many ways. One strict constraint that we have is that we do not allow cooperating agents to choose how they will achieve the goals delegated to them by assuming that the planning agent knows the whole plan in advance. Only one agent is assumed to do planning. In future work, we will try to relax this restriction and to model some interaction protocols that involve multiple planning agents. It would also be interesting to develop tools to support multiagent programming that conform to this specification.

References

1. Cohen, P., Levesque, H.: Intention is Choice with Commitment. Artificial Intelligence, 42:(2-3), (1990) 213–361
2. Cohen, P., Levesque, H.: Rational Interaction as the Basis for Communication. In: Cohen P., Morgan, J., Pollack, M. (eds.): Intentions in Communication. Cambridge, MA, MIT Press (1990) 221–255
3. Dastani, M., van Riemsdijk, B., Dignum, F., and Meyer, J.-J.C.: A Programming Language for Cognitive Agents Goal Directed 3APL. In: Dastani, M., Dix, J., and El Fallah-Seghrouchni, A. (eds.): Programming Multi-Agent Systems, 1st Int. Workshop, PROMAS 2003, Selected Revised and Invited Papers. LNCS 3067 (2004) 111–130
4. De Giacomo, G., Lespérance, Y., Levesque, H., and Sardina, S.: On the Semantics of Deliberation in IndiGolog - From Theory to Implementation. Annals of Mathematics and Artificial Intelligence, 41(2-4) (2004) 259–299
5. De Giacomo, G., Lespérance, Y., Levesque, H.: ConGolog, a Concurrent Programming Language Based on the Situation Calculus. Artificial Intelligence, 121 (2000) 109–169
6. Foundations for Intelligent Physical Agents: FIPA Communicative Act Library Specification. Document 37 (1997-2002)
7. Flores, R., Pasquier, P., and Chaib-draa, B.: Conversational semantics with social commitments. In: van Eijk, R., Huget, M.-P., and Dignum, F. (eds.): Developments in Agent Communication. LNCS (2004)
8. Fornara, N., Vigano, F., and Colombetti, M.: Agent communication and institutional reality. In: van Eijk, R., Huget, M.-P., and Dignum, F. (eds.): Developments in Agent Communication. LNCS (2004)
9. Herzig, A., Longin, D.: A Logic of Intention with Cooperation Principles and with Assertive Speech Acts as Communication Primitives. In: Proc. of AAMAS 02 (2002)
10. Hoare, C.: Communicating Sequential Processes. Prentice Hall Int. (1985)
11. van der Hoek, W., Hindriks, K., de Boer, F., Meyer, J.-J.Ch.: Agent Programming with Declarative Goals. In: Castelfranchi, C., Lespérance, Y. (eds.): Intelligent Agents VII, Proc. of ATAL 00, LNAI 1986 (2000)
12. Huber, M., Kumar, S., and McGee, D.: A suite of performatives based upon joint intention theory. In: van Eijk, R., Huget, M.-P., and Dignum, F. (eds.): Developments in Agent Communication. LNCS (2004)
13. Khan, S.: A Situation Calculus Account of Multiagent Planning, Speech Acts, and Communication. M.Sc Thesis. Dept. of Computer Science, York University. In preparation (2004)
14. Lakemeyer, G., Levesque, H.: AOL: A Logic of Acting, Sensing, Knowing, and Only-Knowing. In: Proc. of KR 98 (1998) 316–327
15. Lespérance, Y., Levesque, H. J., Lin, F., Marcu, D., Reiter, R., Scherl, R.: Foundations of a Logical Approach to Agent Programming. In: Wooldridge, M., Muller, J., Tambe, M. (eds.): Intelligent Agents Vol. II - Proc. of ATAL 95 (1996) 331–346
16. Lespérance, Y., Levesque, H., Lin, F., Scherl, R.: Ability and Knowing How in the Situation Calculus. Studia Logica 66(1) (2000) 165–186

17. Lespérance, Y.: On the Epistemic Feasibility of Plans in Multiagent Systems Specifications. In: Meyer, J.-J.Ch., Tambe M. (Eds.): Intelligent Agents VIII, Proc. of ATAL 01, Seattle, WA, USA (2001)
18. Levesque, H.: What is planning in the presence of sensing? In: Proc. of the Thirteenth National Conference on Artificial Intelligence, Portland, OR (1996) 1139–1146
19. Levesque, H., Reiter, R., Lespérance, Y., Lin, F., Scherl, R.: GOLOG: A Logic Programming Language for Dynamic Domains. J. of Logic Programming, 31 (1997)
20. van Linder, B., van der Hoek, W., Meyer, J.-J. Ch.: Formalising Motivational Attitudes of Agents : On Preferences, Goals, and Commitments. In: Wooldridge, M., Muller, J., Tambe, M. (eds.): Intelligent agents II - Proc. of ATAL 96. LNAI 1037 (1996) 17–32
21. McCarthy, J., Hayes, P.: Some Philosophical Problems from the Standpoint of Artificial Intelligence. Machine Intelligence, 4 (1969) 463–502
22. Moore, R.: A Formal Theory of Knowledge and Action. In: Hobbs J., Moore, R. (eds.): Formal Theories of the Commonsense World. Ablex (1985) 319–358
23. Owre, S., Rajan, S., Rushby, J., Shankar, N., and Srivas, M.: PVS: Combining specification, proof checking, and model checking. In: Alur, R. and Henzinger, T. (eds.): Computer-Aided Verification (CAV 96), Vol. 1102 of LNCS (1996) 411–414
24. Plotkin, G.: A Structural Approach to Operational Semantics. Technical Report DAIMI-FN-19, Computer Science Dept., Aarhus University, Denmark (1981)
25. Rao, A., Georgeff, M.: Modeling Rational Agents within a BDI-architecture. In: Fikes, R., Sandewall, E. (eds.): Proc. of KR&R 91 (1991) 473–484
26. Reiter, R.: The Frame Problem in the Situation Calculus: A Simple Solution (Sometimes) and a Completeness Result for Goal Regression. In: Lifschitz, V. (ed.): Artificial Intelligence and Mathematical Theory of Computation: Papers in the Honor of John McCarthy. San Diego, CA, Academic Press (1991)
27. Reiter, R.: Knowledge in Action. Logical Foundations for Specifying and Implementing Dynamical Systems. MIT Press (2001)
28. Sadek, M.: Communication Theory = Rationality Principles + Communicative Act Models. In: Proc. of AAAI 94 Workshop on Planning for Interagent Comm. (1994)
29. Sardiña, S., Shapiro, S.: Rational Action in Agent Programs with Prioritized Goals. In: Proc. of AAMAS 03 (2003) 417–424
30. Scherl, R., and Levesque, H.: Knowledge, Action, and the Frame Problem. Artificial Intelligence, vol. 144(1-2) (2003)
31. Shapiro, S.: Specifying and Verifying Multiagent Systems Using CASL. PhD Thesis. Dept. of Computer Science, University of Toronto. In preparation (2004)
32. Shapiro, S., Lespérance, Y.: Modeling Multiagent Systems with the Cognitive Agents Specification Language - A Feature Interaction Resolution Application. In: Castelfranchi, C., Lespérance, Y. (eds.): Intelligent Agents Vol. VII - Proc. of ATAL 00, LNAI 1986 (2001) 244–259
33. Shapiro, S., Lespérance, Y., and Levesque, H.: The Cognitive Agents Specification Language and Verification Environment for Multiagent Systems. In: Castelfranchi, C., and Johnson, W. (eds.): Proc. of AAMAS 02 (2002) 19–26
34. Shapiro, S., Lespérance, Y., Levesque, H.: Specifying Communicative Multi-Agent Systems with ConGolog. In: AAAI Fall 1997 Symp. on Comm. Act. in Humans and Machines (1997) 75–82
35. Singh, M.: Multiagent Systems: A Theoretical Framework for Intentions, Know-How, and Communications. LNAI 799 (1994)

Author Index

Lecture Notes in Artificial Intelligence (LNAI)